Mindful Spirituality

ALSO BY DUNCAN FERGUSON

Biblical Hermeneutics: An Introduction
Making the Bible Your Book: Content and Interpretation
New Age Spirituality: An Assessment, Editor
Called to Teach: The Vocation of the Presbyterian Educator, Co-Editor
Exploring the Spirituality of the World Religions: The Quest for Personal, Spiritual and Social Transformation
Lovescapes: Mapping the Geography of Love
The Radical Teaching of Jesus: A Teacher Full of Grace and Truth

MINDFUL SPIRITUALITY

The Intentional Cultivation of the Spiritual Life
A Book of Daily Readings

Duncan S. Ferguson

WIPF & STOCK · Eugene, Oregon

MINDFUL SPIRITUALITY
The Intentional Cultivation of the Spiritual Life: A Book of Daily Readings

Copyright © 2018 Duncan S. Ferguson. All rights reserved. Except for brief quotations in critical publications or reviews, no part of this book may be reproduced in any manner without prior written permission from the publisher. Write: Permissions, Wipf and Stock Publishers, 199 W. 8th Ave., Suite 3, Eugene, OR 97401.

Wipf & Stock
An Imprint of Wipf and Stock Publishers
199 W. 8th Ave., Suite 3
Eugene, OR 97401

www.wipfandstock.com

PAPERBACK ISBN: 978-1-5326-4558-7
HARDCOVER ISBN: 978-1-5326-4559-4
EBOOK ISBN: 978-1-5326-4560-0

Manufactured in the U.S.A.

New Revised Standard Version Bible, copyright 1989, Division of Christian Education of the National Council of the Churches of Christ in the United States of America. Used by permission. All rights reserved.

To Henry and Harper, for whom my love will never end.

Fecisti nos ad te inquietum est co nostrum, done requiescat in te.

Thou has created us for thyself, and our heart cannot be quieted till it may find repose in thee.
—Augustine, *Confessions*, Book I.1.

CONTENTS

Preface | ix
Guidance for Using the Readings | xiii

Section One: Reaching Upward | 1
    January: Reaching Upward for Transcendence | 2
    February: Reaching Upward toward Loving God with Our Whole Being | 35
    March: Reaching Upward for Relationship with God through Faith | 65
    April: Reaching Upward toward Union with God | 98

Section Two: Opening Inward | 133
    May: Opening Inward for Healing | 134
    June: Opening Inward for Emotional Health and Wholeness | 167
    July: Opening Inward for Ethical Guidance and Practice | 198
    August: Opening Inward for Peace and Purpose | 232

Section Three: Expanding Outward | 267
    September: Expanding Outward to Love | 268
    October: Expanding Outward for Community | 302
    November: Expanding Outward in Responsible Living | 334
    December: Expanding Outward for Justice, Reconciliation, and Peace | 366

A Concluding Summary and Course of Action | 391

Bibliography | 403

PREFACE

I HAVE BEEN DEEPLY engaged in both a reflective and active way over the past few decades with several issues, about which there have been intense conversations within the Christian church and the worldwide religious community. One has been about the ways that the leaders of many religious traditions have begun to talk with one another, noting differences, but also finding much in common. A second one is the way that many religions, while causing some of the problems, have given attention and help to solving the overwhelming challenges facing the global community—issues such as global warming and international terrorism. These conversations became so important to me that I felt the need to study them in some depth.[1] Standing behind and foundational to these concerns have been two other issues, one of which is the God problem.[2] I suspect that every generation revisits this issue, as (for example) in the late sixties and early seventies, when the "God is dead" topic got so much attention. More recently, the discussion has intensified once again, and stimulated a vast array of books, articles, and conferences. Even the secular sociologists who gathered in London in 2013 for the British Sociological Association addressed the question "Is God back?" These participants noted that God never fully disappeared in the United States and regions in the Southern Hemisphere, and has reappeared in Europe and, with great energy, in the Middle East. There are the neo-pagan and native faith groups in Europe, fervent evangelical groups in the United Kingdom and the United States, and the Islamic social and militant groups in the Arab world.[3]

While the secular sociologists are more interested in the shape of social movements and describe a return to religiously motivated groups, there are many others who are genuinely asking about the reality of transcendence. Deepak Chopra, the well-known author with Hindu roots, is representative of those who are seeking to re-discover God. He acknowledges that a modest percentage of the human family has

1. See Ferguson, *Exploring the Spirituality of the World Religions*.
2. Bloom, *The God Problem*.
3. Hjelm, ed., *Is God Back?*

PREFACE

a new consciousness and is using postmodern categories of understanding that help to reframe a view of the divine. These people want a construct of faith that is credible and can guide contemporary pilgrims toward a thoughtful and practical approach to spirituality for our time.[4]

There are many, of course (perhaps the majority of religious people from across the world's religions), who have never left the beliefs and practices of their religious tradition. They have followed the ways that their religion understands and worships God and links with transcendence. There is change within these religions, but it is more gradual and almost unnoticed. Many others (and I am one) have earnestly sought to articulate faith in God in a way that takes into account how modern science and social science, philosophy and cosmology, secularism and the rapidity of change in all aspects of our lives, have challenged traditional ways of putting faith together. I join with others across the world's religions in responding to what we sense is a rebirthing of God.[5]

Within Christianity, it has become almost a new Reformation, a movement that has faced the reality that much traditional theological and liturgical language is grounded in a pre-modern view of reality. This new Reformation is concerned about the way the church has often asked its adherents to live schizophrenically, with more orthodox faith commitments in one half of our identity and a postmodern consciousness in the other half.[6]

I am persuaded that authentic religious faith can be integrated with a contemporary cosmology and consciousness. On one level, it can be done with careful thought, the study of new literature, and ways of thinking that address the concern. But on another level, it must go beyond ideas and become an integral part of our identity, a pathway that is thoughtful and invites the engagement of our heart. It asks us to love God "with all your heart, and with all your soul, and with all your mind, and with all your strength" (Mark 12:30)[7]. As we consider the question from this perspective, it intersects with another major issue in contemporary religious life and thought, one that we call spirituality. Two concerns or interwoven issues, then, must be addressed if we are to integrate our faith with our way of viewing the world: (1) understanding the divine in a more contemporary way, and (2) finding ways to live a deeply spiritual life in reference to our view of the divine. These issues become the driving motivation for this book of daily readings.

---

4. Chopra, *The Future of God*.

5. Newell, *The Rebirthing of God*.

6. Keen observers have addressed this reality. See, for example, Bass, *Christianity After Religion*; Stella, *Finding God Beyond Religion*; Pagels, *Beyond Belief*; and Cox, *The Future of Faith*. One author, Daniel C. Maguire, a well-known Christian ethicist, even speaks about *Christianity without God*. I will say a good deal more about this concern as we seek to find our way to a mindful spirituality.

7. This manuscript uses the New Revised Standard Version Bible, unless otherwise indicated.

PREFACE

I do bring the Christian way to these daily readings; it is my faith orientation. I am not exclusive in my outlook and include the wide expanse of spiritual perspectives that are part of the human experience. The Transcendent One, or Cosmic *Logos*, speaks many languages, and we must have the ears to hear and the hearts to follow. There is the risk of selecting, in the supermarket of spirituality, just those items that fit our outlook and needs. There is also the risk of superficiality, if this is our practice. The richness that is present across the great spiritual traditions of the human family should not be ignored in our global context. Our lives can be nurtured by these spiritual practices as we select carefully and work at integration. I do use the Bible for guidance, in that it is foundational for my spiritual pathway. As I do, I generally quote from the New Revised Standard Version, although occasionally I will use other translations. I have also used footnotes to help the reader find other resources for their spiritual journey.

I want to thank those whose help was appreciated beyond measure: Laurie Julian, for guidance early in the process; Barbara Sanford, for her excellent review of the manuscript; Vickie Crupi, for her assistance in formatting; and Dorothy, my wife, for her excellent proofreading. So, we begin.

As a deer longs for flowing streams, so my soul longs for you O God.
(Ps 42:1)

GUIDANCE FOR USING THE READINGS

LIBRARIES AND BOOKSTORES HAVE a nearly endless supply of books and pamphlets with daily readings, entries that inspire and guide. This volume is in that genre. As the many other volumes tend to do, mine also has a particular group of people in mind and addresses the concerns of this group. The group I have in mind is the serious seeker who would like to find assistance in deepening her or his spirituality. Often this pilgrim seeker will be one who wants a guiding focus and center that have been somewhat difficult to find in traditional churches and other religious centers. Not infrequently, the likely reader will be one who is open to a variety of beliefs and practices that take into account the intellectual and cultural currents of our time and is concerned about the overwhelming problems that we face as an earth family. All of course regardless of religious heritage or no religious experience are welcome to read. These daily entries are for everyone.

    I break down the search, as I have mentioned, into the three overarching categories of Reaching Upward, Opening Inward, and Expanding Outward. There are subcategories under each of these larger sections, taking us through the year with a reading each day. At the end of each reading, I frame a question that arises from the reading and urge that the reader to suggest a tentative answer or the beginning of an answer that will need more reflection. For example, in the reading for Day 2, there is an invitation to learn about the shepherd's quest for peace and security as he tends his sheep in the wilderness of Judea, Psalm 23. One question is how this shepherd finds peace and security while he is alone in the wilderness with all of its threats and responsible for relatively helpless sheep that need food and protection. The shepherd, likely David who later becomes a king, finds rest and security in the metaphor of "The Lord is my shepherd." At the conclusion of each month and the end of each major section there is a study guide with questions followed by resources. There is a glossary, additional questions asked and at least partially answered, and further reading suggestions, ones for the most part listed in the footnotes and later in the bibliography.

GUIDANCE FOR USING THE READINGS

To start the day with a daily reading has been nurturing for me. It gives the day some focus and I often think about my reading. This process takes me into subsequent contemplation, meditation, and prayer during the day. The wisdom and inspiration from the readings help center my attention and motivate me to practice the values inherent in my faith. There have been times when I have kept a diary, often for a full year. Writing my reflections on the reading tends to lodge their meaning in my mind and heart. There have also been times when I have started a book of readings designed around the calendar year, but have started mid-year and have missed days and weeks. This set of readings as far as possible allows for this usage, although there is a logical flow and pattern in the readings.

I have also tried to arrange the readings so that they can be read by a group of people who commit to meeting on a regular basis. It may be a weekly gathering, such as a prayer group, and the readings with the questions at the end can be the source of conversation. The readings are arranged so that a group could meet monthly. At the conclusion of each month with a special theme, there is a study guide with discussion questions. In that book groups are fairly common, I would hope that there would be groups of people who might use the readings, commit to living in solidarity and intentionality with others, support one another in prayer, and share insights from the readings. There is also a study guide at the conclusion of each of the three major sections (the four month sections), which invites a review and gives an opportunity for assessing the value of the group and perhaps making any changes that are suggested. It would be my recommendation that the leadership in the groups be rotated, perhaps on a monthly basis, giving each volunteer an opportunity to prepare for guiding the discussion. The groups may want to have some guidelines, and for a start, I would recommend the following:

1. Arrange for time at the beginning for sharing and mutual support.
2. Be sure that all are committed to listen to others without judgment.
3. Avoid the temptation to tell a colleague what to believe.
4. Listen carefully and with empathy.

May you learn, grow, and cultivate a deep spirituality that empowers you to thrive.

SECTION ONE

REACHING UPWARD

As we speak and write about transcendence[1] or the divine, we must often use metaphors and analogies. Human language is unable to describe the fullness of God, and to use abstract rather than anthropomorphic language, such as "ground of being," does not always communicate or lead one to a life of faith, although it may be an accurate and helpful description. The same is true as we speak about a spiritual pathway that guides us in our relationship with the divine. As we go together on our spiritual pilgrimage that we are calling mindful spirituality, we will talk about three different paths using a spatial metaphor. We will describe one of these paths as "Reaching Upward," a second one as "Opening Inward," and the third as "Expanding Outward."

What we are saying in this first section is that we often think of God as being "up there," even though we generally understand God as omnipresent. In using the term "upward," we speak of our belief that God is transcendent and worthy of our worship. We move to the immanence of God by saying that we need to open inward in order to both acknowledge and invite the divine presence within us. By using the directional metaphor of "Expanding Outward," we underline our responsibility to reach out to others in love and compassion. Each of these spatial metaphors captures a dimension of what we are calling mindful spirituality.

As we begin our trek, we quote the Jewish affirmation in Deuteronomy called the *Shema*: "Hear O Israel: The Lord is our God, the Lord alone" (6:4). This affirmation becomes foundational for me as we begin our pilgrimage together, although we may use quite different language as we learn from and refer to the beliefs and practices of other religious traditions.

---

1. I am using the word "transcendence" to refer to what lies beyond the realm of the here and now, above what is present to us through our senses. I will generally not capitalize the words "transcendence" or "divine" unless they are a reference to a personal God. I am aware that our approaches to the divine are within "the cloud of unknowing."

THEME FOR JANUARY

REACHING UPWARD FOR TRANSCENDENCE

Day 1

But the hour is coming, and is now here, when the true worshipers will worship the Father in spirit and truth, for the Father seeks such as these to worship him. God is spirit, and those who worship him must worship in spirit and truth. (John 4:23–24)

I will open on a personal note and say that my spiritual walk is motived by a commitment to the life of the spirit and to the life of the mind (truth). It is the ground on which I walk. I care, of course, about staying physically healthy, and I enjoy sports. But my physical well-being and the pleasures and pains of the body have not been central to the meaning of my life, although always present and sometimes in a challenging way. However, in my heart of hearts I have felt the stamp of the image of God within me, and have known the deep satisfaction of following a spiritual way. I have found great comfort in the affirmation of God as spirit. The root meaning of spirit (*pneuma* in the Greek, *ruach* in Hebrew) is wind, and these words can be translated as either spirit or wind. As the author of John's Gospel teaches us, God's Spirit is always with us, just as the wind is always present and around us. (3:8)[1]

I have also been captivated by the life of the mind, not that mine has been able to grasp all the subtle dimensions of what we think of as truth. I have wanted to have a credible faith, one that both makes sense and matches what we know to be reality. I want my spiritual pathway to lead me to Ultimate Truth, even if I only have a partial understanding and know that my Christian pathway is but one of many and approximate in character. I want it to lead *me* on the right path and enable me to encounter the Transcendent One, who meets me along the way and brings me a peace that passes understanding. In spirit and truth I reach upward for God as I seek freedom from self-destructive and harmful behavior. I seek purpose and meaning across life's way, and serenity as I travel.

How would you describe your mission statement regarding spirituality?

---

1. I do have some discomfort in speaking of the divine in the masculine "Father," but the clear intent of the verses is not lost, especially if we think of the divine as like a loving parent.

Day 2

The Lord is my shepherd, I shall not want. He makes me lie down in green pastures; he leads me beside still waters. (Ps 23: 1–2)

The psalmist—perhaps David, who later became a king—was likely a shepherd in the early part of his life. He had the responsibility of caring for sheep that could easily get lost or be killed. The shepherd's life may have had quiet and peaceful moments, but also the stress of responsibility and anxiety about the future. He sings a beautiful psalm to find comfort. We identify with him because we too feel stress and anxiety as we live in a rapidly changing and demanding world. David found a good measure of peace in reflecting upon his circumstances, picturing himself as a lamb with the care of the Divine Shepherd, quietly resting on the beautiful green grass beside a quiet lake or stream. It was, for him, a time to be free from stress and anxiety as he reached upward to his Divine Shepherd.[2]

In this endeavor, the shepherd psalmist was both mindful and spiritual. He was intentional about remembering and claiming the calming presence of the Divine Shepherd, whose love eased his worries. He relaxed as his soul was restored and he knew that he was on the right path. Another voice also whispered that there was danger; the valleys are dark at night, and evil is lurking in the shadows. For tonight, though, he says, "I will sleep easily, knowing that the Good Shepherd is present and guiding me, taking care of my needs and filling my life with goodness and mercy." His fears began to fade and he knew that God's Spirit, like the gentle wind, would be with him across the days and weeks and years of life.

The shepherd, alone on a grassy knoll by a gentle stream, reached upward to the Transcendent One, rested easily, and slipped away into a sound sleep.

What gave the shepherd a peaceful sleep?

---

2. As we speak of the divine, we often use metaphors. See Bohler, *God is What? What Our Metaphors for God Reveal about Our Beliefs in God.*

Day 3

Let the same mind be in you that was in Christ Jesus. (Phil 2:5)

The word "mindfulness" comes to us from the Buddhist tradition, and it is one central component in the Noble Eightfold Path. It is one of the paths that we must follow as we move toward enlightenment. It is seen as the gateway to wisdom. The Apostle Paul makes a similar point in his letter to the Philippian church. He encourages the followers of Jesus to *think* like Jesus. From these grand teachings, we are encouraged to have the following qualities as we cultivate a mindful spiritual way:

1. Paul's emphasis in his letter to new Christians is on *humility* as he points to the way that Jesus did not assert his status and importance, but emptied himself to be used for the purposes of God. Jesus is our model.

2. In the Buddhist tradition, "mindfulness" has many dimensions, and is quite subtle and complex. A few examples can give us a flavor of Buddhist thought. One dimension of mindfulness is *present-moment awareness*. This is to be alert, in touch, and focused on what is right in front of us (presence of mind).[3] We are to live in the present, not wander off into our past or anxiously worry about our future.

3. Another characteristic of mindfulness is *concentration*: learning how to focus one's thoughts and gain clarity. It is to find a quiet place and listen.

4. Still another characteristic of mindfulness is *intentionality*, or choosing to be in touch with reality and not confused by distractions, such as the needs of the body or the swirl of feelings.

5. One other characteristic of mindfulness is to be *open and teachable*, to give attention to the great teaching of sages such as Buddha or Jesus.

In these ways we can be mindful pilgrims, intentional about making progress on the spiritual pathway. We reach upward for a relationship with the divine.

What does it mean to be mindful in our spiritual lives?

---

3. See Goldstein, *Mindfulness*.

Day 4

By contrast, the fruit of the Spirit is love, joy, peace, patience, kindness, generosity, faithfulness, gentleness, and self-control. There is no law against such things.
(Gal 5:22–23)

We are to be mindful as we seek a spiritual pathway. We need to stay focused in the present and be intentional about seeking God's will and way. Our second word in the title of this book, "spirituality," not unlike the word "love" in English, has a range of meanings. As we travel together on our pilgrimage, it might be useful to provide a preliminary definition of spirituality, one that will get us started and which will expand as we go along. By way of a foundation, we are saying that God is Spirit, and in this declaration we are saying that God is present; all of the earth is filled with God's presence. We live on a planet pulsating with the Spirit of God. We seek to be spiritual by opening our hearts to God's presence, cultivating a God-consciousness by intentional listening, meditation, and prayer. Gradually, we are transformed, leading to our development as a person growing toward wholeness (holiness), insight, and responsible living.

We become persons in process, empowered by God's Spirit. In time, we leave behind the ego's needs for affirmation and importance. We move away from controlling fears and preoccupation with trivial concerns. We find inner freedom and we are liberated and find our authentic self. In time, love and joy become realities for us. Our defense mechanisms drop away, and we discover the life of integrity and find peace and a purpose that guides us into the future. We underline that this is a process, one that is mixed with failures and successes. We will need forgiveness, the care and support of others, and a return to the mode of receptivity, often present in prayer, study, and engagement with other pilgrims. We will know pilgrim's progress and pilgrim's regress. In time, as we reach upward, we will begin to integrate the pieces of our lives, become whole, and flourish as God fills our lives.

What does the word spiritual mean for you? How do you define it?

Day 5

> *It is Love that spins our souls aloft. It is Love that exhorts even the mountains to dance.* —Rumi[4]

As we reach upward for transcendence, we often wonder what it is for which we long and hope to reach. The world's religions give us a variety of answers, and a sampling may be stimulating and helpful as we progress on our pilgrimage. As we do, we will find that other people have taken, and continue to take, different roads in their pursuit of transcendence, hoping that what they discover will bring fulfillment and happiness to them. Just because they are not on our particular path doesn't mean they have gotten lost, but have just taken a different way. We may find that we do not resonate with views that are not our own. However we can deepen our understanding with an open mind and heart and we remind ourselves that our views may be true for us, although partial and approximate in character.

One way that represents a majority of human seekers is rooted in the view of God in the Abrahamic monotheistic religions. It is grounded in the picture that emerges in the Hebrew Bible. In this testimony, we learn about a God who is the one and only true God, a position passed on from the Jewish faith to Christians and foundational for Muslims. There are parts of this testimony that speak sharply against other views, yet it may be possible to see in other interpretations a similar affirmation of one true God or one true undergirding and universal principle of reality. It is also possible to discern in this orientation a tendency toward sectarian exclusivism, a risk for all religions. In our global context, as we relate daily to others with different histories, cultures, traditions, and beliefs, it is possible to hold a view with firm conviction while at the same time respecting others and honoring their religious views. Above all, as Rumi teaches us, God is Love, and asks faithful followers to love all others, in keeping with the One who is Love.

What do we mean when we say that God is love? Do you sense God's love?

---

4. Rumi, a thirteenth-century poet and Sufi mystic, has left us an extraordinary spiritual legacy. See Mafi, *Rumi Day by Day*, 126.

Day 6

But Moses said to God, "If I come to the Israelites and say to them, 'The God of your ancestors has sent me to you,' and they ask me, 'What is his name?' what shall I say to them?" God said to Moses, "I AM WHO I AM." (Exodus 3:13–14a)[5]

The Hebrew people used different names for God, even as we do in English, but the most common name was Yahweh, or, as it appears as a tetragrammaton, YHWH. The origin of this name remains uncertain, and across the generations of belief and practice, the name took on the meaning of divine mystery, freedom, sovereignty, and presence. In time, the Hebrew people began to think and worship God as the creator of all, and engaged in human history. God is both transcendent and present, and as such should be praised and obeyed.

The Hebrew people understood their connection with the Transcendent One in at least four ways: (1) there is no one like Yahweh, the only true God; (2) Yahweh is committed to a relationship with the Hebrew people; (3) Yahweh will be faithful to the people and be in solidarity with them, as expressed in a covenant; (4) Yahweh's fundamental character stands in partial judgment upon the Hebrew people as they violate Yahweh's expectations. The Hebrew Bible essentially tells this story. The relationship of the Hebrew people to Yahweh has the tensions of clear commands and a failure of the people of God to consistently obey them. But within this covenant relationship, God's character does not change. God is understood as: (1) a judge who is fair and firm; (2) a king, with the power to order creation and human activity; and (3) a parent, a father and mother who seeks the welfare of the children. God will be who God is, the Transcendent One who will show mercy and love, heal the wounds and illnesses of the people, and be a shepherd who cares for the people who act like lost sheep.[6]

Do you agree with the way that the Hebrew people understood God?

---

5. This statement might also be translated "I am what I am," or "I will be what I will be." God is and will be who God is.

6. See Brueggemann, *Theology of the Old Testament*, 117–313.

Day 7

In the beginning was the Word, and the Word was with God, and the Word was God. . . . And the Word became flesh and dwelt among us. (John 1:1, 14)[7]

The Jewish people lived with tension in their covenant with God, struggling to be faithful to their side of the agreement, and yet longing for more intervention by Yahweh to free them from the severe difficulties of their lives. They were often ruled by an alien government and experienced the harsh realities of injustice. They expressed their hope in one who might deliver them from their troubles, and referred to such deliverance as the coming of the messiah. Approximately two thousand years ago, a person appeared in their midst who spoke about these concerns and about the wider questions of life. His name was Jesus, and a group of people thought him to be the messiah and formed around him. This group was originally part of the Jewish community, but in time became autonomous, and the people were called Christians.

They, too, reached upward for transcendence and affirmed many of the beliefs and practices of the Jewish community. Jesus, whom they followed, remained a faithful Jew, honoring the God of the covenant and spoke as a teacher and prophet about the need to be faithful to the covenant. He underscored the need to be attuned to the reign of God in one's life and became a model of faithfulness and love. A Jewish leader, Paul, was converted to the view that Jesus was the Messiah (Christ) for whom the Jewish people hoped. Paul, with many others, went beyond his Jewish heritage and taught that Jesus was sent by God, and through the life and death of Jesus, all people might be reconciled to God *by faith*. These early Christians spoke about faith as a way to reach upward for transcendence. They taught that the life, death, and resurrection of Jesus restored the relationship with God. Following Jesus, Christians began to stress the love and forgiveness of God.

Do you agree with the way that Jesus and Paul slightly reinterpreted the Jewish view of God?

---

7. In ancient Greek philosophy, the term *logos* referred to the principle of order that was in the universe. It was central to the thought of the Stoics. John had this concept in mind when he referred to Jesus as the Word.

Day 8

And your God is One God, there is no God but Him, the most Gracious, the most Merciful. (Surah 2.163)

The Christian community, believing that all people may be reconciled to God by faith in Jesus the Christ, endured the persecution of the Roman Empire, and began to thrive and become a significant presence across the boundaries of the ancient Roman world. Their presence, and also the continuing presence of the Jewish community, reached the Arabian Peninsula, a region populated by nomadic people called Bedouins, who traveled by caravan to different Arab cities for trade. One of the cities to which they traveled was Mecca, and it was there that the Abrahamic religious tradition developed further. In Mecca, Muhammad (born c. 530 CE), the Prophet of Islam, went through a religious conversion and believed that God, called Allah, had chosen him to speak out against pervasive polytheism and inappropriate behavior, and to proclaim a radical monotheism comparable to that in the Jewish and Christian religions.[8] Following a time of deep meditation, he spoke about this new faith and his thoughts were recorded and became the central teaching of the Quran, the word of God for Muslim people.

The teaching of the Quran has many layers, but the heart of the Quran is the belief in one true God. This foundational tenet focuses on the character of God and teaches the ways that Muslims should reach upward for the Transcendent One, whom they call Allah. The most fundamental teaching of Islam is what is called the *Shahadah:* "There is no god but God and Muhammad is the messenger of God." In this statement we see the strong belief in the same God who is the focus of belief and worship in Judaism and Christianity, although expressed in a different language and culture. God's will and way come to us through the great prophets and fully and finally in Muhammad. God is the Creator of all, has clear expectations for human behavior, and is honored by submission and obedience.

In what sense is our view of God influenced by our history and culture?

---

8. Muslims affirm that their faith is not derivative, but re-claimed by Muhammad.

Day 9

In a supracosmic view of things, the supreme Reality is alone entirely real. A certain illusoriness, a sense of the vanity of cosmic existence and individual being is normally a characteristic turn of this seeing of things.[9]

The Abrahamic monotheistic religions (Judaism, Christianity, and Islam) believe in a transcendent God who is also personal and engaged in human affairs. Another family of religions, often referred to as transcendent monism, understands transcendence in a slightly different way, stressing that all of reality is essentially one. It is non-dualistic and differs from the view in radical monotheism that God may be understood as separate and qualitatively different from creation and human activity. The spiritual quest, however, is similar in the religions of transcendent monism; it is to find harmony with the One, however it may be understood.

Hinduism is the classic expression of transcendent monism, a religion that is complex and many-sided, and any brief summary runs the risk of distortion. But we might say that, at its foundation, it is the quest for union with Brahman, the universal being, understood not as personal, but the source and energy of the universe. "I am the father of the universe and its mother, essence and goal of all knowledge, the refiner. . . . I am the beginning and the end, origin and dissolution, refuge, home, true lover, womb and imperishable seed."[10] A faithful Hindu will seek this union, believing that the various manifestations of Brahman, often understood as minor gods, have control over nature and the vicissitudes of life, and provide direction for right living and social order. A true seeker may seek access to transcendence in both a devotional way and the way of knowledge. In so doing, the seeker hopes that there will be spiritual liberation (*moksha*) from the cycle of death and rebirth (*samsara*), caused by the pattern of virtuous and non-virtuous actions (*karma*). Such liberation is a state of consciousness (*Samadhi*) that is timeless and beyond all fears and suffering.

Does transcendent monism really differ from monotheism? In what ways?

---

9. Aurobindo, *The Aim of Life*.
10. Mitchell, *Bhagavad Gita*, 116.

Day 10

If we accept that liberation is an achievable goal, how is it possible to achieve it? This question brings us to the fourth Noble Truth, which deals with the true path.[11]

Buddhism was influenced by Hinduism and shares with it the view that transcendent reality is more principle than personal, and that the achievement of enlightenment or *nirvana* comes from accepting and living in accord with the realities or truths of the cosmic order. One might say that Buddhism fits better in the categories of "Opening Inward" and "Expanding Outward," and we will speak of it again in those sections, yet there is deep commitment in Buddhism to be mindful of ultimate reality. The path of the faithful Buddhist is to accept the cosmic order, which is beyond (upward or above) what we see around us in our day-to-day living.

The goal of Buddhism is to reach upward in order to achieve *nirvana*, which may be described as a perfectly peaceful and enlightened state of transformed consciousness in which passions and ignorance are extinguished. It is not always clear whether this state is utter annihilation or perfect peace, and living with some ambiguity is part of the Buddhist way. Buddhists believe it will be better than suffering. The first noble truth is that suffering is the common experience of humankind. The suffering is caused by our attachment and craving, our insatiable desire to have and possess. There can be an end to suffering as we let go of our desire for possessions and attachments. The way to gain liberation from our craving is to follow the law of righteousness (*dharma*) and become detached from greed. The way to overcome our craving is to follow the noble eightfold path, which is to gain a right view, right thinking, right speech, right action, right livelihood, right diligence, right mindfulness, and right concentration. We can achieve these states with appropriate spiritual practices, and can be released from the cycle of *karma* and *samsara*. The Buddhist way is not an easy one, but a noble one, filled with compassion and peace.

In what ways do you find the Buddhist way persuasive? Or do you?

11. Dalai Lama, *The Four Noble Truths*, 115.

Day 11

The Tao that can be followed is not the eternal Tao. The name that can be named is not the eternal name.

—Lao Tzu[12]

Still another expression of transcendent monism is the religion of Taoism, not always thought of as a traditional religion, but more often as a way of life. Taoists tend to be seekers, never arriving and going in many directions. They want to follow the Tao, which they understand in at least three ways. They seek the true path (Tao), understood in the first place as the way of ultimate reality; that which holds the universe together and which cannot be fully described, because it is beyond, and remains a mystery. Secondly, they can say that the Tao is the way of the universe, the transcendent that has become immanent, and which is the rhythm and power of the universe, the cohering principle behind all nature and life. And third, the Tao is the guidance for the ideal way of human life. In short, Taoism is less prescriptive about belief and practice, and more intuitive. It is a way that is found rather than taught or read about in a book, and one that is lived from the soul rather than one that adheres to society's norms and expectations.

Philosophical Taoists do reach upward for transcendence, hoping to preserve their internal resources (*te*) and to learn what it means to live wisely and well. It is a way of not getting sidetracked into needless conflicts and useless activities; it is to focus on one's internal resources, or the gift of the Tao. There is another expression of Taoism that is less philosophical in its orientation, and more religious and devotional, utilizing priests, temples, rituals, and ceremonies. This expression of Taoism brings forward beliefs and practices of an earlier and pre-modern time, using them to be empowered by the Tao. The ethical side of Taoism reflects a belief that the universe should be honored as it appears, and is experienced with elements of *yin* and *yang* that move through the universe and make it change. The ethical goal is to be at rest within this movement and to live in harmony with the Tao.

Do you think that the universe has within it a guiding principle for life?

---

12. Lao Tzu, *Tao Te Ching*, entry 1.

Day 12

Every part of the earth is sacred to my people. Every shining pine needle, every sandy shore, every mist in the dark woods, every meadow, every humming insect. All are holy in the memory and experience of my people. —Chief Seattle

There is another family of religions, one that has sought the divine within nature. The indigenous wisdom traditions from around the world discern and experience the divine in the natural order. I am persuaded and moved by these wisdom traditions and have seen them firsthand within Alaska Native and the American Indian cultures. I have found among these people a profound sense of the sacred, seen directly in the complexity and beauty of nature. The belief is expressed in sacred stories that speak about the way human beings are an integral part of nature and live interdependently within nature.[13]

In most of the expressions of the indigenous wisdom traditions, the sacred stories address how the world was created, and how one navigates through the difficulties of life. These stories often speak about a Great Spirit that is both the Creator and is imminent in nature. It is to this Great Spirit that one reaches upward for guidance in religious ceremony and empowerment for the challenges of daily life. These traditions share a set of religious practices and beliefs. There are clear taboos that can be self-destructive, the belief that spirits and souls inhabit the natural world (*animism*), and *shamans* who have the power to help people to manage life. In North America, many of the native people have been influenced by Christian teaching and have integrated their traditions with Christian beliefs. What has emerged for many of these people is a religious faith that has great respect for nature, and a worldview that is not fragmented. It has integrated contemporary life with the rhythms of nature. They have a spiritual center that is grounded in their belief that there is a divine presence that runs through all of reality.

In what ways does nature point us to the divine?

---

13. See Woodley, *Shalom and the Community of Creation: An Indigenous Vision.* See also Nerburn, ed., *The Wisdom of the Native Americans.*

Day 13

It is intended to raise consciousness—raise consciousness to the fact that to be an atheist is a realistic aspiration, and a brave and splendid one.[14]

There are many other religious perspectives that could be added to the ones we have mentioned. For example, there are the monotheistic religions of Zoroastrianism and Baha'i, the religions of transcendent monism such as Jainism, Sikhism (and, to some extent, Confucianism), and the religions rooted in culture and nature, such as the ancient Egyptian, Greek, and Roman traditions, and the more contemporary expression of Shintoism. The human family has sought transcendence in a variety of ways, often shaped by their history, customs, and cultures. There seems to be a universal need to explore what is beyond, to see if there is another layer of reality that stands above and can help humans to understand life and find their way.

There are those who say that there is no evidence for another layer of reality, a transcendent reality that intersects with humankind. They teach that it is not necessary to be a pilgrim who reaches upward in reference to the divine in order to be enlightened, to find peace and purpose, and to live a life committed to love and compassion. I have taken this view seriously and have discovered that, in order to be a person seeking a mindful spirituality, there is often a need to squarely face the range of challenges to a religious orientation. Not everyone has the need to review these clear challenges; it is enough to be "pure in heart, for they will see God" (Matt 5:8). This insight of Jesus is profound and reassuring. There may be some people (and I am one of them) who will rest more easily with an understanding of these challenges and finding a solid place to stand with a credible faith.[15] So let's take just a little more time to think together about having a mindful faith and spiritual pathway.

How important is it for us to understand the challenges to our faith?

---

14. Dawkins, *The God Delusion*, 1.

15. There are many who have guided me, including Lewis, *Mere Christianity*; Hart, *The Experience of God*; and McGrath, *The Big Question*.

Day 14

> *Humanity, I argue, arose entirely on its own through an accumulated series of events during evolution.*[16]

The religious orientation to life has been challenged across the centuries and with some energy and forcefulness in recent decades. The questioning of religious claims has come from many sources. Perhaps the most poignant ones have come from scientists who see no measurable proof for the existence of God, or Transcendence. Philosophers, too, have questioned whether it is possible to make a logical and coherent claim for a religious outlook. There is also a cogent argument from the social sciences that have found alternative ways of explaining religious beliefs as an understandable way for humans to make sense out of life. At their root, they can be explained better in psychological, sociological or anthropological categories. In our own time, we have felt the turn-off of the conflicts between religions and within a religion based on the conviction that "if mine is right, then yours is wrong."

Even those who stand within a thoughtful and informed faith orientation have had to acknowledge that many religious beliefs and assertions cannot be sustained. More persuasive explanations have come forward and offer a cogent rendering of what is true. In some of the creation stories of many of the religions, it is clear that these are sagas or myths, perhaps carrying a spiritual truth, but which are not to be understood in a literal way. There are accounts of miracles, such as healing, that fit better within the normal pattern we understand as cause and effect. It was the German theologian and martyr, Dietrich Bonhoeffer, who gave us the language of "the God of the gaps," by which he meant that it is not credible to simply insert the word God as an explanation into contexts and situations we don't understand. But while the religious communities of the world have often missed the mark, it doesn't mean that religious affirmations are all wrong. In fact, they can be quite credible.

What makes a religious point of view credible?

---

16. Wilson, *The Meaning of Human Existence*, 15.

Day 15

Two things fill the mind with ever-increasing wonder and awe, the more often and the more intensely the mind of thought is drawn to them: the starry heavens above me and the moral law within me.[17]

The challenges to faith are very real and it is wise for those who pursue a mindful spirituality to have some acquaintance with them. It is beyond the scope of this set of daily readings to take them up one at a time; each one requires a lengthy response. As a way of thinking about these challenges, we might keep the following in mind:

1. Every generation shapes its worldview largely from the predominant modes of thought of their time and culture. Ours is a scientific age, and one learns from an early age that we largely explain the world in a scientific way.

2. Other realities, such as values, beauty, goodness, and personal truth, exist as well. There is being, consciousness, and bliss, which all point to the divine or transcendence.[18]

3. One metaphor that is persuasive for me is that of using maps to explain the cosmos and the world around us. There are different maps to guide us in exploring a region: road maps, geological maps, weather maps, local maps, and world maps. We use them to learn what it is we need to know. There are many scientific maps, cosmological maps, and religious maps, each suited for what they explain. Each is a different kind of truth-telling.

4. In this new era of postmodern thinking and a global context, windows have opened to give us room to explore a faith orientation that is intellectually responsible and has integrity.

As we move through our pilgrimage of mindful spirituality together, we will return to the challenges of having a faith orientation with credibility, and one that is careful about the how the notion of God is understood.

What sort of map do we need to find direction in our spiritual lives?

---

17. Kant, *Critique of Practical Reason,* 123.
18. See Hart, *The Experience of God.*

Day 16

> *It is unfortunate that we do not have at our disposal a more precise word than religion to denote the experience of the sacred.*[19]

Even the most learned scholars have some difficulty defining religion; yet, it is to religion that we often turn in our quest for a mindful spirituality. We know that those who study religion do so for many reasons and from many perspectives. Our interest in religion has to do with the way its many expressions guide us to an understanding of meaning and truth, the essential ingredients in a mindful spirituality. In a sense, religion is the way humans have sought the sacred, that which is set apart as holy and of greatest value and worthy of veneration. Religion, generally, is the reach upward for transcendence. And if religion is the water of life, then spirituality might be the tea we make from the water.

Our spiritual tea generally has at least four components, varying in the life of humankind's many religions and the one we choose to follow:

1. Usually religions have a *creed* or set of beliefs about the sacred and the nature of God, the divine, transcendence, or ultimate concern. Not all religions have God as the center of their creed, such as Buddhism.

2. In addition, religions have a *code* or a prescribed set of values that guide the way one should live. Jesus made love the code of conduct of Christianity, and Islam might say that surrender to Allah is central.

3. Further, religions have *content* or a way of worship that is distinctive. There are practices when they come together; perhaps ceremonies, rituals, liturgies, or guiding reflections from a leader.

4. Nearly all of the religions of the human family have a *community* that gathers, supports, and sustains its members, although there are individuals that choose to sustain their spirituality in isolation.

Are you satisfied with your religious affiliation?

---

19. Eliade, *The Quest,* first page of Preface.

Day 17

> *In our increasingly materialistic world, we are driven by a seemingly insatiable desire for power and possessions. Yet in this striving, we wander ever further from inner peace and mental happiness. . . . What we seem to be missing is a proper sense of human spirituality.*[20]

Roger Walsh, in his helpful introduction to essential spirituality (we might say mindful spirituality), lists seven central practices to awaken the heart and mind. These practices, as they are cultivated and become an integral part of our identity, will deepen our spiritual walk and become a healthy and transforming dimension of our lives. They are:

1. Transform your motivation in order to reduce craving and find your soul's true desire; it will enable you to follow your bliss.

2. Cultivate emotional wisdom in order to heal your heart and learn to love. Most of us carry scars from childhood that need to be healed and which prevent us from being a loving person.

3. Live ethically in order to have a sense of integrity and positive feelings about doing the right thing.

4. Concentrate and calm your mind in order to gain focus and concentration and to instill a deep peace.

5. Awaken your spiritual vision in order to see clearly, focus on reality, and sense the sacred in all things.

6. Cultivate spiritual intelligence by quieting the mind, awakening the spirit, and nurturing wisdom.

7. Express spirit in action by embracing generosity and committing to a life of service.

It is hard to improve on this list, although we can always try. It is wise and helpful and worth a careful reading to catch its depth and utility.

What would you add to Roger Walsh's list of spiritual practices?

---

20. Walsh, *Essential Spirituality*, ix.

Day 18

> *It struck me that religious faith can be enormously powerful in human experience, lead to health, human flourishing, and social responsibility, but also it can lead to an orientation of fear, zealotry, and intolerance.*[21]

In my book, *Exploring the Spirituality of the World Religions*, I speak about spirituality in the categories of life-giving and life-denying. Let me share these characteristics as a supplement to those of Dr. Walsh. The outcomes of a spiritual pathway that are life-giving are the following:

1. It *empowers* the person or the group to behave in constructive ways that lead to love and compassion.
2. It *guides* the person or group to be socially responsible, giving attention to both the regional and global issues of peace and justice.
3. It is intellectually credible and *encourages* the person or group to be open to new ideas. It enables exposure, learning, and growth.
4. It helps the individual or group to *integrate* beliefs and practices. No longer is there a break between values and action.
5. It *sustains* the individual or group in times of difficulty. Who of us does not face profound difficulties in our lives, as individuals and in the groups to which we belong?

I also speak about life-denying characteristics:

1. It is a pathway that is *sectarian* and closed to other points of view.
2. It is overly *ideological* in character and suspicious of other pathways.
3. It tends to *confine* and *control* the individuals within the group.
4. It is filled with mindless *zealotry* about its outlook and way of behavior.
5. It inculcates *fear, mistrust,* and *intolerance* rather than being positive and affirming.[22]

Our goal is to find a mindful spirituality that is healthy and empowers us to flourish.

Again, what might you change or add to these lists?

---

21. Ferguson, *Exploring the Spirituality of the World Religions*, ix.
22. Ibid., 10.

Day 19

> *You have a right to your actions, but never to your actions' fruits. Act for the action's sake. And do not be attached to inaction.*[23]

Those who have sought and continue to seek a mindful spirituality often rely on the great teachings of their religion. As they reach upward, they want to know if they are being heard and if there is a message, perhaps a loving response, guidance, and wisdom. Nearly every religion has a normative narrative, a metanarrative that comes from above and spans across space and time and that guides the faithful. The story of their faith is often found in a guiding and authoritative book, one that can be studied for shaping belief and practice (hopefully beliefs that are credible and practices that are healthy and nourishing). I have been enriched by my exposure to this literature as I have had the privilege of teaching courses in world religions.

Let me give just a few examples of these books and how they are viewed within the religious tradition. Hinduism seeks guidance from the Vedas, literature that contains sacred knowledge for Hindus. This literature was first a part of an oral tradition. In time, the ancient revelations were written down in the form of hymns, rituals, and speculation about the creation. There is an abundance of material, some mythological and some more devotional and philosophical. Special attention is often given to the *Upanishads*, the most philosophical of the literature. In this literature, there is the story in the *Bhagavad Gita* of Lord Krishna and Arjuna, a Sanskrit poem about a warrior and his true love who must make difficult choices as they seek to be loyal to duty. However, the faithful practice of duty may threaten their life of true love. The poem is suggestively ambiguous, yet within it there is a grand metaphysical vision that, for over two thousand years, has inspired a sense of mystery and meaning in the lives of millions of Hindus.

What grand narrative do you use for guidance? Is it helpful?

---

23. Quoted in Mitchell, *Bhagavad Gita*, 21.

Day 20

My experiences are nothing special, just ordinary human ones. Through my Buddhist training, however, I have learned something about compassion and developing a good heart, and that experience has proved very helpful in my day-to-day life.[24]

In Buddhism, Dharma is the spiritual teaching, and it can be found in a variety of sources, chief of which is called *The Pali Canon*. As with most sacred scripture, it is best understood in the original languages, which are, in this case, Pali and Sanskrit. Pali is the language of the Theravadin canon, and Sanskrit is in the language of Mahayana scriptures. *The Pali Canon* consists of three parts, or what are called the three baskets (different books). One of them is the *Vinaya Pitaka* (the Discipline Basket), another contains the discourses of the Buddha, and yet another explains the higher subtleties of the law. It is difficult to date these documents with any certainty, and it is likely that they were compiled over several centuries.

The Pali canon is more systematic in its teaching than the Mahayana scriptures. It divides the suttas (verses) into five collections. There are the Long Discourses, Middle Length Discourses, Kindred Sayings, Gradual Sayings, and Minor Analogies. The Book of Discipline contains guidelines that govern the conduct of monks and historical material relating to social, economic, and religious conditions in India during the formative years of Buddhism. These founding and guiding documents are vast, and provide direction about the whole range of religious concerns: metaphysical beliefs, ethical practices, and ways of worship with rituals and ceremonies. One particular grouping in the Mahayana Buddhist canon, called *The Lotus Sutra*, has been especially influential and helpful for the Buddhists in China, Korea, and Japan. It has attracted more commentary than any other Buddhist scripture.[25]

How important is it for religious people to have an authoritative book or books?

---

24. Dalai Lama, *The Compassionate Life*, 1.
25. Watson, *The Lotus Sutra*.

Day 21

Since the Quran is God's book, the text of the Quran, like its author, is regarded as perfect, eternal, and unchangeable.[26]

In the Abrahamic monotheistic religions, there is even more dependence on the ancient books for guidance. For the Jewish faith, there is heavy reliance on the Hebrew Bible and the Talmud or the commentary and learning of rabbis across the centuries. Christians, too, rely on the Hebrew Bible, and add the New Testament, which is central to shaping beliefs and practices. Islam, of course, pays close attention to the Quran and believes that it is the word of God. Many of us do have some familiarity with the Bible (both the Hebrew Bible and the New Testament); however, except for practicing Muslims, we have less acquaintance with the Quran, and a brief word about the Quran might be helpful.

The Quran (meaning "recitation" or "reading") is thought to be the collected revelations of Muhammad. As these sayings are read in Arabic, Muslims believe they are hearing from above, or directly from God. This recitation is thought to be a true miracle, providing them with a guide for all aspects of living, the pattern for thinking, and essentially a comprehensive vision of history and destiny. For Muslims, it is to hear the true word from the other side. The Quran is understood as the literal word of God, and is therefore honored and read with great care. There is occasional misunderstanding about the Quran by interpreting it as a third and later addition to the Abrahamic religious tradition. Muslims believe that it is a statement about beginnings, even superseding the Bible, and is therefore foundational for true belief, although there is respect for the Bible and the peoples of the book. The great prophets of the Bible are honored, and Jesus has a special place as one of the prophets.

How do you understand relationship between the Bible and the Quran?

---

26. Esposito, *The Straight Path*, 19. The Quran is understood as the word of God in Arabic, although there are translations in English and other languages.

Day 22

All scripture is inspired by God and is used for teaching, for reproof, for correction, and for training in righteousness. (2 Tim 3:16)

Human beings, in the quest to be in harmony with God or the foundational principles of the universe, have longed for a true word from the Transcendent One. At times, they have claimed that this true word is present in the literature that guides their religion. For the indigenous religious traditions, nature's marvelous ways have been more revelatory than the narrative literature, although their stories certainly guide them. The literature of those religions, which we have categorized as belonging within transcendent monism, have sought answers in their great narrative literature, maintaining that it contains an account of transcendent reality, although they have not maintained that every word is the ultimate truth. Insight about transcendence is present, but the stories need not be taken literally, nor accepted in every detail.

The followers of the monotheistic religions have been more dependent upon their great literature, and have seen it as either being or containing the word of God. Yet, there is no universal agreement among these several religions. They agree about the foundational character of the literature, but there are a variety of ways that this literature has been understood and interpreted.

There are diverse views even within each of the religions, and the differences are often expressed in an intense way. For example, within Judaism, one sees differences between the Orthodox and Reformed traditions regarding the Hebrew Bible. The categories of "is" and "contains" (with "is" being the literal word of God, and "contains" being a writing in which the wisdom of God may be discerned) give us some insight into how the foundational literature is understood within Judaism. The same is true within Christianity as well, and I have been immersed in this conversation for several decades. The differences often depend on words such as "inspiration," "critical historical understanding," "liberal," and "conservative." The same conversation exists within Islam, but there is a more profound sense that the Quran is truly the word of God. We do long for the definite word from the Transcendent One.

How important is it for us to have a true word from the other side?

Day 23

Some Buddhists might say that to write a biography of Siddhatta Gotama is a very un-Buddhist thing to do. In their view, no authority should be revered, however august: Buddhists must motivate themselves and rely on their own efforts, not on a charismatic leader.[27]

Foundational literature, read with care, has often been thought to be the authoritative norm for belief and practice of the world's religions. Another source has been the vast and beautiful character of nature. Perhaps as important as the literature or nature representing the word from above has been the founder or the leaders of the religion. In many cases, it is hard to isolate a single individual, though in other cases there is an identifiable person. This is certainly the case with Buddhism and the Abrahamic monotheistic religions. Let's begin with Buddha.

Siddhartha Gautama was born around 563 BCE in the region of the Ganges River in northeastern India. The religious outlook of the region in which he was born was filled with myths, gods, and ceremonies described in the Vedas. Siddhartha was born into the privilege of a royal family and provided with every luxury. The young prince was handsome and gifted, and appeared to have everything one could possibly want in life. But in his late twenties he began to be discontented and troubled by his observation of suffering, that of old age, disease, and dying. These observations and his awareness of dedicated monks who had withdrawn from the world caused him to give up his station in life and seek a religious life that would lead to enlightenment. After some years of extreme asceticism, he discovered a middle way between extreme asceticism and privilege and experienced enlightenment (awakening) under the now famous Bodhi tree. He spent the rest of his life teaching compassion and healing the suffering of his followers. From his example and teaching came the religion of Buddhism.[28]

Are the example and teaching of Buddha good guides for the spiritual life?

---

27. Armstrong, *Buddha*, xi. Note slight spelling change of the Buddha's name.
28. See Blomfield, *Gautama Buddha*, for one of many biographies.

Day 24

The cry of the Israelites has now come to me; I have seen how the Egyptians oppress them. So come, I will send you to Pharaoh to bring my people, the Israelites out of Egypt. (Exod 3:9–10)

One might turn first to Abraham as representative of the monotheistic religions. His story would be a good choice, although Judaism, while having great respect for Abraham, looks more to Moses as the one who shaped Israelite religion. He is the founder and great prophetic teacher of Judaism. His experience and the liberation of the Hebrew people from Egypt are seen as a word from above. The story of Moses is well-known. He was born of a Jewish mother who, in order to save him, left him on the banks of the Nile River. He was found and adopted by an Egyptian princess and had the benefits of growing up in a royal family. He was spared the suffering of his people, who were living in slavery, although he observed their plight. As a young man, he rebelled, and was forced to flee to Midian, a region north of the Red Sea. There he settles down, marries, and becomes a shepherd. But one day, while tending his sheep, he encounters God in the burning bush and is commanded to return to Egypt to liberate the Israelites. He returns and confronts Pharaoh. Following this confrontation, there are plagues in Egypt, the Passover for the Israelites occurs, and Moses proceeds to lead the people out of Egypt in the Exodus. During this event, Moses once again encounters God, this time on Mount Horeb (or Sinai). He then speaks to the Jewish people about the laws of life and the covenant with God.

This story, with liberation, building the law-abiding society and living within the expectations of the covenant agreement between the Hebrew people and God, becomes the prototype of Jewish belief. The eternal God intervenes on behalf of the people, sets them free, establishes a pact with them, and then gives them an ethical code after which to pattern their behavior. They are led to a promised land, in which to live this new and challenging life, a land filled with blessing, and also one in conflict then and now.

Do you find the narrative guiding Judaism to be compelling?

Day 25

For in him all the fullness of God was pleased to dwell, and through him God was pleased to reconcile to himself all things. (Col 1:19–20)

Christianity has tied its faith in God to the coming of Jesus. The Christian Church has taught from the beginning that a true knowledge of God is enhanced by a faith encounter with Jesus, and the study and practice of his life and teaching.

Jesus is viewed as the message of the Transcendent One. In the early centuries, Christians gave attention to the identity of Jesus and understood him as the Christ (Messiah), who was Savior and Lord. They worked diligently to find the best way to speak about how the fullness of God was present in him. The history of his life was not unimportant, but the focus was on the Christ of faith, in whom God was present. The Word "became flesh and lived among us, . . . full of grace and truth" (John 1:14). In time, the concept of the Trinity became the way that the divinity within Jesus was articulated. He had within him the same substance as God.[29]

With the rise of scientific inquiry and the critical historical method, attention turned to the Jesus of history. Hard questions were asked about whether Jesus was divine and performed the miracles recorded in the Gospels. The story of how this inquiry developed is a fascinating one and beyond the scope of daily readings. Suffice to say, this quest for the historical Jesus asked the church to rethink its teaching and the ways that it understands the identity of Jesus. I have immersed myself in the quest, and these historical ways of understanding Jesus have deepened my faith and commitment. This first-century Jew was a compassionate healer, a charismatic teacher, and a radical prophet, and his life and teaching have enriched my Christian walk. I have found ways of thinking about the Christ of faith that enable me to partially integrate the Jesus who lived in first-century Palestine with the Christ of faith who is the second person of the Trinity, although I am still working on it.[30]

Is the Christian narrative attractive and convincing for you?

---

29. The early creedal statements and the writing of Augustine were formative for the church's understanding of the divine nature of Jesus the Christ.

30. See my recent book, *The Radical Teaching of Jesus*.

Day 26

The Prophet of Islam, to whom we shall henceforth refer simply as the Prophet, is for the West the most misunderstood reality within the Islamic universe.[31]

Islam, in part because of the violence associated with radical Islam today, is deeply concerned about the ways that those outside of the Muslim faith understand Muhammad. For Muslims, Muhammad is not viewed as divine, as Jesus is understood to be in Christianity. Even to call him the founder of Islam is not altogether accurate. Muslims prefer to think of him as a prophet and religious reformer. They portray him as a remarkable man and the Great Prophet who received his call from Allah at the age of forty (610 CE). The Quran teaches that he became God's human instrument in bearing the divine revelation, and that he became the model or ideal for human behavior.

As a young man, Muhammad was involved in the caravan trade that passed through Mecca, and he became respected and trusted in his work. He was a reflective person, and in time he felt called by God and received divine revelations (recitations) that were to become integral to the Quran. He associated with others from the Semitic faiths and began to understand his life as a prophet. He became one who warned his hearers to repent and obey God or face judgment. After some difficulty in having his message accepted, a community began to form around him, and the religion he proclaimed became known as Islam (surrender). In part because of opposition and because of his desire to spread his message, he moved his base to Medina. There he began to codify his teaching, setting out the rights and duties of all citizens and the relationship of the Muslim community to other communities. He was later to return to Mecca for the development of this new community, viewed now as not a tribe, but a way of life for all citizens. In time, Muhammad's authority spread to all of Arabia, and the Muslim faith expanded to other regions.

How might the three Abrahamic religions find common ground?

---

31. Nasr, *The Heart of Islam*, 27.

Day 27

So God created humankind in his image, in the image of God he created them; male and female he created them. (Gen 1:27)

During this month of readings, we have been exploring the ways that we reach upward for transcendence, hoping that we will find God or discern the cosmic order, and in these discoveries find guidance for our lives. We reviewed the ways that world religions have spoken about transcendence, whether it is in the form of a personal God with whom we can form a relationship, or an impersonal principle such as the Tao, which sends us clues and signals about structuring our lives. We spoke, as well, about how it is that we hear from the other side or from above. We noted that the indigenous wisdom traditions see the divine within nature and their great narratives that give them categories of understanding. We also spoke about the founding literature of the world's religions, and how faithful adherents hear the voice of the divine in this literature and form their beliefs and practices guided by it. In addition, we spoke about the teachers, founders, and prophets who started these religions and became the source of divine knowledge. We gave special attention to Buddha, Moses, Jesus, and Muhammad. Along the way, we have implied that we sense or hear God within ourselves, and see the divine in those who have been our models and examples in the practice of our faith. As we reach upward we encounter God who meets us and wonders where we have been. We have received a Word from above, and as we think about our own internal lives and the world around us, we sense that transcendence has been with us from the beginning. We might speak about it in reference to why there is anything (being), why we discern meaning in our lives and have values of love and compassion (consciousness), and why we experience happiness and fulfillment (bliss). We have the message from above in nature's beauty and complexity, the founding literature of our religions, the founders and teachers of our faith, and the image of God within us. Our task with all of these messages is to make sense of them.

How do we go about making sense out of these religious teachings?

Day 28

> *The understanding and the interpretation of texts is not merely a concern of science, but is obviously part of the total human experience in the world.*[32]

We have a body of material that we think contains a message from above. The challenge is interpreting and arranging this material in a way that guides us in our present and gives direction for the future. The task of interpretation is called hermeneutics, a term that is used in the fields of literature, philosophy, law, and religious studies. Hermeneutics, while it has a strong methodological component, is more than method; it is the way we read events, experiences, and documents from the past in order to find direction for our lives.[33] The world's religions have a long history of hermeneutics. There is the Talmud in Judaism and the Hadith in Islam, documents that go beyond just critical/historical interpretation of the ancient texts. There is also extensive commentary on them, and additional tradition and reflection that express the quest to understand the original texts and discern guidance and meaning for life. For some people, there is the assumption that one can just read an ancient text or an historical account of an event and walk away with truth or understand what actually happened. I have people tell me after reading the accounts of creation in Genesis, "Well, that's what it says." I listen carefully and honor the sincerity of the comment, but gently remind them that their reading comes out of assumptions about the literature or event and about the nature of the literature. Others might say, "All I need is careful and critical historical work, and then I can provide you with an interpretation that is accurate." I honor this comment and strategy as well, but also want to remind these sincere people that they bring their lives and a range of presuppositions to the task. I often have to remind myself about the challenge of hermeneutics.

What "sunglasses" do we have on as we read this ancient literature?

---

32. Gadamer, *Truth and Method*, xi.

33. There are many fine books on hermeneutics, and the one mentioned above is exceptional. My modest contribution is entitled *Biblical Hermeneutics*.

Day 29

The first and primary work of interpretation is to be conscientious and disciplined in doing the basic work of studying the language and the history of the document to be interpreted.[34]

Across the years, I have had to deal with the hermeneutical challenge in my teaching and writing. Recently, I encountered the challenge in writing the book, *The Radical Teaching of Jesus*. I was faced with literature written several decades after he lived. In addition, the authors of the Gospels were less interested in preserving history than in providing guidance for an emerging church, and they drew heavily on their assumptions that the coming of Jesus was foretold in the Hebrew Bible. Let me provide just a hint of how I faced this challenge:

1. I have done and continue to do the hard *language and historical work*. I understood the genre of the Gospels and the fact that Jesus spoke in Aramaic, which was then translated into Greek. I now read these writings in English.

2. I spent time studying *the types of literature (Gospels) and the creative use of figures of speech* by Jesus, knowing that what he had said came through oral traditions and was used in a didactic and ecclesiological way. There was substantial redaction. I tried to be aware of my assumptions as I read.

3. I spent time on the *cultural and historical background of the region and the setting in which Jesus lived and taught*. I had to cross over to it.

4. I gave special attention to the *people who were his contemporaries and listening to his teaching*. They lived in a particular geographical region, were pre-modern in their understanding of the world around them, and in many cases faced poverty, injustice, illness, and death. Most were Jewish.

5. In particular, I had to look *at their presuppositions as they listened and attempted to apply what he said to their lives*. For example, they believed that miracles were possible and that God was just a prayer away.

What did I forget to do? How might I improve my interpretation?

---

34. Ferguson, *The Radical Teaching of Jesus*, 84.

Day 30

> *The question is this: how can the Christian faith, first experienced and symbolically articulated in an ancient culture now long out-of-date, speak meaningfully to human existence today as we experience it amid a worldview dominated by natural science, secular self-understanding, and the worldwide cry for freedom?*[35]

As we seek and develop a mindful spirituality, we draw upon the resources available to us, usually ones that point us upward toward transcendence. We have briefly mentioned the range of resources available to us, and suggested that we interpret these resources with an eye on how we do it (hermeneutics). The next step is to find a way to put it together in a form that enables us to understand it with head *and* heart, with mind *and* spirit. In many of the theistic religions, this endeavor is called theology, and in other cases it may be referred as *the teaching*. Within the Christian tradition there is a short definition of theology: "faith in search of understanding."[36] We often start our theological inquiry in the present moment, where we currently are, hoping that the word from above will speak directly to us in our situation. We might review both where we are in terms of our personal development and also in terms of our place in history, our culture, our outlook, and where we are in our spiritual journey. For example, we might say that we are in mid-life, in North America, in a global context, in a postmodern moment, surrounded by rapid change, and within a human family that faces overwhelming problems. We then turn to our options for guidance, and often, but not always, to the religious tradition in which we have found meaning and guidance. We turn to its literature such as the Bible, to its teachings and practices, to a supportive community, and hope to receive understanding and guidance for our spiritual pathway.

How confident are you that you can find a true word from God?

---

35. Peters, *God: the World's Future*, 5.
36. A good introduction to Christian theology is Migliore's *Faith Seeking Understanding*.

Day 31

But the wisdom from above is first pure, then peaceable, gentle, willing to yield, full of mercy and good fruits, without a trace of partiality or hypocrisy. (Jas 3:17)

Human beings across time have longed for a voice from God, or Transcendence, one that they can trust and one that gives them hope for a better life. Many people from various times in history and with different cultures and languages have spoken about transcendence, and developed alternative narratives about how the divine voice is heard and what it means. As we have suggested, the voice may be inside of us, present in nature, an integral part of our history, a body of literature, great leaders, and in the exemplary lives of those who surround us. We also mentioned that there are those who argue with some persuasion that there is no voice from beyond; only what we have right in front of us. We wisely give attention to this point of view.

So we maintained that there is a need to listen carefully for the divine voice and interpret it in a way that nourishes us and empowers others to thrive. There is the great risk that we will misunderstand or purposefully distort the transcendent message and use it for our own needs for possessions, power, prestige, and pleasure, and the control of others. In these ways, religion can be harmful and dangerous. A leader of the early Christian community, James, perhaps the brother of Jesus, reflected on what he believed was the way that the divine message should be interpreted and applied. First, and as far as possible, it must be pure, not diluted or distorted by a devious purpose. It should guide individuals and groups to live in a peaceful and gentle way. It should guide followers to show mercy to those in need and bear the fruits of God's Spirit within them. And it should not show favoritism to just a few insiders, but should be loving and compassionate to all. If one acts in this way and guides the group of the followers to act in this way, then all can be sure that the message from above has been heard. One has received transcendent wisdom.

What are the best criteria to use in order to judge a religious view as true?

Study Guide for the January Readings

Questions for Contemplation and Discussion:

1. What are the components of reaching upward for transcendence? How do we do it? What does Psalm 23 suggest as a spiritual way?

2. How would you describe the life of the spirit and the life of the mind? Is it wise to incorporate both in our spiritual journey? Which is most important, or are they both essential and of equal importance? What is meant by mindful spirituality?

3. What do you think the Apostle Paul meant when he urged the Philippian Christians to have the mind of Christ? Is it really possible?

4. What are the various ways transcendence is understood in the several religions of the human family? How important is it to understand God, or ultimate reality, as being personal?

5. What are the most important books that various religions use to understand God, or Transcendence? Do you think that most of these books have helpful insights for the spiritual journey?

6. How important are the various founders and leaders of the world religions? Which one of these great founders/leaders is the most persuasive and provides the best guidance for living a truly spiritual life?

7. What qualities of the spiritual way taught by the great religions are healthy and life-giving, or unhealthy and life-denying? What makes them life-giving, with insights that enable us to flourish?

8. What are the most challenging arguments against belief in God? How important is it for you to understand these challenges? How might the idea of using different maps help us as we deal with these challenges?

9. Do you think that human beings are created in the image of God, and if so, what are the qualities that we share with God?

10. As we seek to develop a theological frame of reference and a spiritual pathway, how might we interpret the literature, teaching, and traditions of our religious orientation? How do we do so in a way that is fair to the teaching and yet brings this teaching forward into our time to guide us? What hermeneutical principles or starting points do we need to make this literature the most helpful?

THEME FOR FEBRUARY

LOVING GOD WITH OUR WHOLE BEING

Day 32

Just then a lawyer stood up to test Jesus. "Teacher," he said, "what must I do to inherit eternal life?" He said to him, "What is written in the law? What do you read there?" He answered him, "You shall love the Lord God with all your heart, and with all your soul, and with all your strength, and with all your mind; and your neighbor as yourself." And he said to him, "You have given the right answer; do this, and you shall live." (Luke 10:25–28)

In January, in keeping with our theme of "Reaching Upward," we focused on what it is we are reaching for, and called it God, or Transcendence. We also spoke about the various ways that humankind has found to reach for the divine. We want to continue with this theme. We will draw upon the Judeo-Christian answer as somewhat representative of the human quest and the specific answer that Jesus gave to the lawyer who asked him about eternal life. The lawyer, like most of us, wondered if his current life could be improved, and whether there was a state of being that might go beyond death.

Though testing Jesus, he nevertheless asked a sincere question. Is there another layer or level where God dwells, and where I might dwell beyond my current earthly life? Jesus, as he often did, answered with a question. What does the law (Torah) teach? The lawyer, probably an educated scribe with knowledge of the law, answered the question by saying that it comes when we love God with our whole being and our neighbor as fully and profoundly as we love ourselves. Though pleased that Jesus said he got the right answer, the lawyer was still in the mood to probe and test: "But wanting to justify himself, he asked Jesus, 'And who is my neighbor?'" As he often did, the great teacher gave the lawyer his answer by telling a story. Jesus was fond of using stories to answer questions, largely because they made his listeners think more deeply and probe the many sides of the answer. This was certainly the case, as Jesus answers with the story of the Good Samaritan, which we turn to in the next few days.

Was Jesus wise in answering the lawyer's question by telling a story?

Day 33

*You have heard it said, "You shall love your neighbor and hate your enemy."
But I say unto you, "Love your enemies and pray for those who persecute you."*
(Matt 6:43–44)

We are exploring the ways that we reach upward for God in order to find guidance for belief and practice. We have acknowledged that there are those who are reluctant to use the word "God" because they are unsure of its meaning, and would rather speak about the divine or transcendence. We honor this position, but hope that the word "God" is acceptable in this context as a way of speaking about what is beyond or above. Alcoholics Anonymous prefers the term Higher Power in order to honor the diversity of beliefs among those who find help with its services. Concerning the context in which Jesus taught (first-century Palestine), the term "God" would have been understood as it was used within first-century Judaism. As Jesus speaks with people, he encourages them to embrace the kingdom of God, by which he meant the power and presence of God, or to say it in a slightly different way, to yield to the reign of God. He encourages his listeners to repent or change the direction of their lives and to follow the will and way of God. It is a simple message, although one that is very difficult to follow. His teaching is transformational in character. In this exchange, God would have been understood as both sovereign and loving. Jesus is saying that God invites all people to become citizens of the kingdom of God. This frame of reference would have been understood in the conversation between Jesus and the lawyer. As Jesus encounters the lawyer, he is aware of the lawyer's spirit of testing and self-justification. Jesus is neither threatened nor impatient with the lawyer. Rather, he is true to himself, authentic and focused, and is able to have empathy with a troubled person. Because God is love, and God is the center of Jesus' life, he demonstrated compassionate love. The word used in the text, coming from the Greek, is *agape*, which is self-giving and sacrificial love, the fundamental quality of one whose heart and mind are open to the fullness of God's love. He wants the lawyer to get it, and tells him a story rather than giving advice.

What does Jesus mean by the kingdom of God?

Day 34

Beloved, let us love one another, because love is from God; everyone who loves is born of God and knows God, for God is love. (1 John 4:7)

It is interesting to observe the way that the New Testament connects love, and what is translated in the Gospels as eternal life. The lawyer's initial question to Jesus is: "What must I do to inherit eternal life?" Then Jesus answers the question with another question, "What is written in the law?" The reply is that we are to love God with our whole being and our neighbor as ourselves. The meaning in this exchange is that eternal life *begins now*; it is in the present as we love God and our neighbors. Frequently, in cultures rooted in Abrahamic monotheism, the answer usually given about eternal life is understood in a slightly different way. Eternal life is often understood as a reward for good works at the end of life. If I do what God expects and requires, then I will go to heaven. I would prefer to think of the teaching of Luke 10:25–37 as the affirmation that eternal life begins now, as we begin to love God and our neighbor, and the loving relationship with God will continue beyond time in eternity. The word eternal does speak of forever, but also speaks of the condition of being surrounded by love, both in time and in eternity. It is not so much a reward as it is a state of bliss that comes from being in the presence of human and divine love. What is also being taught is that our way to eternal life is to love others. The answer given by the lawyer, and then unpacked by Jesus, is that eternal life is to care for those in need. The author of the small letter of 1 John, in quite dramatic fashion, also connects loving others with "being born of God" and getting to know God, because God is love. As we love, we experience the reality of God in this life and are accepted into the loving arms of God as we leave this life.[1] It is difficult for us to know what a loving heaven might be like. For example, will we be with members of our family? One clue may be an existence beyond space and time.

How do you understand eternal life?

---

1. For an honest and careful treatment of the issues of eternal life, see Allison, *Night Comes*.

Day 35

He said, "The one who showed mercy." Jesus said to him, "Go and do likewise."
(Luke 10:37)

It is now time to look more carefully at the story that Jesus tells as he answers the lawyer's question about eternal life. The story is called The Good Samaritan for good reason. Jesus begins the story by saying that a man was taking the fairly dangerous, dusty, and steep road down from Jerusalem to Jericho. It often had the presence of thieves and there was little or no security. The man did get attacked, was robbed, and was left half-dead in the ditch. It is likely that the lawyer could identify with this story because he knew it was a treacherous road. Jesus had his attention and continues the story. He says that a priest went by, saw the man on the side of the road in the ditch and kept walking. No doubt he was busy, and he wanted to be on time for his meeting in Jericho, perhaps one that had been arranged in order to take care of the religious services the following weekend.

It is not difficult to identify with the priest. Often we are in the middle of important work and anxious about time when we encounter a person in need. We might even say to ourselves that what we are doing is more important than getting our hands dirty by taking care of another person. We know that if we do reach out that it will take time and energy and may even be costly and demanding if it is a person without any resources, like the one left beside the road. As Jesus tells the story, he doesn't identify the man in terms of tribe and religion, but it may have been a marginalized person left in the ditch. The person may have been a second-class citizen, perhaps with a different ethnicity, one whom we might today call a Palestinian. The priest's primary loyalty and job description called upon him to serve the religious needs of his own people. He may have said to himself, "I think I'd better pass by on the other side of the road; it will be safer and allow me to get on with my important work." I confess to having some of these feelings as I sprint through my busy days.

Would you have stopped that day to help the injured stranger?

Day 36

If you judge people, you have no time to love them.

—Mother Teresa[2]

Not only did the priest pass by the injured man on the other side of the road, so too did a Levite. Generally speaking, a Levite in the time of Jesus was one who belonged to the tribe of Levi, one of the twelve tribes of Israel. The title of Levite also implied that this person might have been a priest, in that it was common for Levites to choose the priesthood as a vocation. It was also true that, even if the Levite was not technically a priest, this person would be thought of as one who was closely attached to God. It is likely that Jesus is speaking about a priest in this story. The priests were designated to serve in the temple to perform rituals and conduct sacrificial services. In part of the narrative of Jesus, he is described as having reservations about the value of some of the rituals and rites of sacrifice, suggesting that they may be empty and without meaning, and in some cases, even border on hypocrisy. The story says: "A Levite, when he came to the place and saw him, passed by on the other side." I am struck by the phrase "passed by on the other side," and I know how easy it is to ignore those in difficulty and pain and fail to show them practical compassion.[3] The story of Jesus may also imply more than just neglect; he may also be pointing to the ways that we exclude others because of prejudicial attitudes. He may be suggesting that we are inclined, if we do so at all, only to help those who are like us, speak our language, and share our culture. Jesus demonstrates love to nearly all those whom he meets. He even expresses tough love to those who are hypocritical in their behavior and who harshly judge those from a different group, religious tradition, or ethnic heritage, or those just plain down and out. I am sure that, as he spoke with Levites, he would have been sensitive and compassionate; yet he would have also called to their attention that those who represent true and healthy religion must fully live and incarnate the values inherent in their religious faith. Jesus spoke directly to hypocrites.

How easy or hard is it for you to help those in need?

---

2. Mother Teresa, *Life in the Spirit*, 6.
3. See Riley's practical exposition of love in her book, *Practical Compassion*.

Day 37

The best way to find yourself is to lose yourself in the service of others.

—Mohandas Gandhi

Jesus, in order to make his point, gives one other example of a person who was traveling down the road from Jerusalem to Jericho. He carefully selects the person to illustrate his point and says, "But a Samaritan while traveling came near him; and when he saw him, he was moved with pity. He went to him and bandaged his wounds, having poured oil and wine on them. Then he put him on his own animal, brought him to an inn, and took care of him" (Luke 10:33–34). Jesus goes on to say that he asks the innkeeper to take care of the wounded man and then says that he will return the next day and pay the costs for leaving the wounded person at the inn. I want to call attention to three themes in this part of the story:

1. The first has to do with *priorities*. The most important concern for the good Samaritan was to take care of the injured and needy person whom he encountered. He found time, even though he too had obligations in Jericho. It was an inconvenience, yet he knew that the welfare of another human being was what was most important. Love is preeminent.

2. Second, the person Jesus uses to illustrate his point is a Samaritan. The Samaritan was also a *marginalized person*, and the lawyer to whom Jesus was speaking would have caught the reference immediately. The labels we carry, perhaps that of a devout person, do not necessarily mean that we will be true to our values and express the heart of our faith, which is to love.

3. The final theme I want to underline is that the care he gave was *practical and appropriate*. There are times when our heart may be in the right place and we try to help another person, but we miss the true need of the person. We may impose what we think is needed, not what is truly needed. For example, we may judge and give advice, rather than listening with empathy. Not infrequently, we lead with our needs rather than the needs, for example, of the one who has been beaten and is half dead in the ditch on the road to Jericho.

Are there traces of prejudice in your life about people who differ from you?

Day 38

The world is a theatre of love.

—Kashmiri Proverb

The stories that Jesus tell, in order to illustrate his points, tend to be set in the real world, drawing upon the experiences of his listeners. As he speaks about love and compassion with a story, the plot of his story tends to be about an incident that could have happened yesterday in the life of his followers. Love is less about a warm and fuzzy feeling, and more about a positive action that improves the life of one's neighbor. The story of the Good Samaritan, upon which we are reflecting, is a case in point, and even we in the contemporary world can identify with it. The act of loving is hard work, takes time, and costs energy and resources. Our busy worlds are "the theatre of love."

It doesn't take Jesus long to get to the point of the parable of the Good Samaritan, although he may have amplified the story in the actual setting. As he answers the lawyer's question about eternal life, he uses an illustration of a man attacked on the road from Jerusalem down to Jericho. He speaks of those who passed by and one who stopped to help, and then he pauses a moment and asks: "Which of these three do you think was a neighbor to the man who fell into the hands of the robbers?" The lawyer's response is: "The one who showed mercy." And the one who showed mercy was the Good Samaritan. But Jesus doesn't stop there; he has a concluding comment that will get to his point, that to love God (who is Love) is to love our neighbor, who may need help. He says to the lawyer that, if one is really seeking eternal life, a life intimately connected to God now and into eternity, then "Go do likewise." I wish I had been there and observed this exchange. I want to like the lawyer and hope he didn't go away just wanting to argue with Jesus. Or, perhaps even worse, go away with a mild feeling of "That was interesting." My hope is that he went away thinking about the double love commandment, to love God with one's whole being and one's neighbor as oneself. I hope he said, "I have a neighbor in need and I think I'll offer to help."

What feelings does the review of this story create in you?

Day 39

You shall love the Lord your God with all your heart. (Luke 10:27)

The first part of the answer that Jesus gave to the lawyer/scribe when he inquired about how to inherit eternal life was to return the question: "What is written in the law? What do you read there?" As you remember, the lawyer got the right answer. We may want to ask ourselves what the answer truly meant to Jesus and the lawyer. Let's start at the beginning and ask what they both might have had in mind when they quoted the Torah—"You shall love the Lord your God with all your heart. " The word "heart" appears many times in the Hebrew Bible, with the occasional reference to the physical heart, although much more frequently meaning the center or distinctive quality of what is described, such as the heart of God. In the case of human beings, the heart is the center of human emotions, feelings, moods, and passions (it is used 814 times this way in the Bible).[4] Jesus and the lawyer would know and sense this meaning, and in hearing the *Shema*, they would know that we are to love God with our deepest feelings and pure emotions. I find it very perceptive and powerful that the first part of the great commandments begins with our deepest feelings. The truth is that we often do what we feel like doing. If our emotions are not motivating our actions, then we can easily lose interest and neglect what is most important. Our feelings can come and go, be quite fickle, and be subject to fatigue, diet, the range of personal relationships, and the actions and responsibilities of a given day. They can be shaped so much by how we are doing in life, our level of accomplishment, the ways we meet our daily goals, and our level of frustration and of joy about all that is going in our lives. It is true that what I may have experienced in a particular day may put God either in the background or center stage. Likewise, my linkage with God may feel absent or even negative one day, or full of joy and gratitude and the very source of my energy on another. Feelings shape our actions.

How hard or easy do you find it to love God?

---

4. See the article in the *Harper's Bible Dictionary,* 377.

Day 40

The mind emerges from the activity of the brain, whose structure and function are directly shaped by interpersonal experience.[5]

We need to keep our heart finely tuned if we are to love God with our whole heart. One factor in keeping our heart tuned and focused on loving God is to maintain healthy and loving human relationships. There is a linkage, if love is central to our lives, between our love of others and our love of God. While there are differences between loving God in an emotional way and loving another with our deepest and purest feelings, it is still possible to compare the two ways of loving and to view them as somewhat analogous. The great biblical injunction is a double commandment, to love God and love our neighbor. They are related and have a common root. A brief review of the different kinds of love may be helpful for us at this point in our readings.[6] In the English language, the word "love" is somewhat difficult to pin down, in that it describes many human feelings and actions. In fact, as we use our language, we draw upon several words or cognates to clear things up, such as caring, compassion, attraction, and empathy. The Greek language had several words for love, as well, and for clarity, let's look at three of them, in that they are familiar and have crossed over into English. The first one, *eros*, refers to our feelings of being attracted to that which is good, true, and beautiful. The object, such as a beautiful nature scene or fine symphony, evokes our feeling of attraction. A second word is *philia,* and it refers to friendship and the gratification we feel when we are around others with whom we have much in common; they are our friends. The third one is *agape*, and it speaks about unconditional and unlimited care. There are other dimensions of love, but perhaps these three categories will be helpful as we think about loving God with our whole being.

Which of the three kinds of love mentioned is the easiest for you to express?

---

5. Siegel, *The Developing Mind*, 1.
6. See my book, *Lovescapes*, 38–50.

Day 41

Love is patient, love is kind; love is not envious or boastful or arrogant or rude. . . . It bears all things, hopes all things, endures all things. (1 Cor 13:4, 7)

There is a strong emphasis on the importance of love in the New Testament. It is seen as the primary quality of one who has fully endorsed the reign of God in life. While it is a gift of God, a quality that is empowered, it is also one that is nurtured and cultivated by our experience. For example, the relationships we inherit, select, and cultivate play a major role in shaping who we are and who we are becoming. Our relationships are based on many factors and can be healthy and life-giving, unhealthy with negative consequences, or a combination of both. A long list could be made of the qualities that make a relationship healthy and loving. Among them are:

1. Caring/Compassion: a good relationship is one in which there is a genuine concern about the welfare of the other and a tangible expression of this care. Compassion or the concern for the suffering of another is present.

2. Affection: a good relationship has the foundation of positive feelings for the other person. The affection we feel for others can be expressed in tender words, in appropriate physical actions, and the delight we feel with them.

3. Honesty: A healthy relationship will be one in which people are honest with each other; about big things, of course, but also about the small details of life.

4. Trust: Honesty leads to trust, the feeling that one can place confidence in the other person, knowing that the other person will understand and help us.

5. Sharing: In order to fully know and care for the other person, there is the need to share the joys of mutual exchange and common experiences.

6. Forgiveness: Even in the best of relationships, there will be times when we fail to live up to the love we pledge to the other. Forgiveness can heal the wounds when we break the bond of love.

7. Empathy: We need to cultivate the capacity to see the world as the other does, and to identity with that vision and stand in solidarity with the other.

Many other characteristics might be mentioned. What might they be?

Day 42

> *Even though we tell the truth about ourselves, find Real Love, and share it with others, we can quickly lose the effect of those positive experiences if we hit certain obstacles in our lives. We must, therefore, learn to identify those obstacles and deal with them effectively, or they can destroy happiness.*[7]

Unfortunately, all of our relationships are not healthy and life-giving, and even the best ones have some stress and misunderstanding, and lots of room for growth. To illustrate, I will look at each of the positive qualities mentioned in yesterday's reading and explore how these positive qualities can easily turn into an obstacle.
For example:

1. We may not feel like caring because of fatigue or stress, and so we neglect the other's needs and think only of our own.
2. We may not show affection because we are preoccupied with the interests, hobbies, work, and the worries and strains of our own life.
3. We may resort to dishonesty and deception if we violate the norms of the relationship. We then feel shame or guilt, and do not want to be discovered.
4. The trust of course breaks down, and we retreat from one another.
5. We fail to express what we are really feeling, and move into protected silence and keep our distance.
6. We do not ask for or express forgiveness and wounds are not healed.
7. We fail to have empathy for the other, maybe because we feel alienated and our own negative feelings are in control.

It is easy for us to identify with some of these obstacles; we have felt them in our relationships. I would like to invite the reader to think of our complicated relationships with others as somewhat analogous to our relationship with God. It is not easy "to love God with our whole heart" and consistently have positive feelings about God. Many of the Psalms express this reality.

What are the obstacles for expressing love in you life?

---

7. Baer, *Real Love*, 228.

Day 43

Neither my Heaven nor my Earth can contain me, but the soft, humble heart of my believing servant can contain me. —Muhammad

Muhammad expresses two profound truths in one simple statement, that the fullness of God is beyond our comprehension, and yet we can receive God into our lives. One is humbled and overwhelmed by these insights. The great commandment amplifies these insights by saying that we are to love the God within us with our whole soul. Yes, we are to love God with our deepest feelings, but also with our soul. Once again, we have a word, "soul," that is subtle, with different shades of meaning. A critical question for us might be, what did Jesus and the lawyer mean as they used and heard the word "soul," a word likely spoken in Hebrew, although it could have been in Aramaic. Perhaps the best way to understand the word is to think in terms of the very life and identity of the person. The wonderful story of Genesis says that when God created the first person, God breathed in the breath of life, and Adam (as male and female) became a living soul, or a living being with traces of God's breath or spirit.

The wonderful stories of creation in Genesis also say that this soul or person was created in the image of God (*imago Dei*). There have been long conversations across the centuries about the meaning of the affirmation that humans were and are created in the image of God, and at the risk of simplifying a complex issue, let me summarize a kind of consensus that has emerged. If we are to love God with our soul, what is it that is doing the loving? It is a person created in the image of God, a human being with at least four fundamental qualities.[8] I'll list them here and amplify their meaning in tomorrow's reading. Humans, created in the image of God, are rational, moral, relational, and creative. It is these qualities that come into play as we love God with our whole soul.

Do you think that love is innate? Or do we need to learn how to love? Or both?

---

8. One might quote multiple sources, but Peters underlines these four dimensions of the image of God (*God: the World's Future*, 146–49).

Day 44

So God created humankind in his image, in the image of God he created them, male and female he created them. (Gen 1:27)

It is important to underline that the Genesis account says that God created humankind, male and female, in the image of God. There is no ranking; women and men are equal in the sight of God and share God's image and join one another in life. The story in Genesis 1 goes on to describe their activities.

1. They are *rational* beings, able to use their minds and reason about finding solutions to the challenges of life. They begin to garden, raise crops, and find sustenance. They create a place to live, protecting themselves from the weather. They begin to name the animals, providing categories of understanding the different roles and systems that make for an ordered and meaningful life. They are given responsibility to sustain the healthy ecology of Eden.

2. They are *moral* beings and must make choices about good and evil, what will sustain a healthy life, and what might be harmful. The story describes the challenge of what to eat, and the second account of creation in Genesis says they decide to break the rules and not honor the authority of God. Human life is full of choices; many of them sustain us and we flourish, but some are harmful and self-destructive.

3. They are *relational* beings, and in the story, Adam and Eve come together in a loving relationship, are "fruitful and multiply," and connect with the fish of the sea, the birds of the air, and with every living thing. And they talk to God about it all, gain insight, and begin to know one another in an intimate way.

4. They are *creative* beings, and asked to join with God in the ongoing process of creation. They are given responsibility for improving the life of all living beings and to become caretakers of the earth.

Are there other dimensions of our lives that may reflect the image of God?

Day 45

And going a little farther, he threw himself on the ground and prayed, "My Father, if it is possible, let this cup pass from me; yet not what I want but what you want." (Matt 26:39)

The third word that describes how we should love God in the recital of the great commandments is strength. It reads that you shall love God with all of your heart, with all of your soul, and with all of your *strength*. It too is a word that invites a mix of interpretations, and it is wise to review how the word is used in the Bible in order to better understand its use in the conversation between Jesus and the lawyer.[9] What does it mean to love God with all our strength?

1. It suggests that those who are told to love God with all their strength have the *capacity* to obey the command. The capacity includes physical strength, as Jesus had in the Garden of Gethsemane approaching his death, but even more importantly, the psychic strength to sustain love under incredible challenges. It is to have the ardency to overcome obstacles.

2. A sub-point under "capacity" would be that the person has the *courage* to continue to love in spite of circumstances, such as Jesus did as the soldiers arrived the night before his death. Courage is sustained when inspired by a high purpose, and the sacrifice of oneself with a burning passion for a great cause is displayed.

3. Such courage is generated when one has *convictions* about the vision of a better world in which there will be love, justice, and peace rather than armed conflict and the slaughter of innocent people. Jesus knew that he would be arrested and be crucified, yet his deepest values sustained him, as he says in his prayer, "If it be possible, let this cup pass from me, but not my will but yours be done." Jesus was committed to his values.

We are to love God with all of our physical, emotional, and spiritual strength.

Is it possible for us to have love for God fully or do we need to be empowered?

---

9. For thorough discussion of the meaning, see Kittel, *Theological Dictionary*, 397–402.

Day 46

True love has the power to heal and transform the situation around us and bring a deep meaning to our lives.[10]

We are often inspired by the exemplary lives and profound insights of the great religious figures, past and present, that have been dedicated to the ways of love. We often wonder how they found the inner resources to be so dedicated to love "with all of their strength." The New Testament speaks about love as a fruit of the Spirit, suggesting that we do need to be empowered to love. Nearly all of the great religious traditions, in their own way, do speak about ways that *give us* the capacity to love. They also speak about ways that we can cultivate a more loving and compassionate life. Empowerment and disciplined practices are wisely combined. For example, the great Buddhist monk, Thich Nhat Hanh, speaks about the cultivation of the mind (getting in the right spiritual place) and practices that lead to loving and compassionate behavior. He counsels certain practices of mindful spirituality and teaches that awareness leads to commitment and wise action. He writes that:

1. We need to be aware of the suffering caused by the destruction of life, whether it is perpetrated by us or other people. We need to resist it if love is to prevail.
2. We need to be aware of the suffering caused by exploitation, social injustice, and oppression. These conditions fill our world.
3. We need to be aware of the suffering caused by sexual misconduct. We so easily hurt others if we do not treat all people with respect.
4. We need to be aware of the suffering caused by unwise speech and the inability to listen to one another. Words can cause untold harm.
5. We need to be aware of the suffering caused by excessive consumption. Our health is at risk.

What motivates you to be a more loving person?

---

10. Thich, *Teachings on Love*, 1. See as well 123–25.

Day 47

> *When I speak about love and compassion, I do so not as a Buddhist, nor as a Tibetan nor as the Dalai Lama. I do so as one human being speaking with another.*[11]

The Dalai Lama often speaks and writes about love and compassion. For him, the expression of these qualities is the essence of true religion and the best way for humans to live. He often speaks about kindness as his religion. He has been generous in providing guidance on how to cultivate love in one's life. In his small book, mentioned in the footnote below, he counsels that learning how to love is a developmental process and arises out of our motivation, or as he says, the purity of mind. His work deserves careful study and reflection; let me list his seven steps:

1. Step one is to assess our current relationships and to make a commitment to love both friend and foe. One can learn a great deal about love from friends.
2. The second step is appreciating kindness and practicing altruism. He teaches that we must have a basic concern for others and then learn from others who have been kind to us.
3. The third step is to return kindness, by which he means that we should have empathy for suffering and relieve suffering whenever and however possible.
4. The fourth step is foundational: it is to engage in the lifelong task of learning to love. We begin with kindness in spirit, and acts that relieve suffering. In this section, he speaks of the ten conditions that cause suffering, that include lack of respect for life and insensitivity to others with harsh speech and divisive talk.
5. He returns in step five with the need to practice compassion, which is to help relieve the suffering of others.
6. Step six is to make a total commitment to love and compassion.
7. The final step is to seek altruistic enlightenment, to prepare for a life of love. A life of reflection and meditation is necessary.

What are the best ways to learn how to love?

---

11. Dalai Lama, *How to Expand Love*, 1.

Day 48

Do not be conformed to this world, but be transformed by the renewal of your minds, so that you may discern what is the will of God—what is good and acceptable and perfect. (Rom 12:2)

We turn now to the last word in the list of ways that we are to love God, listed in the *Shema*; it is to love God with all of our mind.[12] To love God with our minds is to use reason and critical judgment, and to appraise and to reflect. It is to be open, free of bias and prejudice, and to go to the margin of knowledge and insight. It may involve a paradigm shift, seeing reality in a different way and using new categories that are able to contain complex ideas. It is to be less sectarian, less attached to old ways of thinking, to be more open to alternative points of view, and to engage in the quest to find a new place to drop anchor, although you may still be in the same harbor. It may mean tearing down some walls of narrow, tribal, and cultic secrets that sustain our faith community, and facing falsehoods that give us a sense of security. It may mean being less human and earthbound, and beginning to think of God's engagement in the totality of all that is and will be. It may mean thawing from our frozen or impassable factors of fear, distrust, anger, darkness, and those many layers of meaning that have held our little worlds together. It is to be aware that God is the God of the cosmos, and that our universe may be but one in the realm of multiverses. It is to be informed, educated, sensitive to the digital world, acquainted with scientific theories, and able to begin the hard task of integrating our faith with contemporary knowledge. How is our faith related to evolution, quantum theory, cosmology, and an ecological appreciation of our world? It is also to join with God in the ongoing tasks of creation and, more particularly, our small piece of reality—the earth—and creating a more just and humane world. It is to understand that loving coincides with knowing, in reference to God.

What do you think it means to love God with our minds?

---

12. Note, the various versions of the great commandment list the ways to love God in a different order. Luke uses the order of heart, soul, strength, and mind, which I am following. See Matt 22:37 and Mark 12:30. See as well Deut 6:5.

Day 49

Blessed are the pure in heart, for they will see God. (Matt 5:8)

Yesterday's daily reading may feel like too big of a bite, a challenging task only a few can take on in the course of a busy life. One might ask: how is it possible to read so extensively and to learn all that is suggested in the daily reading? Might it be possible to love God with my full mind without becoming both Saint Augustine and Einstein? Didn't Saint Francis love God with his whole mind as he touched the leper and healed the animals? The answer, of course, is "Yes, one can love God with one's mind without reading through the Harvard Library from A to Z." The key is in the wonderful teaching of Jesus in the Sermon on the Mount: to be pure in heart, for then one can really connect with God and love God. It is important to be as informed as possible in order to nurture one's faith development and integrate it with contemporary realities, but it is not the accumulation of knowledge that is the primary issue. Rather, it is to have one's mind transformed by the Spirit of God so that one can discern the will of God, "what is good and acceptable and perfect" as the Apostle Paul teaches the Roman church. The issue is to clear the mind of conformity to the world, to avoid having one's mind filled with the values of the world, such as desiring possessions, having control over others, seeking the accolades of others, and exclusively pursing selfish and physical pleasures. The ability to love God with one's mind means placing the relationship with God as the highest priority in life and sustaining an intimate relationship with God that will guide the mind to the love of God. To be pure is to be a person of integrity, to have a center that holds life together, and gives one a clear vision. It is to be *simple* in the sense of one-ness, not in the sense of being simplistic. It was Leonard Bernstein that taught us that "God is the simplest of all" because God is purely one. Life can be filled with vast amounts of goodness, truth, and beauty, but the mind that has been transformed can receive this richness, but not be taken over by it.

What did Jesus mean when he said that the pure in heart can see God?

Day 50

> *All those Arhant Buddhas of the past attained to supreme enlightenment by abandoning the five hindrances, defilements of mind which weaken understanding, having firmly established the four foundations of mindfulness in their minds, and realized the seven factors of awakening as they really are.*[13]

There is an abundance of teaching in the Buddhist tradition about mindfulness, and it gives excellent guidance to those who are seeking to love God with their mind. Buddhism puts less emphasis on empowerment and more stress on practical ways of achieving the control and enlightenment of the mind. There are numerous strategies within the Buddhist tradition and a brief introduction may be helpful.[14] One must begin by removing barriers that block mindfulness. The five hindrances to full mindfulness are:

1. Desire, the craving or attachment that causes suffering;
2. Defilement, the way we are inclined to seek immediate gratification;
3. Aversion, the temptation to put off or not seek enlightenment;
4. Sloth and torpor, allowing the mind to get sluggish, unfocused, or weak;
5. Restlessness and worry, allowing anxiety to take over one's thoughts.

In order to resist these hindrances, it is necessary to first identify them, face them directly, decipher the causes, and then explore the conditions for removal. With a concentrated and extensive practice, the seeker should focus on the goal of achieving the qualities of mindfulness, which are as follows: not forgetting (and its opposite, remembering), presence of mind, and the quest for wisdom. Beginning with this foundation of mindfulness, one adds several other qualities, including the discrimination of states of mind, the flow of energy, the need for intense concentration, and a resulting equanimity. This summary does not do justice to Buddhist teaching, but perhaps it will guide and motivate us as we seek to learn how to love God with our whole mind.

Do you find this Buddhist guidance about mindfulness wise and helpful?

---

13. Goldstein, *Mindfulness: A Practical Guide to Awakening*, 225.
14. I am following Goldstein's explanation in ibid., 121-93.

Day 51

> *Those that wish to keep a rule of life must guard their minds in perfect possession. Without this guard upon the mind, no discipline can ever be maintained.*[15]

As mentioned, the great teachers of Buddhism give excellent instruction on the necessary practices that discipline the mind. They provide guidance for the appropriate conduct, focusing on both speech and action. In order to achieve the appropriate level of conduct, the seeker must "tame the wildness of the mind."[16] The primary method for taming the mind is meditation, although there are others.

The Bible also places an emphasis on achieving inner peace (*shalom* in Hebrew and *eirene* in Greek), words that point to health, well-being, and personal security. The New Testament does not deny that this "peace that passes understanding" can be nurtured by discipline, but does stress that such peace is more a gift of God's Spirit or God's presence. In reference to our theme of loving God with our whole being, we would maintain that the mind that is at rest and is quiet is free from distraction and able to focus on God's presence in a loving way. Our mind is easily distracted by the daily demands of life, the ways we approach our responsibilities and our relationships, how we try to quell our fears and anxieties, and the ways we often seek a temporary peace in a variety of counterfeit ways, such as self-medication. We easily depend more on wine than Spirit in our quest to calm our wild mind. But the permanent peace comes from resting in God's love and returning our love for God, both in terms of our inner life and also in terms of the way we seek to find and do God's will. Each day we turn to God, take the divine hand, and then, filled with love, we join God in spreading love to those around us and to those in need. Our minds are renewed daily in the loving relationship with God.

What are the most effective ways for you to quiet your mind?

---

15. Chödrön, *No Time to Lose*, 105.
16. Ibid., 105.

Day 52

Holy, holy, holy is the Lord of hosts; the whole earth is full of his glory. (Isa 6:3)

The prophet Isaiah, with his extraordinary imagination, pictures angels coming into the presence of God and feeling overwhelmed by being in the presence of the Mystery. He uses the language of "Holy, holy, holy" to describe how even angels feel a deep sense of worship and respect in the presence of the Sacred One. This sense of awe about God became integral to the Jewish way of life, and it is reflected by the reluctance to even say the accepted name of God (YHWH). How, then, given this profound respect and awe, does one love God with the mind? Part of the answer is "not easily," but another part of the answer is that we stay with it, as the Apostle Paul suggests: "knowing that suffering produces endurance, and endurance produces character, and character produces hope, and hope does not disappoint us, because God's love has been poured into our hearts through the Holy Spirit that has been given to us" (Rom 5:3–5). We love God because God first loved us and is present in our lives. Though we may feel distant, caused by the grandeur of God, and unworthy because of our failures, God gives us the capacity to return the divine love. If we are filled with Love, we are enabled to love. It is true love because it is freely given. But our struggle to love God with our mind continues across our lifespan. We share with Buddhists the challenging task of controlling our wild mind that so often goes off in directions that lead us astray. We become afraid, so insecure and so needy that all we can do is find ways to protect and reassure ourselves that we are okay. The daily round of life, the demands of our work, and the complexity of our relationships distract us. Our mind focuses exclusively on a swirl of uncomfortable feelings. We too face five hindrances or more, although we may not use the same language of the Buddhist tradition. Let's follow their guidance on dealing with hindrances: identify, face them directly, decipher causes, and explore solutions.

What are the greatest challenges you face as you try to love God with you whole mind?

Day 53

Set your minds on things that are above, and not on things that are on earth.
(Col 3:2)

For the next few days, let's follow the sound advice of the Buddhist tradition on how to tame our wild mind. Let's begin to identify our problems as we try to focus on loving God, face them squarely, decipher causes, and explore solutions. Again, I will be using my Christian tradition in this exploration, but it is certainly possible to use the same principles in another faith tradition.

I have tried to put aside some time daily "to set my mind on things that are above," not by ignoring my daily responsibilities "that are on earth." I am not always consistent, in part because of travel, immediate demands, and the occasional lack of discipline. But somehow, across the years, I have been able to find time to read, reflect, and meditate by using centered prayer.[17] It may be my own internal makeup that has invited me to read extensively, and not everyone will have the same positive experience from reading or even the inclination, but it has been very positive for me. It fills my mind as I read widely, and it softens and warms my heart as I focus on the great literature and the profound spiritual traditions of my faith. Often what I have read stays with me through the day and on into the week and month, and I discover that it has been transforming. I have become a better person, more in touch with God and more loving to those around me. This practice of focusing nearly every day with guided reading and reflection has opened my heart to a longing for quiet meditation. While I live with others and honor their style, I am less likely to turn on the TV as the first action of entering the room. I am more inclined to sit quietly for a while, appreciate the beauty of our surroundings, and "set my mind on things that are above."

What distracts you from "setting your mind on things that are above?"

---

17. I have found the book by Finley, *Christian Meditation: Experience the Presence of God,* a helpful guide. So too are the works of Thomas Keating.

Day 54

Finally, beloved, whatever is honorable, whatever is just, whatever is pure, whatever is pleasing, whatever is commendable, if there is any excellence and there is anything worthy of praise, think about these things. (Phil 4:8)

We are focusing our attention on how we might love God with our whole being, loving God with all of our heart, with all of our soul, with all of our strength, and with all of our mind. We explored, perhaps too briefly, ways of loving God with heart, soul, and strength, and are now focusing our attention on loving God with all our mind. I am spending a bit more time with loving God with our mind, in that I am persuaded that part of our problem in being true to this command is that we struggle with our perception of God.

It is this last concern that we are addressing. One part of our answer is to "set our mind on things that are above." Another part of our answer is to be with others who are engaged in a similar quest. There are certainly those within the Christian tradition that have emphasized that our quest to love God with our mind is a personal one, and indeed there are those who have pursued this quest in isolated and ascetic ways. But I am persuaded that love is mutual and requires relationships with others. We do not love others in isolation, and we might not find it easy to love God in monastic seclusion. We do it more easily when we join with others.

Love is a gift of God, but it is also a learned behavior that can be cultivated and deepened within a beloved community. Not every church, or synagogue, or temple, is a beloved community, and some are even dysfunctional and filled with conflict. But, rather than complaining about the lack of community, I find it wise and nurturing to be a part of the solution, rather than a part of the problem, by practicing loving behavior in the church community and working hard to design systems and programs that encourage loving behavior. In a beloved community, as I am loved and as I love, I learn about God and how I can grow in my capacity to love God with my all my mind.

Are you helped in your quest to love God by being in a loving community?

Day 55

> *We know love by this, that he laid down his life for us—and we ought to lay down our lives for one another. How does God's love abide in anyone who has the world's goods and sees a brother or a sister in need and yet refuses help?* (1 John 3:16–18)

Again and again, as I study the concept of love in the Bible, I discover that our love of God, whether with the heart, the soul, the strength, or the mind, is intimately connected with our being loved by others and our loving behavior toward others.[18] The truth of this experience suggests the there are elements of love common to all of our loving. Of course, our English word "love" is used in ways that are not appropriate for describing our love of God, but if we focus on the Greek word, *agape,* we sense that this kind of unlimited love is universal in scope and guides us as we learn how to love God with our mind. We *know* this love as we reflect on the ways that God loves us. And if we see in the final days of the life of Jesus one who gave his life for us, then we learn about God's love. We Christians believe that God's love was expressed in the way that Jesus lived in solidarity with those who suffer and existed on life's margins. Further, we believe that Jesus understood his unlimited love that took him to the cross as an expression of God's love for us. We see in Jesus that there are causes when love is worth it, even if it means the ultimate sacrifice. The author of 1 John goes on to say that those who follow Jesus and have some wealth and possessions should follow the example of Jesus and give to those in need. He argues the point quite strongly! How can anyone in whom God's love dwells, on seeing a brother or sister in need, not help? We truly love God with our minds as we observe and learn about the causes of poverty and injustice, address the problem in the immediate context, and study the unjust and inequitable structures of the social order. Love engages the mind as we seek solutions. We love God by finding and implementing them.

Is it true that the best way to learn how to love is to begin loving?

---

18. A good summary of love in the Bible is the book by Morris, *Testaments of Love in the Bible.* Though published in 1981, the book still has the ring of truth for our contemporary setting.

Day 56

> *There is no fear in love, but perfect love casts out fear; for fear has to do with punishment, and whoever fears has not reached perfection in love.* (1 John 4:18)

We are exploring the ways that we learn how to love God with our mind. We are suggesting that this command is not all that easy to obey, in that we are so easily distracted by the daily demands of life, unsure of the meaning of the word "God," and perhaps carry some fear of a god that might punish us if we fail to believe all the right things and obey all of this god's expectations. It is interesting to note how many times the Bible (and, in particular, Jesus) says, "Fear not." For example, there is a story in Luke's Gospel in which Jesus says, "Fear not, little flock (sometimes translated "do not be afraid") for it is your Father's good pleasure to give you the kingdom" (Luke 12:32). Here Jesus is saying we need not fear because God's loving presence fills our lives.

I find that fear, in its many forms (guilt about the past, insecurity in the present, and anxiety about the future), blocks my capacity to love. When I fear another person, I have such a range of feelings that I find it quite difficult to step back, regain my balance and poise, and return love to the one whose actions and attitudes have created fear within me. When I project these feelings on the cosmic scale and fear a judgmental God, perhaps by using the term "Father" and associating God with my judgmental father, I do not love God. I am also inclined to be a bit unsure about what I mean when I use the term "God," and therefore find it difficult to love what I don't know or understand. I need to remind myself that, whatever else God may be, God is primarily love, and the perfect divine love casts out my fear. I then learn, using my mind and internalizing this insight, that I can love God with my transformed mind and give my all to God in love. I can rest in peace and return love because I know I am surrounded by and filled with the love God.

What fears do you have that make love difficult?

Day 57

You will be enriched in every way for your great generosity, which will produce thanksgiving to God through us; for the rendering of his ministry not only supplies the needs of the saints but also overflows with many thanksgivings to God.
(1 Cor 9:11–12)

I find it easy to love those who are kind to me. Often, those who are kind to me are people I know well. I am fully aware that my obligations to love go beyond just loving those who are easy to love, those whom I know well and who care for me. When I think about the great commandment to love God with my whole being, I find I am able to fulfill this obligation more fully when I think about my friends, the gifts of God that come to me through those who care for me, and my daily encounter with God in my thoughtful prayers and continual conversation with God across the hours of the day. I find that I am more inclined to love God with my mind when I am thankful for all that God does for me, for those whom I love, those who love me, and indeed for all of humankind. For me, thankfulness is one of the best ways for me to overcome the hindrances to loving God. I still have some problems with sustaining a loving attitude toward God, in part because I do not fully understand why there is so much evil and suffering in the world. As a theologian, I find ways of partially explaining it, but as a humble (and sometimes confused) pilgrim, I often wonder why those dearest to me get cancer, suffer, and die. I also wonder about my finitude as I age. My love for God is not perfect, although I trust that God's love for me is perfect and that God hears and understands my questions. It is for this that I am profoundly grateful, and I am also grateful for so much more. I am grateful for my family, for my friends, for my lifelong work that has given meaning to my life, and for the values that guide me through the perplexities of life. I am grateful for the beauty of the earth and stand in awe of the grandeur of the cosmos. I am thankful for wonderful teachers across history and cultures, giving me insight and wisdom, and knowledge about the earth on which I live. My gratitude to God fills my heart, and I love this Transcendent One whom I daily try to understand in better ways. Gratitude leads to love for God.

Does a sense of gratitude help you to be more loving?

Day 58

Our relationships with one another are not a casual part of our lives; they are fundamental to how our minds function and an essential aspect of brain health.[19]

We are currently exploring better ways to love God with our minds. We have spoken about the hindrances that block our capacity to love God fully and given emphasis to how we might calm our minds and keep them focused. We have also spoken about how our view of God, if distorted, can prevent us from loving God. We have learned from the teachings of Buddhism on how we might identify hindrances, face them, and find good solutions. We said that the human love we experience, our involvement in a beloved community, engaging in acts of loving service, overcoming our many fears, and living with gratitude can increase our capacity to love God. Let's add one more to our list, and it is the need for brain health. In recent years, there has been extensive research about the brain, and the ways a healthy brain can increase our capacity to love.[20] It is not possible in these short daily readings to review all that's being done in neuroscience about how the brain functions, and how a healthy brain can increase our capacity to be happy, gain wisdom, and become a more loving person. Our derivative point here for our daily reflection is that those with healthy brains are better able to love God with their minds, and indeed, with heart, soul, and strength as well. I would take the position that we are endowed with the capacity to love, being created in the image of God, and that to engage in certain practices will empower us to be more loving—loving God, loving others, and indeed loving all of creation. There are others who put more emphasis on the practices and avoid the affirmation of humans being endowed with the capacity to love; but either way, to engage in ways of cultivating brain health is of critical importance. Rick Hanson, quoted above, tells the Native American story about humans having two wolves within them, the wolf of love and the wolf of hate. Both are hungry and wanting attention, and it is for the good of all to feed the wolf of love.

How do feed the "wolf of love?"

---

19. Hanson, *Buddha's Brain*, v.
20. See ibid., 121–225, and my book, *Lovescapes*, 163–88.

Day 59

Be attentive, be intelligent, be responsible, be loving, and, if necessary, change.[21]

We are learning together about mindful spirituality. In an effort to bring some order to this way of life, we have used directional metaphors, working in Section One with "Reaching Upward," Section Two with "Opening Inward," and Section Three, "Expanding Outward," and have set aside four months for each endeavor. We are still in Section One, "Reaching Upward," and devoted January to reaching upward for transcendence. We are now concluding the readings in February with the theme of reaching upward toward loving God with our whole being. As we conclude the readings for February today, let's pause for a moment and remember the path we have followed. The path for January was to reach upward for transcendence. We acknowledged the metaphorical character of our language with the call to reach upward, knowing full well that what we generally mean by transcendence and the divine is omnipresent. But we suggested that reaching upward is the quest to come into a vital and transforming relationship with the divine, the Transcendent One, or the universal principle that is the ground of being. Mindful spirituality is finding and sustaining this personal linkage with what stands beyond, yet imminent in all that has been, is, and will be. Whether Tao or karma, Great Spirit or logos, Allah or Yahweh, and (in our English liturgies) God, we reach upward to be in harmony with transcendence. In February, we have reflected on the great commandment (*Shema*) that is integral to the Abrahamic faith traditions, and is present in nearly all of the religious traditions of the human family. We pondered the meaning of "You shall love the Lord your God with all of your heart, and with all of your soul, and with all of your strength, and with all of your mind; and your neighbor as yourself." Our focus has been on finding appropriate and life-giving ways to love God.

What practices might you add to your life that would increase your capacity to love God?

---

21. Lonergan, *Method in Theology*, 231.

Study Guide for the February Readings

Questions for Contemplation and Discussion

1. Both the Hebrew Bible and the New Testament teach that the essence of the spiritual journey is to love God with our whole being. How do we love God with our whole being, or if we do not believe in theism, how do we undertake a spiritual journey with our whole being?

2. Jesus taught that the spiritual journey involves changing directions and receiving the kingdom of God into one's life. What did he mean, and how do we incorporate this teaching into our lives?

3. Nearly all of the great religious founders and teachers have urged their followers to make love a very high priority in life. How is it possible to say yes to this teaching? What would it mean for our lives?

4. It is well and good to give lip service to love and compassion, but when push comes to shove it is very difficult. How might we be empowered to love? How do we learn how to love ourselves, others, and God?

5. What are the primary obstacles for becoming a loving person, one who cares about others and who takes responsibility for the welfare of others?

6. The Hebrew Bible teaches what is called the *shema*, which is to love God fully with heart, soul, strength, and mind. What does it mean to love God with our heart?

7. What does it mean to love God with our soul? What is the difference in the biblical language between heart and soul? What does it mean to love God with all of our strength, and how is this different?

8. What does it mean to love God with our entire mind? What are the unique challenges in our time and culture for loving God with our mind? How might we go about it?

9. We often sense that fear is present in our consciousness, and at times it can control our attitude toward life and dramatically impact our behavior. How might "perfect love cast out fear" as the Bible teaches?

10. The behavioral sciences, and more particularly brain research, in recent years has learned that the health of our emotions and our brain are interconnected. If they are healthy, it increases our capacity to love. How do we stay healthy in order to love, if love is a high priority for us?

THEME FOR MARCH

REACHING UPWARD FOR RELATIONSHIP
WITH GOD THROUGH FAITH

Day 60

But God, who is rich in mercy, out of the great love with which [God][1] loves us, even when we were dead through our trespasses, made us alive. . . For by grace you have been saved through faith, and this is not our own doing; it is the gift of God—not the result of works, so that no one may boast. For we are what [God] has made us, created in Christ Jesus for good works, which God prepared beforehand to be our way of life. (Eph 2:4–5, 8–10)

Our relationship with transcendence has many dimensions. As we have stressed, it is sustained by loving God with our whole being, with heart, soul, strength, and mind. But it is begun as we receive God's approach to us *in faith*. We understand that it is in faith that we respond to God's gracious invitation and establish a relationship with God. In the Christian faith, three words capture the essence of the relationship as we follow the teaching of the Ephesian letter.

1. The first word is *grace*. The relationship is initiated by God, whose *gracious* invitation comes to us in many ways and is rooted in the coming of Jesus who incarnated the *grace* of God. The Abrahamic faith traditions all point to the ways that God has approached humankind in gracious love—differing in how the primary invitation came, but in agreement that it came.

2. The second word is *love*, similar in many ways to grace, but with more emphasis on how the relationship is sustained from our end. It is held together by and filled with love, our love for God and God's love for us.

3. The third word is *faith*, and while it too has elements of grace and love, the meaning of faith in the relationship is that we believe in and are committed to the gracious invitation. It is an action and a commitment on our part that establishes a linkage with God that is based on *knowledge, trust, and action*. We move now to expanding our understanding of our faith response.

How does one sustain a life of faith in a culture filled with distractions?

---

1. Many translations say "he" for God in this passage. I have chosen to repeat the name God in that I hope we envision God, or Transcendence, while personal, not as a particular gender. Even our metaphors can be gender-sensitive.

Day 61

Hindus all believe in one Supreme God who created the universe. He is all-pervasive. He created many Gods, highly advanced spiritual beings, to be His helpers.[2]

Across the years, filled with global travel, reading, and teaching, I have come to be less tribal in my beliefs and more open to the ways that transcendence, or the divine, is understood in other faith traditions. My Christian faith informs and sustains me, but as I have spoken and engaged in worship with others from different traditions, I sense that God speaks many languages and communicates and extends a gracious invitation in different cultures and historical eras. I have learned this from my Hindu friends and find the teachings in the *Vedas* profound. There is an abundance of wisdom, and progressive Hindus also learn from the Bible, Moses, and Jesus. Though different in content, faith is nearly universal.

From time to time, I have had the privilege of joining with Buddhists in classes, thoughtful discussions, and in meditation. Some Buddhists do speak about a personal God, but the more classical expression of Buddhism is not theistic, and places an emphasis on enlightenment and compassion. Expressed in a non-theistic way, Buddhists do get a profound and gracious invitation from their beliefs. From the example of Buddha, his teachings, and the spiritual community, they find their way. It is also a faith tradition with knowledge, trust, and a life of compassion. And many Buddhists, because of common values, would understand Jesus as a Buddha.

What are the main elements of these faith traditions? While expressed in different ways, there are many common elements. Generally these faith traditions have a set of beliefs or a *creed*. In addition, they would teach an ethical way of life or a moral *code*. Further, they would gather together for worship and education to be nurtured by the *content* of their faith. And, as they gather, they would be encouraged by others and be sustained by a sense of *community*.

What are the practices in Hinduism and Buddhism that nurture spirituality?

---

2. "Introduction to Hinduism," III.

Day 62

Therefore let your visit to that temple invisible be for naught but ecstasy and sweet communion.[3]

Our relationship with God will not always be filled with ecstasy and sweet communion, yet in those rare moments when it is, we sense that we have truly made contact with transcendence. As we look closely at those rare moments of sweet communion, we find that they are based on our sense that we have truly met with God. We cannot prove in an empirical way that we have encountered the Divine One, although we can say that our experience was real and that this faith encounter was authentic. There are three components of this faith encounter that seem to be the essence of what we have experienced.

1. The first is that we have used our minds, and have confidence that such an encounter was truly a connection with God. Faith has a *cognitive dimension,* and we will take time in our daily readings to talk about how and why we believe that God exists, is personal, and receives our leap of faith.

2. In addition, we place our *trust* in the One whom we believe has heard our prayer. For the most part, the trust we offer is in a personal God who hears us and loves us in return. Yes, there are many who do not believe in a personal God, although they too enter into moments of *encounter,* perhaps through meditation, and find rest and peace in the bliss that comes from their acceptance of ultimate reality. It may be called the Tao, nirvana, or moksha, but we humans learn how to trust Transcendence, or transcendence.

3. From this blissful encounter we rise to go into the world, grounded in what we know and trust to be true to live in such a way that we honor the way of life that is integral to our life of faith. As it says in the book of James in the New Testament, "So just as the body without the spirit is dead, so faith without works is dead" (Jas 2:26). We *act* on our faith.

How would describe your encounter with God or ultimate reality?

---

3. Gibran, *The Prophet,* 75.

Day 63

Go to the Buddha, sit with him, and show him your pain. He will look at you with loving kindness, compassion, and mindfulness, and show you ways to embrace your suffering and look deeply into it. With understanding and compassion, you will be able to heal the wounds in your heart, and the wounds in the world.[4]

We have said that faith has been understood in many ways in the religious traditions of the human family, and it is present in some form in nearly all religions. The quote for today suggests the way that faith plays a role within Buddhism. The Buddhist pilgrim believes that, in the teaching of the Buddha, there are ways to overcome suffering and lead an enlightened life of compassion. In fact, all of the components of faith (knowledge, trust, and action) are present. One learns and is enlightened, trust is placed in the Four Noble Truths, and one acts on or follows the Noble Eightfold Path. The follower of Buddha then engages in compassion for those who suffer.

Let's look more closely at these three components of faith, focusing first on having sufficient knowledge in order to embrace a view of reality and a way of life. As one learns and feels confident in a way of looking at transcendence, one is able to endorse it. We are then able to make a whole-person choice that enables us to act on what has the ring of truth for us. We have the confident expectation that what we have endorsed will be true. Then, one is able to place trust in these *truths* and frame one's life around them. The practices of mindful spirituality will naturally follow. It may be hard for many "cultured despisers" to consciously embrace an outlook that includes transcendence.[5] In my experience in the academic world, I encounter people that doubt the truth of religious claims. There are also many who see, in the culture of religion, a measure of superstition and lack of intellectual integrity. To address these concerns seems wise, and we do so by framing a faith orientation in a reasonable way, and then backup the beliefs with a life of integrity in reference to those beliefs.

How do you deal with doubt when it occurs in your life of faith?

---

4. Thich, *The Heart of the Buddha's Teaching*, 5.

5. The term "cultured despisers" comes from Schleiermacher, nineteenth-century theologian, in his book, *On Religion: Speeches to its Cultured Despisers*.

Day 64

> *If we, as human beings, are to lead fulfilled lives, we need more than the partial account of reality that science offers. We need a "big picture," an integral idea of the universe, a richer vision of reality that would weave together understanding and meaning.*[6]

Although we need a big picture for a fulfilled life, that doesn't mean that there is one outlook that is exclusively true. However, I am persuaded that there are big picture outlooks that are convincing. To be sure, there are several big picture outlooks that exist, not all compatible, and therefore not all of them can be true. Yet there can be persuasive approximations, partial in character, and pointing to a transcendent reality. There is a need for some humility in the presence of transcendent mystery, and to claim that your view is the only one and absolutely true is to claim more than is wise. Our views are inevitably tainted by our time and place in history, our culture, our language, and our exposure to a vision of reality that comes from our immediate context.

To integrate our understanding of the natural world and a grand vision of reality can be a challenging and wonder-full endeavor, one that does not require *sacrificium intellectus*. We do not need to sacrifice our intellect, but rather use our intellect to do the hard work of integration. I have loved this journey, and been guided by at least three ways of understanding truth:

1. The first is that a grand vision of reality must not go against what we know to be true in the natural world. It must be integrated and complementary. Religion becomes dangerous when it is rooted in ignorance.

2. Further, my grand view must hold together, have integrity, and not be filled with contradictions. It must have logical coherence.[7]

3. My grand view must be personally efficacious, healing, and encourage me on my way to a more loving, peaceful, and responsible way of life.

What directions are you taking in order to put together a grand view of reality?

---

6. McGrath, *The Big Picture*, 3–4.
7. The work of Swinburne in *The Coherence of Theism* is helpful on this point.

Day 65

> *The impasse in which we find ourselves in today, the inability of ecclesial and cultural systems to cooperate for the welfare of humankind, bears the lack of a fundamental meta-narrative.*[8]

It would be possible to draw upon several meta-narratives from the religious and philosophical traditions of humankind. Because my developing meta-narrative is the Christian faith, I will use it as illustrative of the ways that we might go about the work of integration.[9] It has been done in marvelous ways in other religious traditions.[10] The Christian narrative really begins in the ancient world of Abraham, who left Mesopotamia and traveled west. The narrative affirms that Abraham believed that God was calling him to leave his homeland, and would go with the covenantal promise that he would have God's blessing. The story recounts how God guided him as he traveled and dealt with many difficulties. The Hebrew Bible tells this story and then moves on to the stories of Moses, the kings of ancient Israel, David and Solomon, and the great prophets and their quest for justice. This narrative is the fountainhead of the religions of Judaism and Christianity, and is present in Islam.

The meta-narrative for Christians continues with the coming of Jesus, who lived as a prophetic Jewish teacher. Christians believe that in his life, teaching, death, and resurrection, humankind heard the word of God. The Christian faith and the church emerge from this remarkable story. The centuries have come and gone, and we inherit the story that is believed by many to be one way that God entered into human life. It has not always been easy to re-tell this story in different times, different places, and to the entire human family across time, languages, cultures, and to contemporary people. But it is the case that a profound effort has been made and Christianity is a world religion.

What meta-narrative is most convincing and satisfying for you?

---

8. McGrath, *The Big Picture*, xiv.

9. The work on worldviews by Wright in *The New Testament and the People of God* is especially helpful (pp. 31–80).

10. One thinks immediately of such people as the Dalai Lama and Mohandas Gandhi.

Day 66

> *For God, by definition, cannot be an extra item in the universe (a very big one) to be known, and so controlled by human intellect, will, or imagination. God is, rather, that without which there would be nothing at all; God is the source and sustaining of all being. . . To know God is unlike any other knowledge; indeed, it is more truly to be known, and so transformed.*[11]

There is at least one caveat I need to make as we talk about loving God with our mind and seek a life nurtured with mindful spirituality. It is that we have only a partial knowledge of God, and that part of our faith that is knowledge-based is approximate and has a personal component. There is the risk, as we do serious theology, of feeling like we can find concepts and words that contain God, as if we could put God in a box. We long to know, and our ambition sometimes leads us to think that we can have full knowledge of the divine. In so doing, we feel like we have control and mastery. Here, Einstein's dictum, "The more I know the more I know I don't know," is helpful. Our words are symbols and pointers to the divine, rather than full descriptions. Even words such as "love," "Spirit," and "light" are metaphors that point the way. We need to have our apophatic sensibilities in good order as we think and talk about God. It might be described as "knowing in our unknowing."[12] Further, our knowledge is personal and is spoken about as a relationship. To know another may mean to know about them, but we also speak about getting to know them and mean that we connect with them and form a relationship. So it is with God. We form a relationship and sustain it with worship, prayer, and service. It is not so much the gathering of facts, as it is a life filled with contemplation. We love God with our minds by gaining knowledge and thinking clearly, but we get to know God more on our knees than in the library. The two ways of knowing are complementary, and are the essence of mindful spirituality. They both contribute to the expansion of our spiritual consciousness.

What are the best practices to expand our knowledge of God?

---

11. Coakley, *God, Sexuality, and the Self*, 44–45.
12. Ibid. 45.

Day 67

> *The postmodern subject now knows that any route to reality must pass through the radical plurality of our differential languages and the ambiguity of all our histories.*[13]

Our subject, God, the very ground of being, is out of reach for our minds and concepts to fully grasp and describe. We are wise to say that, when we speak about God, we are pointing to Transcendence, rather than describing the fullness of God in the words that come to our minds. It is not that we shouldn't think and speak about God as our way of loving God with our minds. We should, but we should do it humbly, knowing that in the depths of our love we point to the One we love. It is also true that we reach upward for relationship with God through the tangle of our language, our history, our culture, and all the limitations of our particularity. There are others from different times and places that also reach upward for relationship with God, and express it in the specificity of their setting. It may be just as valid and heard by divine Love with equal receptivity. So we must guard against the illusion that our way of loving God with our minds, our way of thinking and speaking about God, even if profound and coherent, is the only way. Should that quiet us and cause us to retreat into a superficial fideism or passive piety? The answer is no. Rather, we should work that much harder to love God with the best of our minds and our language. There are some ways of putting faith together that are better than others. There are words and thoughts that are better in pointing us and other people to God. It is all too easy to head off in the wrong direction, claim that we are speaking in God's name, and harm others. As Pascal said, "Men never do evil so completely and cheerfully as when they do it from religious conviction."[14] Rabbi Jonathan Sacks underlines this point in his recent book, decrying the violent tendencies of radical religion.[15] As we speak of God, we do so out of the texts that point us to love, peace, and justice.

What language do we use in speaking about our faith in God?

---

13. Tracy, *Plurality and Ambiguity*, 82.
14. Quoted by ibid., 86.
15. Sacks, *Not in God's Name*.

Day 68

> *However, with repeated practice of contacting higher states, your own states of development will tend to unfold in a much faster and easier way.*[16]

Some of the best descriptions of human development are in the pages of the Bible, although it comes to us more through intuition and inspiration. The language of the Bible is not the language of social science. Yet it is confirming and reassuring to learn from developmental psychologists and philosophers that we generally do and can develop across the years of life into a more mature state, one that enables us to be wiser in the practice of mindful spirituality. I find it comforting to know that I can mature in loving God with my mind as I reach upward for relationship with God through faith. I have been informed about how it is that we become more mature. People such as James Fowler on faith development, Lawrence Kohlberg on moral development, and Jean Piaget on intellectual development, have been some of my teachers. Many others could be mentioned who have moved the concept of development to the grander level of a world outlook. Ken Wilber has been very informative to me, as have many contemporary theologians. I will borrow from them as we pray and study together about deepening our walk with God, and will say more about them as we move to the next section of our readings, "Opening Inward."

James Fowler speaks directly to the ways that we mature in our faith and cultivate our relationship with God. While the concept of stages is not used as frequently in current scholarship as it once was, I still find his outline of stages of faith to be very accurate and helpful.[17] In fact, I identify with his stages and find them descriptive of my own spiritual pathway, although I am cautious, as he advises, about seeing them as something I have accomplished. They are stages through which I have passed.

Has your growth in spiritual maturity gone through stages?

---

16. Wilber, *Integral Spirituality*, 11.
17. See Fowler, *Stages of Faith*.

Day 69

It has been apprehended by a more comprehensive vision of truth. It can appreciate and cherish symbols, myths, and rituals in new depth, because it has been apprehended in some measure by the depth of reality to which the symbols refer and which they mediate.[18]

It is not possible to do full justice in our daily readings to Fowler's stages of faith, yet a list of them might be helpful as we reflect on our growth toward a more mature and mindful spirituality. They are as follows:

1. Preoperational: the infant stage of rudimentary empathy and need
2. Concrete Operational: the childhood stage of simple acceptance of roles and reciprocal fairness
3. Early Formal Operations: the teenage and early adult years of interpersonal expectations and acceptance of group beliefs and ethical norms
4. Formal Operations: mutual relationships with a societal perspective ratified by one's own ideological perspective; challenge to accepted norms
5. Formal Operations (Dialectical): openness to other traditions and adherence to a higher law that is universal and critical
6. Formal Operations (Synthetic): with commitment to the commonwealth of all and perceptive of the One beyond the many in the human search for meaning

Each of the stages is explained in some detail by Fowler and is based on extensive research. He notes that many adults tend to *pause* in stage three, and others, especially in the college years, move to stage four as one begins to question inherited norms and a personal frame of reference for beliefs and values. Others do move on to stage five and cultivate an appreciation for the many ways of understanding reality and living an ethical life, believing that there is a more universal norm that can be discovered and followed. Fowler says that few people reach stage six, in which there is universal compassion for all and a deep appreciation for the many ways humans seek to express and live by systems of truth and the ethic of love.

At what stage would you place yourself at this point in life?

18. Ibid. 199.

Day 70

To say that basic human nature is not only non-violent but actually disposed toward love and compassion, kindness, gentleness, affection, creation, and so on does, of course, imply a general principle which must, by definition, be applicable to each individual human being.[19]

I would like to provide one more illustration coming from a developmental psychologist who maintains that it is possible and natural for us to move toward maturity. Lawrence Kohlberg describes the pathway for moral development. As did Fowler, Kohlberg employs the structure of levels and stages, articulating three levels and six stages.[20] They are:

1. Level One: Pre-conventional—the period in which moral judgments are based upon a person's needs and perceptions. At this stage, there are two levels: the first is that of a punishment-obedience orientation, and the second is based on a personal reward for certain behaviors.

2. Level Two: Conventional—the period in which judgment is based on the approval of others, such as family or the laws of society. Once again there are stages, stage three being the reward or affirmation of doing good, and stage four based on laws that are absolute and will be enforced.

3. Level Three: Post-Conventional—the period in which judgment is based on self-determined principles. The fifth stage has the design of a social contract, and the good is understood to be a social arrangement that has merit and should be followed. The sixth stage in level three is when an individual makes moral judgments in terms of conscience, and in reference to universal norms of justice, human dignity, and equality.

In both Fowler and Kohlberg, we see the possibility and motivation to grow toward a more mature stage of development. In terms of our concern, mindful spirituality, I find guidance from these authors, although the pathway is not an easy one to follow.

Where would you place yourself in the categories of Kohlberg?

---

19. Dalai Lama, *Ethics for the New Millennium*, 71.
20. Kohlberg's theories can be found in his book, *The Philosophy of Moral Development*.

Day 71

But the Counselor, the Holy Spirit, whom the Father will send you in my name, will teach you all things, and remind you of everything I have said to you.
(John 14:26)

In Christian teaching, the pathway to mindful spirituality embraces both the ways we are empowered and the ways that our practices help us cultivate a deeper spiritual life. The Christian community speaks of the resources available to us in our journey toward a mature faith as *the means of grace*. The destination of our journey is patterned on the example of Jesus, and the Philippian letter speaks of it as having the "mind of Christ." Paul, the author of the letter, speaks of both empowerment and practice, underlining that "it is God who is at work in you" and "to work out your own salvation with fear and trembling" (2:12–13). John Wesley is quoted as saying, "Work like it all depends upon you and pray like it all depends upon God."

First, then, a word about empowerment: it is the Holy Spirit, understood as the power and presence of God, that is at work in us. This is the way Christians speak about transformation, and moving toward being all that God wants us to be.[21] We open our hearts and minds to the presence of God, and in this relationship, we are empowered to seek and to do God's will. We will say more about inward transformation in our next section of readings. Here, we are simply stressing that we must also do our part by freely choosing God's will and way, and prepare ourselves to follow God's leading. We embrace God's Spirit in our lives and take full advantage of the means of grace. One author, drawing upon developmental psychology, has called our growth "process" in his book entitled *Putting on the Mind of Christ: The Inner Work of Christian Spirituality*.[22] He uses the teaching on the kingdom of heaven as his starting point and then moves the reader to the levels of consciousness in personality development and provides guidance on how to engage in "putting on the mind of Christ."

What are the primary means of grace?

---

21. See the excellent book by Levison, *Filled with the Spirit*.
22. Marion, *Putting on the Mind of Christ*.

Day 72

> *There is no such thing as spirituality in general. Every spiritual search is and must be guided by a particular literature, practice, and community.*[23]

One assumption I am making as we study ways of deepening our faith and cultivating mindful spirituality is that we can learn from the vast world of human understanding and creativity. And, as I am enriched by all that surrounds me, I must do the work of integration with the literature and practices of a specific religious tradition. To move forward I need the guidance and the support of a beloved community committed to the goal of spiritual nurture. I do practice my Christian faith in a specific community of faith and draw upon the means of grace, the exposure to the teaching of the Bible, regular worship including the sacraments, and the faithful engagement in ascetic and contemplative practices, such as prayer. In my reach upward for relationship with God through faith, I draw upon the rich resources available to me, those that empower and practices that nurture. In these ways, I hope to expand and deepen my mindful spirituality. I do not do it alone; I need a *healthy and life-giving* faith community.

At this point, we need to ask: what are those qualities in a faith community that encourage my growth; and conversely, what are those characteristics that might limit it? In my study of the religions of the world, I began to discern the characteristics of the various religions of the human family that were life-giving and those that were life-denying and to make judgments about how a particular religious tradition might be more likely to guide one to a life of inner peace and social responsibility. What I discovered (and it should come as no surprise) is that nearly every religious tradition and specific expression of the religion in a church, synagogue, or a temple usually has elements of both life-giving qualities and life-denying practices.[24] No faith community will be perfect. We will review these positive and negative features in our next entries.

What is healthy about your faith community? Unhealthy?

---

23. Palmer, *To Know as We are Known*, 14.
24. Ferguson, *Exploring the Spirituality of the World Religions*, 10.

Day 73

> *Now there are varieties of gifts, but the same Spirit; and there are varieties of services, but the same Lord; and there are varieties of activities, but it is the same God who activates all of them in everyone. To each is given the manifestation of the Spirit for the common good.* (1 Cor 12:4–7)

Paul, the first-century missionary and leader in the early Christian community, spent much of his time sorting out differences among the members of these new churches. In part because they were new, even a partially new genre, and in part because they were human, they had conflicts. In the Corinthian church, one of the conflicts had to do with the new sacrament of communion. Was it a meal, or was it a ritual? And who should be present? He gave guidance, and was even present as his travels permitted, so he could assist these new churches and help them become life-giving communities. Drawing upon Paul's letters, and my reading and experience, let me suggest some ways that faith communities can assist their members to cultivate a mindful spirituality. I will begin by listing five positive qualities of healthy groups:

1. The healthy community of faith *empowers* both the individuals and the group to behave in ways that lead to love, compassion, understanding, and acceptance of others (those of different social classes and cultures).

2. The healthy faith community *guides* individuals and the group to be socially responsible, and concerned about creating a more just and humane world.

3. The life-giving faith community is intellectually *credible* and *encourages* individuals and the group to be open to new ideas and challenges.

4. The life-giving faith community helps individuals and the group to *flourish* and *integrate* beliefs and practices into a life of coherence, conviction, serenity, and integrity.

5. The life-giving community of faith offers guidance and practices that *sustain* individuals and the church in times of difficulty and challenge.

Admittedly, these goals are a tall order, and they must be kept in front of the individuals in the church as a way to foster health, growth, and transformation.

What positive qualities would you add to this list?

Day 74

> *For just as the body is one and has many members, and all the members of the body, though many, are one body, so it is with Christ. For in the one Spirit we were all baptized into one body—Jews or Greeks, slaves or free—and we were all made to drink of one Spirit.* (1 Cor 12:13)

The Apostle Paul used the body as a metaphor for the ideal Christian church that heals its members and leads them to a mature and mindful faith. He illustrates: "Indeed, the body does not consist of one member but of many. If the foot would say, 'Because I am not a hand, I do not belong to the body,' that would not make it any less a part of the body" (1 Cor 12:14). He longed for a community that would accept others who were different and have a cooperative spirit in these young churches. But they struggled and had some dimensions of their common life that were unhealthy and life-denying. Let me suggest five negative features of their common life:

1. They had started to become *sectarian* and closed to others with different backgrounds and beliefs; there were traces of cultic, tribal, judgmental, and exclusive behavior.

2. A complementary negative dimension was the tendency to become *ideological* in character and suspicious and intolerant of other views.

3. In time, as these negative dimensions of their common life increased, their tendency was to *confine* and *control* the individuals within the community and ask for blind obedience.

4. The community also became filled with *excessive* zealotry about its ways of belief and practice. It led to rejection, and in some cases even violence, and soon the ends of authority and order were justifying the means of control.

5. This outlook created *fear*, *mistrust*, and *intolerance*, and didn't reflect the positive values of personal transformation, compassion, justice, and peace.

Some of the churches that the Apostle Paul founded had elements of these negative features. His writing points to the tendency of some of these communities of faith to lose their way. He tried to help, and counseled love as the more excellent way.

What other negative features have you experienced in a faith community?

Day 75

But strive for the greater gifts. And I will show you a more excellent way. If I speak in the tongues of mortals and angels, but do not have love, I am a noisy gong or a clanging cymbal. (1 Cor 12:34—13:1)

As we belong to and become active in communities of faith, we discover that there are many times of great joy, learning, and supportive love that lead to our growth and development. For these experiences, I am profoundly grateful. At other times there have been fundamental differences among the members that have led to conflict and a toxic environment. There are many causes of this conflict, and one has to do with different interpretations of faith and the subsequent conflict over which values should guide the community. The values we hold are sometimes thoughtfully chosen and based on valid readings of the texts and traditions of the faith. In other cases, the retrieval from the readings has been distorted and the norms of the culture, while sometimes unconsciously affirmed, have been central. There are generally three value orientations present in our gatherings:[25]

1. Based on autonomy: This orientation argues that individuals have wants, needs, and preferences, and that they should be free to pursue these ends. The obligation of the group or society is to provide a context in which individual rights, liberty, and the assurance of justice are honored.

2. Based on community: This orientation affirms the idea that people are members of larger entities such as families, companies, and nations as well as religious communities. These larger groups are real and must be protected, and the members have roles within them that must be sustained. Values such as duty, respect, patriotism, and authority are fundamental.

3. Based on divinity: This orientation argues that we have the divine within us, and have access in our religious communities to understanding the divine will. We understand our responsibilities in reference to the divine.

Which of these three types of community would describe yours?

---

25. Haidt, *The Righteous Mind*, 115-29.

Day 76

Love is patient; love is kind; love is not envious or boastful or arrogant or rude. It does not insist on its own way; it is not irritable or resentful; it rejoices in the truth. (1 Cor 13:4–6)

The Apostle Paul, as he tries to help the new Corinthian church resolve its conflicts and become a life-giving community of faith, guides them to the ethic of love. He maintains that this ethic is God-given and should trump other positions. He knows, as we do, that it is a position that needs to be learned and cultivated. Jonathan Haidt, in his helpful book, suggests five ways that these different value and ethical positions take shape in our groups and in society:

1. There is the care-harm concern: This ethical position puts an emphasis on the ways people take care of others and address their problems and suffering.
2. There is the fairness-cheating concern: In this one, the stress is on the need to treat others equally, respectfully, and honestly.
3. There is the loyalty-betrayal concern: Here, the obligation of the group is to be true to the group's values and live with integrity in reference to those values.
4. There is the authority-subversion concern. In this outlook, people live in a context in which the group's welfare is the highest value, and we honor the community's leaders and norms without ever harming the group's welfare.
5. There is the sanctity-degradation concern: Belonging to a faith community is founded upon and following the divine will. We respect its sacred character and do nothing that would dishonor it, yet discerning it is difficult.

Not long ago, I was working in the national offices of a mainline denomination and found that I encountered these concerns and their underlying values almost daily. My colleagues in this setting were from both progressive and conservative traditions, came from different cultures, and energetically engaged in conversations about very important issues. They discussed how the larger denomination should use its human and financial resources. As I look back upon more than a decade of service, I realized that compassion and justice were fundamental for me.

Which of these orientations is the most attractive to you?

Day 77

Love bears all things, believes all things, hopes all things, endures all things... And now faith, hope, and love abide, and the greatest of these is love. (1 Cor 13:7, 13)

I did learn a great deal from my twelve years at the national offices of my denomination. I had wonderful colleagues, many with more experience and wisdom who guided me in this period of my career. It was a great privilege to serve, but I have to admit that it wasn't the most fulfilling time of my career. I had to adjust to working in a corporate culture and being a good team player. What this meant was that I had to advance my phase of the church's ministry while being loyal to the larger mission of the church. I also had to use my gifts and talents in a setting that was not so much focused on the individuals in a congregation, but on an organization that served congregations. There were times when I had to take one step backward in order to go two steps forward and to become more flexible and resilient. There were weeks in which my attention was exclusively focused on administrative details and committee meetings. As time went along, I did get in touch with these realties, although I still missed opportunities for teaching and writing. My mistakes were my own and not caused by others, and I discovered that the work I was doing, as important as it was, did not allow me to pursue work that brought deep satisfaction. I showed immaturity, partially out of my needs that I didn't fully understand. I made mistakes, did not always work with colleagues in healthy ways, and lived with a bit more stress and anxiety than was healthy. My faith was challenged, and I began to realize that I needed a change, as did my superiors. As I left that position, I sought ways to slay the dragons of stress and anxiety and be true to myself and my needs and longings. I moved into an academic setting in which pastoral counseling, teaching, and writing were central to my work. I realized that I had been caught in a maze of different values, and that my more introverted ways and the pain of growing up in dysfunctional family setting needed acknowledgement and healing. I needed to be in a life-giving community and to give personal attention to health, one in which faith, hope, and love abide.

Is your current work and service done in a setting that enables you to thrive?

Day 78

Now faith is the assurance of things hoped for, the conviction of things not seen.
(Heb 11:1)

We are reflecting on how it is that we reach upward to sustain our relationship with God. We have said that, within the Christian community, it is by faith. In these past several days, in our readings, we have defined faith and said that it has three components: knowledge, trust, and action. We have also said that these qualities are present in other religions as well. We spoke about the cognitive dimension of faith and how it is nurtured. We noted that it develops as we mature and as it is sustained in a life-giving community. For the next few days, we will stay with that aspect of faith that needs reassurance. Have we made a good decision about "the things hoped for, the conviction of things not seen"? A bit later in our readings, we will focus our attention on the trust and action aspects of faith, but first we need to have within us "the assurance" as the author of the Hebrews letter expressed it.

There are thoughtful arguments against a leap of faith. Some might say that it is just a way of meeting our needs for feeling secure and grounded, and that there is really no rational basis for the decision of faith. Others might argue, from an evolutionary point of view, that it is our way of affirming values and belonging that sustain and advance a society. There is the fundamental challenge to a faith orientation from the sciences that there is simply no hard evidence for sustaining a belief in God, especially belief in a personal God that is understood as loving and just. I live with these outlooks almost daily in my reading and research for my writing, and I would like to share some ways that take these challenges to faith seriously and also give one the option of a faith orientation that is credible and has integrity. It will not be so much of a proof in the philosophical and scientific sense, but a big picture view that provides a way of looking at the cosmos and the human experience in a way that is believable. It will suggest a worldview that attempts to hold it all together.

What answer do you give to the one who asks you why you believe in God?

Day 79

Scientists are human beings. Because they are scientists, they have highly developed ideas about how the universe works. Because they are human beings, they also have views on deeper questions such as, among other things, the meaning of their own lives and how to live a good life.[26]

A fundamental issue that needs reflection in our pursuit of mindful spirituality is how we can both focus our attention on life's meaning and values, as well as affirm the vital role of science in helping us understand how the universe works. The argument with science regarding religious belief and commitment is not about the validity of science, but about the "deep existential truths about who we are and why we are here."[27] These questions about meaning and values need answers, and it is a valid quest to pursue answers, even if they are not pursued in a narrowly scientific way.

One way to proceed in the goal to find answers for ultimate questions is to maintain that the answers come from a different source than answers about chemistry experiments. One metaphor we used in an earlier entry, and suggested by Alister McGrath, is that of maps. To understand a region, get to a destination within that region; taking a long hike in the region requires different kinds of maps that will give you the information that you need. One type of map might guide you to the right highway, and another type will provide a description that guides you to your destination. In our daily life and our work, we may also consult maps about why we are doing what we do and what values guide us in fulfilling our responsibilities. Meaning in life and living the good life are very important to us, and it is often to the great religious traditions that humans turn to in order to find meaning, guidance, and serenity. These are maps of life. I have turned to the Christian faith in my quest and have been informed and helped in my exposure to Hinduism, Buddhism, Judaism, Islam, and the seminal insights of the indigenous religions of the Northwest and Alaska—and many other traditions (maps) as well.

What maps do you use in finding answers to the meaning of life?

---

26. McGrath, *The Big Question*, 161.
27. Ibid.

Day 80

Evolutionary spirituality is being born out of the growing realization that the scientific and historical story of our origins actually presents a profound spiritual teaching about the purpose of the universe and our place within it.[28]

I have been encouraged in my quest to find a solid foundation for my faith in the ways that both thoughtful theologians from a range of religious outlooks and scientists with a faith orientation have approached the challenging task of integrating science and faith. At an earlier point in my life, I was exposed to those who were pretty committed and strongly argued for their side of this issue. This activity now seems to me to be more of a dialogue than an intense argument. Early in my Christian journey, I read several books and heard arguments about how science (or scientism) is wrong and that, for example, "there is no proof for evolution."[29] I also read the work of Richard Dawkins, a very able scientist, but not very convincing in books such as *The God Delusion*.[30] I found neither of these *either/or* outlooks very cogent. I did find help in the writings of Pierre Teilhard de Chardin, who held strongly to the view that an evolutionary outlook was compatible with a personal ultimate reality, which was *in* the evolutionary process. I moved away from the positions held by the more conservative scholars, and those who were protecting the traditions and authority of institutional religion. I wasn't comfortable with the view that saw unresolvable conflicts between their foundational religious books, such as the Bible, and scientific understanding. I found resources that set me free. I began to expose myself to people who were engaged in a new movement with many sides, one that was asking the right questions and suggested new ways of articulating faith and understanding transcendence. We move to that story.

In what ways have you thought about the linkage of science and religion?

---

28. McIntosh, *The Presence of the Infinite*, 5.

29. Even Hart's *The Experience of God*, while well-argued, was somewhat condescending toward those who not did believe in God.

30. Nor were the books by Harris (*The End of Faith*) or by Hitchens (*God Is Not Great*) very persuasive.

Day 81

> *There is arguably no more important and pressing topic than the relation of science to religion in the modern world. Science is clearly one of the most profound methods that humans have devised for discovering truth, while religion remains the single greatest force for generating meaning.*[31]

My strategy for exploring ways to integrate my faith with a scientific understanding of the world had two phases. The first was to understand my faith orientation in reference to major developments in certain fields that described the origin and development of the universe. If the universe is 13.5 billion years old, and if the theory of evolution about its development is almost universally accepted, I found myself drawn to those who accepted these ways of understanding, and also maintained that there is really no reason to see these points of view as contrary to a faith orientation. Even these scientific theories had an element of faith. It was in the last days of my university experience and during years in seminary and graduate school that I began the quest for integration in earnest. I have stayed with it for fifty years, bobbing and weaving as new discoveries and theories emerged. Three dimensions of this process stand out for me as I reflect on the journey:

1. First, I did not feel defensive about faith positions, knowing that they were approximate and changing, and every step toward the truth was a step toward God. I did not feel threatened, but felt the freedom to learn and change.

2. I was comfortable with understanding the Bible as an historical account of people of faith and an attempt to frame a religious outlook in terms of their time and place in history. These invaluable insights were framed in analogies and metaphors, and were attempts to guide the believing community.

3. I participated in church and scholarly communities that were made up of people who were more interested in learning and growing than in defending their point of view over against new understandings of reality.

Who and what have shaped your views about science and faith?

---

31. Wilber, *The Marriage of Sense and Soul*, 3.

Day 82

Science sprang not from Greek philosophers or the Brahmin-Buddhist-Taoist East but from the heart of the Christian West. Historically, the foundations of modern science are found in the Judeo-Christian tradition.[32]

As I struggled to put together a thoughtful and informed faith, one with credibility and integrity, I was pleased to learn that the very roots of my faith orientation, the narratives of the Bible, were instrumental in shaping the rise and development of science. The Christian church did not always affirm this insight, and did reject and even punish those on the forefront of the scientific revolution. Copernicus and Galileo paid a price for their discoveries. I can remember, in those interesting years serving in the offices of a mainline denomination, the ways that standards of belief were affirmed. There were carefully prepared ways for disciplining those whose beliefs were outside of the accepted creedal statements. I learned to be careful and thoughtful about what I said, and often heard the words "defend the faith" in one of the statements of faith. Perhaps this was all necessary to maintain order and identity, but it did not prevent me from my lifelong quest to continue learning.

Several topics continued to claim my interest and encourage my study.

1. I was very interested in the origin of the universe, studied the theories of the Big Bang, and saw little or no conflict with—and actually some confirmation of—my faith. If there was a beginning, then perhaps it pointed to a Creator.
2. I was very interested in evolution, and began to view God as within the evolutionary process, not as separate from it.
3. I was fascinated with human development and began to see the growth toward wholeness as akin to spiritual growth.

In the study of these issues and many others, I began to understand God as engaged in the cosmos and human life, not just intervening from outside in a miraculous way.

Are you comfortable or defensive when this topic is discussed?

---

32. Delio, *The Unbearable Wholeness of Being*, 1.

Day 83

From a critical-realist perspective both science and theology are engaging with realities that may be referred to and pointed to, but which are both beyond the range of any completely literal description.[33]

There are several thoughtful and well-researched books that provide guidance in the ways that we might pursue a greater understanding of the ways that theology and science might be integrated.[34] I am in favor of such a strategy, rather than one that argues against the validity of one over the other, especially if there is a lack of understanding, or the risk of distortion or the caricature, of the positions held. What the best have in common is a thorough knowledge in both domains, a commitment to honesty and fairness, and a measure of humility about the complexity of the task and the depth and changing character of areas of study. We are still learning.

In addition to the questions that arise between the hard sciences and theology, there are as many questions about the validity of religious belief in the social sciences. The rise of critical history in the nineteenth century changed the understanding of the origins and the normative literature of religion. Sociology and anthropology began to find more research-based descriptions of religious practices, and psychology has found ways of speaking about religious experience in reference to human need and evolution. While we cannot be scholars in all of these fields, I am persuaded that at least a limited understanding of the issues raised by them in reference to a faith orientation is part of what it means to have a mindful spirituality. As we move along in our readings, we will address the issues raised by the social sciences, and as before, our goal will not be so much to win arguments, but to integrate their best insights with our faith.

What are the most challenging questions for you in your "integration"?

---

33. Peacocke, *Theology for a Scientific Age*, 19.

34. In addition to the ones to which I have already referred, I would add Barbour, *Religion and Science*; Murphy and Ellis, *On the Moral Nature of the Universe*; and the several books by Polkinghorne, and especially his *Belief in God in an Age of Science*.

Day 84

Doctrinal correctness, institutional participation, and religious conformity won't suffice anymore. You need a life centered on... an encounter with the holy mystery and pure loving presence that people commonly call God.[35]

I do not mean to say that one cannot have a vital and life-giving relationship with God without being a widely read scholar. To learn from those who are scholars and authors may be a step in the right direction, and will help place one's spiritual journey on a more sound foundation. Faith is a relationship more than an intellectual assent, although to have a solid foundation for faith gives us assurance that our decision was wise. We have already spoken about the role of thoughtful scientists, philosophers, and psychologists in using the knowledge from their disciplines to help us better understand faith and moral development. Our plan for the remainder of this month is to continue this discussion and to deal with a few critical questions that seem to rise to the surface in any discussion of the foundations of belief. I have a life-long friend who has struggled with whether it is possible to make a religious commitment without checking your mind at the door as you enter the church (or synagogue or temple). In his early years, he was active in a church youth group, and his mother in particular encouraged him in his faith development. But through the college years and the inevitable challenges of family life and a demanding career, he set his faith aside and lived an essentially secular life. As I traveled, I would occasionally stop by and spend the night with him and his wife, talk football and politics, and after the second glass of wine, move on to religion. His favorite question to me was: "Isn't it all bullshit?" We were athletes together, and members of the same fraternity, and this framing of the question was not unexpected. His wife asked the same question, often worded in a slightly different way. I must say that these discussions were both enjoyable and at a fairly sophisticated level, and they did have a measure of trust in me. What I learned from them was how real the questions are in our time and place in history.

What has been the nature of these kinds of conversations for you?

---

35. McLaren, *Naked Spirituality*, 3.

Day 85

I shall discuss Jesus the human being, who lived in a particular time and place, and I shall search for evidence and propose explanations just as does any historian when writing about a figure of history.[36]

For Christians, and other faith traditions founded by extraordinary persons such as Buddhism or Islam, some of the first questions have to do with the historical inquiry regarding the founder. Each of these religions has a measure of difficulty with these questions, some having to do with historical access and some having to do with prescribed formal beliefs surrounding the founder. There are some historical accounts of the Siddhartha Gautama (Buddha), although the historical records do get thin at critical junctures. With Muhammad, there are good historical records, yet they are often framed quite tightly by orthodox beliefs. The same problems exist for Jesus, and for over two hundred years, scholars have been poring over his history. This movement has been called the quest for the historical Jesus, and the movement itself has had several phases. In that I am acquainted with this history, I will draw upon it a bit to illustrate from one tradition the challenges of basing one's faith on an historical figure. We do have the Gospel accounts of the life and teaching of Jesus, but there are questions about how to read and interpret these accounts. They were written at least thirty to fifty years after he lived, and the documents were not intended to be historical accounts, but guidance for the new Christian churches. The authors were not critical historians; they were people of faith who used their faith assumptions to interpret the meaning of Jesus. There was a time in the mid-twentieth century in which scholars were inclined to say that we really do not know too much about the historical Jesus. However, since that time, using the most refined tools of historical inquiry, scholars, while not agreeing on all details, are more inclined to say that we can know quite a bit about Jesus and what he taught. But the larger question for many is whether he was, or in what sense he was, the Word of God, the way through which God spoke to humanity.

How much do think we can know about the historical Jesus?

---

36. Sanders, *The Historical Figure of Jesus*, 2.

Day 86

Thus, for Christians, Jesus is utterly central. In a concise sentence, Jesus is for Christians the decisive revelation of God. Slightly more fully, Jesus reveals and discloses, what can be seen of God in a human life and what a life filled with God looks like.[37]

For some Christians, and indeed for many lay people in other faith traditions, the historical questions are not altogether critical for belief and for faith development. Often, among those who are more conservative in their outlook, there is the conviction that the records in the authoritative texts are divinely inspired, and therefore normative for faith and practice. There is also the belief that the hermeneutical guidance of the clergy and scholars in the faith community is trustworthy. The real issue for most of us is the way the religion and its expression in a local congregation is presented and practiced. Is it truly life-giving? However, from time to time, there are critical questions that arise and need attention, and this attention must be done at the scholarly level for faithful adherents of the faith. For Christians, one of those questions in the past several decades has been the issue of how we understand Jesus and read the records of his life and teaching. The same could be said for Islam as well, as Muslims struggle with whether or not to affirm a moderate reading of Muhammad's teaching or a more extreme jihadist reading. I have had the privilege of teaching and writing in the area of Jesus studies, and I will speak to this concern as general guidance for those who struggle with the classic liberal/conservative division within their religion.[38] The issues are very complex, and these daily readings are not the domain for addressing all of them. However, an informed position may be helpful for those who understand the coming of Jesus as central to their faith. Let me mention five attitudes or conclusions that have given me a place to stand.

What is your impression of how much we can know about Jesus?

---

37. Borg, *Jesus*, 6.

38. My recent book, *The Radical Teaching of Jesus*, is one way I have thought about the question of how we do the historical work and read the records of the life of Jesus.

Day 87

> *No other line of research seems so geared as to making skeptics out of scholars.*[39]

Let's reflect together on the five attitudes or positions I am proposing.

1. There is wisdom in speaking of the *Jesus of history* and the *Christ of faith*. They are connected and integrated in Christian thought, but these two categories make it somewhat easier to speak about both history and faith.

2. Another conclusion that I have reached is that there is *enough trustworthy historical information about Jesus on which to build a faith orientation*. Of course, not everyone is in agreement on all of the details. But reputable scholars who address the issue agree that there is a core picture of the life and teachings of Jesus.

3. Out of this historical core, based on careful research about what Jesus may have done and taught, one might say that the example of the life of Jesus and his extraordinary teaching speak profoundly. There has been a movement within the Christian church that finds guidance and inspiration for faith in the example of his life and in the insight of his teaching. I am one of those.

4. However, the Christian church, from its earliest history, went beyond the power of Jesus' exemplary life and profound teaching. From the beginning (as, for example, in the writings of the Apostle Paul), there was the movement to the Christ of faith. Indeed, the very heart of the Christian Church is the claim, expressed in different ways, that "He is the image of the invisible God" (Col 1:15). and that "God was in Christ" (2 Cor 5:19). It is these affirmations that *require the act of faith.*

5. As a final affirmation, I think it is important to realize that *our Christian faith is based on faith, not factual certainty in every detail.* It is rather a thoughtful commitment to understand Jesus as the Word from God. As the author of John's Gospel says, he is the "light of the world." I can be content with this affirmation and continue to be diligent in my honest and careful scholarship with the New Testament records.

Is it easy or difficult for you to see Jesus as both an historical figure and divine?

---

39. Meier, *The Marginal Jew*, 3.

Day 88

On the face of it, the question "Where is God?" might appear to be an arcane theological notion, but it is, in reality, a profound contemporary global inquiry. Depending on how it is answered, "Where is God?" could be a social and political question with sweeping consequences for the future. To relocate God is to reground our lives.[40]

This section of our daily readings is about the ways we reach upward for relationship with God, and we are thinking together about how we make the connection. We spoke about what we mean when we use the word "God," and then explored what those from different religions and from more secular inquiries mean when they speak about transcendence. We underlined in our second month of readings that the Judeo-Christian tradition speaks about loving a personal God with our whole being. In these past several days, we have reflected on the meaning of the human response of faith as the way we understand and relate to the Transcendent One. We have said that our current time needs an informed faith sustained by a mindful spirituality, and suggested what that might be. We continue on that theme by looking at a small group of difficult questions that need, if not full answers, at least some perspective. In the Christian community, understanding the place of Jesus in our faith journey is critical. So our question for today is, "Where is God?"; or, expressed more traditionally, "Does God exist?" If so, how might we understand the nature of God? Brilliant minds across the centuries have tried to answer these questions, and have to do so not in the sense of a scientific proof, but in the sense of a big picture, or an outlook that gives order to all that exists. We need to reflect as well on the contemporary trend to speak of belief in God as limiting, in that religions may inadvertently tend to reduce our quest for a deep spirituality. They do so by calling for obedience to a patriarchal God and frame dogmas that do not liberate, but confine us. Our goal is to avoid this caricature and give devotion to a loving God who frees us to think, enriches us, and empowers us to flourish.

Are you finding life-giving and credible ways to put your faith together?

---

40. Bass, *Grounded*, 11.

Day 89

It is no good asking for a simple religion. After all, real things are not simple. They look simple, but there are not.[41]

There have been many arguments for the existence of God, some more persuasive than others. Three continue to have some cogency for me.

1. The first one that has been integral to the arguments of many of the great minds that have tried to answer the question is *being itself*.[42] It is as if one gazes initially at the beauty of the earth and ponders the vastness of the universe, and then reflects in wonder about why there is something and why it is so well-ordered and beautiful. There is an inexplicable presence of the universe. Why is there something instead of nothing, and why is what exists so marvelous? Of course, this line of reasoning does not take us to a personal God who is Love and Light, although it may begin to point in that direction.

2. One also needs a second argument to move beyond a scientific reflection on the impersonal forces and energies that stand behind the formation of the universe. A second reason that is often used to claim that God exists is that *there is consciousness*. Late in the evolutionary process, there emerged a human that was capable of thinking, reasoning, and communicating. There were billions of years before there was consciousness, but there came a time when humankind reflected the trend toward personal awareness.[43]

3. There is a third argument, and it has to do with *the presence of values and bliss*. Arising within the human experience is that we understand goodness and beauty, and value it. We create, or perhaps discover, ethical norms, and have experiences that are deeply satisfying. Where do these norms and experiences come from except from transcendence?

Are these arguments persuasive for you, or at least suggestive?

---

41. Lewis, *Mere Christianity*, 32.
42. Hart, *The Experience of God*, 87-88.
43. Teilhard de Chardin, in his book *The Phenomenon of Man*, argues that the appearance of humans is the signal that God is moving the universe toward an Omega Point, or the full realization of the purpose of creation.

Day 90

Father, if you willing, remove this cup from me; yet, not my will but yours be done. (Luke 22:42)

It is not easy to maintain a deep and abiding faith in God and practice the implications of a faith commitment day-to-day. Having a mindful spirituality is essential for our walk with God. The world's temptations are very real; we do occasionally believe that the possession of *things* brings happiness; we often long for immediate pleasure and seek it, even if it is harmful to ourselves and others; and we want to have power and be important and recognized. There are the challenges of maintaining a strong faith as we encounter the findings of both the hard sciences and the social sciences that question the validity of a faith orientation and provide alternative answers in the concepts and language of a different map. I have spent a lifetime with these challenges, found them difficult, and have emerged on the other side of these questions with what I hope is a thoughtful and credible faith. I have also been forced to face another difficult question, which is why a loving and all-powerful God would allow so much evil and suffering. I have no final and definitive answer to the question of evil and suffering, although I find myself moving in three directions that are helpful for me.

1. The first is to separate the evil and suffering caused by human ignorance and by hateful and insensitive people. In short, I make a distinction between what we cause and that over which we have no control.

2. The second direction I go is more theological in tone. It is to affirm that God chooses to be self-limiting. The Greek word is *kenosis,* and it is used in reference to Jesus, who *emptied* himself in order to be fully human and identify with human suffering. He lived in solidarity with humankind. This is often God's way, in both ongoing creation and healing redemption.

3. The third direction I go follows from the second, and that is that God must allow for human freedom in order for human beings to love God in return and to be complete in the expression of their creation in the image of God.

Is the problem of evil a stumbling block for your faith in God

Study Guide for the March Readings

Questions for Contemplation and Discussion

1. What are the fundamental components of faith? How does it differ from belief, or does it?

2. Is it possible to have a deep faith in one's own religious tradition and still be open to learning from another tradition?

3. How do we avoid incorporating indefensible beliefs and even superstitions into our faith orientation? How do we spot them?

4. How do you maintain a strong faith and affirm the findings of science? Do you have to deny some beliefs in your faith or not believe some of what science teaches us?

5. Is it possible to have a meta-narrative that grounds you in your faith, is inclusive of the insights and beliefs of other religions, and is accepting of the findings of science? What does God, or Transcendence, look like in the meta-narrative?

6. Do you find your faith changing somewhat across the years? In what ways? Do you find the research and findings in the behavioral sciences, in both religious belief and in moral growth, good ways to understand the changes occurring in your views?

7. Most religions and spiritual pathways have high moral standards and a strong emphasis on living the ethical life. Is it possible for us to achieve these high ethical standards? Or do we need to be empowered by the means of grace, such as the presence of God's Spirit? What are these means of grace for you?

8. Jesus teaches, as does the Christian church, that attempts to follow the teaching of Jesus mean that love is the most important value in life. Do you think that Jesus got it right?

9. The Christian faith, as well as the faith of its monotheistic cousins, Judaism and Islam, strongly believe that God is personal, and that it is possible to have a relationship with God. Do you believe this as well?

10. How does one begin and develop this relationship with God? Is there an alternate spiritual way for those who do not believe in theism?

THEME FOR APRIL

REACHING UPWARD TOWARD UNION WITH GOD

Day 91

Now during those days he went out to the mountain to pray; and he spent the night in prayer to God. (Luke 6:12)

We continue with our larger theme of "Reaching Upward." For January, it was "Reaching Upward for Transcendence"; for February, "Reaching Upward toward Loving God with Our Whole Being"; and in March, "Reaching Upward for Relationship with God through Faith." These readings across the first three months invited our reflection on how it is we reach upward to establish a relationship with God, or Transcendence. Now we want to focus on how to secure and maintain the relationship, and then in the next four-month section ("Opening Inward") we will reflect and pray together about how to deepen the relationship and make it the center of our lives. Within the Christian faith, and certainly most of the other religions of the human family, union with transcendence or the divine is the starting point and foundation of the spiritual commitment. Our particular goal will be to reflect on how to sustain this union. We will undertake this challenge by giving attention to five domains of the union with God and how we can be mindful about them.

1. We will first give attention to a *definition* of union with God, knowing that this definition will grow and develop as we live out our union with God.

2. We will then speak about the several *dimensions* of the union. We will explore how it is understood in several different religious traditions and attempt to learn from the extraordinary wisdom inherent in them.

3. We will move on to begin our reflection on how it is that we *develop* our union with God across the years of our lives. We will draw again from developmental psychology and explore the stages of spiritual growth.

4. We will then study together the several *demands* that are placed in front of us as we seek to cultivate and enrich our spiritual journey with God.

5. We will also contemplate what our *destination* might be as we sustain our union over a lifetime and then cross over to the other side.

How do you understand your union with God?

Day 92

> *The Father and I are one.* (John 10:30)

There are many names and images for God in the Bible, and if we look beyond the Judeo-Christian tradition to other religious traditions, we discover a multitude of names for the divine or for transcendence. As we begin our reflection on how to achieve union with God, or Transcendence, we should first reflect on how we understand the nature of God/Transcendence. This understanding will shape how we define the union. We will explore several of these views of the divine and explore how union is sought within them. I want to begin this conversation with how union with God is understood within the Christian faith and then expanded to other religions. If we had to summarize the Bible's picture of God, we might say that there are two large categories with numerous sub-categories. In the Hebrew Bible, God is frequently understood as King, a metaphor from the context for one with great power and authority. In the New Testament, while "king," and certainly the phrase "kingdom of God," are very present, God is more frequently spoken of as Father, a familial metaphor. The notion of God as parent and mother are also present in the Hebrew Bible.

Jesus used both metaphors, ruler and parent, although in terms of his walk with God he was more inclined to think of God as a loving Father.[1] He often used the word for "father" from Aramaic, *Abba*, the common language spoken in his setting. For Jesus, the spiritual life consisted of being in union with a God that was personal and whose primary mode of being with humans was to be a loving presence. Jesus freely used other terms to describe the qualities of God. As he walked the dusty roads of Palestine and met a range of challenges, he sensed that his *Abba* was with him. So we might define union with God, drawing upon the teaching of Jesus, as the bringing together of two separate personal beings, human and divine, into one. It is the combination or coalition of two identities, making one. *Abba* was present for Jesus.

What name or image of God are you inclined to use and why?

---

1. Cobb, *Jesus' Abba*, 1. I am sensitive about using the term Father, a masculine parent, although it is accurate to say that Jesus is using the term to describe a loving parent.

Day 93

> *Abba's exercise of power does not reduce human freedom. It liberates human beings to choose. It does not replace the power of human beings. On the contrary, it empowers them. In short, whereas there are indeed massive powers of compulsion at work in the world,* Abba *is not one of those.*[2]

I have read many books on Christian spirituality, and I am so grateful for the ways they have guided me in my spiritual life. Most, of course, use the phrase "union with God" as the central goal of the spiritual life. However, the phrase is used in two different ways, both of which teach a great truth. One of them puts the focus on non-duality as a way of speaking about union. It is a helpful term, but my concern about using it without explanation is that it may suggest that we could lose our identity in the union with God. I know what is being said and appreciate the thought, but I am more inclined to think of our union with God as a relationship that empowers us to find our true identity and to live faithfully by loving God "with our whole heart, and with our whole soul, and with all of our strength, and with all of our mind." In this way of understanding our union with God, our personal identity and freedom are preserved and guided toward union with God. It is established and maintained by our free choice to love; and for love to be truly love, it must be given freely.

I do understand why many gifted and dedicated teachers and authors speak about non-duality, meditation, contemplation, and mystical prayer. They describe the dynamics of active receptivity to oneness with God. We sense, as we engage in these practices, the enlightenment that comes from the union with God; we see and love the way God sees and loves. We are filled with the presence of God, yet I maintain that our identity is still present as well. We rise from our knees to go into the world with compassion and to seek justice and peace. There is a loving union with God and a partnership with God to seek a more just and humane world. Jesus spoke about the union with God as receiving the kingdom of God, by which he meant that we are able to receive the full power and loving presence of God in our lives and to do God's will.

Do we lose our identity in our union with God, or do we find and preserve it?

---

2. Ibid., 139.

Day 94

> *The beloved says from the other side of the door, "Open the door and come in, so we can experience just how one we might become."*[3]

There are many *dimensions* of our union with God, some that are quite obvious and which we take into account as we cultivate our union with God. There are others that are in the background, or deeply buried in who we are as a person. We may not be in touch with them, although they will have a profound influence on how we experience our union with God. Let's sample what a few of these might be. For example, we may seek union with a perception of God that may not be an accurate reflection of who God really is. We may have created a caricature of God that is rooted in a dysfunctional family with a father figure who was untrustworthy. I have struggled with this perception of God seen through the *sunglasses* of dysfunction and unpredictability. I am not sure I can count on a father figure.

Or I may view God as an angry judge who will hold me accountable and make me feel guilty for having the normal feelings of being human. There are churches that draw heavily upon the images of an angry and judgmental God from Scripture and move them to the center of a congregation's understanding of the divine.

Others, drawing upon passages of Scripture that tend toward an exclusive outlook, may teach in a quasi-tribal way that access to union with God is only possible our way, unaware that their way is rooted in their time in history, their culture, and their language. It is certainly approximate and likely distorted.

The fact is that we seek union with God just as we are, and we know that God receives us. God accepts our limited understanding and welcomes us. We reach out to God in faith, rather than with pure sight and full knowledge. We cultivate that union as we bow before the divine mystery, knowing in our heart that God is love and light and will receive us, heal us, and be with us across the years of our lives.

Is it easy or somewhat difficult for you to approach God?

---

3. Finley, *Christian Meditation*, 39.

Day 95

> *That in the winter, seeing a tree stripped of its leaves, and considering that within a little time the leaves would be renewed, after the flowers and fruit appear, he received a high view of the providence and power of God.*[4]

We are reflecting on the many *dimensions* of our union with God. We noted that one dimension is what we bring to God as we seek divine union. We mentioned that there are some aspects of our lives that may make it harder to achieve a healthy and life-giving union, one in which we thrive. It takes time to become aware of these hidden feelings and fears, yet with the love of others and our union with God we can heal and move into a nurturing union with God. Brother Lawrence, the medieval dishwasher in a monastery, did it by practicing the presence of God each day. What qualities may have been present for him to achieve such an intimate union with God? Books could and have been written in answer to this question, but let's at least begin the conversation with a few qualities that make for a healthy union.[5]

1. The union *empowers* the person to behave in constructive ways that lead to love, compassion, and understanding.
2. The union *guides* the person to be socially responsible and concerned about creating a more just and humane social environment.
3. The union is based upon a solid and credible understanding of God and *encourages* the person to be open to new ideas and challenges.
4. The union enables the person to *flourish and integrate* beliefs and practices that lead to a life of coherence, conviction, serenity, and integrity.
5. The union offers guidance and practices that *sustain* the person in times of difficulty and challenge.

Many other positive qualities might be mentioned and, as we think together about our union with God, it will be wise to reflect, as did Brother Lawrence in another time and place, on the life-giving characteristics of our union with God.

In what other ways does your union with God empower you?

---

4. Brother Lawrence, *The Practice of the Presence of God*, 13.
5. I mention several in my book, *Exploring the Spirituality of the World Religions*, 10.

Day 96

> *Typical worldviews among traditional Native Americans are about maintaining harmony or balance in life. This concern over a harmonious existence makes a way for one's happiness, health, and well-being.*[6]

As we remain open and eager to grow and learn, we will be able to incorporate insights and wisdom from religious traditions other than our own. Differences may remain and we need not be threatened by alternative views. Instead, we can find ways of incorporating them into our own faith, knowing that, where there is life-giving truth, there is the footprint of God. In fact the name for God might easily be spelled with two o's—Good. I have found this especially true in my experience with the indigenous religious traditions found in nearly every corner of the earth. Yes, these settings and outlooks should not be romanticized; many people of these cultures suffer from poverty and a clash with the advanced contemporary culture. However, the following dimensions of their spiritual way are but a sample of what I learn from them about union with the divine and wisdom for the spiritual journey:

1. I learn from them that our spiritual journey and union with God is intimately connected with *nature*. We are part of nature and, rather than exploiting nature, we should find our place within nature, and understand the interdependence and ecological balance of nature. It is part of being spiritual.

2. When we do, we find that our lives are *centered* rather than fragmented and alienated. We feel congruent, focused, and ordered in our habitat, and find God's will as we live in harmony with the natural world.

3. Sensing God's presence within nature, we understand the *divine as omnipresent*. We see God wherever we look and sense the divine presence.

4. We can learn from this tradition about an *ethical way of life* that has respect for all of life, cares for the earth, and practices *shalom*. We are only now discovering an ecological outlook that has been present all along.

Do you find the wisdom, which is inherent in the indigenous peoples' outlook, to be inviting?

---

6. Woodley, *Shalom and the Community of Creation: An Indigenous Vision*, 67.

Day 97

But all around us on every side there is an uncharted region, just fragments of the fringe of it explored, and those imperfectly; it is with this that religion deals.[7]

Even as the indigenous wisdom traditions of the world have sought the divine within nature and nature's ways, there are other religious traditions, both ancient and modern, that have sought to understand the divine within their strong emotions and within the cultural norms that control and guide these strong emotions. The religions of ancient Egypt and Greece understood the divine in these ways, with the pharaoh having divine qualities; and the pantheon of Greek gods representing many strong emotions, such as love and wisdom, as well as negative ones, such as anger. The Roman gods had elements of nature and strong emotion, and divine emperors ruled with the other gods. Let's sample one expression of these ideas about transcendence by looking at the mystery religions of ancient Greece. How was union achieved with these gods, and how did one gain acceptance into the cultic community? Often, there were five steps:

1. There was the step of purification with a ritual bathing, an initiation;
2. Then came the instruction in the secret knowledge;
3. There was an exposure to the secret and sacred objects related to knowledge;
4. There was a narration and dramatic reenactment of the sacred story;
5. And finally, there was a crowning, symbolizing full membership and union.

There are obvious risks in identifying the divine with political power vested in a king, pharaoh, or emperor. There are equal dangers in projecting the action of the gods behind the tragedies and triumphs of war or the unpredictable character of storms and natural disasters. But what was sought in these ancient cultures, and to some extent our own, is a divine explanation for what we do not fully understand and cannot control. Nature and culture-based religions explored ways of trying to influence the transcendent cause of these events. We often do it as well.

Are there risks of seeing the presence of God in events that we do not understand or control?

---

7. Murray, *Five Stages of Greek Religion*, 5.

Day 98

> *Two mighty motives run through the mythologies and religions of the world . . . The first and the earlier to appear we may term* **wonder** *in one or another of its modes, from mere bewilderment in the contemplation of something inexplicable to arrest in daemonic dread or mystic awe. The second is* **self-salvation:** *redemption or release from a world exhausted of its glow.*[8]

It is all too easy to cast a denigrating glance at ancient and modern religions that place the divine within nature and culture. However, even the most sophisticated religious outlooks view aspects of the divine in this way. We learn from these less rational traditions about the ways to understand and find union with God. For example:

1. I have learned that God is intimately connected with the life and circumstances that surround me, often difficult to understand;
2. I have learned that God is present for guidance and help with the most pressing problems of life;
3. I have learned that God may empower or endow leaders in the quest for achieving a just social order;
4. I have learned that my union with God takes expression in articulating ethical norms in universal ways and practicing them;
5. I have learned that my spiritual journey is expanded and enriched by the cultural and artistic expression of my faith in art, in music, and in poetic words.

I remain cautious about identifying the divine with the rhythms of nature and the unfolding of national and global political realities. I resist seeing political leaders as anything more than mere humans with some experience and wisdom. And I am certainly not fatalistic, assuming that what will be will be. I do not see anything related to the divine in unethical, self-seeking, and destructive behavior. I believe that God calls us to a life of service in the cause of reducing suffering and building a more just and peaceful world.

How is it possible to see God in the events of our lives? Or is it possible?

---

8. Campbell, *Oriental Mythology*, 35. Emphasis added.

Day 99

> *The Blessed Lord said: Fearlessness, purity of heart, persistence in the yoga of knowledge, generosity, self-control, nonviolence, gentleness, candor, integrity, disengagement, joy in the study of the scriptures, compassion for all beings, modest, patience, a tranquil mind.*[9]

One might summarize the Hindu quest to reach upward for union with the divine (Blessed Lord) as *inner discipline*, a quiet contemplation of what eternal transcendence teaches that calms the spirit and gives one the inner strength to live with purity of heart and compassion for all beings. Unfortunately, the Hindu religion is often described as polytheistic and filled with sacrifices to and leaving food for the gods at a sacred place. Yes, there are mini-gods that are extensions of the one true Brahman, and there are sacred places set aside for honoring Brahman and the expressions of Brahman. Yet the deeply spiritual Hindu, through meditation, yoga, and prayer, seeks a true union with ultimate reality, the source of energy and transformation. The quest is for *moksha*, true spiritual liberation. It is the soul or essence of one's self, *atman*, that will be liberated and freed from the eternal patterns of karma as one follows *dharma*, the cosmic order, in good works.

I find it a bit surprising, although not difficult to understand, how many of the great teachings and practices of Hinduism have crossed over into the western world and been adopted as a healthy way of life. Ultimate reality, in the more philosophical forms of Hinduism, is not personal, although Brahman and the local gods do become personal in what might be called popular religion. It is the practices within Hinduism, almost more than the theological beliefs, which have been adopted. It is not difficult to find classes in churches and synagogues in meditation and yoga, often as health practices, rather than guidance in a religious way. Borrowed from both Hinduism and Buddhism, these practices have helped many people with physical health, and also with the management of anxiety and the desire for a more serene life.

Are you drawn to the wisdom and practices inherent in Hindu teaching?

---

9. Mitchell, *Bhagavad Gita*, 169.

Day 100

> *The religion of the future will be a cosmic religion. It should transcend a personal God and avoid dogma and theology. Covering both the natural and spiritual, it should be based on a religious sense arising from the experience of all things natural and spiritual as a meaningful unit. Buddhism answers this description. . . . If there is any religion that could cope with modern scientific needs it would be Buddhism.*[10]

Buddhism, not unlike Hinduism (and the two religions have common roots) in its most authentic expressions, is also a religion that does not speak of ultimate reality as a personal God. Rather it puts the focus on enlightenment. As one slows the pace of life, engages in meditation, and becomes mindful, it is possible to see and experience the pathway to *nirvana*. Buddhism does acknowledge that it is not an easy pathway to follow, and in fact maintains that we really start our spiritual journey in a state of suffering. The cause of our suffering is our craving, which, if not overcome, keeps us unsatisfied. But when we let go of this craving and follow the eightfold path, we break out of the pattern of karma-samsara (the cycle of death and rebirth) and begin to move toward a peaceful and compassionate life. We begin our spiritual journey by understanding the nature of reality and moving toward enlightenment, following the Buddha, or "awakened one." With the support of three great truths, the Buddha, the Dharma (the spiritual teachings of Buddhism), and the Sangha (the spiritual community), we can become a *bodhisattva* (one who aspires enlightenment in order to relieve the suffering of others). Buddhism offers a peaceful and compassionate way to transcendence. The Noble Eightfold Path includes the right view, right intention, right speech, right action, right livelihood, right effort, right mindfulness, and right concentration. These qualities represent a pathway to union with ultimate reality and enlightenment. There are different branches of Buddhism, and many other practices that guide one in the quest for enlightenment; the heart of the journey is quiet acceptance of reality and seeking enlightenment. It is to follow Buddha.

What aspect of the Buddhist way is most attractive to you, and why?

---

10. Quoted by Das, *Awakening the Buddha Within*, 1.

Day 101

> *The Tao that can be followed is not the eternal Tao. The name that can be named is not the eternal name. The nameless is the origin of heaven and earth while naming is the origin of the myriad things. Therefore always without desire, you see the mystery, ever desiring, you see the manifestations.*[11]

Taoism (now often spelled Daoism), both an ancient and contemporary religion, has some of the same qualities as Hinduism and Buddhism, although it has some aspects that are unique as well. It would also counsel its followers to seek to live in harmony with ultimate reality (the Tao), and makes it quite clear that the Tao is elusive and mysterious. The wise dictum of Taoism is that, if you think you can understand and explain the Tao, then you have not really captured the essence of the Tao. It is a caution similar to the one offered by Augustine, who maintained that, if you think you can describe God, then the God you describe is not God, and not worthy of worship.[12] According to the Taoist tradition, Lao Tzu (its founder) was a keeper of the archives in the imperial court of the Zhou Dynasty, and his life may have overlapped with Confucius (551–478 BCE). They had different perspectives, and Lao Tzu may have been older and a mentor for Confucius. It is hard to reconstruct this history, yet the tradition suggests that Lao Tzu taught a way of life that was removed from the rush of the political and social life of his time. It is not reality, and if one is caught up in it, it would be easy to miss the life of inner tranquility. He counsels that it is best to understand the swirl of government and military life as a distraction that creates worry and anxiety, and which increases the chance that one will not understand the essence of reality or live in peace. As possible, the better life is one that is quiet and reflective, open and contemplative, and willing to experience the Tao, or the principle that gives order and meaning to all of life. Even this quest will not guarantee that one will gain true wisdom, but the search for wisdom is the way that the Taoist pilgrim reaches upward for union with transcendence and a life of meaning and serenity.

Do you think that Lao Tzu was on to something with the notion of the Tao?

---

11. Lao Tzu, *Tao Te Ching*, 1.
12. Saint Augustine, however, did talk a great deal about God.

Day 102

Tsz-kung made the remark: "That which I do not wish others to put upon me, I also wish not to put upon others." "Nay," said the Master, "you have not got so far as that."[13]

Confucius, too, guided his contemporaries into a religious and cultural movement for his time, and one that continues into the present. It is not altogether accurate to call Confucianism a religion; it may be more a way of life, although Confucius does speak about "the mandate of heaven." Confucius does not follow Lao Tzu in advising a quiet life removed from the affairs of a normal life filled with demands and responsibilities. He is more concerned about discerning how the active life should be lived in reference to social order, an order mandated by heaven's will. For him, the life in union with the divine is one lived in propriety and with wisdom. There are a number of books attributed to Confucius, in which he addresses a range of subjects that have in common the description of the ideal life, both for the individual and for the government. One way of getting a sense of his philosophy is to focus on his counsel regarding the norms for human relationships. He frames these norms within the context of what is right, not just in the sense of what is the norm for his time and culture, although we can in see them in that frame of reference. He articulates five basic patterns of human relationships:

1. There is the kindness in the father, filial piety (*hsiao*) in the son;
2. There is gentility in the elder brother, humility and respect in the younger brother;
3. There is humane consideration in elders, deference in juniors;
4. There is righteous behavior in the husband, obedience in the wife;
5. There is benevolence in rulers, loyalty in ministers and subjects.

The paternalism is obvious and needs to be questioned. However, we should not miss his attempt to describe a pattern of life that is in keeping with the mandate of heaven. To follow, it leads to a social order that is free of conflict and makes life acceptable.

How might you rewrite the five patterns of human relationships for our time?

---

13. Confucius, *The Wisdom of Confucius*, 7.

Day 103

> *See, I am setting before you today a blessing and a curse: the blessing, if you obey the commandments of the Lord your God that I am commanding you today; and the curse if you do not obey the commandments of the Lord your God, but turn from the way that I am commanding you today to follow other gods that you have known.* (Deut 11:26–28)

We turn now to the Abrahamic religions and their way of understanding how it is that we reach upward for union with God. The three religions, Judaism, Christianity, and Islam, have many similarities and often use similar words, concepts, and practices as they speak about the spiritual journey with God. Yet, there are some distinctive features that we might highlight, although followers of each of these great religions might say that using only a single word or concept as a description of the journey borders on distortion. It is a risk, but perhaps one worth taking. Let me begin with Judaism. It is one of the first religions to develop a thoroughgoing monotheism with an understanding that the one true God is engaged in human life and history, and invites the Hebrew people (and others as time goes along) to a life-changing and life-giving relationship. In fact, "prayer," or talking and listening to God, is in many ways at the heart of the Judaism. I do want to select one other word as a description of the way the union with God is established and maintained, and it is the word "obedience." The narrative of Judaism begins with God's approach to humankind, and this approach, invitation, and response is called a covenant. The covenant is the promise that God will bless (to confer well-being) on the Hebrew people if they will follow (be obedient to) the expectations of God. These expectations, deeply rooted in justice and wisdom, are seen as the law, or the Torah, as given in the first five books of the Hebrew Bible. The sovereign God will care for and bless the Hebrew people if they are obedient to God's commands. Laws, traditions, and commentaries accumulate as the Jewish people seek to fully understand the Law. On occasion, as with the Babylonian captivity, there is the understanding that the covenant was violated. Even when there is disobedience, God's loving care is never lost, although a price may have to be paid. Faithful and obedient Jews worship and love God.

Do you agree that God does bless humankind, but also expects obedience?

Day 104

One of the scribes came near and heard them disputing with one another, and seeing that he answered them well, he asked him, "Which commandment is the first of all?" Jesus answered, "The first is this, 'Hear, O Israel: the Lord our God the Lord is one; you shall love the Lord your God with all your heart, and with all your soul, and with all your mind, and with all your strength.' The second is this, 'You shall love your neighbor as yourself.' There is no other commandment greater than these." (Mark 12:28–31)

Christianity is, in many ways, intimately connected to Judaism, with the same basic understanding of God and its affirmation of the Hebrew Bible as sacred scripture. But where it differs is seeing Jesus, a first-century Jewish prophet, as the promised Messiah. There may also be a very slight difference of emphasis when it comes to understanding how a faithful pilgrim reaches upward for union with God. Both would affirm that a relationship is possible with the one true God. While the Christian would also affirm that obedience to God's will and way is absolutely vital, the first word often chosen by the Christian to describe the union with God is love. Jesus is quite clear in the response to the scribe, and he does so as a Jewish prophet. The heart of the union is to love God with your whole being and love your neighbor as you love yourself. The four dimensions of love for God are stressed: You are to love God "with all your heart, with all your soul, with all your mind, and with all your strength"; that is, to love God with our deepest affections, with our essential identity as a person, with the way we think about truth and life, and with all the courage and commitment we can muster. It is a response with our whole person. And there is the second commandment as well, "to love our neighbor as we love ourselves." As we love ourselves, that is, as we want to be fully mature; happy; at peace; in harmony with others who are important to us; free from poverty; healthy; free from broken relationships; and free from excessive worry, stress, and anxiety; then we will understand true empathy and desire these same qualities to be present in our neighbor. She may live next door or in Africa, have a different culture, language, and religion, and be quite different from me. As far as possible, our love for our neighbor should stretch around the world.

Is "love" the best word to describe union with God, or "obedience"? Or both?

Day 105

And your God is one God, There is no God but Him, the most Gracious, the most Merciful. (Surah 2.163)

Islam shares many beliefs and practices with Judaism and Christianity. The most obvious is the profound commitment to monotheism, the *Tawhid* (meaning the unity and oneness of God), known as Allah. In addition, there is a statement in the Quran about "the peoples of the Book" and the affinity with Judaism and Christianity in sharing the common history of the Bible, believing that all three religions are descendants of Abraham. There is respect, as well, for the great prophets of the Bible, and an affirmation that Muhammad is in the same line of prophets and the final one. The narrative of Islam, with some roots in the Bible, is found in the Quran, the word of God, best understood in Arabic. In the Quran (meaning "recitation"), God is understood as the Creator of all and in communication with his creation. The fundamental response of humans to Allah is "submission," a word that is a translation of the term Islam. A good and faithful Muslim is submissive to God and God's will, expressed in the Five Pillars and throughout the Quran. The Five Pillars are:

1. The *Shahadah*, or the first Pillar, which is professing one's faith that there is no god but God, and that Muhammad is the messenger of God;

2. The second Pillar, or the fundamental practice of Islam, is *Salat*, the five daily prayers said while facing the Ka'bah, the sacred cubicle in Mecca;

3. The third Pillar is the *Zakat*, obligatory annual alms-giving—the purpose of this giving is primarily to help the needy, and it is also thought of as purification through sharing;

4. The fourth Pillar of Islam is *Ramadan*, or the month of fasting—even as Muslims find a pattern in the day for prayer, so too do they find patterns in the year, with the ninth month as a time to honor God;

5. The final or fifth Pillar of Islam is the *Hajj*, the pilgrimage to sacred places around Mecca and a visit to the sanctuary of the Ka'bah.

Is submission the best word to use to describe our walk with God?

Day 106

O Lord, it is true. According as Thou sayest, so, I beseech Thee, let it be with me; let Thy Truth teach me, itself guard me, and preserve me to an end of safety. Let it set me free from all evil affection and inordinate love; and I shall walk with Thee in great liberty of heart.[14]

We have offered a short definition of what it means to achieve union with God and explored its many dimensions or expressions in a variety of religious traditions. We turn now to a brief exploration of how we develop in reference to our union with God. We will explore briefly the different stages of our faith and how these stages affect our union with God.[15] What we say about stages of faith will be preliminary, and we will expand this topic when we turn to the next section of our readings, "Opening Inward." As we consider the pattern of development, we should understand that it is not always a simple and straightforward growth pattern, but one that is gradual with back-and-forth movement, and elements of more than one stage at any given time in our growth. We may want to say, as well, that it is risky to value one stage over another, although the movement is toward maturity. Yet, each stage has its own value for where we are in our growth. I have personally reflected on the changes in my spiritual journey and have discovered that, while it has not been straight and direct, fundamental changes have occurred across the years. I have wondered if those changes were natural in the sense of the normal pattern of human growth and development, or whether the changes have occurred because of the many external influences at work in my environment. My initial assessment is that the pattern of growth had both: elements that are built into the norms of human development and, given an environment filled with stimulation and support, there were many positive external factors as well.

Are the changes in your growth natural, or the result of external influence?

---

14. à Kempis, *The Imitation of Christ*, 77.

15. I have been informed by Fowler's book, *Stages of Faith: The Psychology of Human Development and the Quest for Meaning*, and Marion's book, *Putting on the Mind of Christ: The Inner Work of Christian Spirituality*.

Day 107

> *The persons, causes, and situations we really love and trust, the images of good and evil, of possibility and probability to which we are committed—these form the pattern of our faith.*[16]

James Fowler, deeply rooted in developmental psychology and the history and practice of Christian formation, speaks of six stages of faith, in part tied to normal human growth and in part the result of exposure to both positive and negative sets of experiences and environments.[17] I have found that his account is a kind of map of my growth, and would invite readers to see how these categories may be descriptive of their growth and development. Having a list with brief introductions to each of the stages will provide us with a reference point as we explore the spiritual journey of our union with God, or Transcendence. We will refer to these stages of faith development again as we move on in our study of mindful spirituality. I'll provide only a brief definition of the stages here.

1. Preoperational: This stage exists in infancy, is rudimentary, and functions in terms of punishment and reward. It is family-oriented with strong dependency on the mother or caregiver, and moves from episode to episode. The character of the person's understanding and experience of the divine will be impacted by the quality of care given to the infant and the sense in the infant of being loved, valued, and wanted.

2. Concrete Operational: This is the childhood stage, in which one sees the world in simple categories; operates with reciprocal fairness, although still egocentric; understands others as like the family; makes sense with a story; accepts a magical outlook or narrative; and is literal and one-dimensional. The child will believe the miraculous stories that are integral to the account of creation and the formation of a religion.

Were the early years of your life positive for the development of your faith?

---

16. Fowler, *Stages of Faith*, 4.

17. Fowler does use six stages. Others, including Jim Marion, add other stages. Marion also identifies the stages with the evolution of human consciousness.

Day 108

Mythic consciousness is the level of consciousness of the child from about age 7 to adolescence; it is the first of the mental levels. It is the consciousness of the child's emerging mind or ego. The child at this level believes that the "God in the Sky," much like its parents, can work every miracle to meet the child's needs.[18]

1. Early Formal Operations: This stage addresses adolescence and early adulthood. It is one in which there are mutual relationships with expectations, experience in groups, and an appreciation for them and their values. The peer group identification is very important. It is also the stage in which there is the beginning development of understanding symbolic or mythic meaning that gives order to the environment. However, the person at this level generally accepts literally what is taught. Many remain at this level into adulthood.

2. Formal Operations: This is the stage of rational consciousness, cultivated in the presence in a self-selected group, often at the college level. The person begins to reflect on the relative character of the group's understanding, and may be informed by another ideological perspective. There is questioning and searching, and in time, meaning is understood and conveyed by symbols.

3. Formal Operational (Dialectic): In this stage, the person becomes more in touch with the values of other groups, recognizes more universal values, and is open to other points of view. There is a willingness to engage in dialectical exchange, and there is an appreciation of the reality beyond the symbol. There is the acceptance of other points of view, and a willingness to acknowledge the limited and approximate nature of one's own beliefs.

4. Formal Operational (Synthetic): In this stage of consciousness, one that few achieve, there is loyalty to the One beyond the many and an appreciation of truth wherever it is found. There is a sense of continual search for the God, or Transcendence, beyond religion, and a measure of comfort and even tranquility in not fully knowing.

Where do you see yourself in these stages of faith?

---

18. Marion, *Putting on the Mind of Christ*, 41.

Day 109

As a new vision unfolds, small groups of people who understand the necessity for change begin to follow a new path; they experiment, create, and innovate with religious, political, economic, and family structures in a search for a new way of life.[19]

Our way of reaching upward for the divine changes across the years of our lives as we go through the stages of development. Our consciousness changes, and we begin to see the world and what is beyond it in different ways. The change of our consciousness happens within us as we grow and develop, and it also changes in reference to our immediate environment, and the culture and history in which we live. Sociologists are fond of naming generations whose outlook is different from that of their parents and the one that they follow. We read these accounts and find ourselves described in quite accurate ways. We also note that those within these categories of generations have slightly changing religious views.

I have been keenly aware that what might be called a new reformation is occurring in our time, one that calls into question traditional ways of belief and practice, and seeks a new way to pursue a spiritual journey and the connection with ultimate reality. There are many sides to this new quest for linkage with transcendence and finding meaning in life. One, of course, has to do with the changing consciousness that occurs as we pass through the stages of development. This new consciousness is also a motivating force for finding God without religion, because traditional religion no longer resonates with these new pilgrims.[20] I have stayed within the church community that understands itself as part of progressive Protestantism, yet I confess to finding additional spiritual nourishment from the gatherings that do it differently. A small example (and it is possible to point to many) is Taize, a quiet, reflective, and chanting (singing) gathering that comforts and deepens. Scripture is read, and there is a common prayer and time for quiet reflection.

Do you find yourself searching for a new spiritual "place to call home?"

---

19. Bass, *Christianity After Religion*, 34.
20. See Tom Stella's book, *Finding God Beyond Religion*.

Day 110

I am a mystic, and so are you. This may seem like an outrageous claim, since in traditional religious thinking, mystics are those rare people who experience the powerful, unmediated, all-consuming presence of God.[21]

I am caught up in both the normal changes that often occur as one moves through life; that is, I am in a stage of faith. I am also influenced by a new reformation that is occurring within the Christian church, and I suspect is occurring in many other religious communities as well. Let me reflect for a moment on the stages of faith and a changing consciousness. Although not raised in a conservative religious context, as a young person, I did experience and was informed by reputable scholarship that the typical conservative or evangelical congregation understands. It articulates its faith largely at Stage Three, with a literal interpretation of the Bible and a theological outlook that is traditional and orthodox. There was some fear of and even judgment in these churches about those who differed from them in belief and practice. I paused for a while at this stage, and found community, groups of Christians, and churches that held comparable views. I felt security with having the truth and engaged from time to time in behavior that was somewhat narrow, in that I had little sympathy for those even in the Christian family who differed from me. I also was inclined to say that those who held other religious views were wrong. In time, with an exposure to a wide variety of views in a university setting and in graduate study, I found myself more open to alternative views, informed by them, and nourished by them in my spiritual life. As a professor, I taught world religions and found myself having profound appreciation for other religions that were true to their history and culture. I was guided by the advice of the Dalai Lama, who said that most people could be nurtured by the profound theology and deep spiritual practices of their own religious tradition. So I stayed within Christianity, but had respect for other world religions. I find that I have moved beyond Stage Three, through Stage Four, and feel comfortable at Stage Five, and sense some movement toward Stage Six. I now easily honor the spiritual journeys of others.

How would you describe your movement through the stages of faith?

---

21. Ibid., 51.

Day 111

> *Aware of the danger, I suggest five categories for naming divisions in American Christianity today: conservative, conventional, uncertain, former, and progressive Christians. In somewhat different forms, these kinds of Christians are found among both Protestants and Catholics.*[22]

I am in this larger family of people who call themselves Christian, and now find myself most at home among progressive Christians. I also have some loyalty to my Presbyterian heritage. It is within this group that I try to give a priority to and practice mindful spirituality. I do find marvelous resources for this endeavor in other religious traditions as well, both in my theological understanding and in my practice. Prayer and meditation seem nearly omnipresent, and I am enriched and deepened in my spiritual journey by an exposure to pilgrims of many faiths. I have found that my movement toward more of an interfaith posture has troubled some of my dearest friends in the more conservative side of Christianity; yet it has also been affirmed by many friends in the more liberal side, and by many from other religions. We have found some common ground.

There has been the occasional question about whether I have had discomfort in my movement across the stages of faith. I admit to some discomfort; yet, the delight in learning from and being with others on different paths has been more than compensating. I usually answer the question about whether I have lost my faith or suffered from doubt by saying that my spiritual walk is deeper and more satisfying, that I have truly learned to love across boundaries, and that doubt is a marvelous way of life. We will never grow unless we doubt our way of putting faith together. My doubt is less about whether there is a Transcendent Other, and more about the reality that my current faith orientation, both theologically and spiritually, is partial and incomplete. I know that, when I speak and write about faith subjects, I often approximate and expect to grow in these understandings. I also find some comfort as I read about the lives of people such as Buddha and Jesus, and sense that they, too, experienced growth.

Are you comfortable with doubt and change in your spiritual journey?

---

22. Borg, *Convictions*, 8.

Day 112

> *All humans crave spiritual experience (properly understood), whether they know it or not. Indeed, an encounter with transcendence can be thrilling and delightful; they can be illuminating and inspiring; they can be heartwarming and comforting; and they can even be awesome and terrifying.*[23]

We have been reflecting together; that is, being mindful about how we reach upward for union with God, or Transcendence. We began by speaking about a definition of what we mean by the phrase "union with God," and then went on to discuss its many dimensions, knowing that we would nuance our definition as we went along. From the discussion of the dimensions of union with God, we reflected on how we develop and grow in a spiritual journey with the divine, pointing to stages of faith and exposure to influences that shape our growth. We turn now to an exploration of the demands of a commitment to mindful spirituality and what is necessary in order to nurture and sustain our union with God, or Transcendence. Forgive the slight pause for review; but let's go back and remember a few of the ways that we spoke about being mindful in our spiritual journey, a journey that is rooted in our union with the divine—with God. We noted earlier in our readings that the starting point for mindfulness is being in the present, or the current moment. It is to put the brakes on the way our mind jumps around to worry about yesterday, what I need to get done today, and anxiety about tomorrow. We might add preoccupation with relationships, wondering if we will have enough money, and the feeling of being overwhelmed with responsibilities—or the opposite, being sad about our loneliness and lack of purpose in life. We stop, breathe deeply, and begin our meditation. In a prayerful spirit and a comfortable posture, we quiet ourselves and listen for the divine voice, monitor our breathing, and get back in touch with our true self. We may continue in our meditation or use a symbol such as a candle to point to the light, or reflect on a reading that takes us to our center and points us to the divine.

What is the best way for you to be mindful about your spiritual growth?

---

23. McIntosh, *The Presence of the Infinite*, 1.

Day 113

Contemplation is the highest expression of man's (or humankind's) intellectual and spiritual life. It is that life itself, fully awake, fully active, fully aware that it is alive. It is spiritual wonder. It is spontaneous awe at the sacredness of life, of being. It is gratitude for life, for awareness, and for being.[24]

I often begin my day with some quiet time, with guided readings, with meditation, and prayer. Of course, there are some days when it is not convenient; perhaps I am traveling, in a hurry to get to a meeting, or need to be a host to our houseguests. It may make a difference in the day, although it is not always obvious. The value becomes more apparent as I am consistent in the practice. I am more at peace, less subject to anxiety, and have less stress or partial depression. To be consistent in the practice, I need to be sure I am ready. It requires that I arrange my schedule so that it is a sort of natural beginning of the day. If I have to force it, with a neglect of some other vital piece of the day such as a conversation with my wife, or it is hurried because I might be late for an appointment or a trip to the airport, then it ceases to be mindful. I go through the motions, but I am not deeply engaged. I also have a place that works for me, an upstairs study filled with the peaceful presence of books that speak to me of goodness, truth, and beauty. There is a comfortable chair that takes away discomfort and helps me relax, and there are windows that allow me to look out on scenes of beauty with water and mountains. Beside the chair is a very functional table with good light and shelves on which are my reflective and devotional books. This room is my study and where I write almost daily, and I need to keep it tidy. Perhaps I have left books out of place, scattered some paper and not put them in files or the right piles, or the computer reminds me that there is one last email that I didn't answer. I remove these somewhat petty preoccupations so that I am not distracted. In short, I make sure that my environment is ready for me to engage in some reflective reading and meditation. I try to be ready to open my heart and mind to my union with God. I engage in mindful spirituality.

Do you have a routine and a setting that work for you?

---

24. Merton, *New Seeds of Contemplation*, 1.

Day 114

Anxiety and discouragement may easily come to people when they see how strict and diligent the lives of our Lord Jesus Christ and his saints have been, and that humanly we are not up to their level, nor even much inclined to be.[25]

As I read the great literature of spirituality in my own Christian tradition and also within the wonderful literature of the world religions and more secular books on being healthy and centered, I find that I am not a lone pilgrim seeking progress. I am among the company of millions who have gone before me and are my contemporaries. I note that most of them have struggled some or are stressed by the demands of our culture, so busy and loud. I take comfort that Meister Eckhart found it somewhat difficult to be intentional and mindful about his spiritual journey. Few have described the human union with God as clearly and profoundly, and I am even just a bit delighted that he suggested ways of sustaining the union that upset the church establishment, often a sign that points to a deeper and more profound way. I have been part of the administration of a mainline denomination, and I know that part of the responsibilities were to guide beliefs and practices. On occasion, I got into trouble, mostly because I was immature and made mistakes, but on rare occasions because I did suggest an alternative way that might have had value.

What I did learn in that setting was that I really did need to be quite intentional about maintaining my spiritual vitality. It was so easy to be preoccupied with duties and responsibilities, including reports, budgets, hiring, and sustaining linkages with the constituency of the church that I served. I confess to the feelings of not being able to keep up with all the work required and inclinations to guide the work (in my case, mission in higher education) in directions that were not always in accord with the larger denomination. I did need to be a good team player, a competent member of the team, and at the same time be very intentional about my spiritual journey and my union with God. The church needed that kind of person, and I did not always feel up to it. Part of the union, thankfully, is forgiveness.

Have there been times in your life when it has been hard to be mindful?

---

25. Blakney, *Meister Eckhart*, 23.

Day 115

I never saw a moor,
I never saw the sea;
Yet know I how the heather looks,
And what a wave must be.
I never spoke with God,
Nor visited in heaven,
Yet certain am I of the spot
As if the chart were given.

—Emily Dickinson[26]

There are times when I am invited to participate in a funeral or memorial service. In general, I am grateful for the privilege of being with those who are suffering the grief that comes with the loss of a loved one. The emotions surrounding the passing of a member of the family or a dear friend are very intense. I am often asked by these people if there is any hope that they might see the deceased person again, or at least some reassurance that their identity will continue into eternity. I do try to be helpful in these settings and with these questions. I find them difficult, in part because I do not have a lot of answers. Additionally, phrases such as "She is in a better place" or "He is resting in heaven" can be a bit trite given the deep grief that is present. I need to have integrity in these conversations, and a reference to clouds and harps does not cut it. But nevertheless, let me go on to the next "d" in our discussion of our union with God: definition, dimensions, development, demands, and now a look at *destination*. As I speak with grieving people and ponder my own mortality, I find myself moving toward the way I understand and experience God. Even in this strategy, the ice occasionally feels a little thin, but I do venture out on the ice and *skate* toward understanding God as Love. Because of God's loving ways, we have grounds for hope. I am unable to describe what eternal life might look like, although I do say that while life after death cannot be described, we can partially envision a way of being that is without pain and suffering, without conflict and tears, and full of the deep love of God. I turn to the vision of the author of Revelation: "and God himself will be with them; he will wipe every tear from the eyes" (Rev 21:4).

Do you hope that one day you will be free from your difficulties and suffering?

26. Dickinson, *Modern American Poetry*, 82.

Day 116

Now faith is the assurance of things hoped for, the conviction of things not seen.
(Heb 11:1)

I think often of my brother, who died in his twenties. He was my best friend, and he and his wife had two wonderful boys. I think, as well, of my parents, who gave me a home and my start in life, and also my grandparents, with whom my brother and I often spent summers. They were far from perfect, yet I am nostalgic about the years of my childhood and being surrounded by their care. It seems like only yesterday that my brother and I played on the farm and in the forests of eastern Oregon, shared high school with common friends, and participated in several sports. It seems like it was only yesterday that my son was born, loved his time in Alaska as a boy, biked all the way across the United States, and received a fine university education. Now, he and his wife (a doctor) are where I sometimes nostalgically place myself: in their late thirties with excellent professions and two beautiful children. These realities invite me to think about my destination, connected as it is with aging and "the remembrance of things past." I yield at times to sadness with the passing of time and my mortality. But I am a bit guarded about this temptation and self-preoccupation. I find myself focusing more on the meaning of hope in my life. It takes at least four directions:

1. One direction is toward my understanding of God as love and the promise of eternal life, although I still would like to know more about what eternal life might mean.

2. The best partial answers for me are found in the present moment, and the ways that eternal life is a present reality. It is being in the presence of God, or to use our current phrase, in union with God.

3. I continue to live, though moving on in years, with a keen sense of purpose. Life is not over; there are tasks to be done, justice and peace to be pursued, and there are people to love.

4. I spend less time thinking or worrying about the future, and try to live in the moment. This posture is the heart of mindful spirituality.

Do you find it difficult to live in the present moment?

Day 117

Well, the time grew on that the pilgrims must go on their way, wherefore they prepared for their journey. They sent for friends; they conferred with them; that had some time set apart, therein to commit each other to the protection of their Prince.[27]

One part of the reformation that we are experiencing within our many religious movements and communities is a strong emphasis on health and well-being. Some have been critical of this emphasis, calling it self-centered and not sufficiently sacrificial and focused on mission. It is a helpful caution, and we might also want to say that self-sacrifice and a commitment to partner with God in building a more just and humane world grow out of being healthy and in union with God. We are most effective in fulfilling our calling or vocation when we are not preoccupied with our own struggle. Even in our mission endeavors, when our own needs are intense, we lose our focus in mission and our own needs clutter the agenda. If we have lost our way with God and engage in pilgrim's regress, we are not able to carry within us the empowerment of God's Spirit, manifesting in love and compassion and a commitment to making life better for all those who suffer from illness, social injustice, natural disaster, and the violence of war. So, as we think and pray together about our destination, we need to find hope in reference to our mortality, but also must find direction (pilgrim's progress) in our immediate future. As we conclude this section on reaching upward for union with God, I want us to reflect on how it is that we reach upward in a wise and life-giving way. In what ways do we need to cultivate our own mental and spiritual health in order to reach upward and connect with God, not just go through the motions and activities of our religious community? In what ways might we improve our mindful spirituality? As we close this section of reaching upward, I would invite us to contemplate how our mental health influences our quest for union with God, and how the spiritual community in which we find guidance and inspiration might provide a solid foundation for mindful spirituality.

Do you have a spiritual community that helps you find your way?

---

27. Bunyan, *The Pilgrim's Progress*, 313.

Day 118

When I was a child, I spoke like a child, I thought like a child, I reasoned like a child; when I became an adult, I put an end to childish ways. For now we see in a mirror dimly, but then we will see face to face. Now I know only in part; then I will know fully, even as I have been fully known. And now faith, hope, love abide, and the greatest of these is love. (1 Cor 13:11–13)

I find it interesting that the Apostle Paul would speak about our need for growth by making reference to our development from the ways of a child to those of an adult. It was Jesus who spoke about having the innocence and integrity of a child in receiving the kingdom of God (Matt 18:3–5). Paul would not disagree with this statement, although he does say that we are moving toward becoming a mature adult as we encounter the divine (fully known). I have read some of the studies that have connected spirituality and mental health, and have demonstrated how a deep spirituality contributes to our mental and emotional well-being.[28] Not infrequently, the link has been described as going both ways; that is, a deep spirituality improves our mental health, and our mental and emotional maturity often deepens our spirituality. Together, the qualities that arise from positive mental health and deep spirituality blend, making it a bit difficult to distinguish the difference.

It is common for the language describing our growth to be selected from both health care professionals and from people in spiritual formation. For example, health care professionals may speak about the formation of our selfhood as the product of our environment, and the religious professional may add that religious education and a religious community increase the positive quality of our spirituality. The developing person may be said to have less preoccupation with selfish concerns, an increased awareness of being connected with the rest of humanity, and being committed to a compassionate way of life. These descriptions from both the side of human development and from spiritual formation increasingly tend to sound alike.

Is being emotionally healthy much like being spiritually mature?

---

28. See, for example, Hanson's book, *Buddha's Brain: The Practical Neuroscience of Happiness, Love, & Wisdom.*

Day 119

Beloved, let us love one another, because love is from God; everyone who loves is born of God and knows God. Whoever does not love does not know God, for God is love. (1 John 4:7–8)

Not all religious education and efforts to encourage spiritual formation are healthy and life-giving. In fact, there are studies and many books that speak of the dangers and damage of religion, and a case can easily be made for harm done in the name of religion. Although not always as visible, the same case might be made for those who have sought healing from health professionals. When I have conversations on this topic, I listen carefully and learn, and I am inclined to look at the positive side. Often, the conversation turns to the nature of the community in which one is helped or harmed.[29] It may be a family, a school, a church, a synagogue, or a temple.

But where true love is present, whether in a religious context or a secular school, there is movement toward the healthy life. As a way of assessing healthy and unhealthy environments, we might review the decades-old conversation about the difference between religion and spirituality. There is an element of truth in the way these two entities differ, although the description of religion is occasionally caricatured. I would like us to think together about some of the ways these two human experiences and settings differ, and how each might contribute to our upward reach for union with God and be integral to our destination. I have drawn from several lists, and thank the many people who have written them.

Generally, religion is a term used to describe an organization that guides people and gives them structure and continuity. Spirituality is often thought of as more informal, and not necessarily needing an organization with a formal structure. It is maintained that spirituality can be expressed in a religious structure, and often is, but it might also be expressed privately. [30]

How do you distinguish between religion and spirituality?

---

29. See, for example, Hitchens' book, *God is Not Great*.

30. My friend Bill Peterson sends out a daily message of support and encouragement, and his list that I have in front of me was taken from the one prepared by the South Points Association for Exploring Religion (SPAFER) on 4/20/2012.

Day 120

My secret is quite simple. I pray and through my prayer I become one in love with Christ, and see that praying to him is to love him, and that means to fulfill his words.[31]

1. Mother Teresa reminds us of the truth, that spirituality can be expressed in the slums of Calcutta, but may also be connected with the structures of the religion, in her case, the Roman Catholic Church. It also points us to our second distinction—that religion often has a hierarchy of power and decision-making that provides the leadership and guidance for religious activity. Spirituality, on the other hand, is more frequently based on a direct relationship with the divine, or God, as was the case in Mother Teresa's prayer.

2. Religion generally utilizes history and traditions, referring to ancient texts and narratives (e.g., the Bible, the Quran). These accounts of how a people worshipped and followed God use myth and metaphor to describe the experience of a people. These patterns become the norms for beliefs and practices in the present. Spirituality may reference these holy books and other resources, but is more in the present moment, and is open to new insights that shape our consciousness, as is taught in mindful meditation.

3. Religion is connected with locations and buildings, has budgets and staff, and makes plans for an orderly week filled with community involvement. It is rooted in an organized community that may be international in character. Spirituality may be practiced anywhere, and focuses on the unseen reality that is knowable in the experience of our evolving consciousness. It tends to be more individually oriented rather than community oriented.

4. Religion is grounded in doctrine and belief systems that shape the life of the community. For many, these beliefs and practices provide security and guidance, but occasionally can be confining and controlling. Spirituality tends to be more universal in spirit, often tied to nature and nature's rhythms and beauty. The life-changing insights are more individual than corporate in character, although both religion and spirituality speak about ethics and service, with a religion generally able to exercise more influence.

---

31. Mother Teresa, *Life in the Spirit*, 1.

5. Religion can be more exclusive, in that certain beliefs and practices are expected within the religious community. Religion often gives one an identity. Spirituality can be more inclusive and open to people of all faiths, or people of no faith. All people may seek a deeper understanding of reality.

6. In religion, God (or transcendence) is clearly defined and named, whereas in spirituality it is not as well-defined and tangible. The universal transcendence is experienced deep within, and one may feel both liberated *and* grounded.

Perhaps you would like to add to this list or nuance it differently.

Study Guide for the April Readings

Questions for Contemplation and Discussion

1. Is one of your goals in life to live in union with God? Or in harmony with transcendence? What does it mean to be in union with God? What metaphors and analogies might you use to *define* union with God?

2. If you believe that you are living in union with God, how do you cultivate and sustain this union? What are the *dimensions* of being in union with God?

3. How does your understanding of God shape your union with God? The Bible speaks about God in many ways, often using metaphors to describe God. One, for example, is King, and another is Father. Both may sound a bit dated or gender-slanted. Are they still acceptable? God is also called Love and Light.

4. What metaphors for God are used by other religions? How might an indigenous wisdom religion, such as Native American, describe God? What names are used for ultimate reality by the Asian religions? Hinduism? Buddhism? Taoism?

5. How does our union with God *develop* over the years of faithful practice? How does it change? How would you describe a mature union with God, one free from the views of childhood and one without the exclusive views of a tribal orientation? Is there one that enables you to flourish as a person?

6. One's union with God carries with it strong expectations about the way life should be lived. What are the *demands* built into your union with God and the way you live out this union over the years of your spiritual journey? How does your religious affiliation frame the expectations?

7. What are the words you use to describe these demands? Among the following terms, which ones are the most attractive to you? Love? Compassion? Faithful? Obedient? Socially responsible? Others?

8. As we live in union with God across the years of our lives, we often wonder where it will lead. What is the *destination* of our lifelong union with God?

9. Do you, for example, believe in eternal life? Do you think you will go to heaven when you die? What will heaven be like? Or will I just return to dust and ashes? Do you think there is some form of reincarnation?

10. Is it possible to think of our eternal destination in ways that go beyond the categories of space and time, such as eternal presence in eternal love?

Study Guide

Section One: Reaching Upward

Questions to Ponder and Discuss:

1. What is the most satisfying way for you to speak about God, or ultimate reality? Is the term "God" the best for you, or do you prefer terms such as transcendence, ground of being, or the divine? What difference does it make?

2. Is it easy for you to be mindful and centered, or does your mind easily drift away to daily responsibilities, troubles from the past, or anxiety about the future? What are the best ways to be more focused in the present?

3. How important do you think it is to be a truly spiritual person? What are the characteristics of a deeply spiritual person, and how does one cultivate a more profound and sustaining spiritual center?

4. Is it possible to learn about mindfulness and spirituality from religious traditions other than your own? Or from secular sources? Are people from different religions able to truly encounter God, understand transcendence, and be harmony with the divine?

5. Do you think that God (or transcendence) speaks different languages and communicates with those whose religion is different from yours? How do you discern what is true and false, and what is healthy and unhealthy?

Key Terms and Concepts

1. Spirit: The term often refers to one's inner life, but also refers to the power and presence of God, and points to the omnipresence of the divine. The Hebrew term for spirit is *ruach*, and the Greek term for spirit is *pneuma*.

2. *Shema*: This is the Hebrew term that refers to the strong affirmation and belief in one God, and that God should be loved with one's whole being. Deuteronomy 6:4 is generally called the *shema*.

3. Mindfulness: This term, central to the teaching of Buddhism, refers to the practice of living in the present; being intentional about not getting distracted; and, through meditation, a way to overcome excessive anxiety and depression.

4. Spirituality: This term, using the understanding of Spirit in the definition above, describes what it is that one seeks, to find inner harmony and union with God, or Transcendence. It is a way of living an ethical and responsible life that empowers you to flourish.

5. God: This is the most common term used for describing ultimate reality or the ground of being, that which is transcendent and infinite.

Study Resources: Please consult the footnotes and the bibliography for more titles:

1. Dalai Lama. *The Compassionate Life*. Boston: Wisdom, 2003.

2. Ferguson, Duncan S. *Exploring the Spirituality of the World Religions*. New York: Continuum, 2010.

3. Eliade, Mircea. *The Quest: History and Meaning in Religion*. Chicago: University of Chicago Press, 1969.

4. Newell, John Phillip. *The Rebirthing of God: Christianity's Struggle for New Beginnings*. Woodstock, VT: Skylight Paths, 2015.

5. Walsh, Roger. *Essential Spirituality*. New York: John Wiley & Sons, 1999.

SECTION TWO

OPENING INWARD

In Section One, our theme was "Reaching Upward," an attempt to understand God, or transcendence. We then turned to the biblical injunction to love God with our whole being, and explored how we link with the divine through faith. Our goal was to achieve a union with God, and live in harmony with ultimate reality. As we reached upward, we were very aware that it required an understanding of what was happening to us in the process. Who are we as we reach upward, what motivates us as we reach upward, and how are we impacted or transformed by the reach upward? In short, we began to realize that it required us to open inward. A certain measure of self-understanding was necessary, and we realized that transformation is tied to new insights about ourselves. We began to ask, how might we express our love for God and our faith in God? In what ways do we seek to achieve and sustain our union with God, or Transcendence? What is necessary for us to rest in God's love?

We now begin to reflect on how we open ourselves to the divine or transcendence. In these next four months, we will focus our attention on four dimensions of our opening inward:

1. We want to open ourselves to *healing*, knowing that our lives can easily be filled with fear, insecurity, anxiety, defensiveness and anger, and a range of emotions that are almost impossible to access and understand. We will explore how opening inward to the presence of God or to the nature of reality can be a healing experience.

2. We want to turn this effort of opening inward to the positive goal of *achieving emotional health and wholeness*, finding the pathway to growth, and beginning to experience happiness, love, and wisdom.

3. As we seek these goals, we do need *guidance and support*, and we will explore together resources and practices that will help us to heal and mature.

4. Our additional goal in this four-month set of readings, prayer, and contemplation will be to achieve an *inner harmony* that brings a peaceful life, and in that process, discern our *purpose in life*, why we are here, and what it is that we should do with our lives.

THEME FOR MAY

OPENING INWARD FOR HEALING

Day 121

> *But the truth is that we can never avoid uncertainty. This not-knowing is part of the adventure. It's also what makes us afraid.*[1]

As we turn inward, we begin to reflect on that which causes us discomfort. There are many causes, and anxiety is one that is especially troublesome. Anxiety prompts us to worry about the future, especially if we face it alone. The hard questions about what might happen remain with us throughout life. We do find some answers that help, but there are still areas of uncertainty. We suggested that the use of maps or the right approaches could be helpful in order to find direction. Yet, we still walk with Abraham, "going without knowing," and as he and Sarah did, we go in faith. To have faith is part of our healing, and our faith takes many forms, as we cultivate our spirituality. For example, it may be *apophatic* (without words), because we judge that the appropriate attitude is humility before the Divine Mystery. At times, our walk of faith may be more *cataphatic*, and we use our minds, our imagination, our language, and our symbols to pattern our faith. There are times when we are *anchoritic* (solitary) in our walk, and at other times we are *cenobitic* (communal) as we gain wisdom and strength from others. Across the centuries, those who have gone before us have left wonderful traditions and strategies for faith development, and we are wise to read about them and to participate in current expressions of them. I find myself nurtured by many of them, and at certain times in my life, when I feel alone, lost, and afraid, they put me back on the path of healing. I sit quietly at home and pray, or I reach out to a friend who listens carefully and wisely. I might turn to my reading, which is a comfort and a guide. I go to a worship service and I am reintroduced to my faith, hear how it might apply to my struggle, and have a sense of belonging to a beloved community. I do not always drive doubt and uncertainty away, but I get a different attitude about it and a different perspective on it. I sense that God, to be God, will remain beyond my full comprehension, and I begin to enjoy the adventure of discovery.

How do you deal with anxiety and uncertainty?

---

1. Chödrön, *Comfortable with Uncertainty*, 5.

Day 122

> *In all of these we find the same principle; the principle of a free spontaneous and creative life as the essence of Reality. Not law but aliveness, incalculable and indomitable, is their subject matter: not human logic, but actual living experience is their criterion of truth.*[2]

We are beginning to explore together by our common reading and our rumination on the ways we seek and find union with God some ways that we overcome those dimensions of life that hurt, harm, and haunt us. We are using the spatial metaphor of "Opening Inward," and in this opening we seek to find ways to accept the healing presence of God. My inadvertent tendency, as I try to be open, is to go first to my mind and try to understand. I sense that, if I can reason it all out and get some clarity, I will be able to relax and have a sense of tranquility. Cognitive therapy works. But always going the route of reason has not always eased my discomfort, although it does help some. What I have learned across the years is that my relationship with God, or my connection with transcendence, has a very personal dimension. In my Christian faith (and many other traditions as well), the linkage is a relationship, and I place my faith in a personal God who *loves* me, not just enables me to think correctly and gather good information. I do not simply believe in and affirm a set of logical propositions that, if correctly listed, incline me to believe in the existence of God, although it helps to have a wisely constructed "*theologie totale*."[3] I return again and again to the Hebrew *shema*, quoted by Jesus, that we are "to love God with all of our heart, all of our soul, all of our mind, and all of our strength." No part of ourselves is left out as we open inwardly in search of healing. Our relationship with the divine is a loving relationship, one that is a whole-person response of faith, and one that opens the heart and mind to the unlimited love of God. It is an embrace.

Are you inclined to feel or to think your way beyond doubt and uncertainty?

---

2. Underhill, *Mysticism*, 27.

3. I have been helped recently in my theological understanding by Sarah Coakley's *God, Sexuality, and the Self*; Katherine Sonderegger's *Systematic Theology*, Vol. 1, *The Doctrine of God*; and Douglas F. Ottati's *Theology for Liberal Protestants: God the Creator*; all efforts of creating a *theologie totale*. Others could be mentioned.

Day 123

While they were talking and discussing, Jesus himself came near and went with them, but their eyes were kept from recognizing him. And he said to them, "What are you discussing with each other while you walk along?" They stood still, looking sad. Then one of them, whose name was Cleopas, answered him, "Are you the only stranger in Jerusalem who does not know the things that have taken place there in these days?" . . When he was at the table with them, he took bread and broke it, and gave it to them. Then their eyes were opened, and they recognized him; and he vanished from their sight. (Luke 24:15–18, 30–31)

At the end of the life of Jesus, his disciples were quite confused and discouraged. Some had hoped that Jesus would be more of a political messiah, overthrow the alien Roman government, and establish a new kingdom, not unlike the one that David had established centuries before. But instead, he was crucified, and the disciples had drifted away in several directions. In this account in Luke's Gospel, two of them had gone a few miles toward their home in the village of Emmaus. The account of Jesus meeting them may be an expanded story, although the fact that it gave them some reassurance, however it occurred, has the ring of truth. There are other stories of his disciples feeling reassured, as well; there was a keen sense that Jesus had left them knowing that God was with them and that they had a mission. I have been with these two people in spirit, discouraged and confused, and doubting the good news about what Jesus did and the empowering presence of God's Spirit. When I reminded myself of the themes of this story, my eyes were opened.

1. The first theme is that Jesus has gone before me and faced down the deepest threats to my well-being and death itself. With courage and love, he gave us the model for dealing with anxiety, doubt, confusion, discouragement, and danger.

2. He demonstrated that God is with us in the most challenging times of life; as he says on the cross at the point of death, "Father, into your hands I commend my spirit." He knew God was with him.

3. All during his ministry, and again at the end of his life, he hands the mission on to us. We are to be people of courage and conviction, and we are to love those who are lost and alone.

Have you been on the road to Emmaus? How did you get to your true home?

Day 124

> *Come to me, all you that are weary and are carrying heavy burdens, and I will give you rest. Take my yoke upon you, and learn from me; for I am gentle and humble in heart, and you will find rest for your souls. For my yoke is easy, and my burden is light.* (Matt 11:28–30)

The world in which Jesus lived was pre-modern, both in terms of the way its affairs were managed and the way in which people made sense of the world. The government was complex with three different levels: the Roman, the Herodian, and the Jewish (Sanhedrin), each with different areas of authority, and all with little concern for the struggles of common people. The ministry of Jesus touched nearly everyone, but was focused on the burdens of common people, whose yoke was heavy.[4] Jesus himself was not from the upper or ruling class, but from the peasant class that had to carry heavy burdens.[5] As they lived and worked with this yoke around their necks, they were not assured about how they would feed their children and deal with disease and injury. Jesus lived in solidarity with these people, and he lets them know that he understands their heavy yoke and burdens. They flocked to him, especially in the early months of his ministry in the Galilee. He helps them with their fears, worries, discouragement, and need for wisdom and guidance. He healed their bodies and their souls, and taught a way of life that was filled with the power and presence of God. His message was direct, never discounting what they were experiencing and with the credibility of being one of them. He says to them that those who are poor in spirit, those who mourn the losses of their loved ones, those who are humble and meek, and even those who are persecuted will inherit the earth, find mercy, and will have their eyes open and see God. They will be called the children of God. He cares about their burdens, addresses them, and invites them to receive the power and presence of God into their lives. He lifts their burden.

In what ways does Jesus give us the capacity to cope and hope?

---

4. Yokes were put on the necks of animals so that they could pull a plow or wagon. A yoke was a symbol of obedience and hard work.

5. See the work of Crossan, *The Historical Jesus*.

Day 125

So now the question is, what is dukkha? What is suffering? Buddhism describes three types of suffering. The first is called the "suffering of suffering," the second is called the "suffering of change," and third is "suffering of conditioning."[6]

Many religions have in their belief system a way of describing the needs and challenges of human beings. The Abrahamic religions, Judaism, Christianity, and Islam, speak about the human tendency to drift away from the will of God and fall into harmful and self-destructive patterns. They then address this drift with a call back to God, and teach how this is done through their beliefs and practices. Buddhism, in its many forms and different branches, speaks less about sin and more about suffering, and how it can be relieved. In whatever way it is described, there is a consensus that we struggle and suffer, and need healing. The Dalai Lama, in his small book on the Four Noble Truths, says that our suffering has three origins or sources. One is the pattern of karma-samsara, in which we feel caught. In essence, we reap what we have sown. In addition, our suffering is tied to the craving we feel for pleasure and possessions, and how we meet this craving. We discover that possessions do not satisfy, even though we think they will bring us pleasure. We often buy the lie. And third, Buddhism says that we suffer from ignorance and that we need enlightenment. These causes for suffering need careful expansion, and their full explanation is beyond the scope of our readings, yet we can look to them as giving us some guidance on why we suffer and need healing. The first cause of our suffering, in Buddhist thought, is that it is built into our very existence. To some extent, we are products of our past, and the past is further back than just the span of our lives. This is a very profound insight, and whether we buy into the reincarnation foundation of Buddhist belief, or whether we just understand it from a more human developmental frame of reference, the universal truth remains—we suffer from what is in our past and we need healing from it. No one escapes it. We need to open inward and be mindful in our spiritual quest in order to find healing.

How do you go about finding healing and reducing your suffering?

---

6. Dalai Lama, *The Four Noble Truths*, 50.

Day 126

When children develop secure attachments to parents, those allow them to go out into the world to explore and develop relationships with others.[7]

Whether one accepts the ontology of Buddhism regarding karma, endorses the notion of original sin, or turns to contemporary scholarship about human development, it seems there is a desire to know why it is that we suffer and engage in harmful behavior that causes suffering. I have found myself drawn less to the notions of karma and reincarnation, or the need to atone for sins, and drawn more to understanding myself in the categories of behavioral science. It is not that I ignore the wisdom of the ages in the great religious teachings; it does, however, describe what I experience, although the way it roots that experience in a distant past is less persuasive. Current brain research and the behavioral sciences give me a better understanding of my struggle. I am less inclined to say that my occasional shyness and tendency to make mistakes are part of my fallen state or the product of a previous life, but more the product of my early years of attachment. I was not exceptionally close to my parents, and am the product of an alcoholic family. I am especially grateful to have discovered that there are resources in my Christian faith and in the healing insights of other religions. When I turn inward and face directly the guilt and loneliness I occasionally feel, I am comforted by the assurance of forgiveness, the love of God, and the wide range of insights from my education and experience. I do find healing in both the beliefs and practices of my faith and my education. This process has the structure of past, present, and future. In my past, there were circumstances that didn't meet all my developmental needs. In the present, I experience a measure of alienation, and want affirmation in order to offset the harm of not having the love I needed. I have been working across the years for a better future, hoping to find patterns of healing and to become healthier. I am grateful that I am finding good ways to achieve wholeness. My mindful spirituality has been a marvelous resource.

Does your approach to healing seem healthy, or just an escape from reality?

---

7. Siegel, *The Developing Mind*, 71.

Day 127

Only when I realize my limitations can I hope to rise above them and glimpse my endless possibilities.[8]

It has not always been easy to realize my limitations, to fully understand my behavior, and accept that there was a better way to live. However, over time I learned why I felt discomfort and had feelings of being unacceptable and unlovable inside of me. I discovered why I engaged in a limited amount of behavior that was partially self-destructive and perhaps hurtful to others. I realized that I wanted to hide it from others in order to be accepted, popular, and loved. I did partially live with two identities: one that was as an achieving, popular leader, and one that was private, afraid, and at times even deceptive. It wasn't a serious situation by any means. I was a fairly normal teenager, and I am grateful that I found ways to understand why I had these two identities and to learn how to become a more integrated person. There was increasing acceptance by others, and I became a trusted friend with many people because of my integrity. It was emancipating, and increased my joy in living.

As I probed the causes of the unhealthy behavior, I discovered that it was rooted in a bundle of related feelings. In its simplest form, it might be called insecurity. I wasn't sure I had an inner place to call home, one in which I felt competent, could manage well, and where I was free from the judgment of others. I suspect it had to do with my father's expectations and behavior. Perhaps it was related to my older brother's achievements. It may have been caused by the way the family moved around; I attended at least six different elementary schools. I did not have a base. Fortunately, I was able to manage, although never free from the fear of not being safe and accepted. Having some academic and athletic ability helped, and I did have good friends. Yet, I lived with the feeling that I was not attractive and was not smart enough to achieve levels of excellence. I was relatively popular, although I had another hidden identity: one that was occasionally afraid and needed the healing power of love.

Have you had times when you felt insecure? How did you deal with it?

---

8. Mafi, *Rumi Day by Day*, 184.

Day 128

> *So do not do not be anxious about tomorrow, for tomorrow will bring worries of its own. Today's trouble is enough for today.* (Matt 6:34)

Regardless of our overarching understanding of reality, we are still inclined to experience a measure of suffering. Understanding doesn't clear it all away. I have bunched my supply of troubles into three categories, in large part because it is a way to talk about them with some clarity. Many of the great religious traditions address human suffering, point to the past as the cause, and underline that it is part of being human. One bunch I noted in the previous reading was insecurity, and I mentioned briefly why this category works for me as an explanation. A second grouping might fit under the category of anxiety and worry. Worry is generally used to describe a specific problem, while anxiety suggests the condition of feeling unsure about the future. The great teachers of human wisdom and insight for healing have pointed to these conditions of worry and anxiety, and suggested some ways of dealing with them that are part of what we are calling mindful spirituality. For example, Jesus met many people in his walking ministry who worried and felt anxious. There were those who were ill and believed that they could not look forward to a good future. Some had relatives that were on the brink of death and asked Jesus to help. Others could not easily manage their day-to-day responsibilities; there wasn't enough money, the social structures of society were stacked against them, and they were unsure about how to cope as they faced severe challenges. Jesus walked and talked with these people and gave them practical solutions and the attitude of hopefulness. For example, in one incident, a leader of the synagogue came to Jesus with the deep worry that his daughter was about to die. Jesus calmly heard his anxious cry and said, "Let's go see." On the way he took time to heal a woman who had a serious hemorrhage, and then continued on with the desperate father. With poise and assurance in the presence of anxious people and with relaxed compassion, he healed the girl. Jesus, wearing a reassuring smile, said, "Give her something to eat" (Luke 5:21–43). This family had less worry and anxiety, and became hopeful.

What do you think gave Jesus a sense of calm and confidence?

Day 129

Therefore I tell you, do not worry about your life, what you will eat or what you will drink, or about your body, what you will wear. Is not life more than food, and the body more than clothing? . . . Your heavenly Father knows that you need these things. But strive first for the kingdom of God and his righteousness, and all these things will be given to you as well. (Matt 6:25, 32b–33)

I find comfort in the words and spirit of Jesus, although I do not find it easy to fully internalize his wisdom. I carry some worry about my immediate circumstances and some anxiety about the life I lead. I trace some of this concern back to my alcoholic father, who made the family's circumstances unpredictable. Maybe he will show up for dinner or maybe he won't. The family spoke openly about the struggle to make ends meet, and so as a child I never knew whether we had enough money for food and shelter. Thankfully, we did, but the anxiety was very real and it has carried over into my adult life. Our current circumstances are quite stable, although I still have some anxiety about the future, especially as I face the realities of mortality. I do try to seek first the power and presence of God; yet I sometimes wonder if this is not a pious platitude. I don't think that Jesus thought it was, and that is why he is better known than I am. His example does live inside of me in quite powerful ways, as does the wisdom teaching of many of the other great teachers of the human family, such as Buddha, or contemporaries such as Pope Francis. I am finding more of my faith orientation taking shape inside of me, relaxing me, and helping me cope and hope. As I reach the fourth quarter of my life (or as my friends say, "You are in overtime"), I am living as much in the past as the present and the future. I am grateful for the good life I have had, my family and friends, my life work, and good health. Thankfulness has been a wonderful companion, as has my education, love of books, and my very modest writing; I do feel fulfilled. I have only a few worries about my immediate future—such as my health, as I age—yet I am not preoccupied with this worry or the health of my family. And while I wonder about the next few years and how they will play out, it is not a burdensome anxiety. In fact, I am experiencing a good measure of fulfillment and inner peace.

How do you deal with the issues of mortality? Are you afraid of death?

Day 130

Do not worry about anything, but in everything by prayer and supplication with thanksgiving let your requests be made known to God. And the peace of God, which surpasses all understanding, will guard your minds in Christ Jesus. (Phil 4:6–7)

My categories of the areas in which I suffer and need healing are not comprehensive, just suggestive. There has been some insecurity, and a measure of worry and anxiety. I have also had some loneliness, and it too has roots in my early life. I had to find some means of coping with a somewhat-dysfunctional family. I do not look back in anger and with blame, but with sadness and empathy for my parents, who struggled and had to navigate their own journey. It did mean that I had to learn how to navigate, as well, and my choice was to go inside, rather than go toe-to-toe with external circumstances and people. My two brothers, older and younger, took the outside strategy and fought back, although they both suffered because of it. My escape was my introversion and the release, even joy, that I felt in being by myself, reading, and keeping my struggles undercover. What I have learned across the decades, of course, is that much of what I kept inside never did get out, except in clumsy ways, and I have lived a fairly lonesome life, partially covered with a friendly smile. Fortunately, I did experience some genuine love, and I found in my religious life (mindful spirituality) some of the healing grace that it promised. For a time, I tried to ignore that I was over on the introversion side of the spectrum. Yet in time, I began to learn how to love myself, even though I often felt unlovable and unacceptable. I did want to be a leader, and had some gifts that nudged me in that direction; as time went along, I realized that it was all right to be who I was. Yes, I could give some leadership, but I didn't need to be a college president, and that a faculty role of teaching and scholarship was more in keeping with my identity. I could be a quite good Secretary of the Board because I thought and wrote clearly, and made sense out of meetings that often went in a thousand directions. I did enjoy leadership, as well, and found quiet strength an asset. I found my way, yet remain a bit lonely, even with a wonderful extrovert for a wife.

Are you comfortable with your identity, or do you wish you were different?

Day 131

Then the devil led him up and showed him in an instant all the kingdoms of the world. And the devil said to him, "To you I will give their glory and all this authority." . . Jesus answered him, "It is written, 'Worship the Lord your God, and serve him only.'" (Luke 4:4–8)

The Dalai Lama and his insightful Buddhist tradition teach that suffering is built into our human existence because of karma. Buddhism also teaches that suffering is caused by our craving. It may be that we crave physical pleasures, possessions, glory and prestige, or power. As we accumulate these, we soon discover that they have limited value, and do not ultimately satisfy us. The story in the Gospels about the temptations of Jesus has a comparable message. The story is told that at the beginning of Jesus' public ministry, the devil dangles all of these possessions in front of him as a means of derailing him from his calling. Jesus has an appropriate answer for each temptation. This story, even if we have a bit of trouble speaking about a personal devil, as I do, nevertheless gets at a fundamental truth: the good life does not consist in the abundance of things possessed. Our culture tends to teach us the opposite. For example, we live in a very materialistic culture, and with the onslaught of advertising—whether it is on television, our cell phones and computers, or in our newspapers—we are told that our lives will be better, perhaps happier and more fulfilling, if we accumulate possessions. The new car or new house will make the difference. It doesn't stop with the accumulation of expensive toys, but goes on to say that other immaterial possessions, such as a beautiful sex partner, or trip to Bali, or power at the office, or prestige and accolades, will give you a life of meaning and bliss. It is not that some of these possessions are not welcome and make life better, but they do not ultimately satisfy us and give us deep contentment. I know that the array of tempting possessions in our culture does paint an attractive picture, and it is hard not to say that my happiness does depend on the abundance of things possessed. The real trick is being able to realize that these possessions may improve our lives, but they do not bring us deep meaning and fulfillment.

Do you think craving as our ultimate motivation in life will cause us suffering?

Day 132

When the young man heard this word, he went away grieving, for he had great possessions. (Matt 19:22)

When Jesus had finished his ministry in the region of Galilee, he traveled to Judea beyond the Jordan River, and continued his ministry of teaching and healing. There were some Pharisees who questioned and tested him, and there were also many sincere seekers who needed guidance, insight, and healing. A young man with wealth came to him and asked what one must do to inherit eternal life. Jesus took the question seriously, and said that one must follow the great commandments of God. The young man replied that he had been devout and faithful, yet Jesus sensed that he was not fully committed to the will and way of God. Jesus then tells him that he must give away his wealth and share it with the poor, and in this way he will have the treasure of heaven. The young man went away grieving, because he had great wealth. In this case, one can almost see Jesus in a board room of a major company underlining the issue of priorities. He was trying to teach the young man that wealth may be a means to an end, but not an end in itself.

The more one has, the more one wants, and it can take over one's life. It is not that having some comfort in life is wrong, or that having a nice home and adequate financial resources to manage life are a violation of God's will and way. It is rather that they enable, even empower us to undertake our vocation in life. I always wanted more education, a better library, and perhaps even a scenic view with which to enjoy the treasures of nature. As these gifts have come my way, they have not taken me from my calling. I have used them in my vocation to follow Jesus and be a teacher, hoping to improve the life of my students. Nor is it the case that all people must become a teacher or a healing prophet, like Jesus or Buddha. The world needs to change, and if it is to change for the better, it needs the skill and energy of people whose work is diverse. It is more about how we do our work and how we use the financial gains from our work than it is what we accumulate. It is how we are grounded.

What are the priorities and values that guide and motivate you?

Day 133

Then Jesus told his disciples, "If any want to become my followers, let them deny themselves and take up their cross and follow me. For those who want to save their life will lose it, and those who lose their life for my sake will find it." (Matt 16:24–25)

Jesus and many of the great religious leaders of the ages have been pretty clear about priorities and values. Buddha taught that those who crave possessions, power, and prestige will miss the mark and suffer. In his early life, Siddhartha, who became the Buddha, did have all the possessions, pleasure, and wealth that were possible in his time. But as he discovered disease, aging, and death, he decided to try another way; first, the way of extreme asceticism, and later, a middle way between craving wealth and the extreme life of denying oneself any comforts. Both Buddha and Jesus sought the middle way, neither the extremes of self-denial or the quest for wealth and possessions. The author of Matthew's Gospel quotes an insightful statement from Jesus that underlines this point: those who try to "save their life" by craving wealth and power, or any possession, will lose focus, meaning, and deep gratification (blessedness). But those that follow the way of Jesus, the way of endorsing the power and presence of God in their life and making love the heart of life, will "find it." Whether one is a Muslim, a Hindu, a Taoist, or one deeply rooted in the indigenous wisdom traditions, the good life is possible by aligning it with ultimate reality and living by the golden rule. We know it is not all that easy to trust the promise that another way will be better, nor it is possible to always feel at home with fundamental change in one's values and patterns of living. At times, one might not even feel the need for a change, and I meet these people quite often. However, there may come a time in your life when you honestly face questions: What is the meaning of my life? Is there a better way that will bring deeper joy and a focused sense of responsibility? Is there a God, or a pattern of ultimate reality or the ground of being with which I can connect and truly find myself? Can I be healed from my suffering? Jesus and Buddha would say yes.

How do we "lose our life" in order "to find it?"

Day 134

Finally, we come to the third type of suffering, the suffering of conditioning. This addresses the main question: why is this the nature of things? The answer is because everything that in samsara is due to ignorance. Under the influence and control of ignorance, there is no possibility of a permanent state of happiness.[9]

We turn now in our contemplation to the way that the Dalai Lama describes another reason for our suffering. We might say that, in the tradition of the Abrahamic monotheistic religions, sinfulness is the reason for our inclination to not follow the will and way of God. Buddhism says that we do not understand that the cycle of death, rebirth, and ignorance keeps us from true happiness, even as the Christian faith teaches that sinfulness (missing the mark of God's expectations) keeps us from knowing true blessedness. The pattern of ignorance, misplaced priorities, and self-destructive and harmful behavior prevents us from living a life filled with meaning, love, and joy. We are not fulfilled, and need enlightenment and transformation.

Other great religious and philosophical teachings describe a similar pattern. They teach that it is so easy for us to get caught up in a way of life that leads to unhappiness and suffering. And the longer we stay with these patterns of life, the more difficult it is to change them. There is some irony in this tendency, in that, in our state of ignorance, we think that a way of life chasing pleasure, possessions, power, and prestige will bring us happiness. But the more this chase takes over our lives, the less likely we are to be happy and fulfilled. It is not that what we pursue has no value; it is rather that what we seek is more of a means than an end. Some pleasure is joyful, some possessions make life better, some power enables us to achieve our goals, and some praise for our life work is gratifying. These are causes for gratitude, not our sole ambition. We pursue a much deeper purpose, living a loving and devoted life with God or in harmony with ultimate reality. In this life of mindful spirituality, we flourish, find joy in our life work, and find peace with a life of integrity and compassion.

How do you balance the values of our culture with the deeper values of faith?

9. Dalai Lama, *The Four Noble Truths*, 53.

Day 135

The urge to do wrong is like fire, its beautiful color pleasing to the eye; yet hidden inside there's a darkness that only becomes apparent once the flames are out.[10]

It was Saint Augustine who observed that the reason we have made a god out of some object in the created world is because the God of all beauty has made the creation beautiful and attractive. He also cautioned us to remember that we should not place our faith in what is in the created world, but in the God of goodness, truth, and beauty. He called this tendency misplaced faith, and observed that it is so easy to misplace our faith, as he illustrated from his own life. Let's reflect for moment on why it is so easy to misplace our faith, as Saint Augustine maintains.

1. The created world, as Saint Augustine observed, is filled with goodness, truth and beauty, created as it is by the God of goodness, truth, and beauty. I do love the beauties of nature and find peace in its presence. It is what I love.

2. The created world is immediately present, and the attractions of pleasure, possessions, power, and prestige are right in front of me. At various times in my life, each of these parts of the created world has had its attractions. The culture in which I live says that I should pursue them in order to be happy. I have sometimes believed my culture and doubted the more abstract promise of true fulfillment in the life of following God's will and way.

3. At times I have been more comfortable in the immediate gratification that may come from giving my body and soul to what is in this world, rather that what made this world. Troubled at times with moderate depression, I have thought that what was immediately available to me was better than the vague promise of full joy in God's presence

4. I do have an investment, in years, of loving the created world, and I do not want to give up this investment. I now know that I do not have to give it up. Rather, I must keep it all in perspective and have clear priorities.

Are you persuaded by Augustine's argument?

---

10. Mafi, *Rumi Day by Day*, 49.

Day 136

The first practice of the Noble Eightfold Path is Right View. Right View is first of all a deep understanding of the Four Noble Truths—our suffering, the making of our suffering, the fact that our suffering can be transformed, and the path of transformation.[11]

In the next few readings, we will continue our theme of exploring how we might find healing with our practices of mindful spirituality. We will devote a good deal of time in our readings to other subjects, as we move through this section on "Opening Inward," but just a bit more time on healing may be wise. We will then turn to positive growth and development and point toward the ethical, responsible, and meaningful life.

First, let's look at basic Buddhist thought about healing, and then we will look at healing in other religious traditions. I am drawn to the Buddhist view, in part because it is so logical and practical. The way out of our suffering is to follow the Noble Eightfold Path that leads away from our ignorance and to enlightenment. Accompanying these eight directions are a wide range of practices that are centered in the life of meditation. The first path toward overcoming suffering and moving toward enlightenment is to understand the process. It is fundamentally to grasp, not just in our minds but also in our emotions, the reality of suffering and its causes. The starting point is the pattern of karma-samsara, that we are products of our past and still in the pattern of death and rebirth. In each of us, there are different seeds or causes of suffering, with each seed or root being either wholesome or unwholesome, and it is, of course, important to cultivate the wholesome seed. The process of healing involves understanding the healthy potential that is inside of us, and begin patterning our life toward the values of integrity and compassion. It is in mindful meditation that we are able to discern what is the right way to live. It is a complex process, and it can be easy to miss our goal, be taken over by wrong views, and dwell in our craving and sorrow. The practice of mindful meditation can give us tools to lead us forward.[12]

Again there may be wisdom in defining mindful. What is your definition?

---

11. Thich, *The Heart of the Buddha's Teaching*, 51.
12. See the book by Bartley, *Mindfulness*.

Day 137

Thinking is the speech of our minds. Right Thinking makes our speech clear and beneficial. Because thinking often leads to action, Right Thinking is needed to take us down the path of Right Action.[13]

We are exploring the ways that Buddhism teaches us about how to overcome our suffering and find healing. As we will learn over these next few days in our readings together, the larger strategy is to follow the Noble Eightfold Path. The first step in the pathway is to have the Right View, to understand the larger process in which we find ourselves. It is by having a clear understanding of what we face that gives us the wisdom about how to proceed. We need to understand our situation as humans, and then think clearly about it and face it directly. Right Thinking follows logically from having the Right View. I was on a call one morning with the Executive Director of a mission agency that is dedicated to seeking a just peace in Israel and Palestine. I serve as President of the Board, and we were discussing the ways that we needed to plan for our work. We spoke about both the immediate situation and, of course, the long-range strategic planning that we had to do in order to propose a course of action in a very complex environment. In this environment, any small mistake can have unfortunate consequences. Different views are thoughtfully and strongly held, and the feelings about these views and the circumstances in the setting are very intense. It would be easy for us to make a hasty decision and to act on a small incident that doesn't represent the larger situation. If we don't have the right view about what is going on, and employ wise and careful thinking about how to proceed, we could easily damage our work and limit our future possibilities to help our effort to find a just peace for the citizens of the region. It is not that our effort is likely going to make a fundamental difference by itself, but with a range of partners we may be able to limit the conflict and help those on different sides to understand each other and find a consensus that will lead to the common good. Right View, Right Thinking!

Can you think of a situation in which right thinking made a huge difference?

---

13. Thich, *The Heart of the Buddha's Teaching*, 59.

Day 138

Mindfulness, the third quality of the mind the Buddha refers to, is the translation of the Pali word, sati, and it holds a central place in every Buddhist tradition. It is what makes any spiritual path possible. Mindfulness has several meanings and functions, all of which are key to the growth of wisdom. Understanding the richness of meaning opens up new potential for its power to transform our lives.[14]

The order is from the right view to right thinking, and then comes the third step in the Noble Eightfold Path, Right Mindfulness. In many ways, right mindfulness undergirds all of the qualities of the Eightfold Path, and it is often thought of as being at the heart of Buddha's teaching. For example, it is a posture and a norm that makes possible right speech and right action. If we have right mindfulness, then right speech and right action will follow. One interpreter of right mindfulness, Jon Kabat-Zinn, offers two short definitions of mindfulness.[15] The first is, "Mindfulness is knowing what you are doing while you are doing it." And the second is like it: "Mindfulness is paying attention on purpose, in the present moment, non-judgmentally." He then offers four dimensions of mindfulness:

1. Mindfulness encompasses both internal processes and external circumstances.
2. Mindfulness is being aware of what is present in you mentally, physically, and emotionally in each moment.
3. With practice, mindfulness cultivates the possibility of freeing yourself of reactive, habitual patterns of thinking, feeling, and acting.
4. Mindfulness promotes balance, choice, wisdom, and acceptance of what is.

Right Mindfulness is the motivation and energy that gives us focus and concentration and brings us back to the immediate present with intentionality and concentration. Thich Nhat Hanh even speaks of it as "the way we cultivate the Buddha within, the Holy Spirit."[16]

Does Right Mindfulness lead us on to Right Speech? How?

---

14. Goldstein, *Mindfulness*, 13.

15. Provided in the syllabus for the course offered by the Cascadia Mindfulness Institute entitled "Mindfulness-Based Stress Reduction" (MBSR).

16. Thich, *The Heart of the Buddha's Teaching*, 64.

Day 139

Speech is such a powerful influence in our lives because we speak a lot. Speech conditions our relationships, conditions our minds and hearts, and conditions karmic consequences for the future.[17]

I have often reflected on the aphorism of my youth, offered by my parents and grandparents as a way of coping when I got my feelings hurt when someone spoke an unkind word to me: "Sticks and stones can break my bones, but words will never hurt me." I look back on this attempt to comfort me as a good effort, although not always persuasive. It has often been the insensitive word that has hurt me the most and stayed with me for the longer time. Occasionally, I am reminded of words from my parents or those close to me that often branded me as incapable or not smart enough to understand or to get it done. Also damaging were words about my appearance, and I worried that I was not attractive. Yet, there were many positive words as well, some that did wonders for my self-image and confidence, and gave me the courage to take on difficult tasks, read complex books, and feel comfortable with others whose acceptance was important to me. In Buddhist teaching, the following descriptions define Right Speech, our fourth step in the Eightfold Path:

1. The first and most obvious quality of the right speech is truthfulness. It is to refrain from saying that which is untrue, but equally important, it is to say that which is credible and has integrity.

2. Right speech also avoids any slander or gossip. It does not demean or use disrespectful language about another. And again, there is the positive side. It gives credit where credit is due and often honors another with kind and descriptive comments.

3. The third dimension of right speech has to do with the emotional tone of what we say. It avoids harsh, angry, and abusive speech and uses kind, courteous, affirming, and soothing tones. It listens well and avoids frivolous talk. It is a helpful contribution for all those who are present.

Do you find it difficult to always be ready for "right speech?"

---

17. Goldstein, *Mindfulness*, 372. Goldstein has guided what I have written.

Day 140

> *Right Action* (samyak karmanta) *means Right Actions of the body. It is the practice of touching love and preventing harm, the practice of nonviolence toward ourselves and others. The basis of Right Action is to do everything in mindfulness.*[18]

Thich Nhat Hanh, a wonderful teacher whose books I have enjoyed reading, maintains that Right Action is intimately linked to Right View, Right Thinking, Right Mindfulness, and Right Diligence. In fact, all eight are interwoven, with a few having a closer link and occasionally bunched around a coordinating theme. In this reading, we are giving attention to Right Action. The emphasis in this category is on both personal ethics and being empowered by awakening or full awareness. Both are essential to live the ethical life. Buddha is quoted as saying, in reference to the ethical life, "Avoid what is unskillful, do what is good, purify the mind."[19] Right Action points to behavior in the following areas:

1. Abstaining from physical harm. It is to practice nonviolence, loving kindness, and learning ways to work for the well-being of all people and indeed for all of creation. It means to give oneself to reducing suffering in all its forms.

2. It is also a commitment to abstain from taking what is not given to us. Right Action means not stealing, acting generously, and encouraging sharing with those in need.

3. As one might expect, it also teaches abstinence from sexual misconduct and abusive behavior. It would be hard to overstate the damage done to people in this domain, and the need for preparing oneself to pay attention to the energy in sexual desire and its link to intimacy needs that go beyond the physical.

4. Right action also includes the emphasis on false speaking, which we are to avoid. This means that we never speak in untruthful ways and that we are always honest. We do not engage in slander or gossip.

5. Also included is the prohibition of the use of toxins. We stay sober and alert.

What would you add to this list of right actions?

---

18. Thich, *The Heart of the Buddha's Teaching*, 94.
19. Quote in Goldstein, *Mindfulness*, 379.

Day 141

> *Right Diligence* (samyak pradhana), *or Right Effort, is the kind of energy that helps us realize the Noble Eightfold Path.*[20]

Not every teacher of the Buddhist way bunches or lists the steps in the Noble Eightfold Path in precisely the same way. This may contain the fundamental truth that all eight are intimately connected. It is obvious that diligence and effort are necessary if one is to follow the Buddhist teaching. These qualities are essential for following not only the other steps in the eightfold way, but for the many other teachings of Buddhism as well. In fact diligence and effort are fundamental values in nearly all religious traditions. I know that this is the case, as I try to follow the teachings of my Christian faith. Within the Buddhist tradition, four practices are generally listed as necessary to be faithful to the call to diligence:

1. The first practice generally listed is the need to prevent "unwholesome seeds" that are present in our consciousness from rising to the surface and shaping our behavior. This is a Buddhist way of saying that there hidden needs and buried impulses that can easily surface, and that we need to be conscious of them and keep them under control.

2. The next practice is to pay attention to the "unwholesome seeds" that have already surfaced and control them so that they don't find expression in harmful and self-destructive behavior. For example, it is to learn how to respond with wisdom and compassion, rather than to react with impulsive anger.

3. Still another practice of diligence and effort is to carefully "water the wholesome seeds" that are in our consciousness, and find ways to let them bloom into the beautiful flowers of love and compassion.

4. Finally, Buddhist teaching urges the careful cultivation of those "wholesome seeds" that are already blooming in our behavior, and finding ways to refine and express them. Let compassion bloom!

Do you find it difficult to always be diligent in speech and behavior?

---

20. Thich, *The Heart of the Buddha's Teaching*, 99–100.

Day 142

> *The characteristic of concentration in both these ways of practice is undistractedness, and it is this steadiness of mind that makes it possible for wisdom to arise.*[21]

Again and again, as one studies the many teachings of Buddhism and its focus on mindfulness, there is an emphasis on concentration. At the heart of our effort to cultivate mindful spirituality would be an emphasis on being aware of what surrounds us and is inside of us. It is to focus on the immediate present and to give attention to the task in front of us. It is an effort to tame our darting mind and unruly emotions, and corral them. It is to gain balance, not to be too excited or too dull, but to have a good and true mind to bring to the present. Right concentration of this kind stabilizes our attention on the single task or context in front of us, and to do so with deepening states of calm and tranquility. Not infrequently Buddhist teachers make a distinction between active and selective concentration, with active concentration centered on what is happening in the present moment, even as it changes. As the poet says,

> The wind whistles in the bamboo
> and the bamboo dances.
> When the wind stops,
> The bamboo grows still.[22]

In selective concentration, we choose one object and hold on to it, such as a painting or a sunset. All around are people, noises, and other distractions, and we need to find ways to block out the distractions and allow ourselves to be deeply present. With this sort of concentration, we can learn, appreciate, and live each moment with wisdom, insight, and happiness. Within the teaching of this step is the guidance of nine levels of meditative concentration. There is much for us to learn.

What ways have you found to concentrate and be attentive in the present?

---

21. Goldstein, *Mindfulness*, 398.
22. Thich Nhat Hanh quotes the Vietnamese poet Huong Hai in *The Heart of the Buddhist Teaching,* 105.

Day 143

So often we separate our work from our spiritual practice, yet the Buddha puts this part of our lives in a central place in our journey of awakening.[23]

The final step in our exploration of the Noble Eightfold Path is Right Livelihood. As we spend so much time daily and in the span of our lives with our work, it is wise to use it as the concluding step in our study of the Eightfold Path. It is not uncommon in our culture to place our work in one category, and our spiritual growth and development in another category. Occasionally, our lives get bifurcated, and we live a compartmentalized life. It is true that, in a given day or week, we do change contexts; we live at home with our family, we work with colleagues in our profession, and we try to attend church or join with our religious community on the weekend. The Buddhist way of life maintains that we need to integrate these domains; if not in terms of actual time spent at a given place, then in terms of our inner life and external responsibilities. It is much easier to do the integration of our lives if our work does not go against the values of our spiritual journey. This bifurcation does happen on occasion. We struggle, for example, with the conflict of values, those of love and nurturing at home and in our fellowship, and those of intense competition in the marketplace and the temptation to cut corners in order to be successful. We are both wise and blessed if our profession and the other parts of our lives are not in conflict in terms of values. Our goals should be to use our livelihood to make our family secure and comfortable, and to use it for the service of others. It is possible to cultivate the attitude of service in nearly any profession, as we think about ways to make a good society and what our role in that mix might be. I am grateful that this has not been difficult in my roles as both an educator and as a minister. But I know that it is been harder for others, and on occasion I have had to choose between values and job expectations. Being mindful regarding these challenges is the framework that will see us through.

Have you had conflicts between your values and your professional life?

---

23. Goldstein, *Mindfulness*, 386.

Day 144

Just then there was in their synagogue a man with an unclean spirit, and he cried out, "what have you to do with us, Jesus of Nazareth?" . . But Jesus rebuked him, saying, "Be silent and come out of him!" And the unclean spirit, convulsing him and crying out with a loud voice, came out of him. (Mark 1:23–26)

The Buddhist way teaches its followers how to be healed from suffering, and to follow a wise and ethical life. This central feature of Buddhism has similarities with the emphasis on healing in the Christian faith. Occasionally, different words and emphases are present, such as the biblical notion of sin causing guilt and distress, whereas the Buddhist religion teaches ignorance and points the way to enlightenment. As one studies the life and teachings of Jesus, it is obvious that healing and reducing suffering were central to his ministry.[24] Jesus was a compassionate healer. An integral part of his mission in life was to restore the health of the people whom he encountered with a range of ailments. Many were brought to him, and others came directly to him without the aid of others. He responded to all with compassion and a healing touch. Questions arise as we read these stories about his capacity to heal, concerning whether there was a miraculous dimension to his healing. Time does not permit a full development of an answer to this question, but a few observations might be helpful. The first is that the stories of healing come to us in three categories: (1) an extraordinary event that is easily understood by a fair-minded observer; (2) an event that offers no reasonable explanation in terms of the way forces operate in our world of time and space; and (3) an event that invites the explanation of a special act of God, doing what no human power can do. Many of the healings of Jesus fit in category one, although others fit better in categories two and three. For example, the healing of the man with the unclean spirit might be placed in category one, if we assume that there may be explanations for these events that make more sense to the modern mind. We will explore this thesis and others in the next few readings.

Do you think Jesus demonstrated miraculous powers in his healing?

---

24. See my book, *The Radical Teaching of Jesus*, 143–47.

Day 145

A leper came to him begging him, and kneeling he said to him, "If you choose, you can make me clean." Moved with pity, Jesus stretched out his hand and touched him, and he said to him, "I do choose. Be made clean!" Immediately the leprosy left him and he was made clean. (Mark 1:40–43)

The passages from the New Testament quoted yesterday and today give us examples of the kinds of healing in which Jesus was engaged. The healing of the person with the unclean spirit might be thought of as therapeutic healing. In the categories of the time of Jesus, it was the norm to define psychic healing as relieving a person possessed by an alien force or unclean spirit. Today, we might use different language, and call it the healing of a person with a mental illness. The healing in the biblical passage for today concerns a person who had a skin disease (often translated as leprosy, but it could have been any skin disease thought to be contagious). Therefore, the person would be isolated from normal life. In this account, the outcast violated protocol and boldly approached Jesus, and Jesus, moved with pity, healed the person. While we do not know the precise nature of his disease, we observe a person who fits our category two, a healing that has no natural explanation. This is a story in which the phrase, often used by Jesus, could be used: "*Your faith has made you well.*" Such a description is recorded in other healings for which Jesus is responsible. A third kind of healing, and the most common one, was for persons whose illness or condition impacted their capacity to function like an able-bodied person. These people have a deformity from birth, or are paralyzed or crippled from a disease or an accident. In one incident, for example, we have a person brought to Jesus who is a paralytic (Mark 2:1–12). This story occurs in Capernaum, Jesus' hometown. Because there are so many attempting to approach Jesus for healing and help, friends of the paralyzed person decide to let him down through the roof, getting direct access. Jesus senses the desperation of this effort and heals the paralytic. Again Jesus demonstrates his commitment to compassionate healing. He restores the person to a normal life. Healing is central to his ministry.

Do you think that this same kind of healing power is available in our time?

Day 146

Jesus stood still and said, "Call him here." And they called the blind man, saying to him, "Take heart; get up, he is calling you." So throwing off his cloak, he sprang up and came to Jesus. Then Jesus said to him, "What do you want me to do for you?" The blind man said to him, "My teacher, let me see again." Jesus said to him, "Go; your faith has made you well." Immediately he regained his sight and followed him on the way. (Mark 10:49-52)

Again, we were not present, nor are the records of these events always complete. There are the inevitable questions. Yet, the story of the healing of blind Bartimaeus does have some credibility, although we still wonder how the healing happened. Perhaps the following observations will be helpful:[25]

1. The healing miracles are in the context of a relationship of faith and love, not a magic show in which the hand moves faster than the eye. In the time of Jesus, there were magicians that claimed healing power. Jesus was not a magician, but a compassionate healer, like our trusted doctors in medical practice today.

2. The person whom Jesus heals has a genuine need or illness, and has no ulterior motive apart from the need for healing. There is not an exchange of money, for example, or an effort to attract attention; the motive for healing was pure.

3. There is, in nearly all cases, openness to healing and the faith that it can happen. The people are eager and ready. This faith and openness in many cases are seen as essential to the healing process. Jesus implies that one must be open to the grace of God. There is an opening inward for healing.

4. With few exceptions, Jesus calls on the power of God and attributes the healing to the grace of God. Jesus does not assume he can claim God's power, but understands the action as the will and action of God.

5. Jesus does not hurt or punish anyone in the healings, and always puts the emphasis on the well-being of the patient.

What is your current view regarding the healing ministry of Jesus?

---

25. Ferguson, *The Radical Teaching of Jesus*, 144.

Day 147

Zacchaeus stood there and said to the Lord, "Look, half of my possessions, Lord, I will give to the poor, and if I have defrauded anyone of anything, I will pay back four times as much." Then Jesus said to him, "Today salvation has come to this house." (Luke 19:8–9)

Jesus was a compassionate healer who healed the physical diseases of many who came to him. He was also concerned about their emotional, moral, and spiritual well-being. He was in the business of making people whole. He was dedicated to relieving suffering in all of its forms, and empowering people to move toward a mature and responsible life. Luke records the story of Jesus meeting with Zacchaeus in Jericho. He was traveling from Galilee down to Judah, and ready to enter into his last days in Jerusalem. The people in Jericho have heard about the ministry of Jesus, about his healings, his profound teaching, and his bold prophetic stances on a range of issues. They want to see and hear him as he comes through Jericho. Zacchaeus, a Jew who had been persuaded to become a tax collector for the Romans, wanted to see Jesus as well. As a short man, he climbed a tree in order to see Jesus pass through the town. To his surprise, Jesus saw him, and asked if he might spend some time with him. They may have had some lunch at Zacchaeus' home and engaged in a heart-to-heart conversation. The outcome was quite dramatic; by the end of the day, Zacchaeus was a different person, transformed from a life of dishonesty and greed. Previously, he had been seen by his kinsmen as a traitor to his people by joining forces with the Romans. We are not sure of all that was said, although it is likely that Jesus, in the spirit of compassion for Zacchaeus and a prophetic concern for justice, must have laid it on the line. Zacchaeus emerged from the conversation with a willingness to totally change his way of life. He not only quit collecting taxes, but was willing to give back four times as much as what he had stolen to the people whom he had defrauded. Here we see from Jesus a different kind of healing, and Zacchaeus genuinely and sincerely opened inward for healing. He recovered his faith in God, was reconciled to those whom he had robbed, and became committed to restoring what he had stolen.

How would you describe the conversation between Jesus and Zacchaeus?

Day 148

People were bringing little children to him in order that he might touch them; and the disciples spoke sternly to them. But when Jesus saw this, he was indignant and said to them, "Let the little children come to me; do not stop them; for it is to such as these that the kingdom of God belongs. Truly I tell you, whoever does not receive the kingdom of God as a little child will never enter it." And he took them up in his arms, laid hands on them, and blessed them. (Mark 10:13–16)

As we learn to open inwardly for healing, we need to be mindful. Jesus is mindful in this tender story about the children; he is fully present and senses what is going on with the children. They are open to his love and he gives it to them. The practice of mindfulness by Jesus and his centered prayer had prepared him to be wise and aware. He can joyfully experience the loving encounter. His disciples, however, are not living in the present, but are worried about the future, schedules, and reacting to the past, remembering that Jesus was sought by crowds of people and often became fatigued. My uptight self would have sided with the disciples. I may have said, "Send the children away; we need to deal with all these adults who have come for guidance and healing." But Jesus gives attention to the children, offers them unconditional love, and even holds them in his strong arms and touches them with affection. Jesus also uses this encounter as a teaching moment. He is aware that the crowds have come for help in dealing with their suffering and discouragement. In this case, he does not chase the children away and begin teaching the adults about how to follow the Torah. Instead he points to the mindfulness of the children, who are fully in the present and enjoying the moment. Jesus says to his disciples, and to the adults who have come to hear him, "Receive the gracious loving presence and power of God into your lives, even as these children have received my love for them." To experience the loving and transforming power of God is to open inwardly to God's love and healing. As we open, we experience the bliss of God's love, forgiveness, and guidance. Jesus urges them to open their hearts, even as these little children have opened their hearts to me. He says, "See in my love for them God's love for you."

Had you been there, with which group would you have sided?

Day 149

For we walk by faith, not by sight. (2 Cor 5:7)

I encounter a lot of people who are doing reasonably well in life. They have fulfilling jobs, good families, and a comfortable home. Yet, they are not altogether free from the need for renewal. They have some worries and anxieties. I also encounter a number of people whose resources do not adequately provide for their needs. They may be unemployed or under-employed, have broken and divided families, and not have sufficient income for the basic needs of food and shelter. Their needs are more pronounced than those that appear to be managing. In conversations with both groups, those who are able to cope with their situation in life and those who are unable to cope and feel desperate, I sense that there is inner longing for a more contented and fulfilled life. There is another dimension of life for all of us that is more than just having our basic needs met. We long for life-giving relationships, a deeper meaning in life, and a more peaceful and tranquil life. The great religions speak to these needs, as well as to having the basic needs of food and shelter met. Christianity, in its variety of ways, invites all who will listen to cultivate a life of faith. This faith commitment gives the assurance of things hoped for and the conviction that what we did not see now will come if we are faithful in our spiritual walk.

Faith might be understood as a way of being mindful. The guiding holy books of the Abrahamic religions (Judaism with the Hebrew Bible, Christians with both the Old and New Testaments, and Muslims with the Quran) are unified in saying that faith in God is the way to overcome suffering and to resist the tendency to engage in harmful and self-destructive behavior. Faith enables us to experience God's forgiveness and unconditional love; it is yielding to love. It leads us to a life of serenity and responsibility. Each of these religions has its own distinctive story, but they agree that faith in God will bring forgiveness, heal wounds, and provide a hopeful future. Faith in God's love is the way to open inward for healing.

How do you access that deeper level of life that gives you meaning and hope?

Day 150

For in hope we were saved. Now hope that is seen is not hope. For who hopes for what is seen? But if we hope for what we do not see, we wait for it with patience.
(Rom 8:24–25)

Christians have taught across the centuries that there are three cardinal virtues that sustain and provide a foundation for the good life: faith, hope, and love. We read yesterday in our daily reading about faith and how it puts us in touch with God, who loves and heals us. Today, we look at the way that hope can renew and heal us in other ways. It is so easy for us to lose hope, as adverse experiences in life drive us into despair. It may be the loss of one's health, the loss of a sustaining relationship, the threat of poverty and lack of suitable and sustaining work, or the approach of death. The Christian faith teaches its followers to have hope, even in the midst of these circumstances. In fact, Christians usually speak about hope and internalize it in the face of severe challenges. On what do Christians base their hope? Let me suggest three foundations for hope:

1. Christians and their cousins, Jews and Muslims, base their hope on the *faithfulness of God in the past*. In the Hebrew Bible, one reads again and again about how God faithfully led the Hebrew people out of slavery in Egypt. Christians base their hope on the past as well, and point to Jesus and his teaching about God's eternal love as the basis of hope. Muslims believe that God has acted in the past in the great prophet Muhammad, who gave them guidance.

2. Christians also live in hope because of the presence of the Holy Spirit, God's power and presence *in their present lives*. Jews and Muslims have similar grounds of hope. The Holy Spirit guides, teaches, encourages, and renews. We hope as we sense the presence of God in our lives.

3. Christians are also given hope, as are Jews and Muslims, in the belief in a good future. *God will help us with our future* here on earth by guiding us, empowering us, and sustaining us. And we can face the end of life with the hope that we will cross over into the loving presence of God.

What gives you hope in difficult and challenging circumstances?

Day 151

No, in all these things, we are more than conquerors through him who loved us. For I am convinced that neither death, nor life, nor angels, nor rulers, nor things present, nor things to come, nor powers, nor height, nor depth, nor anything else in all creation, will be able to separate us from the love of God in Christ Jesus our Lord. (Rom 8:37–39)

Today, we finish our readings on the subtheme of "Opening Inward for Healing." We will continue to address this topic in future readings, but change the emphasis just slightly as we turn to three other subthemes under the larger subject of "Opening Inward." We will not ignore the reality that our need for healing is ever with us, but will shift to the theme of "Opening Inward for Emotional Health and Wholeness." Our transition to this shift is to call attention to the third cardinal virtue, in many ways the foundational one: *agape* love. The Apostle Paul reassures the Roman Christians that nothing can separate us from God's love, and he underlines to the Corinthian Christians that faith, hope, and love abide, but that the greatest of these virtues is love. Jesus, drawing upon his understanding of Torah, says that to love God with our whole being and to love our neighbor as we love ourselves is the heart of mindful spirituality. Because the word "love" has so many meanings in English, we might just remind ourselves again of what Paul and Jesus are saying. Both would honor the meaning of one of the Greek words for love, *eros*, and say that love of all that is good, true, and beautiful is wise and appropriate. They would say, as well, that another word for love in Greek (*philia*, or the love between friends) is important. But what is most important is the kind of love God has for human beings, *agape*, a love that is limitless and unconditional. The Apostle Paul says that he is convinced that nothing can separate us from God's love. Jesus, as well, teaches about this kind of love. It forgives and transforms us, and sets us on the path of following God's will and way. *Agape* love becomes the hallmark of those who have endorsed and received the reign of God into their lives. It is the defining quality of the citizen of the kingdom of God, and it invites us to open inward for health and wholeness.

How does unconditional love contribute to our health and well-being?

Study Guide for the May Readings

Questions for Contemplation and Discussion

1. Few of us are free from some form of pain and suffering. How do you describe your pain and suffering, even if it is mild? Has it ever become severe?

2. What are the causes of your pain and suffering? Is it related to your childhood? Or is it most connected with your current situation?

3. How much are you personally responsible for your pain and suffering, and how much of it is caused by your environment and the conditions in which you live and work?

4. Are there ways that your faith orientation and your union with God help you to cope with your pain and suffering?

5. Some of our pain and suffering is the result of injuries and illness; it is bodily pain. Another part of our pain and suffering is more deeply rooted in our emotional life. Our readings mention insecurity, anxiety, and loneliness. Are these feelings part of your experience? What else would you add?

6. During his temptations and in his teaching, Jesus faced the challenge of priorities. He experienced and taught about the risk of being tempted to place possessions, pleasure, prestige, and power as the highest values in life. What did he say were higher priorities?

7. Buddha also spoke about priorities and values. He said that craving causes our suffering. It is interesting that the very things which Jesus taught were the wrong priorities are what we crave. Is Buddha correct in his assessment?

8. Buddha taught that it was possible to overcome one's suffering and ignorance and be enlightened. It is possible to have a happy and fulfilled life? What were the eight pathways he taught to overcome suffering?

9. Jesus also taught that one could overcome suffering by changing the direction of and receiving the kingdom of God into one's life. What does he mean when he invites us to endorse the kingdom of God?

10. What do Buddha and Jesus teach about priorities and values that should guide our lives? Are there some similarities? How do their priorities help to heal us and make us whole?

THEME FOR JUNE

OPENING INWARD FOR EMOTIONAL HEALTH AND WHOLENESS

Day 152

Abide in me as I abide in you. Just as the branch cannot bear fruit by itself unless it abides in the vine, neither can you unless you abide in me. I am the vine, you are the branches. Those who abide in me and I in them bear much fruit, because apart from me you can do nothing. (John 15:4–5)

During the May readings, we explored together the ways that a mindful spirituality contributes to our healing. We noted that no one of us is free from the wear and tear of life. It comes in many forms. Perhaps it is fear or worry, as one looks forward to the future. Or perhaps it is stress and anxiety, as one anticipates and lives through the day. Or maybe it runs deeper and takes the form of depression and alienation, often the product of negative experiences of the past. It could be physical illness, or a disability. Our reflection was not pessimistic, but realistic in the sense that all of us, while often grateful for good health, do face health challenges. A deep and abiding spirituality can contribute to our healing and give us hope. We shift to this focus as we move into the readings for May and invite a reflection on how our opening inward will keep us moving toward spiritual and emotional health.[1] The practice of mindful spirituality will contribute to our quest to become a healthy person.

As a way of guiding our prayer and reflections this month, we will use a simple outline. We will begin with a modest list of goals for our health and well-being. For example, we will work together to eliminate, at least partially, some of our negative feelings, such as fear, anxiety, and loneliness, and replace them with a sense of being together and content. Second, we will spend some time on the means of achieving these goals. We will explore the values of prayer and meditation and suggest some practices that will cultivate a more hopeful outlook. We will look at mindfulness-based practices in particular, and explore how they will reduce stress and lead to a healthier life style. We will conclude with a modest list of desired outcomes, such as wisdom and serenity.

What does the metaphor of the vine and the branches in John's Gospel mean?

---

1. And our physical health as well.

Day 153

In the Name of God, Boundlessly Compassionate and Infinitely Merciful[2]

—Quranic Invocation

Most of the great world religions teach that unity with God or Infinite Reality is life giving for the pilgrim seeker. The metaphor in the Gospel of John says that our connection with the divine or the vine will produce good fruit. We receive the nutrients of healthy growth by sustaining our relationship with God. In Islam, there is the wonderful invocation, often used in the sacred writing and orally in the teaching, which speaks of Allah as boundlessly compassionate and infinitely merciful. The daily practice of *Salat*, praying daily five times, keeps one connected with the Compassionate and Merciful One. This connection, as the fruit from the vine in the metaphor of Jesus, gives one the family resemblance. The mindful spirituality of daily prayer internalizes the qualities of compassion and mercy. For the faithful Muslim, to share or be infused in the godly virtues of compassion and mercy is to be truly spiritual.

A fundamental and first goal of opening inward for health and wholeness is to become a more spiritual person. There are long lists in many books about what it means to be spiritual, and at the risk of repetition, let me suggest another list as we focus on the goals of becoming a more healthy and happy person. We noted earlier that to be spiritual is to be open to the power and presence of God, or to say in another way, the Spirit of God. As we are open to God's Spirit, we are transformed. The Apostle Paul speaks of the fruit of the Spirit as love, joy, peace, patience, generosity, faithfulness, gentleness, and self-control (Gal 5:22–23). It is a wonderful list of those qualities that describe what it means to be a spiritual person. So our initial goal in our quest to become emotionally healthy and whole is to become a truly spiritual person. Other traditions would use different concepts and language to speak about what it means to be spiritual, and we will explore some of those as well.

What words would be on your list of terms that describe a spiritual person?

---

2. See Rahman, *The Spiritual Gems of Islam*, 51.

Day 154

Love of God and surrender to God are ultimately the same, and constitute the first and primary commandment from God to the human soul. ("If you love me, you will keep my commandments.")[3]

The Apostle Paul names love as the first gift of the Spirit of God, recognizing that the one who has embraced the reign of God will reflect the character of the loving God. The second goal of opening inward for emotional health and wholeness is to become a more loving and compassionate person. The manifestation of true spirituality is to become loving. It is important to keep in mind as we reflect on how to reach this goal is that it is both a gift and a commandment. The gift or the fruit of God's presence is that we now have the capacity to be more loving. As we cultivate a relationship with the God of love and yield to the presence of God in our lives, we are able to express *agape* love to those who fill our lives. It is clear that we need to yield as well as decide. There are many gifts and abilities within, and we must decide to express them and use them for the common good.

In addition, love and compassion are learned qualities. The ways of loving and showing compassion can and need to be learned by practice. For example, we can learn from our parents how to respect the needs of others, as they met our needs when we were children. We can learn from those whose lives have been trained in medicine about how to care for those who are ill. We can learn from those who have empathy how to become a better listener and identify with the suffering of another who needs care. We can learn how to use language, knowing that language that is not harsh and judgmental, but kind, gentle, and accepting of the other, is the true expression of love. We can learn how to live in solidarity with those who are victims of injustice and violence, and work for a just peace. As we learn in these ways, we find that what we have learned is internalized, and we more easily practice what we have learned. We are gifted with love, and we gradually learn how to love and then act in loving ways.

How might we better learn how to be loving and compassionate?

---

3. Keepin, *Belonging to God*, 201.

Day 155

And the ransomed of the Lord shall return, and come to Zion with singing; everlasting joy shall be upon their heads; they shall obtain joy and gladness, and sorrow and sighing shall flee away. (Isa 35:10)

We have spoken briefly about opening inward to reach the goals of being spiritual and becoming a loving and compassionate person. Another goal of our inward growth is to become people of joy and peace. The list of the gifts of the Spirit, given by Paul in his letter to the Galatian Christians, moves from love, to joy and peace. These two attributes could be listed separately, although I have found that they tend to flow together. In my experience, when I am joyful, I am also at peace, and when I am at peace, I tend to be joyful. One reads in the great prophets, reflecting the Jewish captivity in Babylon, that as they were allowed to return to their homeland, the Hebrew people had joy in their hearts because there was the hope for peace and the good life. Not unlike the Exodus leading the people out of slavery, the Babylonian captivity became one of those prototypical experiences that would live in the memory of the Jewish people. As they left their captivity, they felt great joy and gladness.

They also felt a deep peace in their hearts, and they hoped for a more peaceful way of life, one in which they would be free from enslavement and abuse. Peace (*shalom*) is a word that can refer to internal peace of mind, as well as peace between peoples and nations. As they returned home from their captivity, they felt great joy and a sense of inner serenity about their new life. Because of their joy and peace, they could begin a new way of life, one free of threat and conflict.

The lesson I learn from this interesting history is that part of my joy and peace comes from external circumstances, and part of it comes from opening inward to the sense of the presence of God and to appreciate what God is doing in my life. I begin to sense an inner contentedness, one side of which is the joy I feel about the goodness of life, filled with endless blessings. In addition, there is the inner peace I feel about the meaning of my life and my place in the world. I am joyful and at peace about who and where I am.

What brings you joy and inner peace? What prevents joy and peace?

Day 156

Planetary Mind understands that which can be said and knows what cannot be said. Planetary Mind knows in an intuitive sense and understands in a logical sense. Planetary Mind understands and knows humanity's connection with and place within the Infinite, recognizing the Mysteries of the Infinite cannot always be explained, nor must they always be—that there are truths that lie beyond the literal and logical.[4]

We often give labels to the changing patterns of the ways we think, understand, and make sense of our world.[5] For example, there are times, in my writing and speaking, when I speak about the pre-modern, modern, and postmodern ways of life and thought. Over the last several decades, the pace of change has been so rapid that even generations get a special name, because each makes sense of life in a different way. Often, these changes in the way we think are spoken of as a consciousness, underlining that we are living in a time when new patterns of thinking about reality are emerging. We may, for example, be living with new global awareness and the need to think in an ecological way about earth care, cultivating a planetary mind or consciousness. It is therefore important that we add the goal of wisdom as our fourth goal, as we open inward in our quest for health and wholeness. Wisdom will help us understand our consciousness and how we make sense of the world around us. Wisdom is essentially the understanding of what is true, how to move forward with the truth, and how to make good decisions based on truth. Our world is so complex, our challenges so great, and our conflicts so severe, we need to ask for wisdom. We need wisdom for our personal lives, for our region, for our nation, and for our world. We are learning as we watch our national news that the differences in our country are so pronounced that reaching a consensus about a plan that will lead to the common good is nearly impossible to achieve. Some differences are inevitable, but the level of the differences in outlook is so extreme that we are threatened, and we long for leaders who are wise. As we open inward, we must pray for wisdom and cultivate it in every possible way.

What is the nature of wisdom, and how might we become wiser?

---

4. Christopher, *The Holy Universe*, 135.
5. See, for example, the many works of Wilber, such as *Integral Spirituality*.

Day 157

If any of you is lacking in wisdom, ask God, who gives to all generously and ungrudgingly, and it will be given to you. But ask in faith. (Jas 1:5)

We reflected together yesterday about the times in which we live. We noted how complex our situation in the world is, and how difficult it is to reach a consensus about solving our problems and planning for a more stable future. Not only are the world's problems incredibly difficult, but so too is our way of communicating with each other. Too often it is deceptive and cantankerous. We lack civility as we reach across international borders and within our own system of government. There are times when this lack of civility reaches down to our local level and enters into family life. I want to go back and review those gifts of the spirit about which Paul spoke in his letter to the Galatians. Each item on the list has its own meaning, but I would like to bunch a group of them into the category of respectful and civil relationships and communication, and think of these virtues as our fifth goal. They are as follows:

1. Patience: Our relationships and the ways we communicate with each other require that we have patience and understanding of the other. Without it, we will be reactive rather than responsive, and unable to make loving contact.

2. Kindness: Simple kindness means that we listen well, care, and in even the small ways do for the other what we would want the other to do for us.

3. Generosity: Our relationships with others will be open, honest, and respectful as we are generous, not just with financial resources, but with our love and understanding. A generous spirit is a great gift to those whom we meet.

4. Faithfulness: This virtue speaks to the way we build trust with others and open the channels of communication. Faithfulness implies integrity, that we are what we say and that we say what we are. We can be counted on!

5. Gentleness: To be gentle is to be sensitive to the feelings and needs of others, and treat others as those having worth and value.

6. Self-control: We are careful in our communication with others and resist impulsive feelings. We find the right time and place for the right words.

Are there virtues that you would like to add to this list?

Day 158

> *As the Father has loved me, so I have loved you; abide in my love. If you keep my commandments, you will abide in my love, just as I have kept my Father's commandments and abide in his love. I have said these things to you so that my joy may be in you, and that your joy may be full.* (John 15:9–11)

I have one final word as we speak about our goals in our quest for health and wholeness; "responsibility." To be responsible is to understand what is being felt, what people are saying, what is the actual situation, what is needed, and to act in a way that works toward the common good. It is a word we do not generally associate with the words and actions of Jesus; other words such as love are more commonly used. The word love, as it is used in English, may be a bit fluffy and sentimental if it is all we say about the behavior of Jesus. To strengthen the word, I find myself adding other words. One that I occasionally use is responsible. Jesus epitomized the finest expression of responsibility as one who acted wisely and courageously in the most difficult circumstances. He did use the word "love" with slightly different meanings in Aramaic and Greek. He was careful to say that wise and appropriate actions, not just sentimental feelings, are integral to the commandment to love. It is to live by the wisdom of the golden rule.

There is a bit of a risk in understanding our passage for the day as saying that God (and Jesus) will only love you "if you do what I say or command." This is a misreading of the passage. It is rather to say that, because you have been loved unconditionally, and because you return love with your whole heart and soul, you act in a way that is motivated by unlimited love. You are transformed by love and then act out of love. These ways of responding are responsible because they are carefully planned and finely tuned by love; your response is on target and selflessly motivated. As Jesus anticipates the completion of his vocation, he likely did have conversations with his disciples, perhaps not in the literal sense of John 14–17, but in the same spirit. He tells them to keep God's commandments, and that both his joy and their joy will be full. This is the pathway of mindful spirituality.

What are the various motivations that shape your activity?

Day 159

But it was only when I was introduced to certain findings of depth psychology that I began to make the fullest use of their methods for my own religious development and to help others who came to me.[6]

We began this small group of readings by exploring the goals we have for health and wholeness. We carefully read the list of the gifts of the Spirit in Paul's letter to the Galatian Christians and used it as our guide. We then suggested a partial list of qualities that included the following: the cultivation of a deeper spirituality; learning the best ways to practice love and compassion; developing wisdom in order to navigate our complex environment; learning how to practice the ways of respect and civility in communication; and nurturing a keen sense of responsibility for a needy world. These were some of our goals, admittedly drawn partially from my own experience. We could have named many other goals, yet these seemed important to me in this moment, our time and place in our history.

My worry is that these goals may seem lofty and nearly unattainable. I long for them daily, and recently have been stepping up my learning in order to make them a more integral part of my daily life. One of the ways I have tried to actualize these goals was through a class in mindful-based stress reduction. The class was centered on the practices of mindful meditation with direct application to our daily lives. The class was not religiously oriented, although I have integrated the learning in the class with my devotional practices of prayer and contemplation. I worked with two assumptions in the class and in my other efforts to continue the quest for health and wholeness. The first one is that I hoped to have more peace and satisfaction in my life as I grew and developed. The second was equally, if not more, important; it was that I hoped I would be a better person for others as I become more mature. Daily I learn that I can be a more loving and compassionate person when I am freed from my own inner struggles and turmoil. When I am troubled my agenda often gets inserted as I connect with others. I am often less a person for others because I am self-centered.

How much does your personal agenda get inserted into your relationships

---

6. Kelsey, *The Other Side of Silence*, 7.

Day 160

In this list of mind states, the Buddha emphasizes knowing the presence or absence of the three unwholesome roots of mind and how they color or condition our minds. These three roots are greed or lust; hatred, which includes ill will and anger; and delusion or ignorance, which encompasses bewilderment and confusion.[7]

Depth psychology and neuroscience have taught us a great deal about our psychic limitations and healing in these past several decades. The language of these disciplines speaks to me in quite profound ways, and so too does religious language that usually has a moral edge, such as the passage above. Taken together, these outlooks suggest ways and practices that lead to health and wholeness. I want to reference a document that shows two columns of the ways we cope with change and stress, one column representing *reaction* to our discomfort and the other representing a *mindful response* to our stress.[8] In one column, there is a pattern of automatic reaction that is the result of excess stress and how our body reacts and sends us signals. We may become physically ill and experience anxiety and depression. We react with denial, overeating, overworking, hyperactivity, and isolation. We abuse substances such as alcohol, tobacco, and caffeine. It leads to a breakdown with physical illness, exhaustion, and burnout.

In the other column, we see the characteristics of a mindful response. We pause when the feelings of stress become intense, appraise our situation, and remain calm. Our body follows our mindful strategy as we cope. Instead of intense anxiety and depression, we sense new possibilities for growth, and we make good decisions about our care. We make some changes in our behavior and discover that confidence replaces anxiety, gratitude replaces good health, and the joy of living returns. It would be instructive if we could see all the scientific details that constitute the substance of these two columns. However, we can understand and identify with the two pathways; one healthy, leading to wholeness, and one unhealthy and leading to severe burnout.

Our lives may be a mixture of both. What motivates you in your choices?

---

7. Goldstein, *Mindfulness*, 101.
8. Kabat-Zinn, *Full Catastrophe Living*, and Bardacke, *Mindful Birthing*.

Day 161

Mindfulness has several meanings and functions, all of which are the key to growth toward wisdom. Understanding this richness of meaning opens up new potential for its power to transform our lives.[9]

We have set some goals for growth toward health and wholeness. We now need to explore together the means of achieving these goals. Our title, *Mindful Spirituality*, affirms that our means relate to being mindful. We spoke of mindfulness as being in the present—aware, wise, and intentional. We also reminded ourselves how easy it is to become distracted and derailed. It is so easy to lose our way unless we engage in practices that gradually become habitual. It is like the great athlete whose practices build muscle memory. So, too, does the one who chooses to pause and respond in a mindful way need to train the will and emotional memory so that responses are healthy, and not reactions that lead to illness and suffering.

The practices prescribed in mindful meditation are designed to inform and train us to live in a more healthful way. It is a way of life needing years of practice. We can't go into a full description in these daily readings, but we can at least hint at what this pathway might entail. At the beginning, as you would expect, is the practice of meditation, pausing, cultivating calmness and stability, and observing what is happening in the present moment. It does not mean that you become empty; rather, you observe and notice thoughts and emotions. You note them in a non-judgmental way and then move more deeply into what is happening. You might lie down and do a body scan, sensitive to what you feel in different parts of your body. This can be done sitting or walking as well. As your mind and emotions begin to wander, focus on your breathing in order to bring yourself back to the immediate moment. In the class in which I participated, we spent weeks learning how to stop, take a few deep breaths, and observe what is happening with our thoughts, emotions, and in our body. Here and there we would look up and explore other ways of achieving inner calm. In time, the approach was applied to the various activities of the day, such as eating and driving.

How do you generally go about calming yourself and achieving inner peace?

---

9. Goldstein, *Mindfulness*, 13.

Day 162

Yoga can develop strength, balance, flexibility and body awareness. Our mindful yoga emphasizes awareness and balance. Poses are done carefully and slowly and attention is held inside the body.[10]

I have found the practice of yoga quite helpful for inviting me into the present and increasing the awareness of my body. It has also underlined for me the challenges of aging and the need to keep my body as healthy as possible. I do honor the limits of my participation in yoga, aware that I do not move like I did when I was twenty-one. I enjoy pushing myself some, increasing my focus on the present, and gaining more balance. As I go through the several postures, often led by a well-trained instructor, I find the practice guiding me into a more mindful state, sensitive to my breathing, pausing between the postures, and noticing the reduction of my stress. There is a remarkable physiology at work as I stay focused. I try not to be judgmental of my limited flexibility and balance, and to be grateful for what I can do that is good for me. At times, I am aware that I have drifted away, perhaps worrying about some mistake or neglect in the past or some anxiety about obligations and responsibilities of the future. As I catch myself, I do not harshly judge and move on, and rest easily and relax in a particular posture. When there is pain or fatigue, and I do experience these conditions, I try to learn from them. What is the nature of my frustration, perhaps not able to move as well as I used to because of age? Do I fear the aging process, knowing that there will be changes in my body and in my ability to move in agile, flexible, and carefree ways? Yes, I notice these thoughts and feelings, then pause, return to the moment, and focus on the next posture. I find the names of the postures, as they connect with the wisdom and beauty of nature, to be appealing and motivating. I like to "hug the tiger" or "reach for the moon." It helps me to resist becoming angry about my inability to make all the moves with ease and grace. I relax into the moment and live in the now.[11]

Is yoga or its equivalent a helpful way for you to be mindful?

---

10. From the syllabus of a class that I took on Mindful Meditation, 35.
11. See the book by Tolle, *The Power of Now*.

Day 163

Indeed, the sage who's fully quenched rests at ease in every way; No sense desire adheres to him whose fires have cooled, deprived of fuel. All attachments have been severed, the heart's been led away from pain; tranquil, he rests with utmost ease. The mind has found its way to peace.[12]

My mind has not fully found its way to peace, although I am enjoying the process of being on the way. The practices of mindful meditation have helped me make some progress, yet I continue to slip back. I am learning that one does not fully arrive; I remain in process. There are distractions and aversions. The distractions and aversions are both within us and in our environment.

The challenges to growth in the Buddhist tradition have been examined with great care in the literature and in the practices. Again, let us sample some of the teaching, fully aware that a concentrated course is necessary for full understanding and progress. In regard to distractions, we must face our own inner life directly to discern them. The fact that we are all too human, and cannot escape the challenges of becoming a fully actualized person, means that our growth agenda is a long one. There are residual fears and needs that surface and often cause us to engage in self-destructive and harmful behavior. We easily slip into a defensive attitude, justifying and rationalizing what we do and say. As our feelings swirl and our minds become filled with distorted thinking, our behavior can become harmful and hurtful to us and those around us. We easily turn to external distractions. We buy the lie that happiness consists in the abundance of things possessed. We may self-medicate, hoping to escape. Our conscience, and perhaps our friends, invite us back to a centered life, but the aversions, rooted in unpleasant experiences, may lead us to denial and poor choices. But there is a way back to sanity, health, and mindfulness. Family, friends, and our support community will welcome us with open arms. Love heals and wisdom guides. Be open to it. Find a refuge.

What are the distractions and aversions that you face in your growth?

---

12. From the Buddha, quoted in Hanson, *Buddha's Brain*, 79.

Day 164

> *Given the negativity bias of the brain, it takes an active effort to internalize positive experiences and heal negative ones. When you tilt toward what's positive you're actually righting a neurological imbalance. And you're giving yourself today the caring and encouragement you should have received as a child, but perhaps didn't get in full measure.*[13]

We are reflecting together on the means we use to reach our goals of health and wholeness. We have spoken about being keenly aware of our needs and using the disciplines of mindful meditation. In our last reading, we thought together about the distractions and aversions that get in our way and prevent us from achieving health and wholeness. As we close this small unit on the means of progress, I want to speak again personally about how I have been helped. As we underlined in the previous entry, we get help from others, perhaps in a class or support community, or from family and friends. I find some refuge from my storms in being heard by caring others. Just to be with others is somewhat helpful, and meets a deep need to belong. However, it doesn't take me deeply into my struggle to overcome loneliness, act with integrity, and be heard by someone whom I experience as having genuine empathy. I need someone who really pays attention and does not always interject his or her agenda. I need someone who doesn't judge and prescribe solutions before they really understand. I need someone who occasionally seeks clarification in order to understand and who stays with the conversation. I want to be heard.

One other helpful practice for me is to name and note what I begin to understand. When I can identify a problem and understand it, then it becomes less scary. There have been times in my life when I have not understood an unpleasant feeling or a conflicted relationship, and these experiences are very difficult and cause pain. Fully understanding them does not always take them away, but it does make them easier to manage. It also brings them out into the open and I can deal with them, rather than just chasing shadows.

Do you have those who truly listen to you and understand?

---

13. Ibid., 75.

Day 165

He is the living Master who consciously sends the Holy Spirit to dwell within us and to bear witness to his resurrection by empowering us to experience and manifest the fruits of the Spirit and the Beatitudes both in prayer and in action.

—Thomas Keating[14]

The teaching of Buddhism about the healing and nurturing power of mindful meditation is somewhat complementary to the teaching of centering prayer found in numerous Christian teachers of the spiritual way. Thomas Keating, a Trappist monk, has been an important contemporary voice in guiding Christians into a deeper spiritual life, and he draws wisely from many teachers.[15] The idea of centering prayer speaks to our concern to find the means to cultivate emotional health and wholeness as it relates to mindful spirituality. As we turn from Buddhist thought to Christian thought, the difference is in the claim that the Holy Spirit, understood as the presence of God, empowers us to live in a more spiritual way or in a more healthy and mature way. There is not an easy way to distinguish between mature spirituality and emotional health, although both are necessary to help people become mature and whole in the sense of being integrated and fully actualized. The developmental psychologist might say "to achieve one's full potential as a person" and the Christian might say "to become all that God intends for us to be." We'll say more about how these different ways of speaking about growth may overlap.

First, though, let's look a bit more closely at centering prayer as a way of turning inward for emotional health and wholeness. Centering prayer is understood as a means of grace for growth in one's spiritual life. It is the promise of God to receive us as we open our awareness (heart) to God. During this time of prayer, we are open to God's presence, healing, and guidance. It differs from other prayers in that we pause, focus, and become aware of God's presence. It is "resting in God" rather than requesting. It is less about petitions and more about mystical unity with God.

Is centering prayer or resting in God an experience that you have had?

---

14. Keating, "The Method of Centering Prayer."

15. Keating mentions, for example, the enduring fourteenth-century classic of Christian mystical experience, *The Cloud of Unknowing*.

Day 166

> *This is what you are to do; lift you heart up to the Lord, with a gentle stirring of love, desiring him for his own sake and not for his gifts. Center all your attention and desire on him and let this be the sole concern of your mind and heart. Do all in your power to forget everything else, keeping your thoughts and desires free from involvement with any of God's creatures or their affairs in general or in particular.*[16]

The method of centering prayer focuses on the immediate present and calls for awareness and intentionality, or mindfulness. It usually begins with the selection of a sacred word or phrase, or perhaps a sacred symbol such as a cross or an icon. The word or object is used to keep one's attention on being in the presence of God. For example, one might choose from the Lord's Prayer the phrase "hallowed be thy name" or, from the liturgy, "have mercy upon me." It represents our way of being present with God and focuses our attention on God's majesty and forgiving grace. You may want to use your favorite name for the divine, such as Loving God, Lord Jesus, or Ever-Present Spirit. Or, you may want to use a symbol, such as a cross, and as you do, you will want to ponder its meaning.

As with other forms of meditation, it is important that one finds a place that is quiet and free from distractions. Posture is also important. You should sit or kneel comfortably, and then introduce the sacred word or symbol as a way of consenting to be in God's presence and desiring the transforming grace of God in your life. Your choice of phrase or symbol may speak about your current conscious state and needs. Many of those who engage in centering prayer will repeat the phrase many times as a way of staying focused and calming one's unruly mind and emotions. It is wise not to judge what is in your mind or the emotions that you are feeling; just acknowledge and note them, and then return, "resting in God." The length of time is not firmly set in the practice of centering prayer, but perhaps twenty minutes is a good goal, and you may want to engage in the practice more than once per day. The Muslim practice of praying five times a day is a good example.

Is this practice appealing to you, or do you think it is too difficult?

---

16. *Cloud of Unknowing*, 48.

Day 167

It should not be difficult to pray, for prayer is the most natural activity in the world. William James, the great American philosopher, said: "Many reasons have been given why we should not pray, whilst others are given why we should. But in all this very little is said of the reason why we do pray. The reason why we pray is simply that we cannot help praying."[17]

All of our prayers do not take the form of centered prayer; there are many other kinds of prayer. A brief review of them will help us keep in mind the full range of concerns we bring to God in our prayers. Drawing from the example of the Lord's Prayer, we may want to begin our prayers with an invocation, or the way we contact God and invite God's presence. God is already present, and so it is more of a reminder for us that we are now focused on God's presence. For me, it is an easy next step to move to confession, the thoughtful and deeply felt telling of our failures and sorrow about not being more faithful. At this point, I might add the direction I take in confession. I do not focus on "what a wretch I am," so much as accepting my profound worth while acknowledging my failures, and asking for the wisdom and strength to do better. I celebrate God's love for me, rather than focus on my worthlessness in God's presence. The Christian tradition has gone both ways in its teaching about confession, and I think it is important to emphasize our worth.

I often then move from confession to thanksgiving, acknowledging God's unlimited love for me, the joy of living, the wonderful people who fill my life, and the beauty of the earth. I thank God for giving my life meaning, and giving me gifts for pursuing my vocation of teaching and pastoral care. I tell God that I am thankful that my life has meaning and that I am grateful to belong to the team of love. It is then easy for me to move on to my petitions, asking God to strengthen me, inform me, and refine my skills for life and for my particular vocation. From my petitions to be empowered, I move then to the needs (intercession) of those around me, and indeed for all those who struggle and suffer.

Are these dimensions of prayer the ones that you include in your prayers?

---

17. Barclay, *The Plain Man's Book of Prayers*, 7.

Day 168

If you follow Jesus' advice and pray to God constantly, then you will learn to pray well. God himself will teach you.[18]

I find concentrated prayer somewhat difficult. I deal with what nearly everyone must: a lack of focus and concentration. At various points in my life, I would write out the concerns that I felt needed prayer. The script helped me focus my prayers. During one full year, I kept a diary of my prayer life and would return to it from time to time as a means of concentration. Occasionally, I even reviewed what I was doing and underlined certain principles of the life of prayer. William Barclay, the Scottish biblical scholar and teacher, suggested five principles.[19] In my words, they are:

1. We must always be honest in our prayers. We need to be completely open with God, mentioning our fears and struggles. It is a time to truly face what we are experiencing and bring our true self to God.

2. In light of the need to be honest, we need also to be specific and definitive in our prayers. Naming our concerns does help us face them directly and reduce our fears about them. Bring tangible and specific concerns to God in prayer.

3. We need to keep in mind that God wants what is best for us and for those with whom we share life. Therefore, we are unwise to bring selfish requests to God, ones that are ego-driven and which, if granted, would be harmful to us and to others. God does not grant harmful requests. Rather God invites us in the depth of prayer to pray in a loving spirit.

4. It is also true that God will not do what we can do for ourselves. God does not take away our sense of responsibility. God gives us the strength and wisdom to be responsible.

5. I have also learned that God does not invade the natural laws that govern life. We may pray for a miracle, although I seldom see one.

How much of prayer is about our relationship with God, rather than petitions?

---

18. John Paul II, *In My Own Words*, 11.
19. Barclay, *The Plain Man's Book of Prayers*, 10–15.

Day 169

The means of grace, or the media through which grace may be received, are various. The primary means of grace is that of Holy Scripture, from which our whole knowledge of the Christian faith is derived and the chief purpose is to communicate to us the saving grace of the gospel of Jesus Christ.[20]

I use this quote from the *Evangelical Dictionary of Theology* because I know how much the Bible means to the evangelical wing of the church. Other groups within the larger Christian family might speak of prayer or the Eucharist as the primary means of grace, yet all Christians would place the Bible within the various ways we receive understanding and saving grace. A book of readings is not the place to introduce the details of the critical study of the Bible, although it could underline the Bible's primary message and themes. I want to introduce three different strategies in our desire to understand the Bible's message to us and have it function as a means of grace. First, to grasp its message to us, we are wise to ask the following questions as we attempt to understand a particular passage:

1. The first is the language question. What are the words saying? What is the structure of the paragraph or section? What type of literature is it?

2. The second is the historical question. What is the setting from which the passage is written? What particular situation is the passage addressing?

3. The third is the theological question. What is the content and subject of the passage, and what assumptions are inherent in the writing? What is it teaching us about God, and the will and way of God?

4. The fourth is the strategic question. How does what is being said fit into the larger scheme of what Christians believe and how they serve?

5. The fifth question is the contemporary question. How does what is being said jump forward into our time and guide us? How might we apply the message?

6. And, of course, there is the final question, the personal one. How does this passage teach me, as a means of grace, the will and way of God?

How much is the Bible your guide for understanding your spiritual life?

---

20. Elwood, *Evangelical Dictionary of Theology*, 482.

Day 170

"Lectio Divina," a Latin term, means "divine reading" and describes a way of reading the Scriptures whereby we gradually let go of our own agenda and open ourselves to what God wants to say to us. In the 12th century, a Carthusian monk called Guigo, described the stages which he saw as essential to the practice of Lectio Divina.[21]

The second strategy for reading the Bible as a means of grace is a more personal one, although it is wise to use the question strategy in order to increase your understanding of the passage. In the past few decades, as I have explored ways to deepen my spiritual life and used the Bible as a means of grace, I have used the very personal method of *Lectio Divina* and have found it a true means of grace. It has made my Bible reading very nurturing, a special gift to me in that I have spent a career reading it through a more critical-historical lens. Guigo, a twelfth-century monk, suggests four stages in his method of devotional reading:

1. The first stage is the *lectio* (reading) stage, in which we read a section of the Bible slowly and reflectively, hoping that its message will sink deeply into our hearts and minds. The passage should not be lengthy, and should generally carry one thought or message.

2. The second state is the *meditation* (reflection) stage, in which we ponder the meaning of the passage and how it might apply to our lives. It is less of an intellectual reflection, and more a meditation for the heart.

3. The third stage is called the *oritio* (response), during which we try to set aside our pattern of thinking about all of the responsibilities and demands of the day and allow our hearts to hear the voice of God. We assume a meditative posture.

4. The final stage is called *contemplatio* (rest), during which we not only let go of our ideas and plans, but also our tendency to place the passage in our spiritual frame of reference. We assume a more receptive posture and try to hear the voice of God at the deepest level of our being.

Try using this method with "Thy will be done" in the Lord's Prayer.

---

21. Order of the Carmelites, "What is Lectio Divina?", para. 1.

Day 171

In the last several decades, hermeneutics has moved to the forefront of the theological discussion. Today it continues to be a prime concern for all who endeavor to understand the Christian faith. Of particular concern is the way in which the Bible functions as the source of our knowledge about God and God's self-disclosure in Jesus Christ.[22]

I want to underline another concern about how we use the Bible as our means of grace in order to become more mature and deepen our spiritual life. It is the concern about how we interpret the Bible and use it for inspiration and growth. The field of hermeneutics or the interpretation of literature of the past, such as the Bible, is filled with complexity and is a concern in many fields of study. I raise the concern because, as far as possible, we want to understand the Bible accurately and wisely apply it to our situation. Let's glance at a few basic hermeneutical principles:

1. The first is that we exist in a particular time and place in history, live in a particular culture with a first language, and have personal ways of looking at and understanding the world around us. The key word we might use in this observation is that we read the Bible in our *situation*.[23] We read it with frame of reference that shapes our interpretation.

2. We read the Bible in order to understand the ways that our forbears experienced the redemptive presence of God in their history. So, as Christians, we give special attention to the central event, the "happening" of Jesus. We carefully study the coming of Jesus as God's Word to us.

3. As we study the coming of Jesus, we begin to put our faith together; we make a tangible *response* and attempt to read what God is doing and saying to us. All of this is to say that the reading and interpretation of the Bible go beyond the Sunday school saying: "How do I know? The Bible tells me so."

What difficulties do we face as we read and try to understand the Bible?

---

22. Ferguson, *Biblical Hermeneutics*, 3.

23. One thoughtful book on the issues of hermeneutics is Tracy's *The Analogical Imagination: Christian Theology and the Culture of Pluralism*. Tracy uses three words: situation, event, and response.

Day 172

> *For as one body, we have many members, and not all the members have the same function, so we, who are many, are one body in Christ, and individually we are members of one another.* (Rom 12:4–5)

In this subunit of our reflections, "Opening Inward for Growth," we spoke about several goals that might be summarized as the means of moving toward health and wholeness. For the past few days, using Christian concepts, we have been reading and praying about the means of reaching those goals, or the means of grace, in that we asking God to guide and empower us. We have underlined the place of prayer and the guidance of the Bible. We turn today to one other vital way that we sense the grace of God: fellowship. We grow and cultivate emotional and spiritual maturity in our common life in the church. The key biblical word is *koinonia*, often translated as fellowship. The word speaks of the communal association for the mutual benefit of all who join together. The forming of a community around common belief and practice was present among the Jewish community, and was followed as the early Christians came together for mutual support. This community gathered for several reasons; let me mention four, although each of the four can easily be expanded:

1. The first was for the purpose of hearing and learning about the good news (gospel) of the Christian message. Again, there was a Greek word used, *kerygma*—a word often translated as "proclamation." The Christian community across nearly two thousand years gathered to hear about God's gracious love, incarnated in Jesus Christ.

2. They gathered to learn, but also to worship and honor God, and to express their love for God. They participated in the Common Meal, the Eucharist.

3. As they gathered together, they discovered that the members of the community had different skills and gifts, all of which could contribute to the common good. All benefited from the association.

4. And from this base, they went into the world to serve, to "contribute to the needs of the saints and extend hospitality to strangers" (Rom 13:8).

Do you have a beloved community that heals and guides you?

Day 173

Let love be genuine; hate what is evil, hold fast to what is good; love one another with mutual affection; outdo one another in showing honor. Do not lag in zeal, be ardent in spirit; serve the Lord. Rejoice in hope, be patient in suffering, persevere in prayer. Contribute to the needs of the saints; extend hospitality to strangers. (Rom 12:9–13)

As he left the congregations that he had a part in founding, the Apostle Paul would write to them and encourage them to love one another and to serve the needs of the community in which they lived. He spoke to them about the means of grace that would help them grow in their faith, mentioning the need to pray, to study, to worship, and, without fail, to serve. Serving is the one means of grace that is not always mentioned on the list, but I add it because I am persuaded that: "to do it is to learn it and become it." We deepen and nurture our faith by acting on what we believe. We learn how to love by loving, how to serve by serving.

Across the years of my life, I have wanted to learn how to do a number of things. I saw others engaging in a variety of activities, enjoying them, and demonstrating high levels of skill. What I have had to do is to discern which kind of activity was ideal for me, given my opportunities and skills. I couldn't do everything I admired. I did try art, but learned that appreciating art, rather than become an artist, was better for me. I enjoyed music, but as a child I wasn't given opportunity to develop musical skills. However, I was given the chance to participate in sports, and to learn about them. These activities were present in the schools I attended, and in the values of my family. I learned how to expand my skill and how to engage in sports by doing them. So it is with the values of our faith. If love is the overarching value of my faith and the essence of serving, then I need to practice it and become one who loves. Service has become a means of grace for me. I learn by doing.

We set goals for growth and maturity by turning inward and exploring what is the spiritual way for us. We learn about the means that empower us to develop our spiritual lives within a loving community that prays, studies, supports one another, and serves in loving and compassionate ways.

As we do, we might ask, "What are my gifts and how might I serve?"

Day 174

Be like the Bird, that, pausing in her flight, awhile on boughs too slight,
Feels them give way beneath her and yet sings, knowing that she hath wings.

—Victor Hugo

God has given us wings, though like the bird we often seek our security on a fragile branch. During this month, we have been reflecting ("Opening Inward") on how to fly. We have said that, for us to fly, we need to set some clear goals. These goals were to become a deeply spiritual person, cultivate our capacity to be loving and compassionate, open our hearts to be filled with joy and peace, and to seek wisdom. We said, as well, that our lives are filled with all kinds of people, and learning how to be respectful and civil in all of our encounters must be one of our goals. We spoke about the Apostle Paul's listing of the fruits of the Spirit, which include patience, kindness, generosity, gentleness, and self-control. In short, we said that our goal was to become a responsible and loving person.

We went on to discuss the means of achieving these goals, drawing upon both religious and secular resources. We began with the practice of mindfulness, and how meditation and yoga will help us to be more aware, live in the present, and wisely respond to all situations, not irrationally to react to them. We spoke about our tendency to get sidetracked, and then introduced Christian practices that help us stay focused on the will and way of God. As you might expect, we spoke of prayer in its many forms, the study of the Bible as a guide, the richness of fellowship and support in a beloved community, and the need to be engaged in service.

We now come to a small unit in this larger section on "Opening Inward for Emotional Health and Wholeness." It is our third emphasis, following the statement of goals and the means of achieving these goals. We turn now to a reflection on the outcomes of this process. While we never fully arrive, we do make progress. As time goes along, we move toward becoming *spiritually mature, emotionally healthy, mentally alert, and physically sound*. We hope that these qualities will be the outcome of our quest to follow the will and way of God.

Describe in personal terms what you hope will be the results of your journey?

Day 175

When I was a child, I spoke like a child, I thought like a child, I reasoned like a child; when I became an adult, I put an end to childish ways. (1 Cor 13:11)

I promised a brief comment on what might be the difference between being spiritually mature and emotionally healthy.[24] In terms of behavior, I suspect that it might have to do with our values and the way we understand the sources of our empowerment. We find in the religious outlook that the primary values in all of these religious traditions are love and compassion, and they often take the form of justice in a corporate context. These same values may be a priority in a more secular pathway to health, but it would be a self-chosen priority, rather than one understood as given by God. In regard to the source of strength to realize the values of love and compassion in one's life, the religious traditions would speak about the enabling motivation and inspiration that come from the religious teaching. In the case of a theistic religion, it would come from being divinely empowered by God to love and show compassion. But we are all on the way. In the contemporary context, there is a tendency to speak about spirituality as being intentional and centered without the help of a religious outlook, a point of view that has merit. One might almost say that the cultural norm in our secular society is "whatever works."

What has worked for me is a spiritual pathway deeply rooted in the Christian tradition. I am guided and greatly enriched by the extraordinary resources in my faith orientation. However, I know that others with a different outlook have great resources as well, and I have used them in my journey. Developmental psychology and neuroscience teach me, and many of the great faith traditions have brought insight and guidance, often made more persuasive because it is not as familiar. I understand myself as a pilgrim on the way, and I join hands with other pilgrims who are seeking to find a deep spiritual pathway. I try not to judge, but affirm the ways of others if they lead to a life with meaning and a commitment to justice and love.

How do you relate to others who are on a different spiritual pathway?

---

24. See Levison, *Filled with the Spirit*, 7–11.

Day 176

Antiquity has bequeathed to us no writer more enamored of the spirit than the Apostle Paul, whose letters are awash in the spirit, so much so that isolating a single point of entrée is a monumental task.[25]

As I seek guidance in the Bible about the ways of connecting with God and receiving God's enabling grace for my spiritual journey, I have returned to Paul on a regular basis. I have reviewed his historical context and the sources of his view, one of which is the Hebrew Bible. Yet there is also a vast array of resources among other religious movements. I am also aware that some of the teachings of Paul are controversial. But this awareness has not lessened my persuasion that his point of view, taken in its most basic form, is credible. He believes that, as one connects with the divine, one is filled with the divine Spirit. The power and presence of God can fill our lives. He says that the Spirit of God may be working in us, through us, or on us. And, as we yield to the enabling grace of God, we are transformed. So, the first outcome of the spiritual quest is becoming a spiritual person, one filled with the family resemblance as the child of God. We repeat his summary of the Spirit-filled life: "By contrast, the fruit of the Spirit is love, joy, peace, patience, kindness, generosity, faithfulness, gentleness, and self-control. There is no law against such things" (Gal 5:22-23). Earlier, we divided these wonderful fruits of the Spirit into the three categories of relating to God, being transformed within, and our relationship with others. The word "faithfulness" best captures our relationship with God. We reach upward and relate to God by faith and stay in harmony with God by faithfully following the will and way of God. We also open inward for transformation. The manifestation of this inward opening is to be filled with love, joy, and peace. It is these qualities, or fruits, that enrich our lives. And third, we expand outward to love our neighbor as we love ourselves, to do to others what we would have them do to us. We express self-control, patience, and kindness in our relationships, and we are generous with our time, our talent, and our resources for the good of others.

What would add to Paul's list of spiritual fruits?

---

25. Ibid., 253.

Day 177

Emotional processing prepares the brain and the rest of the body for action.[26]

The first outcome in our quest for emotional health and wholeness is to become a spiritual person, one who incarnates those values and virtues that are the best expression of our union with the divine. Following closely and intimately related to being spiritually mature is to become emotionally mature. There are those who make a clear distinction between spiritual maturity and emotional maturity, and there are some differences. I find many overlaps as well, depending on how we define the terms we are using. In addition, as we use biblical language, we are using terms that are religious, rather than scientific, in character. There is wisdom in gaining an awareness of how our emotions, linked as they are to the brain, work in reference to our inner serenity and our motivations to act. I am inclined to see the Spirit of God at work in the process, rather than postulating a whole separate intervention. But, however it works, I find, as I keep myself as healthy as possible and remain open to the presence of the Spirit of God, that my emotional life becomes stable, fills me with the sense that life is good, and motivates me to endeavor to follow the golden rule.[27]

What are the qualities of the person we would judge to be emotionally healthy and whole? What are the outcomes of one who has moved through life to emotional maturity? The list is quite long, and for our reflections, I want to focus on six emotional states that I want for myself and encourage in the life of others. They are:

1. One quality of an emotionally healthy person is that they are attracted to and enjoy the company of others. To make this point in a slightly different way, the emotionally healthy person is not threatened by others and can appreciate the distinctive qualities of others. One can rest easily with others who have different talents, gifts, family backgrounds, ethnic identities, and cultural norms and practices from their place of origin. There is a sense of comfort with others.

Are you comfortable with others or a bit shy and reserved?

---

26. Siegel, *The Developing Mind*, 124.
27. Ibid., 121–59.

Day 178

> *Research also suggests that depression is associated with a decreased capacity to perceive the emotional expressions of others.*[28]

2. A second quality of the emotionally healthy person is that emotions, while alive and well, are easily kept under control and expressed in appropriate ways. It is a wonderful gift to be able to feel deeply and sensitively. Yet, self-control of one's emotions is necessary as well, as we relate to others in healthy ways.

3. A third characteristic of the healthy emotional life is that the emotions are integrated and complementary. They are not expressed in disproportionate ways, with one emotion, such as anger, dominating. Each should be expressed at the right moment and in the right situation.

4. Another quality of the emotional life of the healthy person is that one has an inner feeling of contentment. The emotions one has bring happiness and joy, giving one a deep sense that life is good and worth living. Negative feelings, such as irrational fear, anger, or depression, may be present; however, they are not permanent, and come and go within the normal flow of life.

5. A further characteristic of the healthy person is that emotions can be expressed for the welfare of others. One can feel genuine empathy and be emotionally in solidarity with another person. If there is suffering in another, it is felt not as an intrusion by a disgruntled person with a busy schedule, but an opportunity for the expression of love.

6. Finally, I will mention that the person with a healthy emotional life is able to turn the energy generated from one's emotions to the fulfillment of a calling in life. One thinks immediately of people such as Schweitzer, Gandhi, or Mother Teresa, whose emotions were not always level, but were strongly expressed in their life work. Our world is a better world because of their strong feelings, used in their calling to relieve suffering and pursue justice.

How would you expand this list, filling in numbers 7, 8, 9, and 10?

---

28. Ibid., 129.

Day 179

> *Until very recently, scientists could only speculate about the brain's role in our personality and decision-making skills. We did not have advanced tools to look at the functioning of the brain and thus made many false assumptions about its impact on our lives. With the advent of sophisticated brain-imaging techniques, we are now answering questions . . . that have practical applicability to your life, from relationships at home and at work to understanding what makes you a unique being.*[29]

We are exploring the outcomes of our opening inward for emotional health and wholeness. We have spoken about cultivating a deep spirituality and pursuing a more healthy and integrated emotional life. We will add a third desired outcome as we conclude this unit on opening inward for emotional health and wholeness. We might ask why we use the emotions as the primary area for health and wholeness. I chose the category because, in our common use of language and our cultural understanding, we think of maturity as primarily emotional maturity. But I want to stress that we are opening inward for total maturity or wholeness. We add, then, to spiritual and emotional health, the health of body and mind.

 A good place to start as we think of having a mature mind is with brain health. As the quote by Daniel Amen suggests, there is an explosion of research on brains, and much of it points to healing the brain and insuring that our brain stays healthy. The science is complex, and a thorough discussion of it might take us away from our goals in these readings, So we will focus our reflection on ways of keeping our brain as healthy as possible. A brain scientist at the University of Washington, John Medina, has provided some guidelines for brain health, making it possible for the non-expert to understand. Let me list them with some rewording as enticement for you to read more in this expanding field of research: (1) Exercise boosts brain power, so use it; (2) The human brain has evolved and is remarkable; (3) Every brain is wired differently, and therefore respect your brain and the brains of others; (4) Don't pay attention to boring things; give your brain a rest.[30]

In what ways are you stimulating you mind?

---

29. Amen, *Change Your Brain, Change Your Life*, 3.
30. Medina, *Brain Rules*.

Day 180

All of the evidence points in one direction: Physical activity is cognitive candy. We can make a species-wide athletic comeback. All we have to do is move.[31]

Let's continue with Dr. Medina's brain rules: (5) Repeat to remember, because repetition helps the brain piece our knowledge back together; (6) Remember to repeat, because if you don't, you can forget within thirty seconds. Spaced repetition cycles are essential to remembering; (7) Sleep well, think well. Get plenty of quality sleep; (8) Stressed brains don't learn the same way, and so watch the impact of stress; (9) Stimulate more of the senses. They all work together and, as they do, you will remember more; (10) Vision trumps all other senses; your brain wants to see in order to learn; (11) Male and female brains have some differences. Be ready to accommodate this reality in your relationships.

Brain scientists also make the case that a deeper spiritual life and a healthier emotional life are connected to the functioning of the brain. To say it in a slightly different way, we are an integrated whole that achieves health if all the bases are covered. We might also add, as does John Medina, that our physical health and regular exercise contribute to our total health as well. So we turn inward to better understand how we can become a more finely tuned human being. We need healthy bodies, spiritual depth, integrated emotions, and a fine mind. In the context of our quest for wholeness, we work on all these fronts, knowing that they are profoundly interrelated. We become mindful, focused, and intentional in this quest, knowing that we will find serenity and meaning and develop ways of living in a responsible and compassionate way. This is our road to mindful spirituality.

We turn next to contemplate how it is that we open inward for ethical guidance and practice.

In what ways are your heart, soul, strength, and mind (who you are) being impacted in you practice of mindful spirituality?

---

31. Ibid., 22–23.

Study Guide for the June Readings

Questions for contemplation and discussion:

1. Do you think of yourself as an emotionally healthy person? Or do you think of yourself as one who struggles with old wounds and needs healing?
2. Do you think of yourself as a whole person with the various dimensions of your life fully integrated? Or do you find that there are conflicts within you, with different voices suggesting alternative paths?
3. What do you think are the best ways to achieve emotional stability and integration?
4. Do you turn to spiritual resources for guidance, encouragement, and healing? Or are you inclined to think we are on our own in achieving health and wholeness?
5. Do you think that we can reach a point of emotional health and wholeness and remain in that state? Or do we occasionally slip back when the circumstances of our lives are challenging and difficult?
6. What do you turn to when you need help? Do you turn to family and friends? Do you have a community that sustains you? What do you need?
7. What practices do you use that are helpful and sustain you? Do you occasionally pray or use meditation as a means of dealing with the ups and downs of life?
8. What might be the components of a mindful spirituality that can give you the strength and stability you need to find your way through life?
9. What are the best resources for you as you seek emotional stability and wholeness? Are there books that you have found helpful? Classes?
10. Do you think you might be able to assist another person who asks you for help and guidance in achieving emotional health and wholeness?

THEME FOR JULY

OPENING INWARD FOR ETHICAL GUIDANCE AND PRACTICE

Day 181

> *The questioning part of ethics asks the following: What? Why? How? Who? When? Where? And what are the foreseeable effects and the viable alternatives? Most errors in ethics come from ignoring one or more of these questions.*[1]

We shift our focus slightly, yet continue our strategy of opening inward as a means of cultivating mindful spirituality. We spoke of the ways that mindful spirituality contributes to our healing, sensitive to how we may have been wounded across the years of our lives. We also reflected on how mindful spirituality invites us to engage in practices that lead toward emotional health and wholeness. We open inward as well, as we seek to clarify our values and find ways of living in harmony with them. We seek to be people of integrity, persons who are centered and integrated. As we grow and begin to shape and discover our identity, we learn how to put the pieces of our lives together, to feel less torn between healthy and unhealthy choices, and between that which leads to good ends and which might cause hurt and harm. We come together with a firm set of values and live honestly in harmony with these values. We seek to become congruent, live authentically, and to be ethically responsible.

As we open ourselves to discern what is most important to us and how we can find ways to incarnate these values, we are often called to reach upward for transcendence and expand outward in responsible living. Our integrity, then, means that we are true to ourselves, true to God (Transcendence), and true to others. We live with integrity, are open to the guidance of the ultimate reality, and are responsible and compassionate in reference to others. The question that will arise is how we put these ideals into practice. We need to know how to truly love ourselves, how to hear and follow the divine voice, and what we might do to help others who struggle and suffer. We undertake these tasks within by searching to know the good and to serve it. We are asking the questions suggested by Daniel Maguire in the opening section of his book on ethics, seeking clarity and discerning how these questions will engage us.

Are ethical choices easy for you? Are there some difficult ones? What and why?

---

1. Maguire, *Ethics*, ivx.

Day 182

> *While human beings have attitudes and dispositions in relation to many matters, these things become piety when they are directed toward God. An individual's piety is composed of those attitudes and dispositions that constitute and flow from his or her relationship to the divine. It points to the consistent posture an individual holds toward God and the attitude toward God's world that flow from it. It points to the patterns of action that characterize this relationship.*[2]

Dr. Osmer, from whose book we quote, speaks about the cultivation of a teachable spirit. He argues persuasively that patterns of action, often involving ethical choices, depend upon the spirit within us. His view is that the spirit within us is nourished and informed as we hear the divine voice. He notes that the church needs to create a better context for learning. For Christians, this makes sense. Our goal, however, is to include all who seek to live ethical lives. So we might expand his perspective to include any community to which we turn for nurture and guidance. I hear frequently the very honest statement that the spiritual life can be cultivated apart from a community, and I understand the statement. However, I tend to be a "both/and" person, and maintain that our spiritual lives, leading to a teachable spirit, are shaped by a community and refined by our individual spiritual practices. Osmer's phrase, teachable spirit, is filled with meaning, and it would be wise to examine it and see what is being said. He defines it in reference to the church context, and we might add that any context in which we learn about the cultivation of values is of great importance. It may be a good learning environment, although it might be a toxic environment and discourage a teachable spirit.[3] This subject needs careful attention, and we want to point initially to three positive qualities of a good learning environment:

1. It is open and accepting, a place in which one feels affirmed.
2. The student is engaged in the learning, not just sitting passively.
3. The subjects are contextual, engaging the student with life issues.

Was the environment you had for learning about ethical issues healthy?

---

2. Osmer, *A Teachable Spirit*, 49–50.
3. See Merritt, *Healing Spiritual Wounds*.

Day 183

In everything do to others as you would have them do to you; for this is the law and the prophets. (Matt 7:23)

We are in the process of learning how to be mindful about life. Our attention in this unit is to be mindful about our behavior, and we maintain that we need both to be transformed and to learn. We need to become people of integrity and to have a teachable spirit. The mindfulness tradition addresses both concerns: how to become a healthy and mature person, and then how to live an ethical life. We open inward to grow and develop, and to learn how to live by the golden rule.

We turn first to the Buddhist tradition to learn about the ethical life, and then to other faith traditions to complement and expand what we learn from Buddhism. Buddhist teaching about ethics starts with the foundation of seeing clearly, of gaining insight, of becoming aware, and moving toward enlightenment. There are several truths we need to grasp about this point, and three are foundational:

1. The first is that there is great suffering in the world. The first Noble Truth is that life is filled with suffering.
2. The second is that those who suffer are of great worth, and we need to honor the divine within them; as the greeting says, *Namaste*, or "I honor the divine within you." There is nobility and beauty in all human beings.[4]
3. The third is that there is the interconnection of all things. We belong to each other and we suffer when others suffer.[5]

Once we are able to see and understand, we become motivated to lend a hand. Our hearts are touched, and we deeply feel the suffering of others, in part because we too have suffered and in part because we begin to understand our responsibility to relieve suffering. Compassion is in our nature, and we identify with those who suffer, feel solidarity with them, and begin to sense the motivation in our lives to help.

Are you inclined to help others who suffer? In what ways might you help?

---

4. Kornfield, *The Wise Heart*, 12.
5. Ibid., 23.

Day 184

> *Before we can generate compassion and love, it is important to have a clear understanding of what we understand compassion and love to be. In simple terms, compassion and love can be defined as positive thoughts and feelings that give rise to such essential things in life as hope, courage, determination, and inner strength.*[6]

The heart of the Buddhist understanding of the ethical life is the practice of compassion, and at times, the word love is used with only a very slight difference of meaning. "Compassion" is generally used in reference to relieving the suffering of others, whereas "love" is often used to describe positive thoughts and feelings for another.[7] There is less of the tone of *eros* when the word love is used in Buddhist literature, and more of the sense of *agape*, or unlimited love. The story is told about Siddhartha (the Buddha) who, following his experience of enlightenment under the Bodhi tree, thought of moving on from the world of disease, old age, and death into the state of *nirvana* (the state beyond sorrow, and liberation from suffering and its causes). But instead, he decided to devote his life to teaching what he had learned. He devoted the rest of his life to teaching and relieving suffering. For him, there was a great need for compassion to relieve suffering. This pattern became the model for his followers. A definition of love and compassion began to emerge, as his followers reflected upon the Buddha's life. Four qualities came to be emphasized. They are:

1. *Metta*: friendliness or loving kindness
2. *Kauna*: compassion as in the relief of suffering
3. *Mudita*: gentleness
4. *Upekkha*: equanimity

The first of these values expresses the joy of being in the presence of another. The second is caring about the welfare of the other. The third is that we relate to another person with sensitivity, and the fourth is that we come to them with a deep peace that enables us to be present for them, and not overly concerned with our own needs.

Is compassion a trait that comes naturally and easily to you?

---

6. Dalai Lama, *The Compassionate Life*, 17. See *The Four Noble Truths* as well.
7. See Thich, *Teachings on Love*.

Day 185

> *Spiritual transformation is a profound process that doesn't happen by accident. We need repeated discipline, a genuine training, in order to let go of old habits of mind and to find and sustain a new way of seeing. To mature on the spiritual path we need to commit ourselves in a systematic way.*[8]

We are exploring the ways that opening inward enables us to cultivate a deeper spiritual way. In particular, we are exploring how our mindful spirituality can inform us and inspire us to live an ethical life. Nearly all of the great religions of humankind speak about the need for transformation in order to live in an ethical way and provide guidance about the virtues of the ethical life. We have noted that both Buddhism and Christianity have placed love and compassion at the top of the list, with both providing a means for becoming more loving, as well as guidance for the practice of love and compassion. Buddhism stresses that it is a lifelong quest, and many who follow the Buddhist way affirm that there must be a full engagement in becoming like the Buddha, the awakened and fully enlightened one. They recommend that one be in a community of like-minded people where there is support and encouragement, the Sangha. And, of course, there must be the study of the Dharma, the spiritual teachings of Buddhism. A Buddhist will say, "I take refuge in the Buddha, the Dharma, and the Sangha."

There are specific values and ethical norms for following the Buddhist way, not easy to summarize because of the diversity of Buddhism. Often, there is a list to guide the followers that includes ten norms, the first five of which are for lay members, and the others more for monks. The first five are more universal in scope, and the remaining five are more specific to the context in which the ten norms were developed. The list dates back to the early formation of the Buddhist faith.

Do you have a set of ethical norms that guide your behavior?

---

8. Kornfield, *A Path with Heart*, 31.

Day 186

> *Being mindfully aware, attending to the richness of our here-and-now experiences, creates scientifically recognized enhancements in our physiology, our mental functions, and our interpersonal relationships. Being fully present in our awareness opens our lives to new possibilities of well-being.*[9]

We are listing the ethical norms developed early in the Buddhist tradition, perhaps as far back as the Buddha. We listed, as the first one, the vow not to destroy life, a concept fully developed across the centuries in Buddhist thought. It became a positive statement, and means that all of life is sacred. The list continues.

1. "I take the vow not to destroy life." This ethical norm has meant, of course that one does not take human life and also one honors other life as well and treats it with sanctity.

2. "I take the vow not to steal." As this norm was first articulated, it was in both a community culture that shared resources, and also in one that existed in the context of poverty. It too was often expressed in a positive way, that we honor the right of others to have basic needs met, to have possessions that are valuable, and to have meaning for them and bring joy to their lives.

3. "I take the vow to abstain from impurity." For the monks, this norm meant celibacy, and for lay people, it meant being faithful in the marriage relationship. This norm also moved beyond just the prohibition, and became a norm for the respect of women, in particular, who were abused. For both men and women, it became the goal of purity, beyond just behavior but in spirit as well. The divine in all human life was treated with sanctity.

4. "I take the vow not to lie." Again, the ethical norm developed into the positive affirmation that we are to live lives of honesty and integrity. We are to become those who can be trusted, because we are congruent people who adhere to the values of the community.

5. "I take the vow to abstain from intoxicating drinks, which hinder progress and virtue." The Buddhist way is the way of seeing clearly, of facing reality, and acting wisely. One should never cloud the mind.

How do you respond to these five ethical guidelines? Anything to add?

---

9. Siegel, *The Mindful Brain*, xiii.

Day 187

I also see that, in general, those individuals whose conduct is ethically positive are happier and more satisfied than those who neglect ethics. This confirms my belief that if we can reorient our thoughts and emotions, and reorder our behavior, not only can we learn to cope with suffering more easily, but we can prevent a great deal of it from arising in the first place.[10]

I thought it might be helpful to list the latter five vows as well, in order to get a sense of what was important to the framers of the vows in their time. Our ethics may be based on universal norms, but they get quite specific in our day-to-day lives.

6. "I take the vow not to eat at forbidden times." Of course, the broader application is that we should eat in a mindful way.
7. "I take the vow to abstain from dancing, singing, music, and stage plays." Here, the broader application is to stay focused on one's life calling and not get caught up in the ways of the world. This one does sound a bit puritanical.
8. "I take the vow not to use garlands, scents, unguents, or ornaments." Again, the emphasis is on spirituality, not the way one becomes attractive.
9. "I take the vow not to use a high or a broad bed." There is a good measure of discipline and austerity in the life of the monk.
10. "I take the vow not to receive gold or silver." One should engage in the life of the spirit and service without the concern for money.[11]

In reviewing these vows, I noted that they had both a universal character about them, with guidelines that could be applied across history and cultures, and a quite specific character about them that references the specific context out of which they were developed. I have reviewed other lists of ethical conduct, such as the Ten Commandments and the teaching of Jesus in the Sermon on the Mount. I find the presence of both the universal and the specific in them as well. Our challenge is to discern the universal principles and apply them to our context.

How do you discern between the universal and the contextual norm?

---

10. Dalai Lama, *Ethics for the New Millennium*, xii.
11. I used the list from Hutchison, *Paths of Faith*, 106; as his source, he lists Davids, *Buddhism*, 160.

Day 188

My call for a spiritual revolution is thus not a call for a religious revolution. Nor is it a reference to a way of life that is somehow otherworldly, still less to something magical or mysterious. Rather, it is a call for a radical reorientation away from our habitual preoccupation with the self. It is a call to turn toward the wider community of beings with whom we are connected, and for conduct which recognizes others' interests alongside our own.[12]

Our ethical responsibilities focus on our behavior, and also include the ways we take responsibility for the welfare of others. Deep within, we sense the call to be considerate of others, to respect their wishes and needs, and to be concerned about the quality of their lives. Of course, many do not hear this call, and instead pursue their own pleasure and need for power over others. In both Buddhism and Christianity, there is the call to become a person for others. At the turn into the twenty-first century, the Dalai Lama spoke to the Buddhist world (and indeed, to all the world) about the need for all of us to learn how to respect and care for others. There was the recognition that we are now living in a global context, and awareness that how we live will impact the way that those in other parts of the world will live. He was conscious that the world's wealth and food are not equitably distributed, and that many suffer even if there is an adequate supply of all that they need. The great religions of the world have responded with an eagerness to partner with the Divine Presence in creating a more just and humane world order.[13] As we do, we know there will be resistance, even in the power structures of our religions. There is vested interest, and many in the religious context are finding it difficult to leave their traditional beliefs and customs and turn their energy to caring for the world. The problems we face are overwhelming, and will demand the best minds and spirits of our time to address them. There is global warming, international conflict and violence, world hunger, the plight of immigrants, and gross injustice and prejudice in many regions of the world.

What is our responsibility in helping to create a more just and peaceful world?

---

12. Dalai Lama, *Ethics for a New Millennium*, 23–24.
13. See the book by Thich, *Creating True Peace*, for example.

Day 189

The world is filled with divine sparks. They are hidden, lost everywhere, and it is the responsibility of each Jew to gather some of these sparks and restore them to their place. By doing this, creation can be restored to its original, perfect state. The task of restoring or repairing the world is called the tikkum olam.[14]

In Judaism, there is a very strong emphasis on both personal ethics and social ethics. At the time of this writing, I am teaching the Hebrew Bible to a group of Christians who desire to know more about their historical roots and how Jesus thought about ethics. As I immerse myself in the Hebrew Bible and the literature that has grown up around its interpretation, I discover how grand and rich a resource the Jewish people have developed over the centuries. It is not possible in these daily readings (or in a lifetime) to do it justice, nor am I equipped to do so. Even summary statements run the risk of some distortion, although I am reminded that the great teachers of Judaism have often used the phrase "the law and the prophets." By law, they meant the Torah, or the first five books of the Hebrew Bible. The interpretation of the law took form across the centuries, and it was, in essence, an attempt to enable individuals to understand how to be obedient to God, and to organize society in a way that ensures justice. Once again there was and is an emphasis on both individual and social ethics.

One access point for us to the personal ethics within Judaism is the Ten Commandments, although they speak to social issues as well. Let's remind ourselves of these commandments, one of the most influential listing of ethical guidelines ever developed. The setting in Exodus (they are also in Deuteronomy 5:1–22) is the return of Moses from Mount Sinai, where he has encountered God and received two tablets of the Law. As he descends the mountain, he shares them with the Hebrew people. The Decalogue begins with the reminder of what God has done for them:

Do you think that the Ten Commandments lead to legalism, or are they really helpful to us as a moral guide?

---

14. Diamant and Cooper, *Living a Jewish Life*, 76.

Day 190

Here nothing is either stated or confessed; but orders are given to the one addressed, to the listener. In distinction to all catechisms and compositions resembling catechisms, everything has reference to that specific hour in which the words were spoken and heard.[15]

We are reflecting on the Ten Commandments, and as we do, we note that the scriptural account views the commandments as coming from the one true God.

1. "I am the Lord your God, who brought you out of the land of Egypt, out of the house of slavery; you shall have no other gods before me" (Deut 5:6). It is a call to a weary and unfaithful people to remember the faithfulness of God, to honor God, and to live in obedience to the divine will and way.

2. "You shall not make for yourself an idol, whether in the form of anything that is in heaven above, or that is on the earth beneath, or that is in the water under the earth" (Exod 20:4). In this context, the people may have had tangible idols, often a representation of a foreign god. In our time, our idols are less likely to be an object that is worshiped, but a value that supersedes our love of God and our love of neighbor.

3. "You shall not make wrongful use of the name of the Lord your God, for the Lord will not acquit anyone who misuses his name" (Exod 20:7). The name for God was understood as holy, as representative of the very essence of God. In fact, it was judged to be so holy that it should not even be spoken, and if it was it should be in a whisper. Therefore, do not take the name of the Lord in vain.

4. "Remember the Sabbath day and keep it holy. Six days you shall labor and do all your work. But the seventh day is the Sabbath to the Lord your God" (Exod 20:8–10). This particular commandment became central to the religious life of the Hebrew people as a day for worship and honoring God. Many explanatory regulations grew up around this commandment.

Do you think it is wise to set aside some time to cultivate the spiritual life?

---

15. Buber, *Moses*, 130.

Day 191

The Bible speaks not only of man's search for God but also of God's search for man.[16]

We continue with our reflection on the Ten Commandments.

5. "Honor your father and your mother, so that your days may be long in the land that the Lord your God is giving you" (Exod 20:12). This commandment became central to the family life of the Hebrew people, and it is interesting to read that it is connected to the ways that a stable and loving family life leads to a long life, and even the hint of a stable society that will last.

6. "You shall not murder" (Exod 20:13). This commandment expresses the value placed all human beings; they are created in the image of God. Rabbi Heschel captures in his writing the way in which human beings are valued in the eyes of God. The following commandments also express this great truth, that we honor others in our behavior because all people have infinite value.

7. "You shall not commit adultery" (Exod 20:14). The marriage vows are to be kept, and no deception should exist in the marriage relationship. In this commandment, there is a clear implication of the equality of the sexes, and that the woman is to be respected, a clear challenge to the patriarchal culture in which these commandments were developed.

8. "You shall not steal" (Exod 20:15). Inherent in this commandment is that we should not steal because we respect and love our neighbor.

9. "You shall not bear false witness against your neighbor" (Exod 20:16). An integral part of the spiritual life is to be a person of integrity, one who is honest and speaks the truth in love. What we say can be trusted.

10. "You shall not covet your neighbor's house, you shall not covet your neighbor's wife, or male or female slave, or ox, or donkey, or anything that belongs to your neighbor" (Exod 20:17). Again, there is the commandment to live with integrity and respect for your neighbor.

If Moses had added two or three other commandments, what might they have been?

---

16. Heschel, *God in Search of Man*, 136. We are sensitive of the use of "man" in this quote, but know that Rabbi Heschel meant all people.

Day 192

> *It seems to me that an authentic morality is one resulting from the dialectical tension between two ethics, the ethic of responsibility and the ethic of conviction.*[17]

We have noted that we need to turn inward for ethical guidance and practice. We open inward in order to prepare ourselves for our life calling. Many religions speak of a calling or a vocation, and often it is a reference to the one who is chosen by God to be devoted to serving the mission of a particular religious order. Words such as "rabbi," "imam," "priest," "monk," and "minister" are used to describe the clerical calling. Also, deep within these religious traditions, there is often the understanding that everyone has a calling. While it may not be clerical in nature, it is nevertheless an essential part of the way the world should run. All persons must do their part in order for society to function in an efficient and just way. It may be the calling of a parent, or teacher, or the one who runs a store that provides for the basic needs of life. I often speak with people who are a bit confused about life, and wonder what their purpose in life might be. Often I hear the question, "What does God want me to do?"

The Christian tradition has often used the language of a vocation with the specific meaning of a call to the ministry. The Christian church also has said that all people have a calling, a place and responsibility to fulfill. The Apostle Paul, though a tentmaker, spoke about being set apart before he was born and called by God's grace to proclaim the Christian message (Gal 1:15–16). As Paul speaks about the church, he is clear that each member has gifts to contribute to the common good (1 Cor 12:12–31). The quest for the common good has clear ethical implications. How might we serve, using our talents and gifts, to make life better for those in our circle of nearness and for those elsewhere needing our care and support? As we ponder in what ways we might serve the common good, we need to open inward to the guidance of the Spirit of God and listen for our calling. I have found that writing a personal mission statement has been helpful.

How would you describe your vocation or calling in life?

---

17. Wassmer, *Christian Ethics for Today*, 2.

Day 193

For this is the will of God, your sanctification. (1 Thess 4:3)

As Christians struggle with ethical questions and issues, they often appeal to the phrase, the will of God. As they make a choice, they want it to be the will of God and to represent the way that God is guiding them. It is a very important phrase within the Christian church, and there is a deep and abiding desire to understand it and be obedient to it. One can more easily speak about it in general terms, such as "Do unto others as you would have them do unto you." But as the issues become more complex, it is not always easy to discern what is the best way to follow the will of God. There are many sincere people who want to use the "ask-God strategy" in order to determine God's will, but the answers frequently differ depending upon the presuppositions and circumstances of those asking. The Apostle Paul, as he writes early in his ministry to the church in Thessalonica, uses the word sanctification, which is the process of becoming sacred or like God. We are called to be like God, and we say that the best way to understand how to be like God is to learn from and follow the one whom God sent, Jesus of Nazareth.[18]

Even with this guidance, we still have the challenge of discerning what we might do in a circumstance or ethical dilemma for which we can find no clear example from the life of Jesus. However, a careful study of the life and teachings of Jesus, as difficult as it may be to get to them, reveals a pattern of one who walked close to God, and in so doing became the Word of God to us. Jesus understood his life as the dramatic entry of the kingdom of God, an expression of the God's reign, into human life. Jesus asks his contemporaries and listeners to change directions and endorse the kingdom of God, which is good news (Mark 1:15). Jesus asks his contemporaries and his listeners to change the direction of their lives and endorse God's kingdom. It is a life lived in the presence of God, guided by God, empowered by God, and in the will of God. It is this kind of life to which Christians are called and committed.

How does one endorse or accept the good news (gospel) of the kingdom?

---

18. Hauerwas, *The Peaceable Kingdom*, 75–76.

Day 194

We all like tidy explanations, and that is fine, but when reality is messy, our tidy talk may miss the point. Simplism results, and simplism abounds when people have underestimated the difficulty of explaining the "shalts" and "shalt nots" that are at the heart of morality and culture.[19]

There is some risk in using the phrase "the will of God," in that it can often be a rationalization for doing whatever one wants to do. It does have a subjective side, and we can even hide the truth about our behavior from ourselves when the phrase is carelessly used. A well-known writer and theologian from a previous generation, in light of the confusion about how we can know the will of God, wrote a small book to explain it to his readers.[20] He spoke about three ways of understanding the will of God:

1. There is God's intentional will, or what we might call God's desired choice in a particular situation or circumstance, whether it is personal or corporate in nature. For example, my brother was killed many years ago as a result of an automobile accident. God's intentional will was that this accident should not have happened and that he should have lived a long and good life, one filled with peace and happiness.

2. But the accident points to the second category, God's circumstantial will. Because of human freedom and circumstances beyond our control, accidents and harm occur. When they do we find the best way to deal with what has happened is to care for those who grieve and help them move on to a new way of life. We wisely deal with the circumstances of what has happened.

3. He also speaks about God's ultimate will, by which he means that God will ultimately make the best of all of our circumstances, and indeed all that happens in the cosmos. Ultimately, my brother will rest in God's love.

Can you think of a situation in which all three of these meanings were present? How might they have been present in the life of Jesus?

---

19. Maguire, *Ethics*, 18.
20. Weatherhead, *The Will of God*.

Day 195

I am quite sure that the greatest help available in discerning the will of God is reached when we deepen our friendship with him.[21]

I had a few questions for Dr. Weatherhead as he applied his three categories of understanding the will of God to the life of Jesus. They were theological in nature and they illustrate how difficult it is to discern the will of God. I suspect there will always be questions, and as they arise we might keep in mind the ways that the wisdom of the church over the centuries has suggested we discern God's will.[22]

1. The first, of course, is that we are born in the image of God. We do have a conscience and we are always wise to listen for the voice of our conscience. That voice is often heard when we pray. Deep prayer is discerning!

2. In the same vain, we do have minds with the capacity to think rationally about complex choices and their consequences. We refer to common sense as a way we make good moral choices.

3. We also live in a family and have friends with wisdom. Seeking the advice of a trusted friend, and especially one without a vested interest, is a good way to discern the will of God. Our dear friends who know us well can help us see the right path that has been covered by the brush of defensiveness and fear.

4. There is also an abundance of great literature filled with wisdom. It may be theological, philosophical, psychological, and literary in character. As we read, we find that we are often described. We can learn from the concepts and from the stories that illustrate wise and unwise choices.

5. I did mention that the church has a record of choices and spiritual guidance from its mixed and complex history. Coupled with the accumulated wisdom of the church is the Bible itself, which tells the story of a vast group of people who believed that God was redemptively at work in their midst. The Bible can often be our best guide.

What has been the best way for you to discern the will of God?

---

21. Ibid., 42.
22. Ibid., 42–47.

Day 196

> *For at least twenty-five centuries human beings have been aware of certain distinct differences in human temperament or personality.*[23]

As we have noted in previous daily readings, we reach out for a relationship with transcendence in different ways. We have spoken of a combination of differences, including our time and place in history, our family and cultural heritage, and our inherited religious tradition and its beliefs and practices. We have also underlined that our uniqueness and our temperament are factors as we make decisions. All of these variables come into play as we seek to know the will of God for the direction of our lives and for the ways we make ethical choices.

The Myers-Briggs Type Indicator took the work of Carl Jung and attempted to discern different psychological types, each of which would have a slightly different style of making ethical decisions. There were the two attitudes toward life (extraversion and introversion) and four operating functions (sensation, intuition, thinking, and feeling). Sixteen combinations emerged, based upon whether one was more extroverted or introverted, more trusting of the senses or more intuitive, more inclined to think logically or to sense how a decision would impact the feelings of others, or more inclined to a quick judgment or to wait until one has carefully perceived all the possibilities. This methodology, along with many other personality descriptions, has helped me in discerning how I cultivate my spiritual life and make ethical decisions. For example, I lean just slightly toward introversion (I) and find it easy to be alone and still for extended periods of time. I am somewhat intuitive (N), and trust my inclinations. I have a measure of empathy, and often decide on the basis of how my words and decisions affect others (F). I do make assessments fairly quickly (J), and then can decide what I should do early in the process. In short, I am an INFJ, although, like each of us, we can't be put in simple categories. But these tendencies in my personality will impact my decision-making.

How does your personal style impact your way of making ethical choices?

---

23. Michel and Norrisey, *Prayer and Temperament*, 11.

Day 197

Along with a more advanced theory of mind and an understanding of intention, children also are developing a sense of right and wrong.[24]

While there are those who doubt that the stages of development model is altogether adequate, I admit to finding this model of describing human growth and development a very helpful one. Lawrence Kohlberg has used the model in reference to our growth in moral development. Based on extensive research, Kohlberg maintains that we move through three basic levels of moral development, each with two progressive stages. Let me outline his views:

1. Pre-conventional is the period in which moral judgments are based solely on a person's needs and perceptions.
    a. Stage one is the punishment-obedience orientation.
    b. Stage two functions in reference to personal reward.

2. Level two is the conventional stage in which moral judgments are based upon the expectations of society and law.
    a. Stage three has the good boy/good girl orientation and functions in reference to what pleases others.
    b. Stage four has the structure of law and order, in which the child understands the rules as absolute.

3. Level three is post-conventional, and in which judgments are based on self-determined principles.
    a. Stage five has the design of a social contract. The good is understood in reference to socially arranged agreements and covenants.
    b. Stage six has the orientation of universally understood ethical principles. The good is determined by conscience and reference to concepts such as justice, human dignity, and equality.[25]

Where would you put yourself in terms of Kohlberg's categories?

---

24. Woolfolk, *Educational Psychology*, 98.
25. Kohlberg, *The Philosophy of Moral Development*.

Day 198

> *[Christian ethics] is a form of reflection in service to a community, and it derives its character from the nature of that community's convictions. Theological claims are fundamentally practical and Christian ethics is but that form of theological reflection that attempts to explicate this inherently practical nature.*[26]

We are exploring ways that our opening inward invites us to reflect on personal and social ethics. Our recent daily readings have been more focused on personal ethics. But our ethical responsibility goes beyond the personal domain, and moves to ways that we become responsible in helping to build a more just society and humane world. As we move into social ethics, the issues become even more complex, in that the causes of suffering and injustice reach across our global context. In a former university where I worked, a group of faculty and students participated in a world hunger experiment calculating how what we had for lunch impacted hunger issues in other parts of the world. It was not always totally accurate, yet we were able to estimate our impact on certain parts of the world by what we ate, the way we obtained food, and the waste we left at the end of the meal. Our goals were to eat in a healthy way, attempt to use regionally grown food, and leave as little waste as possible. We didn't change the world, yet we learned how our habits impacted others and how we might be more responsible.

We also learned that ethical choices are not just personal in nature, but are involved in a complex web of imports and exports, government regulations, and the interconnected way the world's people get fed. We learned, as well, that there is enough food in the world even for the expanding world population, but that food distribution was caught up in a tangle of economic and political issues that makes it difficult to move food to the hungry. What this modest experiment did for me was to underscore the need of a sophisticated ethical outlook that deals with the reality of global issues.

How does the food you eat day-to-day impact those without healthy food?

---

26. Hauerwas, *The Peaceable Kingdom*, 64.

Day 199

While there are critical issues in providing food, shelter, and livelihood to the vast numbers of peoples, these issues themselves ultimately depend upon our capacity to sustain the natural world so that the natural world can sustain us.[27]

We will focus our readings in the last major section on "Expanding Outward" in order to live responsibly in our region, our country, and in our world. As we do, we need to reflect on how it is that we prepare ourselves to be ethically responsible in our complicated world. How might we open inward in such a way that we are informed about the overwhelming problems we face and prepared to lend a hand in addressing them? One step is to have a thoughtful ethical frame of reference. This subject is vast and complex, and we might start our exploration with a few brief observations.

We come at this concern from several perspectives. We must look at the hard sciences and the social sciences, of course, and also reflect on our outlook on life. We have the research, and it must be undergirded with logical and persuasive foundational systems of thought. Our very modest goal is to ponder the way that one's religious faith might be our starting point and guide us on our journey. As we turn inward, we should reflect on the following:

1. We need to inform ourselves about the regional and global issues, such as global warming, world hunger, and the violent ways we use to solve conflicts. The list is long and the issues complex.

2. We must reflect on our moral starting point. For many, this may be God's call to lead lives of compassion. There is a shift toward a more empathic world, the nature of justice, and strategies for solutions.

3. We might want to ask ourselves how we could "become a part of the solution rather than a part of the problem." How might we use our gifts and influence to create a more just situation in our region?

4. We should review our limitations and discern what obstacles we might face. We need to be prepared for a wide range of challenges.

Is there a regional social ethics issue on which you might work?

---

27. Berry, *The Great Work*, xi.

Day 200

Much of human history has consisted of unequal conflicts between the haves and the have-nots: between peoples with farmer power and those without it, or between those who acquired it at different times.[28]

Jared Diamond convincingly describes why some civilizations survive, even thrive, and why others fail. His several books are well worth reading. They remove our unfounded prejudices against certain people who live in poverty and suffer from malnutrition. He says that it has to with the quality of the land, and how it has been farmed and managed. A second point, on which he spends less time, but which is certainly implied, is the way that healthier and wealthier countries should learn how to justly distribute the wealth and means for the survival of poorer countries. This responsibility, along with the larger one of earth care, may be the greatest challenge of our time; it is our Great Work, as Thomas Berry says.

This awareness invites us to think about global ethics, our subject for the next section. But in this section, we are saying that turning inward for ethical guidance and motivation is important. I speak often with people who have not had to struggle with their livelihood. They have good health, a quality education, a well-paying job, and a country with strong economy. In one conversation a few months ago, I heard the sentence, "But it is their problem. They have not planned well or worked hard enough to be successful. They get what they deserve." I smiled and said, "But we might want to help them in that we have both the abundance of resources and the means to distribute them." And we do, but having the heart and the will to do it has been a problem. I am persuaded that we are now in a global context in which we need to help others, not only for their sake, but for ours as well, in that we are truly in it together. There are ways to help that do not rob the needy of their dignity or initiative. Nor would our help undercut our economy. A good design can be found to help out, so that everyone benefits. We can "do unto others as we would have them do unto us" and improve the lives of millions of people.

What can you do to help others in a different country improve their lives?

---

28. Diamond, *Guns, Germs, and Steel*, 93.

Day 201

What moral significance does Jesus have for Christians today? There are two brief answers given by believers: "everything" and "not much." They hold down the two ends of the spectrum . . . I will avoid these extremes, while I make a constructive proposal that Jesus Christ is the paradigm for Christian moral life.[29]

Once again, I am turning to the Christian faith for ethical guidance. My spiritual home is the Christian church and I welcome all, regardless of the home (and, of course, the homeless) to explore the ethical norms and practices of Christians. I turn to Jesus of Nazareth for practical guidance, and want to focus on his life and teaching rather than moving toward ethical theory. What were his ethical values?

It is wise to return once again to the way he taught his followers to open inward in order to be motivated and empowered to live what we now call the Christian life. Fond of metaphor, story, and illustration, Jesus selected—in part from his grounding in the Hebrew Bible, and partly from what he saw around him on a daily basis—the metaphor of "kingdom." It is not a metaphor we might choose, in that kingdoms are more rare in our time, and a bit suspect, in that they are often patriarchal and seldom just. But they do represent power and authority in the minds of his listeners. Jesus told those who followed him and listened for his guidance that they need to change their direction and endorse and accept the full power and presence of God in their lives. He called this invitation "good news," or the "gospel," and he says that the good and fulfilled life is lived under the reign of God. It is to say yes to the will and way of God. Of course, his followers had questions about how to know the will and way of God, and so he continued to teach them. One direction he took was to use another metaphor, spirit (meaning "breath" or "wind"), and he said that when you open your heart to God, the very breath or spirit of God will fill you and transform you. The Gospel of John speaks about it in the following way: "The wind blows where it chooses, and you hear the sound of it, but you do not know where it comes from or where it goes. So it is with everyone born of the Spirit" (John 3:8).

Which of the two metaphors for God's presence do you like the best?

---

29. Spohn, *Go and Do Likewise*, 1.

Day 202

When they bring you before the synagogues, the rulers, and the authorities, do not worry about how you are to defend yourselves or what you are to say; for the Holy Spirit will teach you at that very hour what you ought to say. (Luke 12:11–12)

Within Christian thought, the concepts of the kingdom of God and the Holy Spirit have some similarities, in that they both point to the way we are informed, inspired, and empowered to understand and follow the will and way of God. It is at this point that we should return to our central theme of mindful spirituality. The notion of mindfulness has two related meanings: we should be wise and intentional, that is, to use our minds to discern what is the best direction to follow; and we should pause, be in the present, and focus ourselves on what is happening inside of us. It is to be fully present. Spirituality speaks about being fully present to hear the Spirit of God deep within us, or as other traditions might say, the spark of the divine or the inner light. The language of "Holy Spirit" is the Christian way of speaking about the power and presence of God in our lives.

We are saying that the Christian faith teaches that Saint Augustine's prayer is always answered: "Dear God, ask what you will and give what you ask." We seek to know the will and way of God in all of our ethical choices, and as we practice mindful spirituality, we are guided and empowered. In one case, Jesus came to an awkward situation in the temple, where he met a woman who had been caught committing adultery. He began to speak with her, even though there was a group of people ready to stone her for this sin. He challenges this group, and they respond, speaking about the law that says that stoning is the punishment for this sin. Jesus speaks to the group and says to them: "Let anyone among you who is without sin be the first to throw a stone at her." The crowd drifted away in shame, and Jesus said to her, "Woman, where are they? Has no one condemned you?" She said, "No one, sir." And Jesus said, "Neither do I condemn you. Go your way, and from now on do not sin again" (John 8:1-11). One way of understanding this story is to see what is the most important value for Jesus, the law or love. He gives love to the woman.

What is this story teaching us about values and ethics?

Day 203

The practice of Jesus will make clear to us the radical freedom with which he acted, precisely because his activity did not abstract in an idealistic way from the concrete social, cultural, and economic conditions in which it was carried on. On the contrary, the freedom of Jesus demonstrated its history-making power to the extent that it immersed itself in those conditions and went on to transform them.[30]

Jesus was fully engaged and present as he encountered people with profound needs in his historical and cultural setting. His words and actions came together in *praxis*. The ethical norm that comes to mind first as we study his life and teachings is love, translated into Greek as *agape* and on to English as selfless and unlimited love. This kind of love would be very similar to what is taught in Buddhism, and is called compassion, in that so much of the life of Jesus was relieving suffering. In Judaism, the Hebrew word *hesed* has a similar meaning, and is often translated as loving kindness, also a concept in Buddhism (*metta*). In fact, one can find in nearly all of the great religions of the human family the centrality of love as caring for others.

The Gospel of Mark, thought to be the first of the four Gospels, puts the concept of healing love first in his account of the ministry of Jesus. Immediately after calling his disciples, he engages in acts of compassion and loving kindness. He heals the person with a serious emotional illness and then those with a range of diseases. One day, there were so many who sought healing that an ill person was let down through the roof in order to access Jesus. The story is told in Mark's Gospel about a leper who came to Jesus, begging Jesus to heal him. Jesus is described as being filled with pity, a word in English that, on occasion, can be interpreted as condescending, but the word might be better translated as tenderness, loving kindness, or mercy. It is clear that Jesus is moved by the suffering of the leper, and in spite of some laws that controlled the behavior of those with contagious skin diseases, Jesus does reach out and touch the leper to heal him. He then says to him that he should go directly to the authorities and be certified.

Was it wise for Jesus to touch the contagious leper? What motivated Jesus?

---

30. Echegaray, *The Practice of Jesus*, 14.

Day 204

> *Woe to you, scribes and Pharisees, hypocrites! For you tithe mint, dill, and cumin, and have neglected the weightier matters of the law: justice and mercy and faith. It is these you ought to have practiced without neglecting the others.* (Matt 23:23)

The author of the Gospel of Matthew has arranged several of the more prophetic sayings of Jesus into the section now called chapter 23. We are on relatively good historical ground to accept the message of these sayings; Jesus did get prophetic (showed righteous anger) when he saw hypocrisy in the religious realm. He seems to be saying in this passage that the religious leaders should model integrity and be trustworthy. It is to them that people go for spiritual guidance and nurture! And if they do not have these qualities in their behavior, then the people become disillusioned and wonder if the message to follow the spiritual way has merit. The Law is given to provide principles for our behavior, and the leaders seem to be neglecting their own teachings!

One reason why so many were turning to Jesus was because he was an honest and trustworthy person, an authentic teacher with great integrity. He lived what he taught, and the people were amazed and attracted to him. They not only sought him out because he was loving and compassionate, but because he lived and spoke the truth with such remarkable freedom. We see in the several settings in the Gospels a person who was not intimidated by power and authority, but free to speak truth to power and authority. "Woe to you, scribes and Pharisees, hypocrites! For you are like whitewashed tombs, which on the outside look beautiful, but inside they are full of the bones of the dead and all kinds of filth" (Matt 23:25). We have learned in our time about political leaders who have little regard for truth, and we don't trust them and are discouraged about the lack of integrity. Jesus had little patience with phonies who made promises and distorted information to achieve their goals. Jesus, judging from the records we have, never taught that the ends justify the means. He lived and taught that we should speak the truth and live in harmony with our religious values. One might wonder what he would say to our political leaders, and for that matter, to us as we shade truth.

What was it about the religious leaders that was so frustrating for Jesus?

Day 205

*I can do nothing on my own. As I hear, I judge; and my judgment is just, because
I seek to do not my own will, but the will of him who sent me.* (John 5:30)

We are reflecting on the moral compass of Jesus, the ethical norms that guided his life and teaching. We have pointed to love and compassion, the hallmarks of his life and the heart of his teaching. We have reflected on his integrity, and described him as one who was consistently true to his values and trustworthy in all he said and did. We turn now to a third set of qualities that are centered in the notion of justice.

There is a delightful and inspiring story of Jesus encountering a tax collector in the town of Jericho, one that I referred to earlier. In chapter 19 of his Gospel, Luke places this encounter in the final walk of Jesus and his disciples down from Galilee to Jerusalem. Evidently, the word had gotten out to the people of Jericho that the well-known healer, teacher, and prophet was coming through town. A crowd had formed in order to see him, and perhaps some thought they might be able to speak with him and bring him a person with a disease or deformity for healing. Zacchaeus wanted to see him as well and, being short in stature, he climbed a tree to get a better view. As Jesus walked through the main street, he looked up, noticed Zacchaeus, and asked if he could spend time with him and have a conversation. Zacchaeus, caught somewhat off guard, hurried down and welcomed him. We don't have a CNN report on the conversation, but we do have a report on how the conversation changed Zacchaeus. As a tax collector for the alien Roman government, he was asked to collect a certain amount of tax money, and was able to keep whatever might be over and above the amount he had to give to the Roman officials. The whole system was unjust, and Jesus was concerned about it. First of all, it allowed Zacchaeus to collect more from the people than what was required. Second, the money was used to sustain an alien power, one that was in partnership with the Jewish leaders. The people in power got the lion's share of the money, and the system kept the common people in poverty. The conversation between Jesus and Zacchaeus must have been interesting. They probably started over a cup of tea or coffee to talk about what it was like to work for the Romans.

What else do you think Jesus and Zacchaeus talked about that day?

Day 206

Zacchaeus stood there and said to the Lord, "Look, half of my possessions, Lord, I will give to the poor; and if I have defrauded anyone of anything, I will pay back four times as much." Then Jesus said to him, "Today salvation has come to this house." (Luke 19:8–9)

I suspect that Jesus and Zacchaeus spoke at length about what it meant for him to work for the Romans, and become alienated and rejected by the Jewish community, and likely his family. Perhaps they talked about his childhood and the joy he felt in boyhood as part of a family that had elements of support and love. But in adulthood, he may have spoken about being very lonely, and that he suffered from all the resulting feelings of rejection. Jesus probably spoke with him about his faith and the strong emphasis in Judaism on righteousness and justice. There might have been a moment, not unlike the Catholic Christian who has gone to confession, of allowing all the guilt and shame to come out, followed by tears of regret and self-hatred. Jesus may have shared with him about what it means to repent (change directions), and to open his heart to God's forgiveness and love, and to say yes to the power and presence of God in his life. By late afternoon, he was willing to forsake his belief that happiness consists in wealth and the abundance of things possessed. He longed for reconciliation with his family and friends, and for his inclusion in the community. He knew that he must make amends and tells Jesus that he will give half of his wealth to the poor. He understands that repentance is more that just feeling relieved to get it off his chest. He knew that he must do something for the poor who suffered from an unjust social system, so he decided to repay four times more than what he had taken from his people.

It is wise to note that, in this story, there is an emphasis on both the failure of a person and the presence of an unjust social system. Jesus likely spoke about the restoration of Zacchaeus and the need for justice. He was both healer and prophet. Legend has it that Zacchaues become part of the Christian community later in his life, even a bishop. We can't be sure, but it is a nice ending.

What does this story tell us about Jesus' moral compass?

Day 207

People were bringing even infants to him that he might touch them; and when the disciples saw it, they sternly ordered them not to do it. But Jesus called for them and said, "Let the little children come to me, and do not stop them; for it is to such as these that the kingdom of God belongs. Truly I tell you, whoever does not receive the kingdom of God as a little child will never enter it." (Luke 18:15–17)

The Dalai Lama has often answered the question "What is your religion?" with the simple answer "It is kindness." Jesus, too, was a very kind person. He took time for people who needed to express their fears and explain their suffering. He listened carefully, as if he had all day and the person expressing the concerns was the most important person in the world. We know from just a handful of recorded stories that he was especially gentle with little children. Of course, the parents of the children wanted them to see Jesus, and perhaps, if the child was ill or suffering from a birth defect, they wanted Jesus to heal the child. One of the stories tells about some parents who were bringing their small children, even infants, to Jesus. The somewhat-uptight disciples felt that the parents who brought their child were an intrusion on a very busy day. They must have felt that Jesus had better things to do, or maybe he just needed protection because he had had a long day and was tired. But Jesus says to his well-meaning disciples that it is good to bring the children to him. For Jesus, these children have infinite value, as they were created in the image of God. He says to the disciples, "Let the little children come to me, and do not stop them; for it is to such as these that the kingdom of God belongs."

Jesus not only received the children and loved them with tenderness, but also used the setting to gently teach the disciples that the children belong in the kingdom of God. While interpretations differ some on this passage, I am inclined to think that Jesus was really saying that the little children, created in the image of God, have the presence of God within them, and in their innocence and trust are open to the presence of God. They are without fear and bring total trust. They are models for the disciples with these qualities. Kindness, gentleness, and tenderness are present in Jesus.

What does Jesus mean that we must become like a child to receive God?

Day 208

Two others were led away to be put to death with him. When they came to the place that is called The Skull, they crucified Jesus there with the criminals, one on his right and one on his left. Then Jesus said, "Father, forgive them; for they do not know what they are doing." (Luke 23:32–34)

We are exploring the moral fabric of the life of Jesus. We know that there is an extended period of time between when the events happened and when they were put in writing, and that the Gospel writers were not historians, but attempting to guide the new Christian community in their writing. Yet his character and ethical teaching can be seen if we are careful in our interpretations. I draw upon a passage that needs this care. As it is expressive of the character and spirit of Jesus, I find it extraordinary and in keeping with what we read in other sections of the Gospels. In spite of the unimaginable pain that must have filled the body of Jesus in his horrific death of crucifixion, we see a human being that believed deeply in forgiveness and mercy. These qualities are integral to the ethical outlook of Jesus.

It was the Buddha who taught in the first of the Four Noble Truths that all human beings suffer. Jesus, too, was keenly aware of human suffering, and his public ministry was filled with efforts to relieve it. He healed sick and injured people on a daily basis and, with remarkable insight and sensitivity, cared for those with severe mental and emotional disturbances. But even with these guiding values and experience, it is still remarkable that Jesus, feeling the pain of the crucifixion, could care for the soldiers who were implementing the execution. As the story reveals, he also had time to listen and care for one of those that was being executed at the same time, and to speak with John about carrying for his mother, Mary. Death did not come fast in the crucifixion, and so there may have been time to reflect and comment. There was one comment about his own suffering, and why God was allowing it to happen, yet even with the mental anguish and physical pain, Jesus asks God to forgive and show mercy to the soldiers carrying out the execution. Jesus taught and lived the values of mercy and forgiveness.

What were the essential components of the moral matrix of Jesus?

Day 209

Blessed are the peacemakers, for they will be called the children of God."
(Matt 5:9)

The Gospels often describe Jesus as firm and direct in several conversations. He regularly speaks up and resists when he sees injustice or harm being inflicted on innocent people. Of course, we weren't there, and can't know for sure what he said and how he said it. But the picture we have is that Jesus is not only a compassionate healer and a thoughtful teacher, but also a prophet who spoke directly about conflict and reconciliation. He was a peacemaker, and knew that there could be no true peace without justice. He observed conflict, and saw styles of overcoming conflict by the use of force. The flow was as follows: conflict and unrest, to force and violence, to expected peace. But a lasting peace never occurred when this pattern was followed. He advocated another pattern: conflict and unrest—a resolution based on justice—lasting peace. He was aware that the pattern for a lasting peace was not the norm of his time, nor is it often the pattern in our time. So he often resisted injustice in the hope that, if justice could be achieved, peace would be possible.

This reasoning appears to be foundational for his teaching in regard to peace. In the collection of his short aphorisms in Matthew's Gospel, we read that peacemakers will be blessed (their lives will be better by God's presence) and they will be called the children of God. To describe them as the children of God is to say metaphorically that they have the family characteristics, and they belong as children in the family of God. Later in this same section in Matthew's Gospel, called the Sermon on the Mount, the author of the Gospel lists several areas of deep conflict and unrest between people. The author prefaces his comments with a statement about justice inherent in the Law, and then proceeds to the following issues: anger, adultery, divorce, oaths or promises, and retaliation. He speaks of these issues in reference to justice, and then in a concluding paragraph, he is quoted as saying: "You have heard that it was said, 'You shall love your neighbor and hate your enemy.' But I say unto you, Love your enemies and pray for those who persecute you" (Matt 5:43–44).

Are there ways to achieve peace with justice by turning the other cheek?

Day 210

And going a little farther, he threw himself on the ground and prayed, "My Father, if it is possible, let this cup pass from me; yet not what I want but what you want." (Matt 26:39)

I am persuaded that the best way to understand the ethical teaching of Jesus is to focus on the Jesus of history. It is difficult to separate the human Jesus of history from the divine Christ of faith, although it is a distinction made by New Testament scholars. If one moves along the continuum between the two understandings of the Jesus and stress the divine identity, the example of Jesus loses some of its persuasiveness. It is too easy to say, "Yes, but he was divine." I prefer to speak about the human Jesus who fully opened his mind and heart to the presence of God. The account of the end of Jesus' life in the Gospels has power for me, because his prayer in the Garden of Gethsemane is so human. He anticipates his death and prays that he won't have to drink from that cup. I am sure he had good memories of his childhood, missed his siblings, and deeply loved his mother. He would not be able to return to rural Galilee for the simple life in the country. He had a great appreciation for the beauty of his surroundings, and often drew upon nature to tell his stories and to teach about the true spiritual life ("Remember the lilies of the field"). He was grounded in the history of his people, dedicated to the principles of Judaism, and had found a calling as a healer, teacher, and prophet that went beyond his good work as a carpenter. He loved life and did not want to lose it.

But in the end, he sensed that he could not return to these past experiences and share life with family and friends. We read that in the middle of the night, he was alone, fell on the ground, and prayed "Not what I want but what you want." In the end, his choice was to discern and follow the will of God. He opened inward and knew what the foundation of his life was all about; it was to follow the will and way of God. As we open inward for ethical guidance and practice, we would do well to follow the example of Jesus in an effort to discern what God would have us do.

What experience have we had that resembles the one of Jesus in the garden?

Day 211

> *Then Jesus entered the temple and drove out all who were selling and buying in the temple, and he overturned the tables of the money changers and the seats of those who sold doves. He said to them, It is written, "My house shall be called a house of prayer; but you are making it a den of robbers."* (Matt 21:12–13)

Jesus gave us ethical guidance by what he said and by what he did. What is so remarkable about his life is that he incarnated his values and lived in harmony with them. He was a person of great freedom and integrity. And if he truly shared our full humanity, we find ourselves asking how he did it. How did he understand so clearly what his values were and how they matched up with the will and way of God, and how did he live so consistently in harmony with them? My reading, my experience, and my intuition are limited, but I begin with the following observations about this question.

1. He worked hard to understand the will and way of God. He was likely educated in the regional temple, perhaps in Nazareth. He heard the stories of the Hebrew Bible, was familiar with Abraham and Moses, and was reminded of their dedication by his mother. In short, Jesus understood what was important; *he could see clearly.*

2. Not only did he understand, he became motivated to follow in the footsteps of these very human, but also exemplary models. *The stories motivated him.* He dreamed about what his life might be like if he were to move from regional carpenter to national prophet. He left the village of Nazareth at about the age of thirty to visit his cousin John the Baptist, who was a prophet, to learn what might be involved.

3. During the visit, he learned that the work would be difficult, and that he *needed to be empowered*. He was baptized, although John questioned why, and the confirmation came in that experience. He heard the voice of God. He then left for the desert to prepare himself for his life work.

4. Next, he returned to Galilee and *got involved* in his life's work. He learned the will and way of God by doing it.

What has been your pattern for sensing your life calling or purpose in life?

Day 212

Now when Jesus came into the district of Caesarea Philippi, he asked his disciples, "Who do people say that the Son of Man is?" And they said, "Some say John the Baptist, but others Elijah, and still others Jeremiah or one of the prophets." He said to them, "But who do you say that I am?" Simon Peter answered, "You are the Messiah, the Son of the living God." (Matt 16:13–16)

We conclude this unit on opening inward for ethical guidance and practice, and turn to one final unit in the larger theme of opening inward. It is called opening inward for peace and purpose. We have touched lightly on this theme, but need to look at it more directly. As we do, we will reflect on the life of Jesus as the model of one who was a person of peace and purpose. We will put the emphasis on the Jesus of history, while remaining aware of the complexity of accessing the Jesus of history and understanding his inner life. Our biblical text complicates the issue by describing the identity of Jesus as messiah. We are not sure he understood himself as the chosen one, but we are sure that some of his followers thought of him in the category of messiah. We will say more about the identity of Jesus as Messiah in the next unit. But for now, we can be sure that Jesus was the kind of person that his contemporaries may have thought the expected messiah would be. Let's look at four of these qualities as a transition:

1. As I read and study the life and teachings of Jesus, I sense that he was a person of integrity. *He had a single overarching purpose*, and was therefore integrated. He truly wanted to do the will and way of God

2. Because he followed this purpose, we sense that he was a *person of deep peace*, not conflicted by a range of impulses. He had a mindful spiritual life that gave him serenity, even though his public life was demanding.

3. He had deep and abiding values, and as he became engaged in the complexities of life, he called upon *the principle of love*, which gave him the ability to respond compassionately rather than reacting in anger.

4. To say all of this in summary, we affirm that Jesus had *the power* to stay with his mission to the end.

What categories would you chose to describe Jesus?

Study Guide for the July Readings

Questions for Contemplation and Discussion

1. How is our emotional health related to our capacity to follow our moral compass and practice what we believe?
2. In what ways does our spiritual vitality motivate us to live in harmony with our ethical values?
3. In what ways do our past environment and current context shape our ethical values and practices? How much are we influenced by others and the norms of our culture?
4. What is it that motivates us to live lives of love and compassion, and to seek the welfare of others? Does the model of a great religious leader, such as Jesus, motivate you? Is the notion of the golden rule a guide for you?
5. How do we maintain our capacity to be empathetic and to identify with the needs of others? Are you so preoccupied with your own needs and desires that there is little energy left to be concerned about the needs and desires of others?
6. Do you find yourself attracted to the basic guidelines of Buddhist ethical practice? Or do you find these teachings a bit old-fashioned, which only make sense in a former time and for a particular religious group of monks? Is there a way to dust them off for our contemporary life?
7. Do you affirm the basic teachings of the Ten Commandments? Or do you find them a bit outdated as well? And is there a way to reframe them for contemporary life?
8. Do you tend to think that you have the capacity within you to live a moral life, or do you think that you need the empowering grace of God and a community to support you?
9. How do you discern the will of God for your way of life?
10. Are there specific needs in your context that you have the skill to address? What are they?

THEME FOR AUGUST

OPENING INWARD FOR PEACE AND PURPOSE

Day 213

I can do nothing on my own. As I hear, I judge; and my judgment is just, because I seek to do not my own will but the will of him who sent me. (John 5:30)

We will be exploring in this unit the ways that we find inner peace and purpose. Our theme will be developed with the simple logic of getting ourselves together as a person, and from this base of inner stability to discern our purpose and pursue it with energy and diligence. Jesus, as our records indicate, often used this simple logic as he spoke to his contemporaries. He resisted the temptation to claim that what he did was because he was divine (although he was certainly God-centered) and gave God the credit for his extraordinary ministry of teaching and healing. The Gospel accounts give us story after story of a Jesus who is authentic, congruent, and poised, and who knows who he is and lives in harmony with his God-shaped identity. From that center, he carried out his mission of compassion, and incarnated and proclaimed the kingdom of God. As a charismatic teacher, he gave insight and wisdom about the way to live; as a compassionate healer, he tended the sick and physically challenged; and as a radical prophet, he proclaimed the way to establish a just and peaceful social order. He was a person of peace and purpose. Christians, therefore, look to Jesus to find a pattern for a life of peace and purpose. He is their model, and they seek to follow him by "having the mind of Christ."[1] In our previous daily readings, we have spoken to this issue, especially in the unit entitled "Opening Inward for Emotional Health and Wholeness." We want to continue to develop this theme and link it to finding our purpose in life. Five subjects will guide us as we build the base of inner peace and find guidance for our purpose in life: (1) the meaning of wholeness; (2) discerning our gifts and talents; (3) the context of our calling or purpose; (4) our specific role; and (5) sustaining our emotional and spiritual health.

Do you feel content about how you are living your life? Any changes?

---

1. See Reynolds, *Living the Mind of Christ*.

Day 214

Mindfulness attention to any experience is liberating. Mindfulness brings perspective, balance, and freedom.[2]

I have found life-changing wisdom in the Buddhist way. Their practices have helped me to reduce high levels of stress and anxiety. Buddhist teaching and practices have assisted me in both finding and maintaining a level of inner peace and serenity that provide a base for the challenges of each day. I have learned to live more in the moment, not to judge what is going on within me and around me, and to respond to the circumstances of life with a measure of wisdom and compassion, rather than reacting out of disagreement, threat, and fear. Of course, there are many times that I have waivered from being mindful and trusting my spiritual center. However, even in these circumstances, I have been able to look back at them, learn from them, forgive myself, and move forward to another day.

I generally speak about these patterns in my life in Christian language, although the Buddhist vocabulary is very valuable to me as well, and often communicates to others in a similar place in life. As a Christian, I say with Paul, "To set the mind on the flesh is death, but to set the mind on the Spirit is life and peace" (Rom 8:6). The Apostle, in using the word translated into English as "flesh," is saying that we should not yield to the instincts of threat and fear, and react in self-seeking, defensive, and angry ways. The life centered on the Spirit, understood as the power and presence of God in one's life, empowers us to find good ways of preserving our inner tranquility and being wise and compassionate in emotionally laden circumstances. I am able to be kind to myself, and to be kind and caring to those around me. I function best when I am at peace; when at peace, I am able to go forward, grounded in my purpose in life, and express it in the tangible interactions and challenges of a given day and week.

Do you have a tendency to react in challenging circumstances, or are you able to respond with wisdom and compassion?

---

2. Kornfield, *The Wise Heart*, 97.

Day 215

Recognize the mental states that fill consciousness. Shift from unhealthy ones to healthy ones.[3]

On occasion, we have used the word "wholeness" to refer to an inner state of integration, one in which the various pieces of our inner life are integrated and have become a smooth working whole. In that state, there is coherence, defined by Daniel Siegel as "connection, openness, harmony, engagement, receptivity, emergence, noesis, compassion, and empathy."[4] To expand on his definition, to be integrated is to have a coherent center that connects the components of our inner life, gives us openness to the realities of life and ourselves, enables us to find harmony within, and to engage our circumstances with receptivity. We enable what is emerging to become thoughtful (noetic), and with this base, we are able to respond with compassion and empathy. In his book, Dr. Siegel, whom we quoted earlier, traces the ways that mindfulness is both influenced by the brain and the way that the brain is modified by mindfulness. As we are healthy and send the brain mindful messages, the brain being modified sends us wise and compassionate signals in return.

The Buddhist construct of mind is a three-part system, one that describes how we function in a coherent way. The first part is all of the impressions received through our senses: sights, sounds, tastes, smells, touch, and thoughts and feelings. Note that thoughts and feelings are part of our receiving senses. Part two is the actual time that our consciousness receives these sense experiences, the present. The third part contains the mental states such as memory, stability, the feeling states of pleasant or unpleasant, the will, and the energy we put into the response. The goal, of course, is to have these receptions be transformed into wisdom, love, and generosity, enabling us to function and respond with mindfulness, grace, joy, and kindness. It is a somewhat complex outline, and we'll explain it a bit more in our readings.[5]

Do you like this outline of the Buddhist pathway to health?

---

3. Ibid. 50.
4. Siegel, *The Mindful Brain*, 332.
5. See Schonert-Reichl and Roeser, *Mindfulness in Education*.

Day 216

> *The basic ingredients of well-being and compassionate social living are, in fact, teachable. Reflection is the common pathway by which our brains support such abilities, our relationships come to thrive in them, and our minds can achieve a state of internal attunement and sense of harmony.*[6]

We are maintaining that a "state of internal attunement and sense of harmony" becomes the context out of which we begin to discern the meaning of our lives and our essential purpose. Our shorthand for this condition has been health and wholeness, but some additional comments about this state may be helpful. The research suggests that, with mindfulness and careful attention to our goals, our brains learn to anticipate and prepare us for the next anticipated event. In simple language, this is how we learn and manage life with care and compassion. It is also how we are prepared to pursue our intentions. We come together, make order and coherence within, experience a sense of inner harmony and integrity, and find our purpose.

As I look back upon the flow of my life, my sense of togetherness and the reduction of internal conflicts and pulls from different directions have enabled me to discern meaning in my life and have given me a clear sense of purpose. In the Christian context, I have educated myself about the basic Christian values—faith, hope, and love—and found them emerging in the ways I live my life. I am gradually being changed by becoming active in a congregation, preparing for preaching and teaching assignments, and engaging in the disciplines of spirituality, such as prayer and meditation. These activities and practices have been transforming. I have felt "internal attunement and a sense of harmony," or to say in a slightly different way, I have felt a measure of internal peace and a sense of direction for my life. In Buddhist language, "Virtue and integrity are necessary for happiness. Guard your integrity with care."[7] Across the weeks and months and years, I have moved toward integrity and equanimity.

How would you describe your progress toward inner peace and clear purpose in life? Have there been setbacks? What has put you back on track?

---

6. Ibid., 259.
7. Kornfield, *The Wise Heart*, 333.

Day 217

Letting go and moving through life from one change to another brings the maturing of our spiritual being. In the end we discover that to love and let go can be the same thing. Both ways do not seek to possess. Both allow us to touch each moment of this changing life and allow us to be there fully for whatever arises next.[8]

Part of the gradual change that occurs has to do with letting go. The quest for change and a new consciousness can easily become an end in itself, and something that we want to possess. It may be that we want to accomplish something in order to overcome our sense of inadequacy, or have an image that will be admired, or an achievement about which we can feel self-satisfaction and pride. These needs are not totally negative in the sense that they are quite human, and may be the product of our upbringing and our relationship to our parents. We should be aware of their presence. They can even be conditions that motivate us, but to make them the end goal is to be defeated. If fact, we haven't let go. We are hanging on tight to the need to possess. The irony is that this need to possess defeats our attempt to find inner harmony and tranquility. I have learned the hard way that being preoccupied with my own internal psychic dramas soon leads to a life of self-centeredness. I am unable to move out of my preoccupation to a sense of inner freedom and peace, and it reduces my capacity to be a person for others. It is sort of a tricky maneuver to be aware of these needs, and yet be free from them in order to engage in relationships of love and compassion. It is certainly legitimate to get help with overcoming these psychic needs. As they gradually diminish, we find ourselves being able to move in the direction of having integrity with our deepest values, and being empowered to pursue our life purpose.

This tricky maneuver has been my life story. I did experience a somewhat difficult childhood, and grew up with some deep needs for self-acceptance and loving relationships. I got some help and engaged in a number of activities and practices, which have been transforming. I now sense a measure of serenity and tranquility.

How are you doing with letting go, experiencing peace, and learning to love?

---

8. Kornfield, *A Path with Heart*, 15.

Day 218

Maybe the key to Eckhart's spirituality is what he calls abgeshiedenheit, detachment. Letting go of our normal self-centered concerns is the way "to hold ourselves ready": "All attachment to any work that involves the loss of freedom to wait on God in 'the here and now,' will cause us 'to bear no fruit.'"[9]

Stefan Reynolds, in explaining the position of Meister Eckhart, acknowledges that it is difficult to let go and not be preoccupied with our daily concerns. As Eckhart taught, we must free ourselves from attachments; worrying, multitasking, and spending too much time with electronic devices. Even an exclusive focus on the practices of spiritual formation may take us away from the presence of God. Eckhart may be close to holding an extreme position regarding attachments, yet his point is well taken. The means soon can become the ends. The goal is to use the practices to put us fully in touch with God; God as God truly is, not the God of our imagination or an object in time and space, but the very ground of being. So we empty (*ledig*) ourselves as we approach God. This is often as much a goal as a reality, and I am persuaded that it is very difficult. Meditation and centering prayer have been helpful to me, although I confess to frequently having a distracted mind and a concern for the tasks of the day. I have found three ways that have helped in addition to the practices of meditation and centering prayer:

1. The first is to try not to judge myself too harshly in anticipation of a quiet period. I tell myself that I am what I am because of so much that has happened in my life. Yes, I am responsible for what I have done, but I forgive myself and appropriate the deep Christian belief in the grace and forgiveness of God. If I go to my time with God with a measure of self-acceptance and love, then I am freed from preoccupation with guilt and all that I must do to make up for the ways I have failed. It helps me to calm my spirit and be in the Presence.

Are the feelings of guilt and shame constant companions in your time alone in quiet moments?

---

9. Reynolds, *Living with the Mind of Christ*, 115.

Day 219

We seek to know God himself, beyond the objects which he has had made and which confront us as "things" isolated from one another. . . . Our minds cannot set limits to him or to his love.[10]

2. In addition, I try to come to God with my life somewhat planned and organized so that I do not spend all the quiet moments feeling anxious and planning for what I must do in order to catch up or at least stay even. I tend to be a list-maker, and if those lists are in place and up to date, I am free from having my mind dart to all that I have to do today and in the rest of the week. It helps me to have a plan for the day, and a timetable for what I must do to keep life together for the immediate future. I still struggle to stay in the present, and as a Christian to be focused on the Presence, I am making some progress.

3. Further, I find that I am able to engage in contemplative prayer if I can leave all of the suffering of life behind. I find liberation in not going back across the years and reviewing all the ways I have been hurt by others and by circumstances. In particular, I consciously forgive those who may have hurt or continue to offend me in my daily encounters with them. I have some wounds from childhood, and there have been occasional times with colleagues and family that have been filled with conflict and misunderstanding. In quiet moments, it is easy to return to those times, re-live them, and have some negative feelings. I try to focus on forgiveness—not that I can change the past, but I can change the ways I think and feel about the past. For example, I can picture my father as a boy who did not have all the love he needed from his parents. I can envision him as one who struggled with life, not as a person in the role of father who wasn't always nurturing with me. I can feel genuine empathy for him and know that he did not intentionally set out to hurt me. In short, I can let go and let God heal me and fill me with love.

Do you find it difficult to be free from preoccupation with the past?

---

10. Merton, *Contemplative Prayer*, 79.

Day 220

> *Now there are varieties of gifts, but the same Spirit; and there are varieties of services, but the same Lord; and there are varieties of activities, but the same God who activates them in everyone. To each is given the manifestation of the Spirit for the common good.* (1 Cor 12:4–7)

The Apostle Paul, in helping the new Christians in the church at Corinth to find some order and positive rhythms in their common life, writes to them about the distribution of different gifts, services, and activities. To use a contemporary metaphor, he speaks to them like a coach might speak to a team. He says that each person has a place on the team and a contribution to make for the common good. In another section of this chapter in the Corinthian letter, Paul uses the metaphor of the body, and says that all parts of the body are necessary for its health and efficiency. He remarks, "The eye cannot say to the hand, 'I have no need of you,' nor again the head to the feet, 'I have no need of you.'"

As we open inward, we seek a place of quiet peace in order to discern our purpose in life. We ask ourselves what we might do for the good of the team, the health of the body, and for the common good. We begin to assess our gifts and talents as we seek a place in society. Paul's wisdom suggests that we should look at a range of qualities and characteristics in our lives. He speaks about gifts, for example, and he says that they are God-given. We have taken Paul's notion and made it an integral part of the way we often describe people. We speak of them as being "especially gifted" and imply that the gift comes from the Creator. Of course, our notion of being gifted has a secular and scientific application as well. We often say that the gifts that a person possesses are genetic and inherited from the parents.

Paul has a particular application of this notion of gifts as he writes to the Corinthians. It is evident from the letter that there was some conflict in the church over who had particular responsibilities, and some questions about who made decisions. He seeks to guide them with his metaphors of gifts and the body.

How would you describe your gifts, and how do you use them?

Day 221

> *We have gifts that differ according to the grace given to us: prophecy, in proportion to faith; ministry, in ministering; the teacher, in teaching; the exhorter, in exhortation; the giver, in generosity; the leader, in diligence; the compassionate, in cheerfulness.* (Rom 12:6–8)

The Apostle Paul also wrote to the new Christians in Rome about the distribution of talents and gifts for the welfare of the church and the common good. I am struck by his choice of talents and gifts that illustrate his point. I suspect he could have listed several others, but he selects just a few as examples to make his point. The first is the gift of prophecy. We often think of prophecy as predicting the future. Prophecy may point to the future, but does so from the perspective of the present. The prophet is the one in the community in this case; the community being the church, which has the responsibility to ensure that there is justice and fairness. The prophet may say, often speaking to leaders, that if there is not a change, it is likely that there will be conflict and people will suffer. In our time, we often think of people such as Martin Luther King Jr., who, in his prophetic role, pointed to the racial injustice that existed in the United States and called on the leaders of the nation to pass laws insuring justice for all. It is not an easy role, and requires a good measure of faith, as Paul says: "prophecy, in proportion to faith."

Paul goes on to illustrate his point about the distribution of gifts for the common good. He speaks of ministry, the role that all people have to help others heal and move toward maturity. Often, when we use the word "ministry," we think of those who have been educated for the professional life of the ordained ministry, but Paul is more inclined to say that all people in the church (and to extend his point, people in society) can contribute to the well-being of others. It is the ordained minister who may have special responsibilities within a congregation, but all are called to some form of ministry. He continues with his illustrations, and speaks of the teacher who has a special talent for communicating helpful information and for leading people to life-changing insight. In both the church and society, we have a desperate need for excellent teachers.

What do you think your special gifts might be for the common good?

Day 222

Do not neglect the gift that is in you, which has been given to you through prophecy with the laying on of hands by the council of elders. (1 Tim 4:14)

In the early church community and in the larger context of the church, there was a great respect for the wisdom of elders. There was a meaningful tradition and custom of laying hands on a person, which symbolized the passing of wisdom from one generation to another. As the young Timothy assumes responsibility, the church confirms his calling and gifts in this fashion. With this tradition in mind, we return to Paul's illustration of the nature of gifts for the common good. The next one that he mentions is the gift of exhortation, the ability to inform and inspire others to use their gifts for the well-being of all. I am grateful for those who exhorted me in my early years of formation. There were those whom I admired, who seemed to always have the right ideas expressed in clear and profound ways. I was inspired and guided by them. Now, in my senior years, I know, especially as I look within, that they too were not perfect, yet they used their gifts for the common good.

Paul goes on to mention two other gifts. He says that there is the gift of giving, which should be done with generosity. Whether it is the widow's mite (Mark 12:42–44), or the rich young ruler who went away sorrowful (Matt 19:16–22), there is the clear message in the teaching of Jesus that we are to share our wealth and help those who have so little. The widow, rather than the rich young man, was the generous one. Paul goes on to speak about those with the gift of leadership. The current emphasis on the cultivation of the skills of effective leadership is extremely welcome, and there are ways to develop these gifts of leadership. Paul could have used several words to illustrate the practice of leadership, but his choice of one word is significant; the leader has the quality of *diligence* and gives careful attention to what is required for progress. His final illustration of the distribution of gifts for the common good is compassion. The common good does require those with compassion, the capacity to see the suffering of others and to do something to remove the suffering. There is no greater gift!

How might you discern your gifts, and how might you enhance them?

Day 223

> *The Buddha... introduces the mental qualities necessary for walking the path: one needs to be ardent, clearly knowing, and mindful, free from desires and discontent in regard to the world.*[11]

The Buddhist tradition is somewhat different from the Christian way, as it guides its followers in opening inward for peace and purpose. I have found it very stimulating to compare and contrast the ways of the two traditions. Both have a source to consult, the Bible for the Christian and the Dharma (the spiritual teachings) for the Buddhist. Both affirm that following certain principles and virtues will lead to a peaceful and purposeful life. Both also affirm that each person has the capacity for growth and the development of certain qualities that will lead to a serene and meaningful life. Let's turn to brief review of the Buddhist way.[12]

In the first place, the Buddhist tradition teaches that one must be ardent, dedicated to pursuing the path that liberates the heart and mind. In using the term ardent, they say that one must engage in a balanced and sustained effort, one with attachment, commitment, and a passionate enthusiasm to the way. One does not achieve gratifying levels of enlightenment without an ardent effort. A second quality necessary for progress toward peace and purpose is to study and reflect on the principles of growth and development. There is the need for clearly knowing and cultivating deep comprehension. We need to be able to envision where we are going (toward enlightenment) and how to get there (a range of practices). Awareness of motivation plays a central role in the path toward liberation, and requires a good measure of self-understanding. It is when we slow down, become less judgmental of ourselves, less selfish in reference to the way we try to meet our needs, and become calm in spirit, that we begin to make progress toward peace and purpose, inner tranquility and loving kindness. It is possible to become calm, give attention to the present moment, have integrity, and be true to our values.

What are the best ways for you to be calm in the presence of life's storms?

---

11. Goldstein, *Mindfulness*, 4.
12. Ibid., 3–23.

Day 224

> *Mindfulness is this aspect of the quality of bare attention, of non-interfering awareness, which we're familiar with from our enjoyment of music. When we're listening to the music, our minds are open and attentive, not attempting to control what comes next, not reflecting on the notes just past.*[13]

The third quality of the pathway to peace and purpose is mindfulness, that quality of life about which we have already spoken, one that has many levels of meaning. As we have underlined before, it is present-moment awareness, the capacity to live in the present and have presence of mind. The Pali word *sati* also implies that we must remember the principles and practices that lead to peace and purpose, and direct us on the path of awakening. If we don't remember them, it is very easy to slip back into the harmful habits of being narrow-minded, closed-hearted, and selfish; to worry about the past; and to be anxious about the future. To be mindful is to have a balanced perspective and be able to see the dangers of self-destructive behavior. It protects us from yielding to the alluring temptations of our materialistic culture. Mindfulness has a supervising and guarding function, enabling us to guard against unwholesome states of mind. A fourth attribute in the Buddhist tradition that we need to cultivate to achieve high levels of peace and clarity about purpose is concentration. To concentrate on the virtues and practices of the Buddhist way will empower and enable us to find composure and be focused; we can unify the many dimensions of our mind. It will give us freedom from unhealthy desires and the discontents that so easily creep into our consciousness. There are several ways to maintain high levels of concentration that are common to most of the great religious traditions of humankind. We need to engage in meditation and prayer, continue our daily reading, and participate in the disciplines integral to yoga. It is also important to join a community of support, the Sangha, and gain wisdom and encouragement from others on the same pathway. It is then possible to move into the confusing mix of everyday life with the maturity and freedom to show compassion for those who suffer and are lost.

What can you learn from Buddhist way, even if you belong to another religion?

---

13. Ibid., 14.

Day 225

> *The first is* Islam, *which means "surrender in peace." What we are surrendering is attachment to our ego so that there is space for God in the center of our lives.*[14]

Islam leads with the answer to the question of how we open inward to find peace and purpose. It is contained in the Five Pillars that make Islam an easy religion to understand, at least at its center. As with all religions, however, there are many details in Islam that take a lifetime to learn and to practice. The first Pillar says, "There is no god but God, and Muhammad is a Messenger of God." To affirm and commit to this statement is to become a Muslim, and to rest in faith on this affirmation is to find the peace of God's love and to surrender to God's will (purpose). To sustain such a commitment is to make prayer an integral part of your life (second pillar). Muslims are commanded to pray five times per day as a way of keeping one's faith and commitment firm and at the forefront of one's life. The third pillar is to give alms and live generously by helping those who are in need and marginalized. In addition to total surrender to God, praying five times per day, and give giving generously, there is, as a fourth pillar, a month set aside for the discipline of the spiritual life and for self-purification (Ramadan). The fifth Pillar, the Hajj, also points to dedication, and requires that all able-bodied Muslims make at least one pilgrimage to Mecca in the twelfth month of the Islamic calendar. It means to visit the holy site in the presence of millions of other Muslims, and to sense that one belongs to a universal religion. The word *jihad* is a more general term, comparable to commitment, and means to commit to the ways of faith and to protect the faith. In these ways, spelled out in detail within the faith community, Muslims discover the way of turning inward for a life filled with peace and purpose. As with other religious traditions, these beliefs and practices are sustained by teachers (imams) and by regular attendance at the weekly worship held on Fridays. It has been my observation, as I have spoken to many faithful Muslims, that they feel they are on the right path. They have found peace and purpose.

Why do you think that Islam is one of the fastest growing religions in the world today?

---

14. Rahman, *Spiritual Gems of Islam*, 8.

Day 226

> *Beloved, do not believe every spirit, but test the spirits to see whether they are from God; for many false prophets have gone out into the world.* (1 John 4:1)

The Christian church, especially in its early years of formation, was concerned with making sure that her adherents did not lose their way. In fact, most of the world's religions have had this concern, and have attempted to guide the faithful and keep them on the right path. Some religions have said there is more than one path to follow, and have had the spirit of leniency in guiding followers. Others have maintained that the path is narrow, and have attempted to keep their followers on the true path. To a large extent, the guidance from those in authority has had two dimensions, the general direction that one should follow, and the specific direction that each individual should follow. For example, within the Christian faith, there is the broad direction of believing in God, accepting the life and teachings of Jesus, and making love the central virtue. In addition, there is the belief that each person has a specific calling in life.

It is so easy to get lost along the way and to follow a direction that leads to self-destructive behavior. The author of the first letter of John speaks about "spirits," and likely believed they were literally present, inviting us to follow a false way. I am more inclined to take this passage in a metaphorical, rather than literal, way; that is to say, that there is a tug on us to go in a direction that will be harmful to us. The author of 1 John had a specific movement in mind as he writes his letter. The movement was called Gnosticism, and it maintained that there was a special knowledge and a pattern of life that was different from Christian belief and practice; he urges his readers to "test the spirits" to make sure they are not led astray by a sectarian movement. He goes on to speak about the nature of God and the way of life that flows from one whose faith is in the true God. He speaks of God as light and love, with light being a metaphor for truth. He maintains that truth and love are the central components of our faith, with truth guiding our way and love the heart of our relationships and way of life. I have found that a life focused on reality and the truth, as well as a commitment to make love the primary value in life, keeps me on the right path and gives me peace and purpose.

Are there times when you have lost your way, and do you know what caused it?

Day 227

> *This is the message we have heard from him and proclaim to you, that God is light and in him there is no darkness at all.* (1 John 1:5)

We might think for a moment about the fundamental questions we are asking as we turn inward for peace and purpose. I find myself generating tentative answers to four questions:

1. What is the frame of reference and the context I am currently in as I seek answers?
2. What is my worldview, and how is it articulated in what I believe?
3. What is the way of life I am choosing in making a commitment to a worldview and a spiritual way?
4. What do I need to do, and what steps do I need to take, to live with integrity in this spiritual journey?

Let's begin with question one. We all live in a certain time and place in history. It is different than the one in which Buddha, Jesus, or Muhammad lived. This time and place suggests a way of viewing reality, makes assumptions about how to know what is true, and uses a certain method and a language to describe what is true and good. There are also many cultural norms that we assume are the way to live, although we occasionally will challenge the prevailing cultural norms and patterns of life, and move into a more counter-cultural style of life. I will illustrate from the Christian frame of reference that I have chosen, not because it is the only way, but because I know it best, and have some grounds for speaking about it. It could be done from one of the other great religious or philosophical traditions, but I speak with more knowledge and some integrity about the Christian way. I expect readers outside of the Christian way to make an application within their outlook on life. Let me also add that, within a large worldview such as Christianity or Islam or Buddhism, and even within a postmodern and scientific outlook, there will be a family of partial outlooks that shape one's beliefs and practices. For example, not all Christians have the same views.

In a few sentences, how would you describe your worldview?

Day 228

Beloved, let us love one another, because love is from God; everyone who loves is born of God and knows God. Whoever does not love does not know God, for God is love. (1 John 4:7–8)

Let me begin, then, with some thoughts about how Christians might begin to answer the four questions listed in yesterday's readings. Again, I want to underline that Christians who live in different times and places are exposed to alternative outlooks and ways of understanding the Christian faith. They function and make sense of life from within different cultures that will give them slightly different answers. Of course, there are followers of the many different spiritual pathways of the human family (including Christians) who may say that their way is the only way. I confess to having some difficulty with these fundamentalist views, but do affirm the people who hold them if their outlook brings them deep peace and a life-giving purpose. I prefer an attitude that is more willing to say that God, or Transcendence, speaks many languages and communicates within the narrow band of everyone's language and culture. I share the outlook of the Dalai Lama, who has said in many different ways that Jesus was a Buddha, and Christians should follow the way of Jesus.

Here are a few words, then, about how I as a Christian might begin to answer the four questions and how they help me find peace and purpose. The first question is about the frame of reference in which I start and the context in which I currently reside and reflect about life's basic questions. There are a few obvious answers. For example, I start with living in the first half of the twenty-first century and live in the United States. Because I do, I have a certain way of understanding that helps me find my way, far different than those of Moses or Buddha. I have traveled in about seventy-five countries and observed different ways of belief and different ways of life. It has helped me to understand that my ways and beliefs are relative, although I hope that some of what I believe, say, and do points to ultimate reality and Holy Presence. As I ponder this notion of transcendence, I learn from my tradition, read the Bible, and find the affirmations of the author of 1 John, that God is light and love, quite convincing.

How would you describe your frame of reference and context?

Day 229

In the beginning was the Word, and the Word was with God, and the Word was God. . . . And the Word became flesh and lived among us, and we have seen his glory, the glory of a father's only son, full of grace and truth. (John 1:1, 14)

In my worldview, I bring together and integrate the description of God as light and love in 1 John and the beginning of John's Gospel that speaks about the Word. The author says that the Word came in human form as grace (love) and truth. I believe that God spoke in a variety of ways to humankind, and profoundly and redemptively in the personal word of Jesus of Nazareth. The notion of the "word" (*logos* in the Greek) was current in the time of Jesus. It was used in Stoicism, and it referred to that which gives order and meaning to all of creation. *Logos* was seen as the coordinating and integrating principle of the cosmos, giving it order, design, and meaning. The human task is to understand it and discern its meaning for guidance in life. The author of John's Gospel uses *logos*, and says that the God of truth and love has spoken (word) in the coming of Jesus; and in his life, teaching, death, and resurrection, we find peace and purpose in life. This brief paragraph is partial and only suggests a direction.

From this direction, I begin to answer question two about my worldview and how it is articulated. I think about it in a different way than these first-century authors did. I am on this side of the rise of science, and have a sense of the complexity and grandeur of the cosmos. It is a bit of a reach to believe that the one who spoke of Jesus as the Word two thousand years ago adequately explains the cosmos or even the tiny speck in the cosmos, earth. Yet for me, it is a place to start and to use the notion of *logos* as a hint about meaning and order. I also read the literature of other great religions, and I sense that they too only give hints, and in many very helpful ways these hints complement my own views. The big picture in the Vedas and the psychology and ethics of Buddhism do not so much challenge my view as they do complement it. So too does modern evolutionary theory, whether it speaks about the cosmos or human development. I work at integration, and join with people from other religions, philosophers, and scientists, asking them for guidance.

How do you tell others about what you believe and how it helps you?

Day 230

He has told you, O mortal, what is good: and what does the Lord require of you but to do justice, and to love kindness, and to walk humbly with your God?
(Mic 6:8)

From the context and environment in which I live come a variety of influences on me and several choices about the values that will shape the color and direction of my life (question three). I suspect that I am more affected by these factors that I am able to recognize. There are many assumptions I make about goodness, truth, and beauty that are built into my culture and language, some of which I may not see or at least go deep enough to observe their influence. In my daily walk, there are a variety of choices, and I sense that I have the freedom to make these choices, even though the voices from my background and surroundings will echo in my conscience. Let me give an example. I might dislike another person and seek quite intentionally to harm them. I might impulsively choose to return evil for good, even though this person has really done nothing to harm me except to cause some discomfort or irritation. I hear several voices about how I might respond. If another person actually harms me in some way, I might choose to see the person who has inflicted the harm as an enemy and sense that I should get even. I could also reply in kind and feel that there is some kind of legal basis for my response. But there is a third response rooted in the example and teaching of Jesus; I return good for the harm done to me. I forgive, cleanse my soul of resentment, and treat the other person as having values and feelings as one created in the image of God. I hear the voice of Jesus, who taught: "But I say to you, Love your enemies and pray for those who persecute you" (Matt 5:44). It is this way of life that is implied in the Christian worldview that I have chosen. I may have to say no to the voices of impulse and culture, rise above protective instincts, and choose kindness rather than revenge.

Due to the worldview I have chosen, I am motivated to rise above some instinctive feelings, even some norms in my culture, and choose to love my neighbor as I love myself. Opening inward, I see the ways that I need love, and especially that I need to forgive in love if I violate my values and intentionally hurt another.

Are you able to make choices to love, especially in the moment of being hurt?

Day 231

"Teacher, which commandment in the law is the greatest?" He said to him, "You shall love the Lord your God with all your heart, and with all your soul, and with all your mind. This is the greatest and first commandment. And a second is like it: You shall love your neighbor as yourself. On these two commandments hang all the law and the prophets." (Matt 2:36–40)

As I choose a Christian worldview, I need to be sure that I have good answers for the last question about opening inward for peace and purpose. The question is, how do I sustain a consistent pattern of life that has integrity with the values of the Christian way? How am I able, with the many currents of my culture that suggest an alternative way, to truly love my neighbor? As I measure my own levels of maturity and sense that there are miles to go before I reach levels of maturity, I continue to ask how I can truly love my neighbor. As I try to answer this question, I find myself thinking about four categories: (1) the model of the life of Jesus that inspires and teaches me; (2) personal practices that cultivate the motivation and ability to practice loving kindness; (3) the community of the church that informs and sustains me in pursuing the Christian way; and (4) the movement into the world to serve, giving attention to individuals I encounter daily and also being conscious of the ways I may help to secure a more just and humane social order for them.

By my choices to engage in the life of the mind and the life of the spirit, I have been able make some progress in understanding the model of the life of Jesus and to grasp the radical nature of his teaching. My pattern is not the norm for everyone; not all need to do advanced studies and research Jesus extensively.[15] But it has been a way for me as I sought ordination and chose to do doctoral studies in Christian origins. It has been a good way for me, yet the vast majority of people will not select this route. However, some exposure by reading, by taking classes, and by reflecting on the life of Jesus as a compassionate healer and radical prophet will inevitably guide and inspire. A reading of the New Testament, especially the Gospels, captures the heart.

How much are you inspired and guided by the example of another person?

---

15. See Ferguson, *The Radical Teaching of Jesus*.

Day 232

Let love be genuine; hate what is evil, hold fast to what is good; love one another with mutual affection; outdo one another in showing honor. Do not lag in zeal, be ardent in spirit, serve the Lord. Rejoice in hope, be patient in suffering, persevere in prayer. Contribute to the needs of the saints; extend hospitality to strangers. (Rom 12:9–13)

The Apostle Paul, in writing to the new Christian community in Rome, takes up our question of how to sustain the Christian way with integrity. He guides them and suggests several personal practices that will motivate them. He leads with love and underlines that love must be genuine. The feelings of attraction we have for others on occasion can be mixed, especially when we are sexually attracted to another. Paul does select the term *agape*, rather than *eros*, in speaking about genuine love, and says that this kind of love must be pure in its desire to enhance the well-being of the other person. He uses a strong word, often translated as hate, and it implies avoiding and resisting that which harms another. He counsels that we should seek the good that will lead others to lives of peace and purpose, and do so by expressing loving ways and honoring their worth. In addition, be zealous about it, not passive. Paul employs a word translated as "ardent" that has the connotation of deep commitment. In these ways, we serve the Lord. In a setting where confusion and discouragement could be contagious, he says to be hopeful while enduring the inevitable suffering that nearly all of us feel at times. He moves to the personal practice of prayer, that mode of life that seeks dialogue with God and maintains constant communion. Paul then urges them to be generous and to take care of those in need, and he goes on to urge them to be hospitable with strangers.

In these ways, as they become a constant pattern of life, we are able to have integrity in our spiritual journey. Living spiritually does require constant practical and ethical choices, and it also becomes easier as we are more habitual in our practices. It is like the muscle memory of the great athlete who naturally does what those with lack of practice will never be able to do. Paul's counsel anticipates that this group of Christians in Rome will face severe challenges, and even persecution.

What are some ways that you might improve your spiritual practices?

Day 233

> *The gifts he gave were that some would be apostles, some prophets, some evangelists, some pastors and teachers, to equip the saints for the work of ministry, for building up the body of Christ. We must no longer be children, tossed to and fro and blown away by every wind of doctrine . . but speaking the truth in love, we must grow up in every way into him who is the head, into Christ, from whom the whole body, joined and knit together . . is working properly . . building itself up in love.* (Eph 4:11–16)

The Ephesian letter continues the trend to help these new churches find their way and help their members to continue on their spiritual journey. We follow the example of Jesus and engage in spiritual practices to cultivate our faith. In addition, we belong to a community of like-minded people called the church. It is in this beloved community that we are informed and sustained in our faith. Nearly all of the great religions have a community that meets to guide and nurture their members. The Jewish people in the time of Jesus had such communities. It is likely that Jesus received some of his education in a Jewish synagogue. These new Christians, many of whom still thought of themselves as Jewish, met on regular basis for support and encouragement. As the Gentile churches began to flourish, this same model prevailed. It is in the church that we continue to be supported and learn about our spiritual journey. The letters of Paul, who helped to found and serve the Gentile community, lay out a partial design for these congregations. He says that there will be those in the churches with different gifts to take on a variety of responsibilities. He knows that many of these new Christians need guidance, cautions them about being taken in by the range of viewpoints in the settings of these new churches, and urges people to gather together in a loving spirit and support one another.

To sustain our spiritual lives and live in harmony with our values, we too need a supporting community. We can be tossed to and fro in the multi-cultural and pluralistic culture in which we live. Time alone in prayer and contemplation can be very good, but we also need to be a part of supporting community with good teaching, pastoral care, and a loving spirit. While our faith journey is personal, it will not be sustained in isolation.

In what ways does a church or community of like-minded people sustain you?

Day 234

From now on, therefore, we regard no one from a human point of view, even though we once knew Christ from a human point of view, we know him no longer in that way. So if anyone is in Christ, there is a new creation; everything old has passed away; see, everything has become new! All this is from God, who reconciled us to himself through Christ, and has given us the ministry of reconciliation. (2 Cor 5:16–18)

As Christians, we sustain our spiritual journey by following the example of Jesus, with disciplined practices, and supported in a community life filled with love and guidance. Jesus added another dimension to the spiritual journey as well, that of service. We can be thankful for sensing God's gracious love; we are reconciled to God and have been given insight and guidance about sustaining this relationship. We have been invited into a loving community in which we find support and guidance. We are now called to share this good news with others. Note that what we are called to share is reconciliation. There are some risks in this task. There are some parts of the Christian church that believe they must convert those who have not embraced a particular Christian way. I do honor these movements, although at times feel uncomfortable when they harshly judge the beliefs of other religions and say that if they don't convert to Christ, they will be condemned. I feel that there is a better way, which is to take seriously the ministry of reconciliation. Yes, we need to be in harmony with God, but there are many ways to experience the grace and guidance of God. At times in our quest to convert others, we build barriers rather than reconcile with others. We are called to serve, not out of the arrogance of believing that we alone have the truth, but out of humility and service to those in need. People may endorse our way of faith, but our task is to build bridges of understanding, to bring people together for the common good, and to make life better for the marginalized. We will say more about this ministry in the next section. But for now, we are saying that part of our growth and development in our spiritual lives is to find ways to serve and share in the wider ministry of the Christian church. It is a ministry of love and mercy, not a ministry of saying we are right and you are wrong. We incarnate God's gracious love for all of life in the acts of service. We find a way to contribute to the ministry of reconciliation.

What might be some ways that you can engage in the ministry of reconciliation?

Day 235

Pause before judging. Pause before assuming. Pause before accusing. Pause whenever you're about to react harshly and you'll avoid doing and saying things you'll later regret.

—Lori Deshene

We are exploring the ways we engage in looking inward in order to achieve deeper peace and serenity and to discover the ways we are called to live. We have named this endeavor of opening inward for peace and purpose. We have implied that we need to pause from time to time to remind ourselves that there are some currents in our lives that shape our attitudes and our demeanor, and we need to understand them. Our joy in life and the joy we bring to others are the result of the ways we have done the hard work of growing more mature, a process that has no end in this life. We need to cultivate an inner harmony, a spirit that is based on both self-reflection and practices that help us to become people of integrity and compassion. We have also said that the worldview of our time and place in history and the context in which we serve will guide our decisions and our way of life. There is also wisdom in further reflection on our gifts and talents, and how they shape the direction of our lives. We then can explore how it is that we sustain our emotional and spiritual health, as well as have a gracious spirit and the energy to live as a person for others.

A biblical way of thinking about this process of opening inward for peace and purpose is to say that we have general talents and are given specific spiritual gifts for the common good.[16] Some groups within the Christian church make a clear distinction between talents and gifts, suggesting that all people have an array of talents to be used to make their way in life. But each of us is given specific gifts as well by the Holy Spirit in order to serve the church and wider society. I have discovered that the general context in which I live and work, and the needs and challenges present in this context, often shape the way my gifts and talents develop and blossom. They make my life of service tangible and specific. There is a clear relationship between our gifts and our course of life.

Do you sense that what you are doing in life matches your gifts and talents?

---

16. See Brueggemann, *Journey to the Common Good.*

Day 236

Vocation does not come from willfulness. It comes from listening. I must listen to my life and try to understand what it is truly about—quite apart from what I would like it to be about—or my life will never represent anything real in the world, no matter how earnest my intentions.[17]

It took me a while to let my life speak to me about what I should be doing with my energy and talents. I was interested in sports as a boy, and I began to think about ways I might become a coach when I had passed the stage of playing. Through the college years, this interest subsided, largely because my competitive playing years were over and I was drawn to the life of the mind. I was especially interested in the history of ideas, and wondered if teaching might be a good direction. I also got involved in a variety of Christian groups, attended conferences and summer camps, and began to think about the life of the spirit focused in the professional ministry. Following my university education, I chose to go to seminary, and thought ministry would be my vocation. After a few years in campus ministry, my place of work in and adjacent to a university, the call to the life of the mind re-emerged and I moved on to graduate study. I was listening to my inner life and noticing my talents. Following my doctoral studies, I did bring my interests and my talents into a career in church-related higher education. For a while, I thought that I might go the route of senior level administration, but in time I realized that my greatest joy came from teaching and writing. With the occasional wrong turn and the challenge of just living in a healthy way in the culture of the United States, I think now that I have been on the right course in my life with both the life of the spirit and the life of the mind playing the central roles. Coupled with these themes was the motivation to be a person for others, and to use my modest talents and gifts for the well-being of others. All of this is not to say that it has always been easy; there have been some mistakes and failures. I did consider other alternatives, and now believe that I let my life guide me.

Do you think you have "let your life speak" in your choice of vocation?

---

17. Palmer, *Let Your Life Speak*, 4.

Day 237

Today we live in a blizzard of another sort. It swirls around us as economic injustice, ecological ruin, physical and spiritual violence, and their inevitable consequence, war. It swirls within us as fear and frenzy, greed and deceit, and indifference to the suffering of others.[18]

As we pursue a mindful spirituality that will give our lives tranquility, integration, maturity, order, and meaning, we will need to find our way of lending a hand in healing our broken world. I find it relatively easy to have a partial understanding of nearly all of the overwhelming challenges we face as a global community. I know I can't make a contribution to all of them, because there isn't enough time in my life, and my skill set and life direction do not match up with more than a few of the challenges. What has given me some comfort is to give vocal and financial support for many of these causes, and then to decide in what ways my gifts and talents might be used in one or two of them, ones in which I am able to make a genuine contribution. I care deeply about world hunger, about the suffering caused by war and violence, and about global warming. I learn as much as I can about these concerns and several others like them, but have decided that I can best use my gifts and talents, as well as my inner motivation and passion, in advancing education and addressing injustice. I have had to get specific about helping reduce human suffering, in all of its myriad forms, in the ways that match my life. It is been my great privilege to work in the cause of transformational education and justice in a variety of places: at home, of course, in the United States, but also in Northern Ireland, India, Pakistan, and Israel and Palestine. My contributions were limited; I was at times just a spectator, yet I have felt so privileged to be present and make a small contribution to both education and justice in these regions of the world. I was and currently am involved with tangible and specific endeavors that seek to improve the lives of people by provided high quality education and challenging injustice. As I serve in these ways, I have become keenly aware of how important volunteers can be in these endeavors.

What steps have you taken to be specific in your effort to help others?

---

18. Palmer, *A Hidden Wholeness*, 1.

Day 238

That the geological structure of the Earth and the number of species should be so vast, so diverse, and their interaction so intimate is the wonder of the known universe.[19]

Thomas Berry's observation in *The Great Work* is that our generation's essential task on earth is to save the earth, and all that dwells on it. It is possible to help in small ways by living so that we do not contribute to ecological deterioration. This I can do, as well as by being supportive of causes that reduce global warming. Yet, my scientific knowledge and my skill set are not as helpful in dealing with "The Great Work" apart from my support and lifestyle. I have found that the goal of being supportive of many of the great global challenges we face is important, and I also believe that I need to use my energy, gifts, talents, and refined skills to solve other problems that may need my expertise. So I have plunged into transformational education and the concerns of social justice. I am giving time, some talent and training, and my experience in crossing cultures to improve the educational quality of marginalized students, and to engage in efforts to achieve justice for those who live with discrimination daily. I want to help students to be educated in ways that lead them to healthy, productive, and fulfilling lives, and also teach them to accept and affirm those who are different from them, racially, ethically, or religiously. For example at the Mar Elias Educational Institutions, a small school district with K–12 education for approximately three thousand students in the region of the Galilee in Israel, I support the effort to educate students to celebrate, not resist, the presence of Jewish students, Arab Muslim students, and many Palestinian Christian students. I help with both financial support and with consultation in strategic planning. It is a way for me to use my advanced knowledge of these religious traditions, my experience in education, and the years of traveling internationally and crossing cultures. I can make an informed contribution that matches my life. Earlier, I had a similar opportunity to spend several weeks as a consultant to Forman Christian College in Lahore, Pakistan.

What specific contributions might you make to create a more just world?

---

19. Berry, *The Great Work*, 87.

Day 239

> *True maturation on the spiritual path requires that we discover the depth of our wounds: our grief from the past, unfulfilled longing, the sorrow we have stored up during the course of our lives.*[20]

I do not find it all that easy to speak about the wounds that continue to linger in my life. It sounds too much like being self-preoccupied, the strategy of getting attention with "Oh poor me" statements. On the other hand, there are times when my injuries that linger from the past really do limit me. I easily slip away into depression or turn to the extra glass of wine, both self-defeating strategies. I have looked for good settings in which to find healing for my wounds, and more often than not, I find myself hearing about the worries and wounds of others. I know, as the popular song says, "It's my own damn fault," but is only partially helpful to acknowledge that. My spouse is helpful, although I can't put the whole burden on her; she has too much vested interest. Perhaps that is why I often want to be of help to others, a good listener with helpful insight, and a wounded healer with deep empathy because of my own sorrow.

What I have discovered is that my own healing is integral to my capacity to embody a loving and wise spirituality that contributes to the healing of others. As Jack Kornfield says, "Unhealed pain and rage, unhealed traumas from childhood abuse and abandonment, become powerful unconscious forces in our lives. Until we are able to bring awareness and understanding to our old wounds, we will find ourselves repeating patterns of unfulfilled desire, anger, and confusion over and over again."[21] I continue to work on my own healing in a variety of mindful ways, living more in the present, directly facing the wounds from the past, staying physically healthy, and cultivating warm and caring relationships. Across the years, I have gradually become a better wounded healer and an empathic person for others. I am listening to my life, finding limited serenity and some clarity about purpose.

What are your wounds, and how are you finding healing from them?

---

20. Kornfield, *A Path with a Heart*, 41.
21. Ibid., 42.

Day 240

> *Do not neglect the gift that is in you . . . Put these things into practice, devote yourself to them, so that all may see your progress. Pay close attention to yourself and to your teaching, for in doing this you will save both yourself and your hearers.* (1 Tim 4:14–16)

The Apostle Paul had several colleagues as he worked diligently to carry out his sense of vocation, and what he deeply believed was his God-given mission. One of his colleagues, a younger man named Timothy, was special to Paul, perhaps like a son that he never had. Paul was a teacher and a tutor for Timothy, helping him to develop his gifts for his life calling. It was a relationship of affection, honesty, trust, and respect. In the literature we have, there are two letters addressed to Timothy, and the traditional view is that these letters came from Paul.[22] It is more likely that the letter came from another mentor, yet they are nevertheless special words to Timothy. In the first place, the author does acknowledge the talents and gifts that make Timothy effective in his mission. He uses that Greek word that has now found its way into English, "charisma." It was the deep conviction of Paul that those called to serve God are given *charismata*, or gifts to be effective in this work. The author urges Timothy to not neglect his gifts and to cultivate them. He says quite directly that Timothy should use them and devote himself to improving them in order to make progress and be ready for all the challenges of his calling. The message is clear to us as well, as we discern our gifts and talents for our life work. Richard Foster, in his fine book on Christian discipline, categorizes the steps of cultivation in three categories: The Inward Disciplines, The Outward Disciplines, and the Corporate Disciplines.[23] In the category of inward disciplines, he lists four, ones that we have thought about in discussing mindful spirituality. They are meditation, prayer, fasting, and study. The letter spoke to Timothy about these practices and urged him to incorporate them into his life. These inward disciplines are essential in sustaining the spiritual life.

What are your gifts, and how do you cultivate and practice them?

---

22. New Testament scholars are not sure who was the author of the Timothy letters.
23. Foster, *The Celebration of Discipline*, table of contents.

Day 241

One might think that silence would be valued in our religious communities, since they purport to bring us face to face with the sacred mysteries. Yet real silence is rare in most churches I know: more often the air is filled with words or other sounds.[24]

Richard Foster lists the outward disciplines as simplicity, solitude, submission, and service. I find it interesting that he would place solitude and submission as outward disciplines, in that they are practiced in the privacy of one's own heart and mind. The fact that he did place them there invited me to ponder why. In reading about them, I discovered that he links them to the preparation to move into the world in service. His outline works for me in the following ways:

1. The simple life clears away the distractions from giving attention to the cultivation of mindful spirituality and from focusing on one's purpose or mission in life. I have learned that I can't do everything, and I can hardly do anything if I do not focus my attention on the immediate task. I can carry heavy responsibilities when I have set priorities.

2. It is in solitude that I can determine what is most important. Having quiet moments away from the cacophony of contemporary life, I begin to hear the quiet voice of God, calming me, guiding me, empowering me, and directing me to do what is most important.

3. As I hear the divine voice, or perhaps read about it, I move toward submission to the divine will and way. From the peace that comes from my solitude and submission, I am energized and focused, able to move into the day with my purpose and goals clearly in mind.

4. I am guided, then, drawing upon the focus of the simple life, the comforting solitude with God, and the clarity that comes from the submission to the will and way of God to service. I am ready to take on the challenges and risks of service that may involve me in careful planning, interaction with complex people, and the barriers to serving the common good.

What are the distracting challenges you face on a typical day?

---

24. Palmer, *A Hidden Wholeness*, 159.

Day 242

Then the devil led him up and showed him in an instant all the kingdoms of the world. And the devil said to him, "To you I will give their glory and authority; for it has been given over to me, and I give it to anyone I please. If you, then, will worship me, it will be yours." Jesus answered him, "It is written, 'Worship the Lord your God, and serve only him.'" (Luke 4:5–8)

Richard Foster lists four corporate disciplines as he concludes his list of disciplines for the cultivation of the spiritual life. These are confession, worship, guidance, and celebration, all of which are to be affirmed as essential for our spiritual journey. As he gained clarity about his mission in his baptism by John, Jesus goes to the desert wilderness to prepare himself for his life's work. It is there that he faces those temptations that could distract him from his life mission. There are physical temptations, the temptations for possessions and power, and the great temptation to neglect the call to place God first in his life. Jesus has convincing arguments to fend them off, and he knows he is at peace and ready to fulfill his purpose in life. The account may be a kind of parable about what can draw us away from the life to which we are called. For Jesus, it was a life of service as a compassionate healer, a charismatic teacher, and a radical prophet. He did not yield to the temptations, and was true to his vocation. We follow his example:

1. By confessing the ways we fail and being restored to health and wholeness;
2. By worshiping God only, and always giving God's will and way the highest priority;
3. By seeking the guidance of God from the sisters and brothers who know us best;
4. And by celebrating the joys of the spiritual journey that brings us tranquility and meaning in life.

For these past several weeks, we have focused on opening inward: we are opening inward for healing, opening inward for emotional health and wholeness, opening inward for ethical guidance and practice, and opening inward for peace and purpose. As we do, we are finding our way and becoming what it is that God wants us to be.

Are there ways still locked away in your heart and mind that need to open?

Study Guide for the August Readings

Questions for Contemplation and Discussion

1. What are the most effective ways of cultivating deep inner peace and a life of tranquility? What spiritual practices are most helpful to you in this quest?
2. What are the most effective ways of discerning your life's purpose? How does your discernment relate to mindful spirituality?
3. How do your talents and gifts suggest a direction for your life? What is your life telling you?
4. What sort of clues does your environment (time and place in history, culture, family setting, etc.) give you about a direction in life?
5. What sorts of talents do you need to develop in order to fulfill what you understand to be your purpose in life?
6. What are the particular challenges and growing edges on which you need to work on in order to gain inner peace and meaning in your life? What are the spiritual components of this quest?
7. What are the primary sources of inspiration and empowerment for you as you seek a more peaceful life, filled with purpose and direction?
8. What are the best ways for you to be mindful in your relationships and your life work? How do love and compassion guide you in these relationships, and how are they cultivated?
9. Are you the kind of person who naturally responds in appropriate and compassionate ways, or do you tend to react impulsively in situations that have an element of conflict and tension? Do empathy and compassion come easy for you, or do you need to cultivate these qualities?
10. What steps can you take to continue growing into a person with a full measure of inner peace and clear purpose?

Study Guide

Section Two: Opening Inward

Questions to Ponder and Discuss

1. What are the areas in which you need healing?
2. How will you go about seeking the healing you need?
3. What resources are available to you in your community to cultivate emotional health? Are there some resources in your religious community or in the region in which you live?
4. Are you pretty well-settled in living by a set of values and norms, or do you still want to gain clarity about the values that guide your life?
5. Are you a person who is living with a sense of inner peace and knowing pretty much what is the purpose of your life?

Key Terms and Concepts

1. Mysticism: the experience of encountering the divine or ultimate reality in a direct way without the intermediaries of clergy, liturgy, or holy book.
2. Attunement: to be aware and to bring into harmony, often applied to the integration of the person.
3. Reconciliation: to restore friendship and harmony, healing the break in relationships.
4. Islam: title of the religion, which means "surrender in peace."
5. Sangha: the spiritual community in Buddhism, offering guidance and support.

Study Resources

1. Goldstein, Joseph. *Mindfulness: A Practical Guide to Awakening.* Boulder, CO: Sound True, 2013.
2. Kornfield, Jack. *A Wise Heart: A Guide to the Universal Teachings of Buddhist Psychology.* New York: Bantam, 2009.
3. ———. *A Path with Heart: A Guide through the Perils and Promises of Spiritual Life.* New York: Bantam, 1993.
4. Reynolds, Stefan Gillow. *Living with the Mind of Christ: Mindfulness in Christian Spirituality.* London: Darton, Longman and Todd, 2016.

5. Siegel, Daniel J. *The Developing Mind: How Relationships and the Brain Interact to Shape Who We Are.* New York: Guilford, 1999.

6. Foster, Richard. *The Celebration of Discipline.* San Francisco: Harper, 1978.

SECTION THREE

EXPANDING OUTWARD

As you well know by now, we have divided our daily readings on mindful spirituality into three sections. The first is "Reaching Upward." We devoted four months of our readings to the ways that we understand God, or Transcendence, and how it is that we relate to or make connections with the divine or ultimate reality. We noted, among many other points, that our belief in and understanding of transcendence or, in contrast, being at peace with the idea that there is really just one layer of reality, has a profound impact on our lives. Those that affirm the reality of either of these views are generally nurtured—but may be hurt—by it, depending on how they frame their worldview.

We then turned to Section Two: "Opening Inward," and focused more directly on our need for healing and the cultivation of emotional health and wholeness. In our readings, we underlined the ways that mindful spirituality has the capacity to guide and cultivate practices that lead to a life of tranquility and meaning. We spoke as well about our need for identifying those values that enable to us to make wise and ethical decisions that lead us to a sense of integrity and purpose in life.

We turn now to Section Three: "Expanding Outward," and we will invite reflection through the readings on the place of love and compassion in our lives, and the ways that belonging to a community provides needed support. We will also reflect together on the ways we fulfill our life purpose by embracing and acting on our sense of vocation, and how we can live responsibly in reference to our calling. Then we'll explore the ways we can engage in our life work by addressing the extraordinary challenges to the earth community, ones that invite the best we have to give in terms of wisdom, commitment, and expertise. These challenges may be global in character, but have local, regional, and national expressions. We will explore how we can make a contribution by expanding outward.

So, together, let's think, pray, and grow in order find our way to respond (expand outward) to a world in need.

THEME FOR SEPTEMBER

EXPANDING OUTWARD TO LOVE

Day 243

The spirit of the Lord God is upon me, because the Lord has anointed me; he has sent me to bring good news to the oppressed, to bind up the brokenhearted, to proclaim liberty to the captives and release to the prisoners. (Isa 61:1)

The Hebrew people, following the founding of Jerusalem as the capital during the reign of David, longed that the city would be free from external conflict, a region in which there was peace and justice. As the challenges came and went, the great prophets would speak to the welfare of the people with the hope that, somehow, the leaders of the state and city would facilitate the common good.[1] The eighth-century prophet Isaiah was a most profound writer, one who saw the deep need and captured this eternal hope for a just and peaceful place for the people, a hope that continues until this day in that region. He continues in his expression of hope, "to comfort all those who mourn, to provide for those who mourn in Zion—to give them a garland instead of ashes, the oil of gladness instead of mourning, the mantle of praise instead of a faint spirit. They will be called oaks of righteousness" (Isa 61:2b–3a).

In this passage, there is the grand vision and hope that those who mourn (and we all do) shall be comforted. Note three points that apply directly to our lives:

1. Isaiah feels that he has found his life purpose; he has been called to bring the good news. The word "chosen," translated as anointed, resonates with those who believe that Jesus had a similar calling, that he was also anointed for the task of bringing the good news to suffering people.

2. There is deep and profound suffering on the part of the people; the prophet's teaching is not just a casual observation that there are needs, but a description of people who are oppressed and brokenhearted. They are a suffering people who mourn the loss of the good life. They hope for a setting in which their needs are met, and where peace and justice prevail.

3. There is a need for leaders as strong as an oak tree who will heal the wounds of the people and proclaim liberty to all the captives of injustice.

How might you lend a hand to those who mourn in your region?

---

1. Brueggemann, *Journey to the Common Good*, 73–113.

Day 244

For I the Lord love justice, I hate robbery and wrongdoing; I will faithfully give them their recompense, and I will make an everlasting covenant with them.
(Isa 61:8)

A fundamental condition at this time in ancient Israel was that the people had lost all hope. The need for good news was very pronounced. As they faced invasion by alien forces and injustice in their own country, the Hebrew people wondered if life could ever be good again. They may have had memories of better times when families could live together, little children could play, and the basic needs of food and shelter were met. There are times when we look back to moments of peace and happiness. We are inclined to say, "It seems like only yesterday that we were together, enjoyed our lives, and felt a measure of happiness and contentment. But now we are afraid, there is violence, we are unsure about where our next meal will come from, and the children are sick." Part of the mission of the prophets was to give hope and to project a better future. Isaiah writes, "They shall bind up the ancient ruins, they shall raise up the former devastations; they shall repair the ruined cities, the devastations of many generations" (Isa 61:4). He continues: "I will greatly rejoice in the Lord, my whole being shall exult my God; for he has clothed me with garments of salvation, he has covered me with a robe of righteousness... For the earth brings forth shoots, and as a garden causes what is sown to spring up its shoots, so the Lord God will cause righteousness and praise to spring up before all the nations" (Isa 61:10a, 11).

Ponder the wonderful metaphors and foundations of hope:

1. Our hope resides in a loving and just God;
2. Who gives us garments of salvation and a robe of righteousness;
3. And causes the garden to grow in the rich and fertile earth;
4. We will then see righteousness and praise spring up before all the nations.

Perhaps we will once again be a nation among equals, one that is just, preserves the peace, and insure that the basic needs of housing, food, health, and education will be provided. God will be true to the covenant made with the Hebrew people.

How would you describe the components of your hope for the future? And what part do we play in achieving our preferred future?

Day 245

For God so loved the world that he gave his only Son, so that everyone who believes in him may not perish but may have eternal life. Indeed, God did not send his Son into the world to condemn the world, but in order that the world might be saved through him. (John 3:16–17)

The prophet's role in the Hebrew Bible was to proclaim that God loved humankind, and that those in power should create a setting in which there was justice and peace. One part of the prophet's message was that God loved individuals and sought communion with them. The message was also a challenge to social structures that were unjust and caused the people to suffer and be marginalized. The New Testament confirms this message and proclaims that the God-given vocation of Jesus was to proclaim the good news of God's love, that *all* (God so loved the *world*) were loved by God, not just those in power or of any one ethnic, religious, and social class. The verse in John 3:16, and the particular phrase "eternal life," is often interpreted to mean will go to heaven after death. It does refer to reconciliation with God that will be eternal, but it is also a reference to the present. Eternal life begins now, and that God's love, as expressed in the coming of Jesus, is comparable to the Hebrew prophet's message—that all of God's children deserve the good life here and now. It is the beginning of eternal life. Jesus was a Jewish prophet, among other callings, and he had compassion for all those whom he encountered; the hungry and the sick, those who mourn, and those who were victims of injustice.

Jesus gathered a band of followers, including some apostles and a large number of disciples, and he challenged them to get engaged in the mission of compassion. "As he walked by the Sea of Galilee, he saw two brothers, Simon, who is called Peter, and Andrew, his brother, casting a net into the sea—for they were fisherman. And he said to them, 'Follow me, and I will make you fish for people.' Immediately they left their nets and followed him" (John 4:19–20). Jesus begins his mission to take his God-given calling of love and compassion to the people, to "fish" for people who suffer and are victims of violence and injustice. For Christians, this is the meaning of the church, the beloved community, to expand outward in love.

In what ways might we begin to fish for people with love and compassion?

Day 246

Love is reckless and carefree; small, trifling minds seek profit, but true lovers lavish everything on love and never expect benefits in return.[2]

Nearly all of the great religious traditions of the world have given love and compassion a central place in their teaching. In October of 2007, an open letter was sent from thirty-eight Muslim scholars to His Holiness, Pope Benedict XVI. It was sent in the name of God, the Compassionate, the Merciful. The letter was copied to many other Christian leaders as an invitation to the Christian community to join Muslims in finding a way to foster peace and justice in the world. It begins with the observation that Christians and Muslims make up "over half of the world's population" and share the common commitment to love the One God and to love one's neighbor. The document, while written from the Muslim perspective, is careful to reference support for these beliefs and practices in both the Quran and the Bible. The closing line in the introduction to the letter says: "Thus in obedience to the Holy Quran, we as Muslims invite Christians to come together with us on the basis of what is common to us, which is also essential to our faith and practice: The Two Commandments of Love." The two commands are to love God with our whole being and our neighbor as we love ourselves. Comparable affirmations of the love commandments are present in Judaism, Hinduism, Buddhism, Sikhism, Baha'i, the Indigenous Wisdom religions, and the Asian religions of Taoism, Confucianism, and Shinto. Common to many of them is a deep belief in some form of the Golden Rule.

Yes, it is true that "trifling minds seek profit" (and we might also clarify power, prestige, and possessions), and often do so with many forms of oppression and violence. In addition, there are those who think regionally, nationally, and tribally, and seek to protect and advance their country or region. But we have reached the point in human history in which we must now think globally. We are interconnected and interdependent, and what happens in one place on the globe will impact other places.

How is it possible to care for our own and still think and act globally?

2. Mafi, *Rumi Day by Day*, 187.

Day 247

Be generous in prosperity; and thankful in adversity. Be fair in thy judgment, and guarded in thy speech. Be a lamp unto those who walk in darkness, and home to the stranger. Be eyes to the blind, and a guiding light unto the feet of the erring. Be a breath of life to the body of humankind, a dew to the soil of the human heart, and fruit upon the tree of humility.

—Baha'i Prayer for Peace

The Hebrew prophets saw great need in the settings in which they lived, and Jesus as a radical prophet also saw profound need as he walked the dusty roads of Galilee and down to Judah. So, too, have the prophets of many traditions been moved by the suffering of those near and dear to them. Our time is no different; people are suffering, and the harsh realities which humankind must address are challenging, perplexing, and alarming. They are challenging in the sense that they demand solutions that require political will, international cooperation, and enormous costs. They are perplexing because the size and complexity of the problems are beyond the scope of what humankind has ever had to address before. They are alarming because even the proposed solutions contain risk, and because the numbers of people suffering is so large. For example, there is the challenge of feeding 7.5 billion people, and while there may be enough food on earth to feed all of the people of the world, it is not easy to distribute food equitably across country and continental boundaries, and underlying equitable food distribution is the distribution and scarcity of water.[3]

At this point, we will not go deeply into the range of challenging problems we currently face. Instead, we will highlight a few of them in order to better understand why the great human vocation of our time, to be loving and show compassion, is so important and so challenging. Let me list a few of these profound challenges that call us to service. To begin with, let's list the global concerns: (1) the issues dealing with global warming and climate change; (2) the issues dealing with immigration; (3) the issues dealing with poverty, hunger, and disease; (4) the issues dealing with a global economy and international justice; (5) the issues dealing with war and violence.

What other concerns might we list as we think about global management?

---

3. See Ferguson, *Lovescapes*, 3–27. In these next few entries, I will be using the interfaith prayers of a Unity conference, "Celebrating Oneness, Healing the World."

Day 248

To begin: the first quality to come into view in our state seems to be wisdom.

—Plato[4]

On a more regional and local level, we need to address the following challenges: (1) the challenge of receiving adequate health care; (2) the challenge of gaining access to high-quality education; (3) the challenge of having an adequate income; (4) the challenge of adapting to rapid change; (5) the challenge of maintaining good mental health. I have reflected a great deal about how these challenges might be addressed by governments and by private initiatives. As I read historical accounts of how these concerns have been addressed, I notice that there are at least three different strategies, each containing a multitude of sub-strategies. The first is to try to take them on in a collaborative way through government structures. These government structures, whether local, regional, national, or international, carry with them the complexity of changing leadership, arranging for financial support, setting priorities, reaching a consensus on how to address the problem, and determining what level of government has the responsibility. As I write, I am watching the somewhat-awkward and inefficient way the Trump administration is attempting to deal with the range of responsibilities usually managed at the national and international levels. There has been a dramatic change in leadership, a shortage of available funds, arguments about priorities, deep differences about how to address the problems, and the debate about which level of government should take on the challenge. The angry give-and-take, the devious and dishonest reporting, the subterfuge, and the America-first philosophy have been disillusioning and disheartening. I have to acknowledge how difficult it is to manage the federal government of the United States. It is challenging, but I would still maintain that the larger principles of governance should be based on integrity and compassion.

How should government agencies be guided by integrity and compassion?

---

4. Plato, *Republic*, 121.

Day 249

Lead me from death to life, from falsehood to truth. Lead me from despair to hope, from fear to trust. Lead me from hate to love, from war to peace. Let peace fill our heart, our world, our universe.

—From the *Upanishads*

It may be misguided and naïve to speak about integrity and compassion guiding the affairs of government, especially at the international level. It is true that the work of government is the art of the possible, and that compromises are inevitable. Running a government, especially the most powerful in the world, does involve dealing with deception and conflict among the several goals of governments that need to protect and meet the needs of their people. There will be many days that one must take one step backward in order to go two steps forward; resiliency, commitment, and patience are absolutely necessary. I am persuaded that having a guiding set of values as one labors in this baffling arena gives one the courage, fortitude, perseverance, and guidance to make wise decisions. I place "love," defined as the care for the welfare of the people being served at the top of the list. Its companion, "compassion," in the sense of having a special concern for those who suffer, is a close second, and an integral part of *agape* love. To lead, one must earn the trust of the people, and that trust is earned with honesty and integrity. There will be situations that need confidentiality, and times when one cannot say everything and when hard decisions that hurt some people will need to be made. But they will be made more wisely and with a better chance of success when love, compassion, and integrity are integral to the process and evident in the lives of the people who serve.

To what ends should the government consistently work? There will be as many immediate goals as there are issues, but these goals need the larger vision of creating a society that meets the basic needs of its people in the context of a just, humane, and peaceful social order. People need equal opportunity to have excellent health care, access to a quality education, adequate housing, and good and fulfilling work that earns a fair wage. This can only be done in a society based on peace and justice, and it can only be accomplished in a collaborative way.

How would you describe the ideal government and its leadership?

Day 250

May our brothers and sisters, human and non-human beings, born in every form sharing the web of life, be safe, be happy, and be free. May true peace of the heart bring peace among all the peoples of the world. May all beings everywhere find joy and blessings. May I and all beings awaken together.

—Buddhist Prayer

In addition to solving our many perplexing problems through the collaborative strategies that are the foundation of various levels of government, there are two other approaches that might be called private and individual strategies. A recent movement on the part of some of the wealthiest people in the world to use their wealth to build a just and humane world has been very encouraging. One of the assumptions of this group is that there are some very important changes that need to be made for the welfare of all the people of the world that cannot be done by governments. The governments are seen as too inefficient, too bound by restrictions, and unable to respond quickly enough to issues that need immediate attention. In addition to this initiative is the presence of an abundance of private foundations that have great wealth and can target particular concerns to match their mission and goals. As one living in the Seattle area, I have watched with joy at the way the Gates Foundation has addressed so many needs in the world, particularly in the field of health. In a much more modest way, I have been a part of organizations that have sought financial support from foundations, received this support, and were able to accomplish many goals in the field of education that local and regional governments were unable to address. For example, I have worked a number of years on the quest for a just peace in Israel and Palestine. One strategy in this endeavor is to educate children to respect and honor those with a different ethnic and religious background. We were able to find a private foundation to grant us five hundred thousand dollars for a new high school building, a great gift with a life-changing vision.

Love and compassion may motivate an individual as well, one who uses the God-given talents to engage in a range of service ministries that transform the lives of needy people. We turn next to the way that love may motivate an individual.

What sort of service would you most like to contribute to help your region?

Day 251

Lord, make me an instrument of your peace. Where there is hatred, let me sow love. Where there is injury, pardon. Where there is doubt, faith. Where there is despair, hope. Where there is darkness, light. Where there is sadness, joy. O Divine Master, grant that I may never seek so much to be consoled as to consol. To be understood as to understand, To be loved as to love. For it is in giving that we receive. It is in pardoning that we are pardoned. It is in dying that we are born to eternal life.

—Prayer of Saint Francis

Love has been interwoven in most of what we have read together in our readings, and because the term has so many meanings, especially in English, it might be well for us to return to our much-used word "love," and be sure we keep in mind how we are using the term. I wrote a book of over two hundred fifty pages on the term, and knew as I finished that there was more to say.[5] Fortunately English (as well as many other languages) has a number of synonyms and cognates for love, so we are able to use the concept in very descriptive and specific ways. As I think of cognates—words with a similar meaning—the following terms come to mind (and I am sure there are many others): care, trust, acceptance, compassion, attraction, affection, attachment, tenderness, sympathy, empathy, communication, benevolence, devotion, dear, cherish, and altruism. Perhaps these will suggest how rich and subtle is the concept of love.

At the risk of repetition, let me go to the three Greek words that are often used as definitions of different kinds of love: *eros*, *philia*, and *agape*.[6] The Greek word *eros* has the meaning of attraction, and may refer to the physical and sexual attraction we have for another person, hence the word erotic in English. But to limit *eros* to this meaning is to miss its more subtle meaning. The full-orbed meaning comes to us in a profound and elegant way in the writings of Plato, and in particular in his book called *Symposium*. In the dialogue of this book, Socrates is in conversation with several thoughtful people about the nature of goodness and human love for the good. The wise Socrates takes their arguments one by one, and he won the argument that day by saying that love is noble as we use our mature reason to search for beauty, truth, and goodness.

Do you think Socrates is on the right track as he speaks of love in this way?

5. Ferguson, *Lovescapes*.
6. Ibid., 38–50.

Day 252

> *Peace and universal love are the essence of the Gospel preached by all the enlightened ones. The Lord has preached that equanimity is the Dharma. Forgive do I creatures all, and let all creatures forgive me. Unto all have I amity and unto none enmity. Know that violence is the root cause of all miseries in the world. Violence, in fact, is the knot of bondage. Do not injure any living being. This is the eternal, perennial, and unalterable way of the spiritual life. A weapon, howsoever powerful it may be, can always be superseded by a superior one; but no weapon can, however, be superior to non-violence and love.*
>
> —Jain Prayer

As Socrates spoke with his friends, he maintained that *eros* is developmental in character, and that the early phases of this form of love were often selfish and linked to sexual attraction. He explained that, over the years of growth toward maturity, one begins to love that which is good, true, and beautiful. The nature of these qualities is discerned, as our reason guides us to value them above all else. Our problem is that we have seen only shadows rather than the truth. Plato, on the lips of Socrates, explains that, early in life, we see reality in terms of our own needs. We are dependent and view those around us as existing to make sure our needs are met. We are attracted to what we think will make us happy, and there are times when our parents must intercede and point us in a wise and healthy direction.

Socrates goes on to speak about our deep needs as we grow and develop, and how easy it is to think that we will be happy if we have praise, possessions, and power. We are attracted (*eros*) to that which we think will fulfill us and make us satisfied. It is during these years that erotic love has great power over us. But in time, we see that, while these stages are necessary to our growth, they do not contain what will ultimately satisfy us. As we mature, we are attracted (*eros* again) to what is universal, to goodness, truth, and beauty. He even adds, on occasion, the concept of justice. To love these eternal values, that which is truly good, ultimately real, and truly beautiful, will fulfill us. We can say, "I love this human being because she is good," "I love that perception because it is true," and "I love that landscape because it is beautiful." He would add, "I love this form of government because it is just, protects the people, and gives them a good life."

In what ways do you use the concept of *eros* when you say, "I love?"

Day 253

Our next subject must be friendship. This is necessary because such love has somewhat the character of a virtue, or at any rate involves virtue. Besides, it is one of those things which life can least afford to be without. No one would choose a friendless existence on condition of having all other good things in the world.[7]

It was Aristotle who was more inclined to use the word *philia*, translated as "friendship," to describe the highest form of love.[8] He used three categories of friendship to make his point. The first is when a so-called friend pretends to care, but in fact is using you for personal gain. This person may be polite, but has a hidden motivation and really wants to use the other person to gain her or his objectives. The next level of friendship is when we exchange favors with another person in normal everyday human encounters. He speaks of these kinds of favors as false friendship, in that another person is being used for gain or pleasure, not as a valued person who deserves respect. A true friendship is one of mutual concern and active care. We may, in fact, gain and find pleasure in this kind of friendship, and it is built upon the deep and abiding trust that each party has for the other and the sincere concern for the welfare of the other person. Such an attitude and spirit will also contribute to the good of society. This kind of friendship is an excellent expression of what we mean in English when we speak about true love.

Thomas Aquinas, the great medieval theologian, used this concept of love in developing the command of Jesus to love God and neighbor. His word choice is the Latin term *caritas,* from which we derive the term "charity" in English. The King James Version of the Bible translates our third Greek word, *agape*, from 1 Corinthians 13 as charity: "So faith, hope, and charity, abide." Aquinas, in choosing the Greek word *philia*, does allow in his description of love the presence of joy in each other's presence, and that we experience deep joy in our friendship with God and that God has joy in our presence as well.

In what ways are good friendships based on Aristotle's understanding of love?

---

7. Aristotle, *The Ethics of Aristotle*, 227.
8. In the *Nicomachean Ethics*.

Day 254

No, in all these things we are more than conquerors through him who loved us. For I am convinced that neither death nor life, nor angels, nor rulers, nor things present, nor things to come, nor powers, nor height, nor depth, nor anything else in all creation, will be able to separate us from the love of God in Christ Jesus our Lord. (Rom 8:37–39)

The understanding of love in the Christian tradition, while not discounting the great value of *eros* and *philia*, has focused on *agape*, understood as unlimited and unconditional love. It is the heart of God's identity, and the divine care for humankind and all creation. It is used in the translation of the teaching of Jesus, and the word chosen by Paul, as well as the authors of the Gospel and letters of John. One well-known and widely respected theologian of an earlier generation, Anders Nygren, has contrasted *agape* with *eros* in a persuasive way. However I am inclined to see them as different dimensions of a larger reality. If there is a fundamental difference, it has to do with *agape* as "a form of love that extends beyond the normal limits of human interaction and selflessly reaches out to all of humanity, and indeed to all sentient beings, and goes to the point of need with a caring and healing response. It asks nothing in return and cares only for the well-being of those within the circle of exchange."[9]

One aspect of this definition is the need to distinguish between appraisal and bestowal. Love that is generated by appraisal views the object of love as worthy and having attractive features that evoke a loving response. *Agape* love is bestowed on all people, including the unattractive and those not inherently loveable, yet in need of the response of love. It is the sort of love that is bestowed on the person or persons needing love. In this sense, *agape* participates in the love of God, which has a forgiving and healing aspect in reference to all of humankind. In a way, many of those that strongly affirm the unconditional character of *agape* still maintain the worth of those on whom they bestow love, often referring to the needy person as created in the image of God and of infinite worth because of the divine that is in all humans. The quality of empathy is often associated with the capacity to bestow this kind of love.

Do you think that loving the attractive and the unattractive are the same?

---

9. Ferguson, *Lovescapes*, 43.

Day 255

Other-regarding love is usually considered the hallmark of both a moral and spiritual way of life because it is perceived to be both a human virtue and an aspect of Ultimate Reality.[10]

I would like to draw upon the understanding of love in the writing of Pitirim Sorokin, a Harvard professor of sociology of an earlier generation, who founded an institute for the study of love at Harvard. Stephen Post, a current scholar in the field of love, has developed Sorokin's work.[11] They identify five essential qualities of *agape* love:

1. Polite and respectful behavior is expected in normal relationships, but *agape* has the additional and essential aspect of being *intensive*. Love becomes intensive when it is ardent, focused, and moves beyond self-interest. People such as Mother Teresa demonstrated this form of love in settings where mere politeness would have been inadequate. In her case, it was showing intensive compassion for the poor and sick of India. The people whom she served were not easy to love, given their lives of poverty and illness and having no resources. She opened the door to them as they came to her center in the sprawling city of Calcutta. They were (and continue to be in her center there and in other parts of the world) welcomed, given food, provided with basic health care, and made to feel accepted as human beings created in the image of God. And, as death approached, they were given spiritual comfort. In her work, she gave aid and dignity for the dying. For her work, she was award the Nobel Prize. Her simple prayer captures her beautiful spirit:

   Lord, open our eyes, that we may see you in our brothers and sisters.
   Lord, open our ears, that we may hear the cries of the hungry, the cold, the frightened, and the oppressed.
   Lord, open our hearts, that we may love each other as you love us.
   Renew in us your spirit,
   Lord, free us and make us one.[12]

In what ways might we make our love more intensive?

---

10. Post, *Unlimited Love*, 133.
11. Ibid., 15–35. I list the qualities of love they identify in Ferguson, *Lovescapes*, 44–45.
12. Mother Teresa, *Life in the Spirit*, 11–12.

Day 256

> *Therefore I appeal to every one of you—poor and rich, young and old—to give your own hands to serve Christ in his poor and your hearts to love him in them.*[13]

2. *Agape* love also has the quality of being *extensive* and should be extended to all those in need. Mother Teresa was especially concerned for the poor, and her love extended to all forms of poverty. She writes: "Who are the Poor?"

   The poor are the materially and the spiritually destitute
   The poor are the hungry and the thirsty
   The poor are those who need clothing
   The poor are the homeless and the harborless
   The poor are the sick
   The poor are the physically and mentally handicapped
   The poor are the aged
   The poor are those imprisoned
   The poor are the lonely
   The poor are the ignorant and the doubtful
   The poor are the sorrowful
   The poor are the comfortless
   The poor are the helpless
   The poor are the persecuted
   The poor are those who suffer injustice
   The poor are the ill-mannered
   The poor are the bad-tempered
   The poor are the sinners and the scoffers
   The poor are those who do us wrong
   The poor are the unwanted, the outcasts of society
   The poor are somehow or other we ourselves.[14]

In her work, Mother Teresa made love extensive, reaching out to all those in need, the down-and-out as well as the up-and-out. She took seriously the call to love our neighbor with all the care and sensitivity with which we love ourselves.

How extensive is the love you have for those beyond your circle of nearness?

---

13. Ibid., 14–15.
14. Ibid., 15–16.

Day 257

The madness of love
Is a blessed fate;
And if we understood this
We would seek no other:
It brings into a unity
What was divided,
And this is the truth:
Bitterness it makes sweet,
It makes the stranger a neighbor,
And what was lowly, it raises on high.

—Hadewijch of Antwerp

We have reflected together about the ways that *agape* love is both intensive and extensive. We continue our reflection on the many dimensions of true love.

3. Further, *agape* has *duration*, and does not end when the situation becomes complex and demanding. The Apostle Paul speaks of this aspect of love in his letter to the Corinthians: "Love never ends" (1 Cor 13:8). He spoke from experience, in that his life as a mission worker was so full of challenges. Often, his life was threatened, and he may have died as a martyr in Rome. His message was not welcome in large measure because it was radical. It challenged the accepted norms of Judaism, the religion of his birth, and because it called into question in a prophetic way the practices of the Roman leaders and their policies. Yet he never gave up. He deeply believed that the love of God, grasped by faith in the life, teaching, and death of Jesus, is the great message of the ages. We are transformed as we understand and receive the *madness* of God's love as expressed in Jesus, and then make this kind of love ours. It is what I have tried to do in my life, although I continue to fail. With the example of Jesus and Paul in front of me, my mission has endured, even as it had duration across the years of their lives. While on the cross, Jesus took time to honor a thief being crucified next to him, and to speak to John the Apostle, asking him to take care of his mother. He then prayed for those carrying out the crucifixion.

Does your love endure through the challenging moments in life?

Day 258

> *Love is patient; love is kind; love is not envious or boastful or arrogant or rude. It does not insist on its own way; it is not irritable or resentful; it does not rejoice in wrongdoing, but rejoices in the truth. It bears all things, believes all things, hopes all things, endures all things.* (1 Cor 13:4–7)

We continue to reflect on the many shades of the meaning of love, as articulated by Pitirim Sorokin and Stephen Post.

4. In addition, they say that *agape* has the quality of *purity*. It is free from hidden motivations, and from any form of deception. The person who loves is honest to the core and has absolute integrity. One can trust what is said and done by the person who truly loves. The Apostle Paul says that love "rejoices in the truth." There are some quite obvious ways that we shade the truth with those whom we love and those whom we should love. Often we are motivated to protect ourselves, and believe that if we tell a white lie about something we have done, we will not be discovered, and we will be accepted without the other's judgment and disappointment about our behavior. I am not suggesting that we have to say everything, but that which we do and then hide will often erode the levels of openness and trust in the relationship. As I have done this in the past, and then countered with an honest acknowledgement, I have generally been forgiven and affirmed. All of a sudden, there was a deeper connection in the relationship, and even empathy from the one I may have offended. There are other times when the offense is not minor, but major, and may indeed threaten the relationship. It is in these cases when the guilt and shame are too great for us to easily bear, and a true confession might genuinely threaten the relationship. I do not have complete wisdom about these kinds of situations, and on occasion, I have even counseled those who have asked that it may be necessary to bear burden of guilt and shame. The trump card in this kind of situation is *agape* love. We must ask what is true love in these situations, and be pure with ourselves if not always with those whom we may have violated.

How should we love purely in those situations that are especially difficult?

Day 259

So many expressions of love in the world are well intentioned but ineffective and unwise. Love can be successful or it can fail terribly, and one important measure of this is the efficiency of love. Of love, it can be said that "the road to hell is paved with good intentions." Any person who wishes to live a life of love must become competent to achieve fitting goals.[15]

Love is difficult. There are times when is hard to know what sort of attitude or action would be most appropriate and the best expression of true love. We must be wise and add still another quality of *agape* love. Post and Sorokin suggest that love must be *adequate* as well.

5. So another quality of love is that it must be *adequate* and *appropriate.* The response of the one who truly loves is on target, and addresses the need of the one who longs for love. Note that I have added the additional word "appropriate." I am somewhat amazed as I read the Gospels and see the many different ways that Jesus expresses love. Invariably it is adequate and appropriate.[16] I have experienced the difficulty in finding just the right words or the most appropriate action that expresses true love, and not something trite or inappropriate. I have learned a great deal about adequate and appropriate love by watching those who are more skilled than I am, and by reading and reflecting on those great teachers of love, such as Buddha and Jesus. I have also observed those trying to love me, often doing so in awkward ways or trying to meet their own needs, rather than mine. As I move into a day, I try to stay attuned to the deeper realities of expressing a love that is healing and life-giving to all whom I encounter. It is a life-long journey.

Are these qualities of love present as you meet those in need of love?

---

15. Post, *Unlimited Love*, 153.

16. I am aware that the Gospels were written many years after the life of Jesus, and that the authors were writing them as extended sermons and not as critical historical biographies. They also wrote them prior to the rise of critical history, and want to speak in a positive way about the inherent message in the life and teachings of Jesus. See, for example, the first three chapters of my book entitled *The Radical Teaching of Jesus*.

Day 260

Oh Great Spirit of our Ancestors, I raise my pipe to you. To your messengers and the four winds, and to Mother Earth who provides for your children. Give us the wisdom to teach our children to love, to respect, and to be kind to each other so that they may grow with peace of mind. Let us learn to share all good things that you provide for us on this Earth.

—Native American Prayer

Daniel Day Williams, a thoughtful Christian scholar, has also expanded and deepened the understanding of love. In his book *The Spirit and Forms of Love,* he describes *agape* in five descriptive ways.[17]

1. He maintains that *agape* has the essential quality of *individuality*; it is a unique response to the individual, not one that is generic in character. As we meet others, and especially those needing loving attention and guidance, our response is unique to the individual, carefully wrapping around the identity of the person and addressing their distinctive needs and concerns. A mother provides a careful and selective love, selfless and given in a special way to each child. We can learn a great deal from mothers about love. It is interesting to me that Buddhists and the Dalai Lama in particular invite those with a desire to expand their capacity to love to turn to the example of their mother's love. He offers a way of meditating on the mother's love as a way of learning how to love in a specific way.[18] In this volume, and in several books written from the perspective of Buddhism, there is also a great emphasis on friendship and the need to give a particular form of love to each person. Of course, there are some basic practices of being polite, cordial, and respectful to every person we may meet. If we are to be those who love, this is the first step, but in time, as we get to know the person better, we will find ways of expressing love that are specific to the identity and needs of that one who is immediately present.

What are some specific ways that you need to be loved?

---

17. Williams, *The Spirit and Forms of Love,* 114–22; these I also list in *Lovescapes,* 46.
18. Dalai Lama, *How to Expand Love,* 44.

Day 261

> *But when we consider not only the beginnings of love, but its full course, we must affirm freedom as one of its categorical conditions.*[19]

Love, to be true, must be individualized for each person that we meet. We are careful to find a way to love that is appropriate to their lives in all of their many dimensions. In addition, we join with Daniel Day Williams and affirm the following:

2. *Agape* is given in *freedom*, and is not driven by the needs of the giver. It will come with the context of the relationship. There will be feelings of duty and responsibility, but it is still the free choice of the one who loves. I know there have been times in my life when I have felt some form of pressure to at least be polite and cordial, and have done so out of the expected norms of my context, and not out of my deep convictions. I may have been fatigued or out of sorts in some way. Love is more than good manners, although good manners are essential to a loving relationship. They are a way of respecting the other person. I, then, truly love when I freely act out on my convictions. An action that is forced is not an action of love. There are three reasons why expressing love freely is necessary, if it is to be a true expression of love. One is that we act in a specific context, and our love must grow out of that context if it is to be appropriate and individualized. We sense the environment which we are in, and how an expression of caring might best be expressed in this particular setting. Second, to offer love freely is to honor the individuality and the freedom of the other person. We recognize their distinctive qualities and offer love in reference to them. And third, if the other person senses that we are giving a response of love because it has been predetermined or is required, then the person may sense that it is not sincere or from the heart, but only coming from the demands of the setting. We give our love freely out of respect for the other person.

In what way is love only true love when it is given freely?

---

19. Williams, *Spirit and Forms of Love*, 115.

Day 262

To love and lose might be better than never to have loved; but most of us, when we lose a love—not through death but through love's demise—would be hard-pressed to find this oft-repeated Tennyson quote very consoling. Love is a risky business.[20]

Love must be tailored to the person and the context in which it is offered. It must be given freely without external coercion. In addition, love is an act of the will, often an action, and it will not always be received with grace and gratitude. In fact, as Williams teaches us, it may create discomfort.

3. In most cases, the giving of *agape* will be an action that involves *a dimension of suffering*. It may also be one of sheer joy and delight, although in many cases, the person in need of love will ask for a response that will mean sacrifice and demanding attention to the healing process. When we love, we run the risk of suffering and selfless giving without positive reinforcement. The suffering may take a number of forms. It may be a rejection on the part of the person to whom we have offered love. This is not uncommon in romantic relationships, and ironically, even in relationships in which the kind of love offered is selfless. A second form of suffering may occur when the love we offer is based more on our need for love than on the well-being of the one to whom we offer love. We should not expect the other person to always be able to discern our need or, as is often the case, assume that other person will return our love even if they do discern our need. *Agape* is a form of altruism or selfless love that is given without the expectation that it will be returned in kind. Our offer of love may not even be viewed as love, if those to whom we offer love are suffering from illness, poverty, or injustice. It may in fact be misunderstood. Love is indeed risky, and to offer unlimited love must come from our deep commitments that to love others is the essence of life and our most fundamental value.

Have you ever extended love to another and been misunderstood?

---

20. Greeley and Durkin, *The Book of Love*, 361

Day 263

In a famous scene from Victor Hugo's Les Misérables, Jean Valjean, a desperate man just released from nineteen years in prison, is taken in by a kindly bishop. The cynical ex-con repays his hospitality by stealing the church silverware in the dead of night. But when Valjean is caught by the gendarmes with the cutlery in his sack, the bishop lies that he had given it to him as a gift, pressing upon him two more silver candlesticks. Valjean's humanity is reawakened by the single gesture, and he begins a new life of virtuous service to others.[21]

As we extend outward in love, we do more than just feel warm inside. We often express our love in words and actions. We learn, as Daniel Day Williams reminds us, that love makes change.

4. As one gives *agape*, one must be prepared that the giving is *an action that may cause change.* As the parent loves, the relationship will change, and perhaps the child will smile in such a way that the day is different for both the parent and the child. As the friend expresses gratitude for a gift or kind favor, the situation changes, both in terms of emotions and courses of action. In most cases, the expression of *agape,* such as the bishop's intervention on behalf of Jean Valjean, will produce a change in attitude and spirit. A good parent and a kind friend will see that the spirit and actions of love have caused the one who receives love to be happy and flourish. I remember a situation when I was teaching in which a student came to my office with a confession that he cheated on the exam. We talked about it, and the student expressed the fear that a poor grade would lessen his chances to be accepted into graduate school. I showed a measure of empathy for this fear, offered an opportunity to retake the exam, and the student diligently studied and did well on the makeup exam. The action of empathy had a positive outcome. But not all actions of empathy have a positive outcome. The change could have been that the student would cheat again. As we love, we must be ready for both possibilities.

Have you ever had your offer of love appreciated? Or betrayed?

---

21. An illustration given by Barasch in *The Compassionate Life*, 210.

Day 264

> *Theologians, philosophers and scientists who speak of* agape *typically believe it means something beyond or distinct from the simple word* love. *Many adopt* agape *to distinguish their notion of love from romantic or popular understandings [of love].*[22]

Daniel Day Williams offers one other perspective on *agape* that will help us better appreciate its many dimensions.

5. The giving of *agape* must also be done in an *impartial and rational way* without advancing one's own agenda, especially with a parent and a child. He maintains "that there can be no real love without the rational function which aims to transcend personal bias, and which assesses objectively the human situation, including that of the lover, the beloved, and their relationship."[23] He does not exclude the affective, or even the mystical, side of love, but wants to make sure that what we offer to the valued other person or the actions we take are thoughtful and well-reasoned actions. Love offered without objective knowledge is more likely just sentimentality, and not the expression of care for the well-being of the person or those who are marginalized. If we are to marry another person, warm feelings are wonderful, even necessary, but care should also be given to the nature of the relationship, the family environment, ancestry, and financial foundations. When we step into a social context in which there is injustice and human suffering, we must know about the causes of these conditions, assess how they might be changed, and design careful strategies to make change. In this case, we should anticipate some resistance by vested interests. We can also expect a range of opinions about strategies. Making social change is very difficult. In addition, we may even inadvertently impose our assessment, and therefore miss the perspective of those who suffer. In any case, it will be complex!

When you say that love is needed, what are you really suggesting?

---

22. Oord, *Defining Love*, 33.
23. Williams, *Spirit and Forms of Love*, 120–21.

Day 265

> *But I say to you that listen, Love your enemies, do good to those who hate you, bless those who curse you, pray for those who abuse you. If anyone strikes you on the cheek, offer the other also; and from anyone who takes away your coat do not withhold even your shirt. Give to everyone who begs from you; and if anyone takes away your goods, do not ask for them again. Do to others as you would have them do to you.* (Luke 6:27–31)

I find this teaching of Jesus quite difficult. The primary reason is because what the other person does when s/he strikes me and steals from me is to invade and violate my personhood. These actions, in essence, say that I lack value, and yet I feel deep inside that I should be treated with respect. My way of dealing with this kind of offense is to try to get inside the person who has offended me and understand the reasons for these inappropriate actions. There are times, of course, that we should resist and challenge the mindset and social systems that may produce this inappropriate behavior. Jesus speaks to this concern as well, and it should be balanced with the lesson of this passage on turning the other cheek. Five concepts come to mind that may enrich and deepen our understanding of *agape* (selfless love):

1. The first is captured in the term *altruism,* which may be defined as a form of helping behavior that provides no anticipated benefits to one who turns the other cheek. The term, coming from the Latin *alter,* meaning "other," carries the meaning of showing love for the other for their sake.

2. A second term is *compassion*, that quality of one's life that reaches out to reduce the suffering of another. Jesus in this passage is pointing to compassion.

3. A third concept is *empathy,* that capacity to understand the experiences, feelings, and thoughts of others and to be sensitive to them in an explicit way.

4. A fourth idea inherent in this teaching of Jesus is *care,* a form of love that is specifically making a tangible response to a person who is obviously troubled and in need. It is a patient response, an action to take care of the person.

5. A final word that deepens the understanding of this teaching of Jesus is *forgiveness*, a response that means reactions of offense and resentment subside, and the person is welcomed back into the circle of communication.

What strategies do you have to cultivate these qualities of love in your life?

Day 266

Be generous in prosperity, and thankful in adversity. Be fair in judgment, and guarded in thy speech. Be a lamp unto those who walk in darkness, and a home to the stranger. Be eyes to the blind, and a guiding light unto the feet of the erring. Be a breath of life to the body of humankind, a dew to the soil of the human heart and fruit upon the tree of humility.

—Baha'i and Middle Eastern Prayer

We have only begun to understand all of the dimensions of selfless love, though we may have reached some clarity about the concept of love. Human languages, especially our English language, enables us to speak wisely about its many dimensions. In my research for the book *Lovescapes: Mapping the Geography of Love*, I discovered that nearly every culture across human history has had a slightly different take on love, and has defined it in reference to the customs and practices of their language and culture. I devoted a small section to these various descriptions. A few illustrations from across history might expand our understanding.

Love in the preliterate and classical eras focused on seeing love from the perspective of human need, and what emerged was a description of love that was rooted in human survival and understanding the complexity of human emotions. Love was important in human reproduction and healing. It was attributed often to one of the gods in both the Greek and Roman pantheons. For example, Aphrodite (Venus) was the goddess of love and beauty. In some cases, as mentioned, thinkers such as Plato, Aristotle, and several others elevated the concept of love, with Plato stressing *eros* (deep attraction) as the ideal form of love, and Aristotle lifting *philea* (friendship) as the highest form of love. In the Middle Ages, love had some of the same overtones of the classical era, but it also had the addition of the Christian understanding. Augustine's view about misplaced love was quite influential. He maintained that the created world and the richness of human experience often claim our primary love. He acknowledges that the world is beautiful and good, as created by God, and human love is often focused on the created world. However, we should never give our full love to these lesser gods, but reserve it for the one true God, an act that provides order and meaning in life.

How and where do you give your deepest love? Why?

Day 267

A night full of talking that hurts,
My worst held-back secrets:
Everything has to do with loving and not loving.

—RUMI

From the late Middle Ages, and on into modern times, there was the addition of romantic love, the deep and powerful feelings of attraction to another person. Romantic love has continued into the present, and is viewed as a great gift, although often acknowledged as based on unrealistic expectations and the projection of ideals onto the other person. Yet it stays with us, and is very present in literature and media.

As the modern era advanced, motivations for love and other values associated with the feelings of love have been questioned. With the rise of science, and especially the development of critical history and social science, our understanding of human development has matured. We know that sexual love may contribute to a deep abiding union with another person, although this expression of erotic love has been carefully studied. It was Sigmund Freud (1856–1939), probing beneath the surface into the depths of the human psyche, who dramatically called into question the validity of sexual attraction and romantic feeling. Other social scientists followed in his wake, and offered alternative views of human love. By the mid-twentieth century, love had become an important subject of scholarly inquiry and artistic expression.

Social critics such as Theodore Reik and Erich Fromm, and philosophers such as George Santayana and Jean-Paul Sartre, examined the many dimensions of human love. Novelists such as D. H. Lawrence and Marcel Proust wrote about the wonder and magic of love that fills human life. We have mentioned already the work of Pitirim Sorokin, but should add as well the work of Abraham Maslow, who spoke about two types of love, B-love (which focuses on the love for the other person) and D-love (which is driven by needs and deficiencies). More recently, moving into the twenty-first century, there has been an emphasis on brain research that shows that love is linked to the workings of the brain and the nervous system. Brain health is a factor in our capacity to love. It is good that our understanding of love is expanding!

How would you assess your capacity to be a truly loving person?

Day 268

The essence of love is to affectively affirm as well as to unselfishly delight in the well-being of others, and to engage in acts of care and service on their behalf; unlimited love extends this love to all others without exception, in an enduring and constant way.[24]

There are many definitions of love, coming from nearly every stage of history and diversity of culture. So as we try to tidy up our definition of love, we are wise to explore what others have said and done in the name of love. This has been our goal in the last few readings as we have explored the meaning of love. I find the word *agape* especially helpful. We might conclude this brief section on the nature of love by once again reviewing the several components of *agape:*

1. We lift up *agape* as being one of our *deepest values* as we attempt to live a responsible and spiritual life. It is the heart of mindful spirituality.

2. It is based on *understanding* as we try to make our way through the challenges of life. We need to know why and what we are doing, or we will lose our way.

3. It involves *communication*, as we interact with others and attempt to love them in responsible ways. This communication may come with words, but it also may be expressed in acts of service and in becoming a healing presence.

4. In general, the expression of *agape* will bring *appreciation and delight, even celebration*, to those whom we love. We want to bring joy to their lives.

5. In addition, the love that we express toward others should *empower* them to move from a state of discouragement, confusion, and depression to a positive outlook on life. We love in order to make life better for those who need love.

6. The love that we give to others may mean that we have to be able to *unconditionally accept and forgive them*, and manage other interpersonal complexities. Loving others will make life more difficult, and may cause us discomfort and even suffering.

7. Finally, in my view, the capacity to love is increased as we are empowered by God, who is love. We become those who love as we are *in communion with God*.

Are there other components of *agape* that you would add to this list?

24. Post, *Unlimited Love*, v. I also use the list of Jean Vanier in ibid., 49–52.

Day 269

> *As the heart expands in gratefulness, we feel a natural desire to repay the kindness we have received, to give it back somehow. Gradually this develops into a basic wish that all beings be well, that the world live in peace, that everyone find true peace, that everyone find true satisfaction. This is what Buddhists call loving-kindness. And out of loving-kindness arises compassion—not wanting anyone to suffer needlessly.*[25]

Loving-kindness that leads to compassion is a fundamental value and virtue in many of the great religions of the world. The word *hesed* in Hebrew, used frequently in the Hebrew Bible is often translated as loving-kindness or steadfast love. And as one might expect, many of the great teachers of religion have not only spoken theoretically about loving-kindness, but have also provided counsel on how one can cultivate this virtue in everyday life. The Dalai Lama, in his book *How to Expand Love,* provides several steps that help one put loving-kindness into practice. A summary of his guidance may be helpful to us as we seek to expand outward to love.[26]

A foundational step is to learn from friendships. Nearly all of us have close friends, people that we care about and who care about us. As we examine these relationships, we can discover what it is about them that fills us with care and compassion. It may be that we have spent a great deal of time with them, have common interests, and have learned a lot about their lives. In this gift of friendship, we have likely shared our deepest feelings, our joys and dreams, our fears and sadness. Over time, we have learned to care deeply about these people and want them to be free from suffering and to be happy. The Dalai Lama, as do other Buddhist teachers, suggest that we meditate on these friendships This practice of meditation will be transforming, empowering us to see all people as friends and reach out in love to them. In our meditation we may want to place two people in the thought process, one for whom we have deep affection and another whom we have found difficult. The comparison may help us understand why caring for another is hard for us.

What are some patterns of love that you might learn from friendship?

---

25. Welwood, *Perfect Love, Imperfect Relationships*, 95.
26. Dalai Lama, *How to Expand Love*, 29–49.

Day 270

> *In this second step, you reflect on the kindness that others individually afforded to you when, over the course of lifetimes, they were your parents and you were a child.*[27]

Meditation and reflecting on the nature of one's experiences are basic ingredients of the Buddhist's path to a deeper spiritual life; for them, it is mindful spirituality. In this second step for deepening and widening the circle of love relationships, the Dalai Lama invites us to meditate and reflect on a relationship of love that has existed over a lifetime. He suggests that we may want to consider the ways that our parents have loved us from the beginning and been kind to us. I find this suggestion very helpful, in that once again we can reflect on how much we have been loved, but also the ways that we wish we would have been loved. In most cases, our parents were kind to us, although somewhat mixed and different from our mother than from our father. In my case, to reflect on the ways my parents loved me has expanded my understanding and capacity to love in many ways. Let me mention four ways in particular. First, my basic needs were met. I had a nice home, adequate health care, and a fine education. We are truly kind to others if we make sure their basic needs are met, and mine were. I am grateful to my parents' kindness to me in these many ways. Second, they supported me as I engaged my several interests such as sports, reading, and graduate study. They were kind even when it took time away from their activities and stretched the budget. Yet there were times when they did not fully understand, especially as I became interested in a life of faith. A loving relationship is able to understand another person's world. Third, I think they wanted to be close, have open conversations, and really enjoy family life, but often it became difficult, especially with my father's alcoholism. My brothers and I felt embarrassed and hurt. A loving relationship avoids life patterns that hurt others. Fourth, I occasionally felt unloved, unaccepted, and shamed; perhaps not intentionally, but I have had to deal with this reality. Love finds ways to accept others as they are, and aids them in growth and development.

What do you learn about love as you reflect on your parents' love for you?

---

27. Ibid., 51–70.

Day 271

> *It is in fact Christian love which discovers and knows that one's neighbor exists and that—it is one and same thing—everyone is one's neighbor. If it were not a duty to love, then there would not be a concept of neighbor at all. But only when one loves one's neighbor, only then is the selfishness of preferential love rooted out and the equality of the eternal preserved.*[28]

If is important to note that the Dalai Lama underlines that love is not just feelings, but kindness, and kindness involves acting in a loving way toward others. We can celebrate warm and tender feelings, even romantic feelings, but love does not stop with feelings. It pushes us beyond preferential love and asks us to be kind to our neighbor. Danish philosopher Soren Kierkegaard states this very clearly in his profound book, *Works of Love,* a title that suggests his point of view. He draws upon the teaching of Jesus, that we should act on behalf of others in the same ways that we want to be treated. The verse begins with "do unto others," not just "feel attracted." There is so much that we can do; the needs are all around us.

The Dalai Lama, in his third step in expanding our circle of love, again turns to meditation and reflection as the means of cultivating kindness and undertaking acts of love on behalf of our neighbor. He suggests that we should meditate on the relationship we have with another (perhaps our mother) and picture her as blind and walking along the edge of a frightful cliff without a guide. The kind action (the act of love) is to take her hand and help her along the path so she does not fall. He also suggests that we should then take this mediation further and apply it to others in our circle of nearness, helping them walk a safe path and avoid a fall over the cliff. Our worlds are filled with cliffs. As we ponder this responsibility, we might reflect on the lives of our friends and neighbors and ask ourselves how we might help. We can say, "I will do whatever I can for these beings—my own nurturing friends—stricken by such suffering."[29] We might add another practice—that of praying for those who walk along the path next to the cliff.

What specific actions might I take in the near future to help another person?

---

28. Kierkegaard, *Works of Love,* 58.
29. Dalai Lama, *How to Expand Love,* 72–73.

Day 272

Having dealt with the theoretical aspect of the art of loving, we now are confronted with a much more difficult problem, that of the practice of the art of loving. Can anything be learned about the practice of an art, except by practicing it?[30]

The Dalai Lama, as he writes about how to expand our capacity to love, underlines the point made by Eric Fromm, that we must begin to practice it. In time we will get our "love legs" and we will have "love memory," much like the athlete who practices daily and gains muscle memory, doing naturally and almost without thought what is required in the sport. He suggests in step four that we need to begin to think about each person we meet as a friend, one to whom we can show sensitivity and kindness. Of course, we cannot devote time to everyone we meet; for example, when we buy groceries and take them to the check stand, there is not time to engage in a long conversation with the person who is helping us, although we can be kind in spirit and share a few words. A smile and an inquiry such as "How is your day going?" will deliver the message of kindness. The Dalai Lama also underlines the risks of being rude and harmful. The act of kindness contains both dimensions, the positive attitude and act that affirms the other person, but also the avoidance of rudeness and impatience. We listen with empathy, even if the answer is but one sentence. Perhaps, as we move to the parking lot with our groceries, we encounter an elderly person who has difficulty getting their groceries in the car. A smile and helping hand are acts of kindness.

As you would expect, the Dalai Lama suggests that we will increase our capacity to love and be kind by meditation and reflection.[31] One suggestion is that we may want to focus in our meditation on how we have suffered in our life, and how we have been hurt by those that have been unkind to us. I find this practice extremely helpful, and have discovered that my feelings are not all that different from the feelings of hurt and loneliness in other people. Such a meditation has increased my capacity to be empathic around the people I encounter on a given day.

Are there changes I should make in my everyday conversations with others?

---

30. Fromm, *The Art of Loving*, 90.
31. Dalai Lama, *How to Expand Love*, 75–95.

Day 273

> *Discipline, it has been suggested, is the means of human spiritual evolution. This section will examine what lives in back of discipline—what provides the motive, the energy for discipline. This I believe to be love.*[32]

The Dalai Lama moves on to the fifth step, and maintains that love is more than just basic kindness and respect for those whom we encounter on a daily basis. The fifth step for cultivating and practicing love is compassion. As he uses the word, it takes on the meaning of understanding the suffering of others and finding ways to reduce or eliminate the suffering. It becomes integral in our quest to improve our practice of mindful spirituality. As he says, "Compassion is crucial in the beginning, middle, and consummation of spiritual practice. It is like the seed of enlightenment."[33] I reflect from time to time on the extraordinary suffering in the world. I wonder how people endure in countries where there is so little water, in places where there is war and people are being killed daily, in settings that are so impossible that migration is the only course of action, and in families in which there is sickness of loved ones about to die from cancer. In my setting, I see illness more frequently than the violence of war or the lack of food and water. But as I check the news on a daily basis, I am reminded of the terrible plight of so many in our world. I do feel compassion, and I ask myself what I might do to help. I know that I can't do everything, yet I can do some things, and I focus my energy on what it is I can do. Among them are:

1. Help those who are hungry in my community by supporting the food bank.

2. Encourage those who represent me in the government to take actions that shape policies of compassion for those who are afraid and suffer.

3. Use my gifts and talents to teach, helping others to learn in ways that enrich their lives. I have been a teacher most of my adult life, and have learned insights and knowledge that may help to transform the lives of others.

4. I can work internationally on issues of peace and justice.

Are there specific ways that you can show compassion to others?

---

32. Peck, *The Road Less Traveled*, 81.
33. Dalai Lama, *How to Expand Love*, 134.

Day 274

Knowledge of these basic facts makes realistic the assumption of responsibility to help others on a vast scale. Since you understand that all afflicting obstructions can be removed, it is realistic to decide to help all beings do this. With these realizations you can make the altruistic decision from the depths of your heart and mind, which in turn opens the way for full spiritual development.[34]

The Dalai Lama's final two steps in widening the circle of loving relationships and practicing mindful spirituality are to make a total commitment to the life of love and to continue seeking altruistic enlightenment. As we expand outward in love as part of our practice of mindful spirituality, we need commitment and understanding. These suggestions by the Dalai Lama absolutely ring true for me. It was because of my Christian faith and the study of the life and teachings of Jesus that I formed a commitment to attempt to be a loving person. It has not always been easy, although there has been some progress. What progress has been made has come about because of spiritual practices of prayer, reflection, and the responsibilities of being a pastor. It has also come about by the range of relationships I have formed across the years, such as loving my family (my wife and son), the several friendships that have enriched my life, and working with colleagues in a variety of settings in the church and higher education. I look back upon this array of connections with people, and I know I have been loved and learned how to love. In addition, my obligations to care for another who was ill or facing difficulties helped me to understand the meaning of empathy.

I am now committed to a life of love, and I know that I also need to expand my understanding of what this commitment entails. I have read some of the literature about love and learned from this reading about love's many dimensions. I have also taught courses on love and have written a book on the meaning of love in the human experience. I am making progress in altruistic enlightenment, and will continue to pursue it. This writing of daily entries has reminded me of how much I need to learn and move my learning into practice.

How have you learned about kindness, love, and compassion?

---

34. Dalai Lama, *How to Expand Love*, 157.

Study Guide for the September Readings

Questions for Contemplation and Discussion

1. In what ways does the Hebrew Bible ask us to respond to those who suffer and are in need?
2. In what ways does the Hebrew Bible help those in despair and give them hope?
3. What was the "good news" that Jesus proclaimed and brought to people in despair and suffering?
4. What is the "double love commandment" and how do we share it with other religions?
5. How should we apply the double love commandment locally, regionally, nationally, and globally?
6. What are the major social problems we face regionally and globally? Which are most intense and need immediate attention?
7. How much should our different levels of government be involved in solving these problems, and how much is it the responsibility of individuals or private organizations to solve these problems?
8. What are the several ways that love has been defined? What is your definition of love?
9. What are the primary characteristics and dimensions of love?
10. How do we cultivate love in our lives? How much is it a matter of commitment and discipline, and how much do we need to be empowered to be more loving?

THEME FOR OCTOBER

EXPANDING OUTWARD FOR COMMUNITY

Day 275

How do I love thee? Let me count the ways.
I love thee to the depth and breadth and height
My soul can reach when feeling out of sight
For the ends of Being and ideal Grace.
I love thee to the level of every day's
Most quiet need, by sun and candle light.
I love thee freely as men strive for Right.
I love thee purely, as they turn from praise.
I love thee with the passion put to use
With my lost saints—I love thee with the breath,
Smiles, tears, of all my life! And if God choose,
I shall love thee better after death.[1]

We do not love in a vacuum; we love in relationships and community. We love others and they love us. As the Irish proverb says: "It is in the shelter of each other that people live." Elizabeth Barrett Browning, in reflecting on her love for her husband Robert, speaks of their love as the essence of life. She was perhaps a bit of an introvert, yet even those of us who value time alone need others. We need both warm and personal relationships, and also a sense of belonging in a community.

I remember a fairly recent move my wife and I made for our retirement. We longed for a return to the region in which we grew up and had so many good memories of childhood and a sense of belonging. We left Louisville, Kentucky, which had been our home for eighteen years, with some sadness; it had been a good place for us, both in terms of our employment and our family life. But it wasn't quite home as it was for many of our friends whose families had been there for generations. We made at least two trips to the Northwest, with Seattle and Portland as our places of birth. We loved the beauty of the mountains and the water that had brought so much joy to our early years. We finally settled on Whidbey Island—a quiet place that was free from the rush of traffic, was situated on the Puget Sound, and was a short ride to the mountains and to Seattle. It has been a good move for us. We feel at home.

What are the places in your life where you feel most comfortable? At home?

1. Browning, "Sonnets from the Portuguese." From *The Oxford Dictionary of Quotations*.

Day 276

Having a map and directions from spiritual books and texts is not enough. We do not know where our spiritual life will lead us, but it always requires us to go into that which is difficult and unknown. Those who attempt to practice alone are almost inevitably more confused or lacking in spiritual depth than those who have practiced under a skillful teacher.[2]

Having arrived in a new location, even with years of experience in a variety of places in the United States and around the world, I discovered that several needs surfaced. The first was finding some friends from the past and forming new friendships. My wife and I both began to reach out for those people with whom we had much in common, perhaps past experience, and also current interests and shared values. It was a bit easier for my wife, the extrovert, than it was for me with my introverted tendencies. We found these friends in a variety of ways, and these friendships continue to give us joy and support. Having had a career in higher education and the church, it was natural for me to seek a community in religious and educational settings. It wasn't long until we found a sense of community, meeting the second need. Mine was in a progressive church that allowed me to be myself, a person who is never quite at rest, who asks questions, and likes the challenge of continual learning. I found others who liked to put faith together in different ways, and enjoyed the challenge of linking spiritual growth with the new world in which we live.

I began to meet a third need, that of finding a way to use my life experience, my skills, and my interests. I had thought I would find a place in a progressive learning center on Whidbey Island, and I did explore connections to this institute and a community college. As it turned out, it was not easy for me to find a role in either situation. In time, this need was met by the soulful environment of the island. It turned out to be a setting in which I could continue my research and writing, teaching, and use of my pastoral skills. The fourth need, intellectual and spiritual development, was met in this soulful environment and my own initiative. It has been a good setting for us.

Are your needs for friends, community, a clear role, and growth being met?

---

2. Kornfied, *A Path with Heart*, 229.

Day 277

Soul is not a thing, but a quality or a dimension of experiencing life and ourselves. It has to do with depth, value, relatedness, heart, and personal substance.[3]

Across the years I have been a person who has sought a deep and meaningful life. I have pursued this quality of life largely within the Christian community and local congregations. There have been times that the expression of the Christian community in a local congregation has not been an exceptional source of nurture and growth for me. Good and gifted people have led them, and welcomed me as a friend and one who could help. Where I have had some discomfort is the ways that the liturgies and worship have sounded dated and drawn from a previous era. The language did not always take me to the places I need to go to continue my personal growth and to find guidance in linking my faith to current realities. In some cases, the theology has been a bit defensive, arguing for a faith orientation that has not come to terms with contemporary life.[4] I also confess to the tendency of moving into leadership roles, rather than relaxing and having my needs met. Perhaps this has become a way of meeting some of my needs as I tend to put the growth and well-being of other people at the center, and find fulfillment in this ministry. It is possible that I expect too much. My quest for a mindful spirituality will have to continue within the limitations of my own community life, and with the people that share the common goals suggested in the pregnant expression "mindful spirituality." Buddha and Jesus reached their levels of mindful spirituality in the daily give-and-take of imperfect communities. These communities are filled with people not unlike me who occasionally feel less-than-fulfilled, face vague depression, remain unsure about their deepest values, long for more personal fulfillment, and look to the church and other religious communities for a deep meaningful spirituality. It is often in life together, to use the phrase of Dietrich Bonhoeffer, where this happens.

Have you found a community of faith that encourages your spiritual growth?

---

3. Moore, *The Care of the Soul*, 5.
4. Many people are addressing this concern; for example, McLaren, *A New Kind of Christianity*.

Day 278

Because the spiritual process is not a random one, guides and teachers drawing on ancient traditions can understand and assist our journey when we ourselves are lost.[5]

There have been many times in my life when I have been confused and sensed that I was losing my way. I have been most fortunate to have friends, mentors, teachers, and pastors who had the patience to pause in the rush of their lives and lend a hand to help me re-orient my life and stay on track. Looking back on these relationships, I have noticed several patterns; some healthy and life-giving, and others not so helpful. The first pattern is when these kind interventions were empathic and wise. There was genuine care, a true listening, and helpful guidance. I felt no condescension, but affirmation as a person. A second pattern that was occasionally present was that I began to feel some dependence, and wanted to be like those who were helping me. I gradually learned that I needed to be true to and apply the counsel of these mentors to my journey. As I chose this direction, I freed myself from excessive dependence. I also learned that these mentors were not free from the risk of co-dependence, a relationship that inadvertently encourages unhealthy dependence and continues harmful practices inherent in the relationship. As the years passed, I began to better understand the difference between being present for another for their welfare and the risk of taking over the agenda and self-referencing every comment. I also began to observe and learn the great truth that in these relationships, one needs to respond with understanding and compassion, not judgment and advice.

There are several roles, ranging in character and importance in different religious traditions that are essential to our growth. For example, we all need good teachers, people who take us to new ways of understanding. We also need mentors, those who lead by example and friendship over extended periods of time. Many people have benefited greatly from spiritual directors, people who are well-trained, able to guide us on our spiritual journey, and who often serve as counselors.

Who has helped you along the way, and what was their role?

---

5. Kornfield, *A Path with Heart*, 231.

Day 279

Trust and risk are closely related. In fact, they are bound or linked together. You cannot have one without the other. You cannot trust someone unless risk is involved. And you cannot risk being vulnerable unless you can trust someone. In short, without trust there is no risk, and without risk there is no trust.[6]

In addition to the personal one-on-one relationships that sustain us, there is also a need for support groups. Those who have chosen the monastic life have them built into their daily routines, but those of us who do not have them provided should be diligent about finding one. Those in the Buddhist tradition give the Sangha, or the spiritual community, a rightful place when they elevate it to the point of being one of the three foundations of their faith. Alcoholics Anonymous speaks of the small support group as essential to healing. The first-century Christian church consisted of small groups, gathered in homes for worship and supportive fellowship. My own experience has taught me about the value of a small group where there is openness, honesty, and high levels of trust. During those stretches of time when I have been without the small support group, I have been less motivated and, at times, discouraged.

As Tom Kirkpatrick suggests in the quote above, such a group functions with the presence of risk (I hurt and need some help) and trust (please hear me and come alongside). If such a group is for healing and nurturing, one must overcome the almost inevitable fear that there may be those who will not have my well-being in mind. We may fear rejection and lack of confidentiality, and we wonder if our sharing of needs will be interpreted as self-centered, or even devious, and a quest for attention. The best small groups anticipate these kinds of fears in their members and promise that certain guidelines will prevail, such as empathic listening with no interruptions, no judgments, and confidentiality. There must be high levels of trust in order for us to talk openly about struggle and a willingness to listen with compassion to others in the group. We learn that we are not alone in our struggle, and have friends who care.

Are you presently in a small group, and if not, would you like to be?

---

6. Kirkpatrick, *Communication in the Church*, 59.

Day 280

> *I am by no means alone in arguing that the process of coming to faith and growing in faith takes place in the context of community and that God uses community as a means of grace. Indeed, a near consensus prevails among religious educators that faith communities have formative power in the lives of people, nurturing faith and giving shape to the quality and character of their spirits.*[7]

In order to move toward health and wholeness, one needs a mentor, a support group, and a larger community in which to belong. It is easiest for me to illustrate this point from the perspective of the Christian faith, in that the practice of faith in the Christian tradition is sustained in the community called the church (*ekklesia*, meaning "assembly" or "gathering"). It can be illustrated, as well, from nearly all of the great religions. It has been very informative for me to be present in the gatherings of many of them, including Jews, Muslims, Hindus, and Buddhists. Let me mention four primary qualities of these groups, noting that they are more suggestive than comprehensive.

1. The communities gather to be informed and reminded of their *creeds*, the essentials of what they believe. Often this is done in the context of a worship service, and in most cases worship is a time of remembrance, hearing about the founders, their teachings, and the experiences of past and present followers and faith communities.

2. In addition, those gathered are informed and reminded of the ethical *code*, and informed about what it means to live as a faithful Jew or Muslim, inspired to live an ethical life and empowered to be a true disciple or follower.

3. Further, as people gather together, they *act out the content* of their faith. They go through ceremonies and experiences, often involving more than just hearing. For Christians, the Eucharist (or the communion service) is an example of the community re-living the redemptive acts of Jesus Christ.

4. The gathering also provides a strong sense of belonging, a *community* that gives one an identity and values by which to live.

What sort of experiences have you had in a faith community?

---

7. Dykstra, *Growing in the Life of Faith*, 83.

Day 281

I, therefore, the prisoner of the Lord, beg you to lead a life worthy of the calling to which you have been called, with humility and gentleness, with patience, bearing one another in love, making every effort to maintain the unity of the Spirit in the bond of peace. (Eph 4:1–3)

We are reflecting on the ways that we move out into our living environments to make a positive contribution to the common good. We have said that we need to prepare ourselves for this responsibility, and maintained that having a mentor or teacher, a supportive small group, and a larger community in which to belong are the ways that we are nurtured and move toward spiritual maturity and responsible living. We noted that we move toward maturity and responsibility by being informed about our foundational beliefs, guided in our moral life, motivated by regular worship and attention to the content of our faith, and sustained in an active fellowship of sisters and brothers in our faith tradition (code, creed, content, and community).

We underlined, in reference to community life, that it gives us a sense of belonging, an identity, and set of values that guide our lives. But not all communities to which we belong provide the support and guidance that we need. The Apostle Paul, as he founded new churches (communities of faith), often spoke to them about the ideal way of life in these communities. For some of them—the Corinthian church, for example—it was hard to come together as a unified community. They argued about leadership and abused the communion service. In the letter to the Ephesian Christians, the teaching about community life (life together) is summarized.[8] The author begs them to lead a life worthy of their calling. The true marks of the healthy Christian community are humility, gentleness, patience, and unlimited love. If these qualities prevail in the church (or nearly any community), there will be unity. As members of the community are led and empowered by the Spirit of God, there will be the bond of peace. I am grateful for the ways that communities have nurtured me!

What are the primary values that undergird your faith community?

---

8. New Testament scholars have questioned whether Ephesians was written by Paul, but do affirm that it contains the thoughts of Paul.

Day 282

> *But each of us was given grace according to the measure of Christ's gift . . to equip the saints for the body of Christ . . until all of us come to the unity of faith. . . We must no longer be children, tossed to and fro and blown about by every wind of doctrine. . . But speaking the truth in love, we must grow up in every way into him who is the head, into Christ.* (Eph 4:7, 12–15)

The author of Ephesians (perhaps Paul or one of his followers) is quite clear about the foundations of a healthy faith community and the values that guide it. The author makes six points, as relevant today as they were in the time of Paul.

1. The first is that each of us has a skill, a gift, or a special contribution to make which can be helpful to the entire community; in this case, the new churches in the region of Ephesus. We have been *graced* to contribute to the common good.

2. Our goal is "to equip the saints for the work of ministry, for building up the body of Christ." We are essential to the health and well-being of the church community, so it can carry out its ministry.

3. There will be unity in the community of faith if all are truly led by the Spirit of God. They will be fully able to engage in their ministries, rather than get bogged down by the distractions of petty conflicts.

4. But all too often we act like children, want our way, and are easily influenced by whatever anyone says (tossed to and fro). It is so easy to get lost.

5. As we grow and mature, we learn how to speak the truth in love. The phrase "speak the truth in love" captures so perfectly the way we need to relate to members of our community, and indeed to all of the people whom we encounter. It contains what every comment should have, truth and love, truth for insight and guidance, and love so it can be heard and applied.

6. But the capability to speak the truth in love must be learned and developed as we grow in every way toward our great model and example, Jesus. In every way, he spoke the truth in love to all those that he encountered.

We know we have a gift to contribute to others for their well-being and to help them mature. We do so by living and speaking the truth in love.

What is your gift to use in your community of faith—or any community?

Day 283

In the power of the Holy Spirit the church experiences itself as the messianic fellowship of service for the kingdom of God in the world.[9]

I have chosen to speak about the Christian faith in these daily readings about mindful spirituality. I have done so because it is that community of those seeking the spiritual life with which I am most familiar, and the one that has nurtured me. Yet there are other communities of faith, and we will draw from them as well, as we explore together how we deepen our spiritual life. We are currently focusing on the theme of "Expanding Outward," and began this section on the subject of love. We soon learn as we try to love how much we are helped in this endeavor by participating in a community that loves and supports us. So, our subtheme is "Expanding Outward for Community." We have begun to sketch this community by suggesting the characteristics of a supporting community. What should the community provide for us as it becomes a base for the cultivation of mindful spirituality?

I come to this subject with a variety of experiences in the church, having served in a congregation, its international mission, its national offices, and its related schools and colleges. Each of these assignments has provided a slightly different perspective, and I will draw upon these perspectives as we ask what the spiritual community provides for its members. I have both appreciated belonging to a religious community, in my case a Protestant denomination called the Presbyterian Church (USA), and I have also struggled with its limitations and my failures within it. I do not easily find a single word or concept that summarizes my life in the Presbyterian Church and the way it has provided for my spiritual life, although the one that comes the closest is the way it became a home. I belonged to a community of faith that sought to extend the mission of Jesus, that of love, justice, and peace in the world. Has it always been easy to be in this home? Of course not; nor have I always been a good member of the family. But it has been *home*, a place to struggle and grow.

Have you found a community that feels like home for you?

---

9. Moltmann, *Church in the Power*, 289.

Day 284

> *When the day of Pentecost had come, they were all together in one place. And suddenly from heaven there came a sound like the rush of a violent wind, and it filled the entire house where they were sitting. Divided tongues, as of fire, appeared among them, and a tongue rested on each of them. All of them were filled with the Holy Spirit and began to speak in other languages, as the Spirit gave them the ability.* (Acts 2:1–4)

The Book of Acts describes the formation and early development of the Christian Church. It is quite a remarkable story, told in the categories and metaphors of its time. It is this community that provides a home, and in the home are people who are becoming friends. The description given by Luke in Acts has several components:[10]

1. The first is the affirmation that *God was present* in a quite dramatic way. Those who have had mystical experiences have not easily found language to describe them. Luke chooses to use the metaphor of tongues to describe the way that these people began to communicate, even though they spoke different languages. God enabled them to understand each other and make contact.

2. This new community was a *diverse* group. Luke's description says that they came from a vast region and brought with them not only their language, but also their culture and customs. The church community was inclusive.

3. What they had in common was a *unique and profound experience*. All of them felt like they had encountered God in a deep and transforming way. They had shared this experience together, and all were eager to understand it.

4. Though a diverse group in terms of language and culture, they nevertheless felt a *great affinity with one another and remarkable unity*. What was very surprising was that they could understand one another, even though they spoke different languages. They became spiritual friends (*anam cara*).

5. Some who were present or nearby were not impressed, and said, "They are filled with new wine." This observation may suggest an ever-present reality, that *those who have not had the common experience may doubt its reality*.

In what ways does a common experience make friends and create community?

---

10. There are some questions about who was the author of the Book of Acts.

Day 285

> *But Peter, standing with the eleven, raised his voice and addressed them.*
> (Acts 3:14)

Fortunately, for this mixed group of people who needed understanding, a leader stepped forward and gave them *understanding and guidance*. A community is held together by leadership that provides insight and guidance, and invites the members to reflect on their experience and share it with others in the group. The first part of Peter's address (sermon) was to call attention to the immediate moment. He says to this group that those who are observers, not participants, have accused us of being drunk, but it is not so, for it is only nine o'clock in the morning. Peter goes on to explain that what has happened to them has been expected. The great prophets, Joel in particular, have said that the time will come when "God declares, I will pour out my Spirit upon all flesh, and your sons and your daughters shall prophesy, and . . . everyone who calls on the name of the Lord shall be saved" (Acts 2:17, 21).

Peter then goes on to explain to them that the current experience is the outgrowth of the coming of Jesus. Peter describes the way that the people of Israel dared to hope that the messiah would come, and Jesus is that expected Messiah. Jesus did all that God expected in this role: there were "deeds of power, wonders, and signs that God did through him among you." Then he was crucified outside of the law, but was victorious over death, giving them hope. We are that new community that is forming around his life, teaching, great works, death, and victory over death.

It is doubtful that all of those present fully understood what Peter was saying. Yet, many responded to the message of God's love expressed in Jesus, and "about three thousand persons were added" to the new community that was later to be called the Christian church. Peter explains to them that what they have experienced together is good news, that God has acted in Jesus on their behalf, and that the Holy Spirit, the very presence of God, will empower them to experience a new way of life. They were reassured that God had not forsaken them, that the messiah had come, and that God will be with them as they face the challenges of life.

How would you have felt if you had been there on the day of Pentecost?

Day 286

> *All who believed were together and had things in common; they would sell their possessions and goods and distribute the proceeds to all, as they had need.*
> (Acts 2:45)

The early Christian community that would soon be called the church provided a spiritual home for these new converts. In this home, they found supportive friends who were like an extended family. They were a bit confused as they began this new way of life, patterned on the life and teachings of Jesus. The early leaders, such as Peter, helped them to understand their new faith and gave them guidance.

The next characteristic of this new community was that the members gave to and received care from the community. An early practice of sharing all that they had did not last indefinitely, but was integral to the early formation of the community. It was their way to ensure that all the basic needs in life were provided. They needed housing and food, and while it is not specifically mentioned, they likely needed health care. The center of this new community was spiritual care, which Luke underlines: "They devoted themselves to the Apostles' teaching and fellowship, to the breaking of bread and the prayers." Further, as Luke notes, "Day by day, as they spent much time together in the temple, they broke bread at home [in homes] and ate their food with glad and generous hearts, praising God and having the good will of all the people" (Acts 2:42, 46–47). It was a beloved community.

The churches that I have served have provided care for their members in these many ways. The church in which I am currently active has a care committee that meets on a regular basis to review the needs of its members and those in the surrounding community. There is housing available on cold nights, right in the church's fellowship hall, and food is available. The teenagers have a special program just for them in the basement of the church. There is a pattern of making calls on those who are ill or unable to leave their home because of age. Small groups meet on a regular basis to "devote themselves to the Apostles' teaching" (bible study) and prayer. And while it is never sought, there is a great deal of goodwill in the surrounding community about the good work that is done by the church.

Do you have a small community that provides these services?

Day 287

> *Now there are varieties of gifts but the same Spirit; and there are varieties of services, but the same Lord; and there are varieties of activities, but it is the same God who activates all of them in everyone. To each is given the manifestation of the Spirit for the common good.* (1 Cor 12:4–6)

As this new community of the church became a home filled with friends who cared for each other, they looked to their leaders for guidance on how their common life might be organized. They needed to get it together in order to meet the needs of their members and proceed with their mission. As the Apostle Paul became involved with these new churches, he gave them sound advice on how to organize their affairs. He assumed that everyone in the new church would have a role, and he lays out a design that should help the members accept their new responsibilities. His first observation about this design was that God had gifted certain individuals for essential tasks for the common good. He mentions that some of the people are especially wise, and others have important knowledge. These people should be in positions of leadership in order to help this new community find its way into the future. He goes on to say that others have a deep and profound faith, and are able to keep this new community centered in its beliefs and its way of life. Others have the gift of healing, and are able to care for the health of those in the community.

In addition to the need to give leadership to those who are especially gifted, Paul reminds this new community that that they will be involved in a variety of services, all of which will need planning, implementation, and coordination among the members. Meetings and events will need to be scheduled, planned, and organized. The people in the church will have needs, and the mission of the church is to reach out to the region (Corinth) with its message of faith, hope, and love. As the church begins to understand its mission, it will want to provide a range of activities, both for its members and for people in the region. Worship services must be planned, prayer groups formed, and study groups must be arranged to help understand their new faith orientation. Churches are busy places, and everyone must help and be involved.

What are your gifts, and how might they be used to help others?

Day 288

> *Now when they heard this, they were cut to the heart and said to Peter and the other apostles, "Brothers, what should we do?" Peter said to them, "Repent, and be baptized every one of you in the name of Jesus Christ so that your sins may be forgiven; and you will receive the gift of the Holy Spirit. For the promise is for you, for your children, and for all who are far away, everyone whom the Lord our God calls to him." (Acts 2:37–39)*

The new community was forming; people had found a new home; they were making spiritual friends, even among those from other cultures who spoke different languages; they were being cared for, and their needs were being met; they were being asked to use their talents and gifts for the common good; and they were receiving information and guidance about their new commitment to the life of faith.

In the swirl of all this new insight and activity, there was likely some doubt about it all, and a high degree of physical and emotional fatigue. Inevitably, the question came to the apostles: "Brothers, what should we do?" Peter, generally ready for a comment, responds in order to keep them inspired. He reminds them of what has happened, and underlines five points. The first is that they have repented or need to repent. Unfortunately, the word "repent" has come to mean almost exclusively feeling sorry for one's sins. There is this dimension in Peter's charge to them, but the more essential point of the word is to change directions. He reminds them that they have changed their hearts and their lives. He then says, secondly, that this reality of life change needs to be acted out or celebrated, as they join this new community of people. He guides them to be baptized as an expression of this change and becoming a part of the church of Jesus Christ. Thirdly, he notes that baptism is the expression of having been forgiven and cleansed from sin, or the old pattern of life that didn't have God at the center. Fourth, he says that all of this activity means that you will receive the Holy Spirit, by which he meant the power and presence of God. It will fundamentally transform you and give meaning and direction to your lives. And fifth, he says this new faith is for you, your family, and for all whom the Lord calls to this new way of life. They recover their energy and are inspired to continue.

In what ways have you been inspired to continue your life of faith?

Day 289

Day by day, as they spent much time together in the temple, they broke bread at home and ate their food with glad and generous hearts, praising God and having the good will of all the people. And day by day the Lord added to their number those who were being saved. (Acts 2:46–47)

This new community was developing, and its many pieces were falling into place. People felt at home and were making good friendships, and their basic needs were being met. The leaders were providing guidance, and each person was beginning to understand what their role might be. At this early stage, most were inspired and felt that God was truly at work in their midst. The challenge, of course, was whether this new movement could be sustained. I know that I have been to conferences in which I learned, made good friends that I thought would last, heard inspiring stories, and gathered wisdom by reading important documents and books. I began to see how I might find a role in a new and challenging endeavor that would change hearts and minds for a better way of life. I then caught a plane home, and as the days came and went, I discovered that I was no longer as inspired by the new and grand vision I had heard about at the conference. Life had its daily challenges, and it was all I could do just to keep up with the demands of my life, my family, and my job, in which I earned only enough to hold life together. I had the best of intentions. The early Christian community was inspired by a grand vision, and many of its members sustained their motivation for developing the movement, even as they went home to the context and routines of their former life. The beliefs and practices of their new life were sustained, and I have wondered, as I read about the growth of the Christian community, how they remained faithful. What motivated them? As one reads the history of the early church, one sees that several factors were present that sustained the new Christians. We will describe these factors in our next entry.

Have you had a similar experience full of vision, and then gone home and lost it?

Day 290

I thank my God every time I remember you, constantly praying with joy in every one of my prayers for all of you, because of your sharing in the gospel from the first day until now. I am confident of this, that the one who began a good work among you will bring it to completion by the day of Jesus Christ. (Phil 1:3–5)

We are reflecting on the ways to sustain a vital Christian life and community.

1. One was that they had a conversion experience and sensed that God was now present in their lives. They were truly transformed by their new faith. Their hearts and their lives had been fundamentally changed. It was more than just a high from a weekend of inspiration and joy. They had life together.

2. They formed small house churches for worship and fellowship. They were encouraged by the presence of others who were following the same spiritual path. There was a continuation of what they had experienced in Jerusalem.

3. In that the majority were Jews, they linked what had happened at Pentecost as an extension of their current religious outlook. Of course, there were those who did not have a Jewish background (Gentiles), and they were persuaded that what had happened to them did have continuity with Judaism and its history.

4. There was a group of leaders who sustained them with wisdom about how to have a mindful spiritual life and guidance for organizing their new church.

5. In addition, there was an oral tradition filled with the life and teachings of Jesus, and they heard about how others were finding ways to be the church in their respective cultures. An embryonic New Testament was circulating.

6. As important as any factor in the growth and development was that they were asked to take responsibility. They learned a version of the commissioning of the first group of disciples; Jesus had said, "All authority in heaven and on earth has been given to me. Go therefore and make disciples of all nations, baptizing them in the name of the Father and of Son and of the Holy Spirit, and teaching them to obey everything that I have commanded you. And remember, I am with you always, to the end of the age" (Matt 28:18–20). These precise words came later, but this message sustained this first group of Christians. They were to spread the love of God (as expressed in Jesus) and invite all to endorse this new way of life. They belonged to a new community of faith and had a role to play.

Picture yourself in one of the house churches. What would be going on?

Day 291

> *When they had finished breakfast, Jesus said to Simon Peter, "Simon son of John, do you love me more than these?" He said to him, "Yes, Lord; you know that I love you." Jesus said to him, "Feed my lambs." A second time he said to him, "Simon son of John, do you love me?" He said to him, "Yes, Lord; you know that I love you." He said to him a third time, "Simon son of John, do you love me?" Peter felt hurt because he said to him the third time, "Do you love me?" And he said to him the third time, "Lord, you know everything; you know that I love you." Jesus said to him, "Feed my sheep." (John 21:15-17)*

It is difficult for many of us to speak openly about our faith. I expect it has never been all that easy. In our time, there is the pervasive value of respecting the views of others, and I agree with this value and honor it. In the story that we have of the conversation between Jesus and Peter,[11] we have a thoughtful exchange about how the followers of Jesus might tell the story. In the story, Jesus used the metaphor that would have been easily understood in that culture of caring for sheep. Note that Jesus first asked about motivation with the question, "Do you, son of John, love me?" It is asked three times, and Peter felt a little hurt that Jesus repeated the question. Commentators have offered a number of interpretations of this passage, most attempting to explain the pathos in the exchange. Both Jesus and Peter knew that this would be one of their last conversations, and Peter would have felt a great deal of sadness and wanted Jesus to understand how much he was loved. I suspect he also wanted some guidance about how to proceed with the mission when Jesus was not present. It is likely that more was said in the conversation than is recorded in this small paragraph. Jesus was very suggestive with his question and the metaphor. He pointed to motivation, and then told Peter how to help in continuing the movement. The motivation will be love and the mission is to feed and tend the sheep (to care and nurture). I find help in this passage about why and what I might say as I am asked about my Christian faith.

Why does Jesus ask Peter, "Do you love me?" and what does he mean by "feed my sheep?"

---

11. New Testament scholars view this passage in John, and indeed the whole Gospel, as being quite late in the formation of the literature of the Gospels. The passage may have been added to the original manuscript of the Gospel of John, but it is a thoughtful addition in keeping with the spirit of Jesus.

Day 292

> *Instead, by speaking the truth in love, let's grow in every way into Christ, who is the head. The whole body grows from him, as it is joined and held together by all the supporting ligaments. The body makes itself grow in that it builds up with love as each one does their part.* (Eph 4:15–16, CEB)

We are reflecting together about how we might be involved in the life of a religious community. We have spoken about how a community sustains us, gives us a home, provides spiritual friends, cares for us, and offers us guidance. We learn about our role in the community, find inspiration and motivation from it, and then are asked to be a part of its mission. One part of its mission, when our community is the church, is to share the message of God's love with others. We underlined that our motivation in this endeavor is love. The heart of our mission is "to feed and tend the sheep," or to invite others in the spirit of love to be fed by God's love and be nurtured by those in the flock. Our challenge will always be to "speak the truth in love" and to make sure the body "builds up with love."

I have had some association with those within the Christian community who are quite direct in the way they invite others into the church community. I am reluctant to judge other sisters and brothers in the community. However, there are times when I feel uncomfortable with a particular strategy that says all must accept Christ or be lost for eternity. My discomfort is caused by the presumption of this judgment. First of all, it is a judgment rather than an act of love. With its quite literal interpretation of certain verses in the Bible, the judgment is made that God will punish those who do not have a correct set of beliefs. I have listened carefully to this point of view, and I do not think it contains the central message of the New Testament of God's love for all people. It also assumes that the way they read the Bible is what the Bible and its central message are telling us. We must be careful about the presumption that we can capture God and the divine way with our thoughts and words derived from the worldview of our time and place in history. Our knowledge of God is always approximate and limited. We love and invite, rather than judge.

What are the best ways to share the story of God's love for humankind?

Day 293

In the beginning was the Word, and the Word was with God, and the Word was God... And the Word became flesh and lived among us, and we have seen his glory as the father's only son, full of grace and truth. (John 1:1, 14)

The author of the Gospel of John maintains that God has lovingly communicated to the human family in and through a first-century Jewish Palestinian. He draws upon a current philosophical movement of his time, Stoicism, that maintained that the universe has order and purpose, a principle called *logos*. *Logos* has been translated as "word," in that this foundation of the universe is discernable just as a word communicates. The author, whom we call John, says that Jesus epitomizes this personal communication from God, and we see him as both grace (love) and truth. I learn from this teaching that the way we carry out the mission of the church is to always be sure that the way we represent the church is filled with grace and truth.

As we feed and tend the sheep, we do so in the spirit of unlimited love, and with the conviction that we must always be truthful, even if the truth is that we are not sure and don't quite know how to say it in all of its complexity and profundity. The way this has played out for me is that I have found ways of understanding the Christian message as grace and truth for me. I also know that others from different backgrounds, traditions, cultures, and beliefs may find love and truth elsewhere and in a different language or religion. I learn from and am enriched by them, and I have learned to acknowledge that God speaks many languages and that and there are many ways to speak about ultimate reality. I share my views in the spirit of love and the desire to be truthful. I do so with some humility before the Great Mystery, grateful that the Christian faith has given me a home. I feel profoundly privileged to have been in settings in which questions were welcomed, genuine doubts honored, and the way of holding convictions and beliefs flexible. New language and concepts were accepted. The articulation faith was in language more in keeping with current realities and the new world that is being born almost daily. I have enjoyed exploring these hermeneutical challenges that are so demanding in our time.

How do you make faith rooted in history become contemporary?

Day 294

> *Then Paul stood in front of the Areopagus and said, "Athenians, I see how extremely religious you are in every way. For as I went through the city and looked carefully at the objects of your worship, I found among them an altar with the inscription 'To an unknown god.' What therefore you worship, I proclaim to you."* (Acts 17:22–23)

As we talk with others about religious subjects, I have found that several attitudes or ways of communicating help the flow of the conversation and make it meaningful. The first is to acknowledge the context, understand it as far as possible, and speak within its framework. I think that it was very wise of Paul to speak with the Athenians by recognizing that they were a thoughtful people who had an extraordinary heritage, were comfortable with hard questions, and impatient with simple answers. Paul knew that day in front of the Areopagus that he was speaking with people who were familiar with the great philosophical traditions of Greece.

In addition, Paul was well-informed. He knew about the Greek culture, and had lived in it and absorbed the ways that it put reality together. He also understood the Greek way of thinking about religion, knowing that there were many gods, a whole family of them depicted in the Pantheon. He also knew his own primary base, that of the Hebrew Bible and first-century Judaism. In addition, he had thought a great deal about his own life experience—how he learned about the life and ministry of Jesus, and how he came to believe that Jesus was the Word from God.

Further, Paul came to these people as an honest person who was centered and authentic. His congruence as a human being caused the Athenians to trust him. They would have said, "This man speaks truthfully." There was no hypocrisy or deception in him. Perhaps they thought, "We may disagree with him, but it is wise to hear what he says. He understands us, and is knowledgeable and smart." So they listened, and as he left, they said, "We will hear you again about this." At this point, Paul left them gratified, knowing that some were persuaded, had become part of this new community called the church, and began to follow Jesus. From Athens, Paul went on to another Greek city and found a good reception there as well.

What are the most satisfying conversations about religion you have had?

Day 295

> *Again he began to teach beside the sea. Such a large crowd gathered around him that he got onto a boat on the sea and sat there, while the whole crowd was beside the sea on the land. He began to teach them many things in parables.*
> (Mark 4:1–2)

I learn from the stories that describe the way that Jesus met with groups and spoke with them. Often he had quite large groups, and he was able to communicate with them very effectively. I learn a great deal from the subjects he addressed, and I also learn that he communicated with people on several levels, not exclusively about the concerns of the religious life. Often I place myself in the crowd who listens, and I try to picture myself in that setting. I sense that he is communicating on at least three different levels. The first level has to do with caring about the comfort of the people who have gathered, making sure that their basic needs are met. In the brief account we have used from the Gospel of Mark, we observe Jesus finding a good way to be heard, arranging a way for the people to listen without distraction. In other situations we find him caring about those who were hungry, grieving, and perhaps ill. Level one, as we speak with others, is making sure they are safe, comfortable, and as much at peace as possible. We want them to be able to truly hear what is said.

Secondly, Jesus introduces an important topic for conversation. He does so in very interesting ways, often telling a story or a parable. He may talk about the religious situation in which the people find themselves, or the tradition and customs used in caring for the religious life of the people. He may speak about a topic on the people's minds, such as the Law, how to manage anger or divorce, or the need to be direct and honest. He finds a way to grab the attention of his listeners and get them engaged. At times, there are questions, even disagreements, and people wonder about his wisdom. Generally, Jesus moves on to a level three, which is to find ways of making what he is talking about very personal. He makes sure that the people can apply what is being said to their lives, the lives of their families, and the situation in which they live. They get it when he speaks about the Prodigal Son and the Good Samaritan. They listen when he gives them the Lord's Prayer and the Golden Rule.

What can we learn from Jesus about how we speak with others?

Day 296

After Jesus had left that place, he passed along the Sea of Galilee, and he went up the mountain, where he sat down. Great crowds came to him, bringing him the lame, the maimed, the blind, the mute, and many others. They put them at his feet, and he cured them, so that the crowd was amazed when they saw the mute speaking, and the blind seeing. And they praised the God of Israel. (Matt 15:29–31)

As Jesus ministered to people, he made sure that his message of love and compassion was not just words, but was backed up with action. The old saying, almost a cliché, is that "actions speak louder the words." If, when using this saying, we mean that actions speak more poignantly and powerfully than words, I do believe that it is true. I think this short aphorism is especially applicable in a religious context. Generally, those who have responsibility for guiding people in a religious setting speak about the virtuous life. They exhort people to live by the fundamental values of the religious tradition. But if they do not practice the values about which they preach, then the message becomes less persuasive. It is very easy to say that if a teacher or pastor/priest does not practice the values, then s/he is a hypocrite. In the case of Jesus, and many other great religious teachers, the fundamental values were integral to life. Often, he demonstrated his faith in God before he invited people to the life of faith in God. Even in the face of danger, he acted with hope before he asked others to place their hope in God. He lived the life of love and compassion before he encouraged others to be committed to that life and love their neighbor.

Jesus himself spoke directly about hypocrisy, and maintained that it was present in the leadership of the religious community. Matthew's Gospel has placed these sayings of Jesus in one section, chapter 23. It begins as follows: "Then Jesus said to the crowds and to his disciples, 'The Scribes and the Pharisees sit on Moses' seat; therefore do whatever they teach you and follow it; but do not do what they do, they do not practice what they teach'" (Matt 23:1–3). He does not question what they teach, but notes the hypocrisy of their actions. If we are to be a part of a beloved community such as a church, then we the members must practice what we teach.

Have you ever had difficulty practicing what you believe and teach?

Day 297

Be kind, compassionate, and forgiving to each other, in the same way God forgave you in Christ. Therefore imitate God like dearly loved children. Live your life with love, following the example of Christ, who loved us and gave himself for us. (Eph 5:1–2, CEB)

The author of the letter to the Ephesians, attributed to Paul, has a great deal of affection for the members of the new church in Ephesus. He longs for them to have a beloved community that will provide them with a spiritual home with supportive friends and with care and guidance. He wants so much for them to be inspired by their community and motivated to carry out its mission. He underlines the need to be sensitive to the context in which they live and work, well-informed about their new faith, and to communicate with those whom they serve with sensitivity and integrity. So he writes to them with a full heart, filling his letter with loving wisdom. He reminds them to conduct themselves with humility, gentleness, and patience, to accept one another with love, and to make an effort to preserve the unity of the Spirit with the peace that ties them together (Eph 4:2–4). He goes on to remind them that they have different gifts and talents, all of which should be used for the common good.

He closes his letter with two exhortations. The first is to be filled with the Spirit, the power and presence of God. As the new church gathers together, they share the wisdom of the psalms, sing hymns and spiritual songs, and "make music to the Lord in your hearts."[12] The second exhortation is to put on the armor of God by which the author asks them to put on the belt of truth, the breastplate of justice, and shoes that will enable them to spread the good news of peace. And above all, carry the shield of faith, the helmet of justice, and the sword of the Spirit that is God's word (Eph 6:10–17). The author wants them to be ready to face any challenges.

What more contemporary allegory would you suggest to make the same point?

---

12. The author of the letter to the Ephesians, perhaps Paul, speaks about the relationship of husband and wife, underlining love and respect. One part of this passage, 5:22–33, does raise some questions about authority and submission. I understand the passage as encouraging order and unity, but also carrying the prejudice of the patriarchal culture. There is a similar problematic passage about slavery (6:5–9).

Day 298

> *If then there is any encouragement in Christ, any consolation from love, any sharing in the Spirit, any compassion and sympathy, make my joy complete: be of the same mind, having the same love, being in full accord and of one mind.* (Phil 2:1–2)

The Apostle Paul had many roles in the early Christian community. One of his most important roles was to be a missionary and establish new churches. In his writings to these new churches, he spoke directly about four concerns: (1) the nature of this new community; (2) what it provides for its new members; (3) the way it reaches out to extend its mission; and (4) what sustains it across months and years in the face of dramatic challenges. We have reflected this past several days on the first three of these concerns. We now move to the fourth concern, or what will sustain these beloved communities called churches. We have already indirectly suggested what these sustaining qualities are, but let's try now to summarize them in one place for easy remembrance and reference. As we do, I want to say once again that I am inclusive, and suggest that these qualities apply to many types of groups, not just Christian churches. I illustrate from the Christian faith because I know it best, and because it has been a setting in which I have found a spiritual home. I speak as an insider, rather than an outside observer, as I illustrate from Christian communities, and I invite you to apply these basic dimensions of a beloved community to your settings.

Let me borrow from Paul directly, and repeat what he says to one of these new communities, the one in Philippi, a city in northeastern Greece. As he writes to them, he begins by expressing gratitude for their faithfulness, and prays that their love may overflow with knowledge and insight. As he moves along, he says that the health of the beloved community will be sustained by unity, by having the same mind as Christ. He urges them to follow the example of Jesus and to do nothing from selfish ambition, but by acting in humility to place the interests of others first. He is not saying that one should seek unity at any cost, however, and does urge them to have humility and listen to others. Unity, rather than a self-seeking will, enables a beloved community to sustain its life.

How have you coped in groups that have had deep conflicts and divisions?

Day 299

> *I am astonished that you are so quickly deserting the one who called you in the grace of Christ and are turning to a different gospel—not that there is another gospel, but there are some who are confusing you and want to pervert the gospel of Christ.* (Gal 1:6–7)

The early Christian community had to face the challenge of sustaining a good measure of unity. It could have easily fallen apart because of the diversity of cultures and languages. One particular concern, in that it was a child of Judaism, was how to honor its Jewish heritage and yet extend its mission beyond Jewish borders. The very first followers of Jesus were Jews, and saw themselves not as a new religion, but as an extension of Judaism following a radical Jewish prophet whose name was Jesus. Paul got into the middle of the struggle, believing that the gospel (the good news) should extend beyond Judaism and become available for everyone. His concern is that the message of Jesus about God's gracious love for all people should not be lost. Much of his time was devoted to preserving the gospel of grace. There were many Jewish followers of Jesus who said that the customs of Judaism should be integral to this developing new movement. Paul worked hard to articulate the key message of the new Christian faith, which is that all people may be in relationship with God through divine grace that is received by faith in the life and work of Jesus Christ.

The second quality necessary for sustaining the new community was clarity about the message. This concern is present in various forms in all of the writings of the New Testament and especially in the writings of Paul. He sought to articulate the message in continuity with the Hebrew Bible and Judaism, and also to make it understood by those outside of Judaism. "For by grace you have been saved through faith, and this is not your own doing; it is the gift of God—not the result of works, so that no one may boast" (Eph 2:8–9). It is God's gracious invitation to all people to form a loving relationship based on the Jesus event. This basic understanding may be the primary reason that the Christian church has existed for two thousand years, even with its many challenges.

In what sense did the Jesus event clarify the human response to the divine?

Day 300

> *Now after John was arrested, Jesus came to Galilee, proclaiming the good news of God and saying, "The time is fulfilled, and the kingdom of God has come near; repent, and believe in the good news." (Mark 1:14–15)*

The Christian faith and its beloved communities called the church have continued across history somewhat remarkably. I am persuaded that they have continued for several reasons. We have noted two of them: their unity within diversity and the clarity of the message of God's universal love. A third contributing factor in the church's longevity has been its mission of proclaiming and living out the belief in God's universal love, as expressed in Jesus.

As Jesus carries this message of God's love, he does so in language and categories that would be understood by his listeners and followers. The Gospel of Mark explains the mission of Jesus with four key ideas. The first is that it is good news (gospel) to people who did not always hear good news. In many ways, the people to whom Jesus was speaking were people who daily had to be concerned about feeding their families, and dealing with illness without any hope of getting well, as well as governments which did not assure them of basic services or justice. So they listened carefully to the good news of Jesus. As Jesus spoke about the good news, he underlined that it arrived in him, and now was the time to listen and apply what he is saying to them. The heart of the good news that arrived in the presence of Jesus was the kingdom of God, a term that refers to the reign of God. While the term had some political and apocalyptic implications, it also had immediate personal application, that one can receive the power and presence of God right now. The power and presence of God in one's life is transforming, changing one's inner life, motivations, attitudes, and spirit. But the catch is that it requires that one change directions, beliefs, attitudes, and perspectives. The word Jesus uses is "repent," a term that has some moral and ethical implications, but more specifically points to a fundamental change of attitude and outlook, a change that places the reign of God at the center of one's life.

In what ways does Jesus teach "mindful spirituality"?

Day 301

> *The message of Jesus is a presupposition for the theology of the New Testament rather than a part of that theology itself. For New Testament theology consists in the unfolding of those ideas by means of which Christian faith makes sure of its own object, basis, and consequences. But Christian faith did not exist until there was a Christian kerygma; i.e., a kerygma proclaiming Jesus Christ—specifically Jesus Christ the Crucified and Risen One—to be God's eschatological act of salvation.*[13]

We are reflecting on how the Christian church both survived and thrived. What were features that enabled it to become so central to the human experience across the centuries? We underlined that it managed to achieve a good measure of unity within diversity. We said as well that its message was refined, and became understandable and persuasive for many people. We stressed that this message affirmed that God spoke to the human family in the person of Jesus, who proclaimed God's universal love, the good news, and that Jesus invited his listeners to open their hearts to God's love, to repent and receive the power and presence of God into their lives.

One of the most influential New Testament scholars of the twentieth century, Rudolf Bultmann, draws upon a particular New Testament word to describe how this message was communicated. It soon became one of the four primary components of the identity of the new Christian church. The word used is *kerygma*; it is often translated as "proclamation," and has the deeper meaning of both the message and the way it is delivered to people who were eager to hear good news. It becomes the foundational starting point for those who attempted to understand and make sense out of the Jesus event. It is the life-changing message about the life, teachings, death, and the defeat of death in the resurrection of Jesus. This basic message, called the good news (gospel), was proclaimed far and wide in the broad expanse of the Roman Empire and even beyond in the immediate years at the close of the life of Jesus. It was truly believed that God did speak the Word, a message that was not just words, but incarnated in the person of Jesus, who became what was heard and endorsed by faith.

In what sense do most religions and worldviews have an essential message?

---

13. Bultmann, *Theology of the New Testament*, 3.

Day 302

> *At times like this the church is challenged to think radically about its origins, to lay hold decisively on its charge and to return to Christ's future form its now flawed and dying form. In a situation like this, the theological doctrine of the church cannot simply be expressed in abstract terms about the church's timeless nature. It will have to provide points of departure for reforming the church, for giving it a more authentic form.*[14]

The *kerygma*, the core message of the church, is its foundation, and has helped to sustain the church over several centuries. The second quality of the church, enabling it to survive and thrive in changing and challenging times, is *koinonia*, a term often translated as "fellowship." The term, however, implies much more than having coffee in the fellowship hall following the service. Books have been written about this subject. For purposes of our mindful reflection, let me suggest three essential dimensions of *koinonia*:

1. The first is that it is a *beloved community of people with a common bond of belief and practices*. We do live in difficult times, and often we get lost. We find it difficult to navigate the rapid changes and severe challenges of our time in place in history. We do need a community of love that supports and sustains us. The church and other religious communities give us a home with care and guidance.

2. The term *koinonia* also has the meaning of belonging to a *worldwide community that links us to the purposes of God that are planetary in scope*. I find great comfort in sensing that I have been invited into a fellowship of world citizens who are attempting to discern the will and way of God in the world. I find meaning for my life in this fellowship of global citizens and hope for our troubled world. I do not see it as the only way that God is present in the world, but it is one way.

3. And thirdly, I begin to frame my life purpose around the church's mission in the world. *We join with God in this endeavor.*

Do you think of yourself as living in harmony with the divine plan for the world?

---

14. Moltmann, *Church in the Power*, 2.

Day 303

> *This book builds on a simple premise: good teaching cannot be reduced to technique; good teaching comes from the identity and integrity of the teacher.*[15]

We are exploring together those qualities that enable a community of people to sustain their common life and mission across the years of change and challenge. We have said that one aspect that encourages continuity and longevity is its core message. We have also said that the core message is the proclamation of the life and teachings of Jesus, called the *kerygma*. We have also affirmed that coming together in community, as the Sanga within Buddhism or *koinonia* within Christianity, sustains an organization. A third quality that helps a community to sustain its life and mission is teaching. In the Christian church, two words with somewhat comparable meanings are used. The first is called the catechetical process, by which Christians are given instruction on those qualities that enable the learner to live a full Christian life. The subjects of this instruction will include biblical knowledge, the identity and mission of the church, and the foundations of Christian belief. This education will include ways for students to reflect on their behavior and experiences in light of the gospel. It will also include experiences that are formational and transformative, empowering the person to live the Christian life in a faithful way.[16]

Another word with comparable meaning is the Greek term *didache*, which (as a verb) means to "teach" or "instruct." It is certainly one of the most prominent features of the life of Jesus. He was known by his contemporaries as a rabbi, a term referring to a religious teacher. People marveled at his teaching, in that it was done in a way that changed the life of his listeners. They were taken by his integrity and authenticity: "Now, when Jesus had finished saying these things, the crowds were astounded at his teaching, for he taught them as one having authority, and not as their scribes" (Matt 7:28–29). The followers of Jesus, the leaders of the new Christian community, were also teachers, and teaching the faith was central to the church then, as it is now.

What do you think are the primary characteristics of a lasting community?

---

15. Palmer, *The Courage to Teach*, 10.
16. Hauerwas and Westerhoff, *Schooling Christians*, 266–71.

Day 304

> *There are two distinct types of call, and they are discovered or discerned in different ways. First is the "spiritual" or "general" calling to become a Christian, be baptized, and take up the duties of the Christian life. It is this call to faith and discipleship that is prominent in the New Testament.*[17]

A fourth dimension of the church's life, foundational to its continuance as a vital and life-giving community, was the call to service. The Greek word for this call is *diakonia*, with the original meaning of "waiting on tables," but which soon became in the New Testament the "discharge of service" in genuine love.[18] The church began to teach that all of its members had the general *calling of se*rvice, a responsibility that was seen as a fundamental component of discipleship or following the Christian way. My experience has been that those groups that have asked me to take some responsibility have claimed my loyalty and commitment. Other organizations that I have joined that did not ask me to be engaged in the mission of the group were sooner or later squeezed out of a busy schedule. I became active in the church for at least three basic reasons:

1. It was a community that *helped me to grow and develop as a more mature human being*. The church helped me to set goals for becoming more responsible, more sensitive to the needs of others, and more compassionate. It began to free me from my self-centeredness.

2. The church not only asked me to take responsibility for its mission of loving service in the world, but also *provided me with training and education*, so that I could make a genuinely helpful contribution to the mission of creating a more just and humane world.

3. The church gave me a *community of support*, theological guidance, and inspiration to use my life in compassionate service, rather than exclusively seeking my own selfish goals.

Do you have a community that guides, sustains, and inspires you?

---

17. Cahalan and Schuurman, *Calling in Today's World*, 58.
18. Kittel, *Theological Dictionary of the New Testament*, 87.

Study Guide for the October Readings

Questions for Contemplation and Discussion

1. In what kind of a setting are you most comfortable? What is the nature of the group in which you feel at home and free to be yourself? In what kind of setting do you feel uncomfortable? What makes you uncomfortable?

2. What sort of role do you usually play in a group? Are you a natural leader, or do you prefer to be less visible but still have a helping role?

3. In what kind of a setting or community gathering do you find the most help for your spiritual growth? What sort of groups assist you in your quest for mindful spirituality?

4. What kinds of people have been most helpful to you in your desire to cultivate mindful spirituality? Have they been teachers? Religious professionals such as pastors, priests, rabbis, or imams? Have they been small group leaders? What are their qualities?

5. Are you fairly secure in a small group and feel like there is a high level of trust? If so, how was this trust cultivated? Or are you cautious, even afraid that you might be hurt, rejected, or misunderstood? Why does that happen?

6. What are your most natural gifts and talents? Is it easy for you to use them in your various communities?

7. What are the marks of a fine leader? What is it about them that attracts you and gives you confidence that the group or organization is moving forward and accomplishing its mission?

8. Are there people in your life that you would call spiritual friends, in that you can speak openly about spiritual concerns and help one another on your respective spiritual journeys?

9. What is it that motivates you to stay in a spiritual community? What are the marks of a healthy spiritual community?

10. Does your spiritual community have these qualities?

THEME FOR NOVEMBER

EXPANDING OUTWARD IN RESPONSIBLE LIVING

Day 305

Learn to do good; seek justice, rescue the oppressed, defend the orphan, plead for the widow. (Isa 1:17)

We have explored two directions in our metaphor of "Expanding Outward" in the practice of mindful spirituality. The first and foundational one was "Expanding Outward to Love." We then turned to the theme of "Expanding Outward for Community, and stressed the importance of having a supportive and guiding group of caring people, one in which there is love and that inspires us to love. We now turn to the subject of cultivating our sensitivity to the needs of others, both as individuals and the conditions in which they live. I move to this concern with commitment and energy because of what I have experienced over the last several years of my life, the suffering of so many people that I observe.

Over the past several decades, I have had the rare privilege of observing the quest for justice in several strategic areas of the world. It was not that I was central to these quests, although my work in education did take me to these regions. The first setting was in the 1990s in Northern Ireland. I saw how the troubles in that region were as much or more about economic structures as they were about religion. During this time, I also traveled to Lahore, Pakistan, working again in education. I observed there how minority groups, with some difficulty, sought an excellent education in order to find employment and provide a good life for their families. More recently, I have been engaged with the issues of a just peace in Israel and Palestine, focusing again on how education can be of help in finding solutions to the divide between the government of Israel and the Palestinian people. These experiences have been educational and life-changing for me as I have observed the suffering caused by injustice and oppression. The issues are complex, often rooted in centuries of tradition and practice. I couple these experiences with what I learn daily about suffering in other parts of the world, and I want to help.

Are there some ways that you might lend a hand to help those who suffer?

Day 306

> *These questions are not only about how individuals should treat one another. They are also about what the law should be, and about how society should be organized. They are the questions of justice.*[1]

The questions about the nature of justice are numerous and complex. Occasionally, we run into them in our own life when we feel that we have not been treated fairly. As we begin to probe the reasons for being treated unfairly, we soon discover how difficult it is to rectify the situation. I recently spoke with a person who did not have adequate health care coverage, a situation that severely limited his ability to function. The more we talked, the more I began to understand why he was so frustrated. As I reflected on his situation, I found myself understanding it in the following ways:

1. The first and most obvious problem was that he was partially responsible for it. As he consulted with others, there were omnipresent comments about what he should have done along the way. The persistent questions of "did you?" and "have you?" only deepened his guilt and frustration.

2. But he went forward with his concern, and learned that the reason for not being able to get health coverage was a matter of history, politics, and the way laws and regulations are made. He was told: "That is the way it is and there is not much this office can do about it." He learned that making basic social changes to improve services for ill people is incredibly difficult, and he was told that "You may have to live with it."

3. He was given modest help and guidance. There were some health services available, a person to talk with about it, an office to call, and an email to send. But full coverage for the serious condition was dependent upon the federal government and congressional action, and he was impatient.

As we talked, our conversation went toward the subject of how difficult it is to navigate our current social order, how the current laws only approximate justice, and how many people feel unfairly treated. I learned that I needed to be educated to help!

What are some ways to learn about how to help in creating a more just society?

---

1. Sandel, *Justice*, 6.

Day 307

There is but one law for all, namely, that law which governs all law, the law of our Creator, the law of humanity, justice, equity—the law of nature, and of nations.[2]

Edmund Burke (1729–1797), a teacher at Trinity College in Dublin, wrote about the issues of law and justice. He knew that the law was a tangible expression of the ideal of justice, and sought in his philosophical works to apply his reflections to the expanding British Empire. In reading his works, it soon becomes clear that he is both brilliant and yet a child of his times. He notes how hard it is to govern justly with all the twists and turns of the human drama in his era. This is true in our era as well, yet it continues to be our goal, to insure that our government of the people, by the people, and for the people seeks to order society in a just way. As I engage in the pursuit of this goal as part of my journey of mindful spirituality, I soon discover that I must be a learner and educate myself in order to seek justice in wise and helpful ways.

As I have mentioned previously, I have been engaged in a range of peace and justice concerns in Israel and Palestine. I have read extensively about the conditions that exist in this region, and have traveled there on a regular basis over the past two decades. I feel empathy for Jewish people, who tell me that they need a safe haven, given the ways that Jewish people have been persecuted across the centuries. I speak with Palestinians who see Palestine as their homeland, and that they are the indigenous people with rights. Both groups live with fear, and those with the most power have the upper hand. That the settlements continue to expand in the Occupied Territories is a case in point. The best diplomats in the world have been unable to find a resolution for the conflict. Those of us who help in a small way have learned that we can provide some assistance to those who suffer injustice and live in fear, but sense that the quest for a just peace will continue to be a quest. Our best help is based on having knowledge of the region. Being uninformed or having a strong bias often leads to more suffering.

How does mindful spirituality guide us in these challenging circumstances?

---

2. Edmund Burke in his comments on the impeachment of Warren Hastings, May 28, 1794.

Day 308

> *To ask whether a society is just is to ask how it distributes the things we prize—income and wealth, duties and rights, powers and opportunities, offices and honors. A just society distributes these goods in the right way; it gives each person his or her due. The hard questions begin when we ask what people are due, and why.*[3]

A few years ago, Michael Sandel, a Professor of Government at Harvard University, taught courses on justice to overflow enrollments. In the course, he asked the basic question: What's the right thing to do? His book on justice reflects the content of the course and the challenge of finding the right thing to do, so that each person is given his or her due. I wish I had taken a similar course when I was in college. It would have helped me as I have continued to work on issues of law and justice. What I have discovered in my pursuit of wisdom on law and justice is how hard it is to know how to order a just society that gives all persons their due. I have learned that there will be endless disagreements, although being informed as much as possible about the place of law and justice in the specific context will gradually inch us forward. Informed people have helped to increase justice in Northern Ireland!

I have also learned that justice is achieved not by external intervention, although wise counsel and other forms of support are appreciated. Rather, it is achieved as the indigenous people find their way. I return again to my work with one small agency that makes its contribution by supporting high-quality education for Palestinian students, both in Israel proper and in the West Bank. We are committed to working collaboratively with many groups, most of them led by Palestinian people. The goals of these schools and other programs are to improve the life of the Palestinian people, and especially to educate in a way that teaches respect for differences and how to pursue a more just and humane society. We raise money for scholarships and other financial needs of the schools and programs, and as appropriate, we offer encouragement and consultation. Our work is not always easy, and we have made mistakes, but we stay with it and continue to learn.

How do you answer the question of "Am I my sister or brother's keeper?"

---

3. Sandel, *Justice*, 19.

Day 309

> *Like Caesar's Gaul, all of justice is divided into three parts. There are three ways in which to give each his/her own. To miss out on even one of these is to be unjust. The three forms of justice are commutative, social, and distributive.*[4]

To watch the work of the Supreme Court is to learn how difficult it is to fully understand the many sides of justice, and how it is applied to society. Daniel Maguire's three categories of justice are helpful to us. The first of these is commutative justice—or to say it in a slightly different way, it is the honest exchange between two people. It has to do with the commitments and promises people make to one another. It also has the components of freedom and equality, in that we make a promise to another person freely, and the exchange assumes that there is equality between the two people. It is not just if it is forced or coercive. For example, we might say, "I will cut your lawn for ten dollars, and when it is cut you will pay me." It is a just exchange.

The second type of justice is social justice, which aims for creating the common good with justice at the heart of the social order. The common good is understood as arranging the social structures so that human life and the rest of nature can flourish. As these conditions are met, then people feel respected and have hope for a good life. How this all happens is complex, and making it happen requires extraordinary care. The human family has gone in several directions in order to approximate social justice.

The third type of justice is distributive justice, and describes how people receive the goods and services they need. This kind of justice is generally managed by governments, corporations, schools, fine arts organizations, churches, synagogues and other religious institutions, and individual citizens and citizen groups. In a relatively free society like the United States, I am free to secure sufficient wealth and then select what I need from the range of options. I know that I can generally get what I need to keep my family healthy. I feel that I am treated justly if I can get what I need to flourish. But when I do not have sufficient wealth, power, or access, then I feel like I am treated unfairly. The last several decades in the United States tells us this interesting story.

How have we done in the United States, with regard to ensuring that all people receive their due?

---

4. Maguire, *Ethics*, 55.

Day 310

Plato's point is that to grasp the meaning of justice and the nature of the good life, we must rise above the prejudices and routines of everyday life.[5]

There have been many views on how best to achieve a just society and advance the common good. A brief glance at a few of them will put us in touch with the challenges of achieving a strategy that is accepted by a majority of the people. As I write, we are living in the early period of the Trump presidency, and this period illustrates the pronounced differences of opinion in our democratic society.

We might look briefly at the classical Greek period in history, in that the views the Greeks developed have been influential across history. They faced the issues of justice, one of which was finding the best leaders to govern. The quote above suggests that Plato believed the best way to the common good was to have enlightened philosophers govern, in that they would be above prejudice and rule for the good of all. Their reflections on goodness, truth, beauty, and justice give them the right virtues and deepened their commitment to a just society. Aristotle also advocated for finding the right leaders, people who fully understood the purpose of governance. He maintained that these people understand how to give people what they need and deserve. Wise people are able to understand the *telos*, or "end goal," of the social order. The aim, then, is to find leaders who fully grasp the reason for good government, and have the right virtues to take care of the just distribution of goods and services. In China's classical era, Confucius was influential, and spoke about the best way to order society. He maintained that the key to a good and just government was maintaining appropriate relationships (*li*), beginning in the family and going all the way up to emperor. Propriety and respect should prevail in order to achieve the common good. We observe a form of democracy in ancient Athens, and it was contrasted with military strength in Sparta. We also observe a federal government in early Rome, and see as well the rise of imperial government and the Caesars.

What sort of leaders are best able to govern justly in our time and place?

---

5. Sandal, *Justice*, 29.

Day 311

> *Let every person be subject to the governing authorities; for there is no authority except from God, and those authorities that exist have been instituted by God. Therefore whoever resists authority resists what God has appointed.*
> (Rom 13:1–2)

The rise of Christianity, built upon the foundation of the Hebrew Bible, underlined the place of religious commitment and values in ordering society in a just way. Justice was a central value and goal. It was clearly expressed by many of the great prophets, often in terms of the judgment of leadership. Frequently, defensive justification was offered for, and loyalty demanded toward, certain governments by claiming divine authority. Many of the emperors of ancient civilizations not only claimed divine sanction of their leadership, but actually claimed divinity.

Christians gave attention to the theological foundations of good governance during the Middle Ages. The church was instrumental in the transition from the decline of the Roman Empire and the transition to the *Holy* Roman Empire. Popes and kings did a sort of dance, claiming power in certain domains. The literature explaining this point of view is extensive. We can only point to a few examples. No less a person than Augustine gave attention to issues of just governance.[6] He lived during the decline of the Roman Empire, and had less confidence in the ways that governments ensure justice and the common good. He contrasted this human city, filled with human sin, with the City of God, which is a spiritual domain. He said that we must learn to live with the limitations of human government, and counseled that Christians should live in hope for the eternal city of God. The prevailing Christian position sided with Paul's guidance in the Book of Romans, in which it was argued that the authority to rule was given by God, and that we should honor our rulers, in that their authority is granted by God. This view was challenged in large measure because not all rulers were just. It became clear that there must be a way to resist corruption and oppression. There were soon voices justifying resistance to injustice and oppression.

What are our rights, and what should we do if government rule is unjust?

---

6. See Augustine, *The City of God*, for his reflections on the two cities.

Day 312

We hold these truths to be self-evident, that all men are created equal, that they are endowed by their Creator with certain unalienable Rights, that among these are Life, Liberty, and the pursuit of Happiness.

—Declaration of Independence

A third theme, in addition to finding appropriate leaders and understanding the religious dimensions of governance, was the assertion of human rights. One of the more dramatic events in which this occurred was the American Revolution. It was John Locke (1632–1714) who formulated the philosophical foundations which justified political resistance and revolution. Locke, an English philosopher, wrote on many subjects, but one was in the area of political and economic thought. He was bold enough to challenge the divine right of kings and the authority of the Bible and the church. He provided a philosophical foundation for the thesis that political sovereignty rests with the consent of the governed, and that ecclesiastical authority should be based on reason, not God-given power. He was an ardent defender of freedom of thought and speech, and it was to John Locke that Thomas Jefferson and others who led the American Revolution turned.

Other English philosophers were among those who recognized the right to resist tyranny, and they suggested alternative forms of government that might be more just. One point of view, advanced by Jeremy Bentham (1748–1812) was to find that form of social order that maximizes the greatest happiness. He wanted to shift the balance of pleasure over pain. His view is called utilitarianism; that is, to utilize that system that produces the most happiness and prevents suffering. Another English philosopher, John Stuart Mill (1806–1873), added the need for liberty and suggested that less government was the better way. Thomas Jefferson advocated this view, and articulated it in the Declaration of Independence. The American and the French revolutions illustrated these several points of view and ushered them into the Western world; they continue into the modern period. The debate about how to achieve a just society exists with equal intensity in other parts of the world as well.

What is the best possible government structure for the common good?

Day 313

> *Act only on the maxim whereby thou canst at the same time will that it should become a universal law.... So act to treat humanity, whether in thine own person or in that of any other, in every case as an end withal, never as a means only.*[7]

German philosophers also addressed the issues of ethics and just governance. It was Immanuel Kant (1724–1804) who argued for a universal rule, and who maintained that the social order should never treat human beings as a means to an end, but always as the end in terms of justice. While Kant did not focus his attention exclusively on the need for just governance, he did add this fourth feature to the modern discussion: all rational beings should be treated with dignity. Across the centuries, philosophers argued how this universal law of respect for all people can be the foundation of just governance. Various governments in all parts of the world have struggled to implement a social order that honors the dignity of all people. Tracing these trends in the modern world is well beyond our scope, but again some illustrations may be helpful. One possible way to reflect on our concern to advocate just governance and to serve the common good, is to suggest three major types of government: the centralized (authoritarian), the democratic, and the socialist or social democratic.

As one looks back upon the last three centuries, it is easy to point to governments with centralized power as, for example, at the close of the nineteenth century with Napoleon in France, and at the first half of the twentieth century with Hitler in Germany. We might also point out that some governments, based on more socialist principles, also became authoritarian in practice, with the USSR (Union of Soviet Socialist Republic)'s communist government as a prime example. The obvious risk of these forms of government is that there is little separation of power, and almost no system of checks and balances. It would be hard to overstate the harm done to humankind by these authoritarian governments and their corrupt leaders. You may know of examples from other parts of the world that would also serve to illustrate the risks of centralized power.

How is possible to maintain social order with shared power?

---

7. Kant, *Critique of Practical Reason*, quoted by Albert et al., *Great Traditions in Ethics*, 208–24.

Day 314

> *But the United States was committed to the principle of democracy by the logic of the Revolution and, as a consequence, the framers established their government in frank Lockean style upon the consent of the governed.*[8]

We are suggesting in our reading that one essential component of a profound and committed mindful spirituality is to extend outward and assume some responsibility for a just social order. If compassion is integral to our spirituality, then we must be concerned about helping to shape social structures in a way that protects the rights of all people, gives them liberty, and provides the means to build a constructive and meaningful life. I know that some would say that being spiritual is fundamentally a personal concern. It is a means to be centered, and to become a healthy person who lives in harmony with God, or ultimate reality. We affirm these truths, and we are also suggesting that one needs to be responsible for the context in which one lives. We are using the metaphor of extending outward in responsible living to underline this component of our spiritual journey.

We have noted that justice embodied in laws and the structures of social order is one goal of this responsibility. We looked briefly at the nature of justice, spoke about the nature of leadership that ensures justice, and listed three different types of justice: commutative (individual), social, and distributive. We are now reflecting on the ways that justice takes a tangible form in governments, and how various forms of government may be better able to maintain a just social order. We have just spoken about authoritarian governments and now turn to the democratic model. The government of the United States is one example. From the beginning, it has attempted to be democratic in character. Its founders and many of its leaders have believed that a democracy is the best way to ensure justice, seek the common good, and empower their citizens to flourish. I agree with their convictions. However, I am aware of how difficult it is to be a truly democratic society and sustain a just social order. It is incredibly challenging, and there have been many dramatic failures.

Do you think that American democracy is living up to its ideals?

---

8. Gabriel, *The Course of American Democratic Thought*, 12.

Day 315

The workers have nothing to lose in this [revolution] but their chains. They have a world to gain. Workers of the world, unite![9]

The other major form of government also driven theoretically by justice is the socialist model. The writings of Karl Marx on socialism and communism influenced the Russian Revolution and the governments of several other countries, including China and Cuba. We are inclined to be harsh in our judgment, because the tangible manifestation of his thought in governments did not emancipate them from economic oppression and institute a just social order. The ideas themselves—as, for example, the role of the government to insure economic justice—are worth reflection. These ideals have been very hard to implement, and the tendency has been to centralize governmental power and then to resort to forms of totalitarian oppression to govern efficiently.

I have traveled in the countries of Scandinavia and observed their socialist democratic governments. I have observed and read about their way of life, the levels of justice, and the degree of happiness of the population. No setting is perfect, and the contextual situation such as the homogeneity of the population may make governance easier. Nevertheless, there appears to be a commitment to the common good and relatively high levels of satisfaction in these countries.

In every setting, there continues to be marginalized people who long for more opportunity and a better way of life. Major social problems continue to exist, and the quest for peace, justice, liberty, and equal opportunity is never-ending. I am persuaded that one part of our mindful spirituality is to find a way to contribute to the well-being of others. It may be a modest responsibility for each of us, such as helping a child with homework or giving an elderly person transportation to see the doctor. Others may have more political influence or money to contribute to the cause of justice. We can all do something and lend a hand to help others.

What unjust conditions exist in your region, and how should they be addressed?

---

9. Marx, last words of *The Communist Manifesto*.

Day 316

Why is equality so assiduously avoided? Why does white America delude itself, and how does it rationalize the evil it retains?[10]

We are reflecting together about how to deepen our spirituality and make it more intentional. We are currently engaged in the process of understanding how our spiritual commitments will lead us to care more deeply for those who are marginalized and suffer. We know that mindful spirituality invites us to reach upward for unity with God. In the Christian tradition, this reach is often described as a three step process: (1) to become quiet and purge ourselves of all that would block us from union with God; (2) to find the best way or to gain illumination on how we achieve unity with God; and (3) to arrive and achieve union and blessedness. Saint Bonaventure says, "Purgation leads to peace, illumination to truth, and perfection to charity."[11] We also know that mindful spirituality invites us to open inward, seek healing and pursue wholeness, and continue on the spiritual way that leads to peace and purpose.

We are now in the third direction of mindful spirituality: expanding outward to love, finding community, and taking some responsibility for creating a more just and humane world. It is this last concern that is not always stressed in discussions about finding a spiritual pathway. It is, however, definitely present in the great spiritual traditions of the human family. Compassion is at the heart of Buddha's teaching, justice the core of the teaching of Moses, love at the center of Jesus' teaching, and *Zakat*, or "giving to the needy one," on the five pillars of Islam. The quest for intentional and mindful spirituality asks us to care deeply and wisely for the suffering of others, and to address the conditions in the world that cause suffering.

One of the most pressing concerns in our world today is racism, the view that those who are different in appearance, ethnicity, language, or culture are somehow inferior and not worthy of all the rights and privileges of a given society. Martin Luther King Jr. championed this issue, yet years later it has still not gone away.

What forms of racism still exist in the United States and other parts of the world?

---

10. King, *Where Do We Go From Here*, 5.
11. McGinn, *The Essential Writings*, 153.

Day 317

The God-given diversity of the human family was twisted by sin into the destruction of human community long before the first slaves reached American shores. And though the unfortunate development of race as a classificatory system is modern, ethnic "othering" is traceable as far back as the biblical narrative.[12]

We are living in a time when many forms of racism, both acknowledged and unacknowledged, are evident. Hardly a week goes by when there is not some violent act based in part on a racist and prejudiced outlook. I have been particularly aware of the ways that the police forces of our large cities have a tendency to treat African American and Hispanic people in different ways than they treat white people.[13] It is always important to be aware of how difficult the work of law enforcement is in our diverse country, and that the vast majority of the professional police do challenging and dangerous work to provide security and protect the rights of all citizens. But there continues to be situations in which black or Latino people are treated unfairly and even harmed or killed. All lives do matter.

It is also the case that minority populations do not always receive the best educational opportunities or have access to the finest medical services. Standing beyond these harmful conditions is a long history of prejudice and poverty. I was greatly privileged to assist the work of schools and colleges that served black, Latino, and Native American students. I met gifted and kind people who were committed to providing the best possible education for their students. They would occasionally ask the organization for which I worked for more financial support. I can remember one conversation when the senior leader of the program agency asked me to come in his office and do all that I could for these schools and colleges. He meant well, yet I sensed that his primary concern in this one conversation was to avoid any negative publicity, an understandable concern. His parting words were "just fix it," and I wondered how to fix a situation that has existed for two hundred and fifty years.

How would you have responded to the charge to "just fix it"?

---

12. Gushee and Stassen, *Kingdom Ethics*, 397–98.
13. The *Seattle Times* headline on June 20, 2017 is "Questions and Anger after Mother Killed by Police." See Westneat and Matthews, "Questions and Anger."

Day 318

The universal message of God's love for all humankind will continue to be heard through the power of the Holy Spirit, but the fashion in which it is heard depends on our willingness to speak and act the Word in ways concretely addressed to the struggles and longings of women and men today. Today, that speaking and acting can no longer ignore the existence of women as part of the people of God. Women are no longer willing to be invisible partners either in the work and life of church and society or in the interpretation and proclamation of the gospel.[14]

This observation by Dr. Letty Russell was made several years ago, and it was prophetic in character. It had great influence as she and her many women colleagues called attention to a form of prejudice in the life of the Christian church. A great deal has been done to rectify the situation, but as with racism, more needs to be done. Prejudice against the leadership of women in the church and in society continues. Again, it is wise to note that laws have been changed and many practices reformed. The pastor of the church that I attend is an extremely gifted and well-educated woman whose leadership, teaching, preaching, and pastoral care are superb. I know she is in a minority of people who guide the denomination. Even more to the point, she may be an exception to the trend in terms of opportunity and leadership in the society.

I also would call attention to another controversial issue in church and society, the access to positions of responsibility and leadership by members of the LBGT community. The debate about whether members of this population have chosen this lifestyle or are adjusting and accommodating to the realities of their birth identity is nearly over. It is clear that this population has not only accepted the reality of their sexual identity, but also embraced it and asked to be fully welcomed into the mainstream of society. To discriminate against these people in church and society is no longer justifiable. It never was! From a theological perspective I side with those teachings that speak of God's unconditional love for all of humankind.

What are your thoughts and feeling about these issues in church and society?

---

14. Russell, *The Living Word*, 14–15.

Day 319

A basic way of describing evil in the New Testament uses the term cosmos, the world, which primarily refers to the order of society and indicates that evil has a social and political character beyond the isolated actions of individuals.[15]

I have thought and struggled a great deal about the ways that the world religions—and in my case, Christianity—have spoken about the two ways, one that leads to self-destructive behavior and one that leads to a life of serenity, purpose, and responsibility. I have also projected the notion of the two ways onto the structures of society and the world. I have looked carefully at my own life, felt the tug of both ways, and have seen the same tug in organized religion, the area in which the good way is supposed to be present. I have placed my journey of mindful spirituality within this frame of reference, knowing that as I do I run the risk of using a trite generalization. I do know that there are many ways, not just two!

As we think about expanding outward for responsible living, the two-way construct can be useful. We are arguing that the true spiritual way is the way of compassion and justice, a way that resists the tendencies of the way of the world in the biblical sense, the way that is self-seeking. I have just applied the spiritual way to the religious context in the areas of racism and discrimination against women and the LBGT community. The true spiritual way also endorses religious understanding and interfaith cooperation. It deeply saddens me that we should be prejudiced against those with a different religious heritage. We know that the two ways are present in organized religion, but we should be those who side with the way of understanding and collaboration. I am especially concerned about Islamophobia and the way it caricatures a major religion.[16] Does Islam have problems and failures? Yes, but I urge that we work together to solve our common problems and to join together in creating a world of cooperation and reconciliation. I speak not just from theory, but also as one who has spent a great deal of time in Muslim countries.

Do you like the construct of two ways as a general way of thinking about life?

---

15. Mott, *Biblical Ethics and Social Change*, 4.

16. Another headline in *The Seattle Times*: "Attack on Muslim Shakes London." See Westneat and Matthews, "Attack on Muslim."

Day 320

In this world hate never dispelled hate, only love dispels hate. This is the law, ancient and inexhaustible. You too shall pass away. Knowing this, how can you quarrel?

—Buddha

Thich Nhat Hanh, a well-known Vietnamese Buddhist monk, poet, and peacemaker, has written extensively on Buddhist thought and the subject of human suffering. His foundational point is that we all suffer, and the central ethical component of Buddhist thought is to relieve human suffering. He leads, as we would expect, with the two Noble Truths: (1) all humans suffer; and (2) this suffering is caused by our attachment and craving. Because of these realities, the goal of the true follower of Buddha, the Bodisattva, aspires to attain enlightenment in order to relieve suffering.

Thich Nhat Hanh speaks of three kinds of suffering: (1) that associated with pain and unpleasant feelings; (2) the suffering of "composite things" or the reality that nothing is permanent; and (3) the suffering associated with change and the reality that we will grow old and die.[17] Buddha himself recognized these realities and chose to spend his life following his enlightenment, teaching the ways to cope with suffering, and finding peace within. His insights and teaching are profound and liberating, and not easy to summarize in just a few paragraphs. But one way to point to them is to again list the eightfold path that leads to the cessation of suffering and brings spiritual liberation and enlightenment. The path includes the following trails:

1. The right view, having understanding and seeing things as they are
2. The right intention, having a pure aim or goal
3. The right speech, speaking the truth in love
4. The right action, the art of living in a positive and constructive way
5. The right livelihood, earning a living in a way that makes life better for all
6. The right effort, intentionally seeking to do that which is constructive
7. The right mindfulness, living in the present moment (mindful spirituality)
8. The right concentration, being focused on the goal of enlightenment

How would you compare this spiritual path with that of other religions?

17. Thich, *The Heart of the Buddha's Teaching*, 19.

Day 321

While these are chaotic and turbulent times, they are hardly crazy ones. There is rhyme to both the reason and the unreason. Those who have eyes to see, ears to hear, and . . . their minds to understand, will rest easier knowing the sky is not falling after all.[18]

As part of our mindful spirituality, we are looking at the challenges of being responsible and seeking justice. As we do, we are sometimes overwhelmed. Our circumstances close at hand and the chaotic condition of the world seem impossible to get under control, let alone shape into a just social order for the common good. But the call to love and show compassion becomes all the more urgent in these turbulent times. When we look closely and study carefully, we find ways to understand and strategies to help shape the patterns of our society and move global infrastructure toward justice. We have noted the levels of suffering in our world, and have explored the nature of justice and its relationship to law and governance. We have underlined the goals of finding wise and virtuous leadership, explored the interplay between religious thought and government, and stressed the need for government and, indeed, all of society's institutions to honor the rights and dignity of all people.

Another subtheme that we should reflect upon together regarding responsible living and seeking justice is the way we cultivate the values and virtues that we need in order to do our part in living ethically and effectively. What are the ethical norms that should be integral to our lives as we help to create a more just and humane social structure, one that has justice as its foundation and the goal of the common good? The organizations in which I have worked and observed have often created standards of ethical conduct. I have a few of them in front of me and as I look at them, I discover that they often reflect the nature and purpose of the organization, and the time in which they were written. However, there are some common themes, ones that, if internalized, will prepare us to be responsible agents of creating a more just and humane society and world. I will borrow from some of their wisdom as we continue.

On what basis would you begin to write standards of ethical guidance?

18. Beck and Cowan, *Spiral Dynamics*, 17.

Day 322

> *Values express what a person believes should happen or ought to happen, and they are relatively stable and enduring from situation to situation, though they can also change and become more complex, particularly as a person gains more experience.*[19]

We maintain that an integral part of our mindful spirituality is to develop and live an ethical life. In addition, we maintain that we bring our ethical maturity to our responsibilities as we expand outward to improve the lives of others. Continually, we remind ourselves that this dimension of spirituality should not be ignored. Yes, the deeply spiritual life is the mystical ascent to the Transcendent One, and it is the resulting peace and joy that fills us in the ascent; it is the "peace that passes understanding." It is also an invitation to engage in compassionate service, to extend outward and initiate those acts of service that lead to justice and the common good. So we ask ourselves, "What is the ethical life?" Our summary answer is that "In everything do to others as you would have them do to you; for this is the law and the prophets" (Matt 7:12). We repeat it in order to deepen our understanding: "You shall love your neighbor as you love yourself"; and "But I say to you, Love your enemies and pray for those who persecute you, so that you may be children of your Father in heaven; for he makes his sun rise on the evil and on the good, and sends rain on the righteous and the unrighteous" (Matt 5:44–45).

As I have said, I find that my worldview and deepest values within the Christian faith and similar injunctions are present in other traditions. The command of Jesus to love your neighbor is from the Hebrew Bible, and similar ethical injunctions are in many of the sacred books. The challenge for us then is to understand the standards of ethical conduct and engage in the process of incorporating them into our lives. The process of incorporating or internalizing them is sometimes long and difficult, but also one that it is deeply gratifying as we sense that we are finding the Way. We are realizing what it means to be created in the image of God.

What two or three ethical norms do you most want to have in your life?

---

19. Anderson, *Organizational Development*, 36.

Day 323

As a member of the Presbyterian Church (U.S.A.), in obedience to Jesus Christ, I accept Christ's call to be involved responsibly in the ministry of the church, confirm that Jesus Christ is the pattern for my life and ministry, and relying on God's grace, commit myself to the following standards of ethical conduct.[20]

Those who follow the Christian way come in all sizes and shapes and have different ways of expressing ethical guidelines. The Presbyterian Church (USA) and the larger worldwide Reformed family of churches have guided me in this area. I am committed to ecumenism and interfaith understanding, although my commitment comes from a context, the PCUSA in shorthand. I try with both integrity and commitment to follow its ethical guidelines. I will use it as a model for ethical guidance, not primarily because it is one that should guide everyone, but as an example of the many that are available to those in a different time and place. In the PCUSA, there are general guidelines for all members, more specific ones for employees and volunteers in the church, and quite demanding ones for those who are ordained. I will have these different sets of guidelines in front of me and draw more heavily on the Integrated Version. These documents are referred to as "Life Together in the Community of Faith." I will generalize and rephrase the principles in an attempt to make them more applicable to other settings.

The first guideline has to do with being guided by the Bible, the Church's creeds (historical *Confessions*), affirming that Jesus is the pattern for life, as well as the need for grace to empower us to live up to the standards of ethical conduct. Three points become the foundation of the ethical guidelines: (1) the mega-narrative of the Bible, summarized in the creeds; (2) the model of the life and teachings of Jesus; and (3) the need for grace to live consistently with the ethical norms. Most religions would have a grand narrative describing why it exists, a suggested pattern for the ethical life, and ways to embody the values inherent in the worldview of the narrative. The need for empowerment is present in many as well, but especially in the Presbyterian one.

Where do you get your inspiration and guidance?

---

20. "Standards of Ethical Conduct," 1.

Day 324

Show yourself in all respects a model of good works, and in your teaching show integrity, gravity, and sound speech that cannot be censured; then any opponent will be put to shame, having nothing evil to say of us. (Titus 2:7–8)

The small letter of Titus is not all that well-known as a document of the New Testament. It is attributed to the Apostle Paul who writes to his colleague, Titus, who was doing mission work in Crete.[21] Paul, or one of his followers, is instructing Titus to live with integrity to the values of the Christian faith, and says that there are those who might resist his teaching if there are any traces of hypocrisy in his lifestyle. The documents used by the PCUSA have a comparable concern, and ask of their members and ministers to affirm the following: "I will conduct my life in a manner that is faithful to the gospel and consistent with my public ministry."[22] The contemporary church has a similar concern as it guides its members in ethical conduct. There is the general counsel to be a model of good works. There is the more specific counsel, if one is in a teaching role, to have three qualities: (1) Integrity—live consistently with what you teach others or your words will be hollow and have no impact. It is a clear statement that our deeds will speak as poignantly and powerfully as our words; (2) Sound speech—there are two pieces of advice in this phrase, to be both clear and truthful. What we say must be understood and an accurate reflection of the Christian way; (3) Gravity—the intent of this word is not to be seriously boring, but to introduce depth into one's teaching. Titus is urged to take his students beyond the obvious, to places where they have not yet advanced in their understanding.

In these ways, Titus will be advancing the goals of the church and assisting new Christians to understand the faith and be transformed by it. It will also place him in a position to avoid being criticized by those that may be resisting the new movement known as Christianity.

Is this sound advice? What might you add to offset the charge of hypocrisy?

---

21. Some New Testament scholars question whether the letter is from Paul, and suggest that it may have been written by one of his followers. It does reflect a pattern of thinking that suggests later developments, after Paul's death, in the life of the church.

22. "Standards of Ethical Conduct," 6.

Day 325

You shall not bear false witness against your neighbor. (Exod 20:16)

A second ethical guideline in the "Standards of Ethical Conduct" is to be honest and truthful in all relationships with others.[23] It is amazing how easy it is to not speak the truth or to shade the truth to the point of deception. As I examine my own life, I trace my capacity to always speak the truth in a developmental pattern. It is not that I was oriented to being dishonest as a child or when I moved toward adulthood. It is rather that I made choices about what to say out of quite pronounced needs. For example, if I had made a mistake or done something I was not supposed to do, I may have not been truthful because I was fearful that I would be punished and afraid of not being accepted and loved. As I moved into the teenage and young adult stages of my life, I began to understand better the moral character of being truthful, although I still wanted to be accepted and well-liked, needs that at times urged a moment of bragging or taking credit for something I didn't do. As I moved into my adult years, and incidentally to a faith orientation, the urge to be honest and truthful, both in speech and behavior, increasingly became more internalized. I discovered that being honest in a loving way was profoundly liberating, even if it did mean that there were complex feelings to navigate. The old feelings of the need to be accepted and loved and the fear of being rejected if I admitted doing something wrong have not altogether disappeared. I am learning how to internalize the value of being honest. I have increased my own self-esteem and built relationships of trust and openness. One area in which I have been especially sensitive is in religion. I realize that, as I speak about my faith, I should always do so with integrity. I know that I will always be a learner, and I do not have all the truth. So I am sensitive about being honest and fair with other faith traditions and not "bearing false witness" by referencing them in negative ways. For example, I speak about a small minority of those who claim to be Muslim, who engage in violent activity. I honor the vast majority of Muslims who are sincere.

Has it been a development process for you to become increasingly honest?

---

23. Ibid., 7.

Day 326

Be faithful, keeping covenants I make and honoring marriage vows.[24]

Our ethical responsibility expands and deepens as we form relationships in work, the organizations we serve, and the many promises we make to a wide range of people. We do have a covenant relationship in these settings, in which the expectation is that we will be honest in what we say and live in accord with the norms built into our professional duties. Covenant is a powerful word, and carries a meaning that goes beyond the word contract. It suggests that we not only follow the letter of the law, but become truthful in our relationships as well. Covenant, drawn from its biblical usage, means that a relationship of trust is formed between God and the people of God, with God promising them well-being if the people live in a righteous way, often meaning in accord with the Law (Torah). The notion of the covenant underlines the notion of being faithful to promises when it is applied to the marriage vows as well. Marriage is more than a contract; it is primarily a relationship of faithfulness and trust. As one breaks the marriage vows, communication and trust break down and are difficult to restore. The word "covenant" implies a relationship of trust, and a commitment to honor the spouse in all ways.

Our promise is that we will honor our primary relationships in the family and the relationships we form, as we go to school or work and interact with a range of people. In the role of a leader, we have a special responsibility to have integrity and to be true to our covenants. I have discovered in my work in different parts of the world on issues of peace and justice that I am only effective if I am truthful and honest. Trust is absolutely essential as we cross cultures. When there is no trust because of a violation of a covenant, written or unwritten, then the work of finding a just peace in Israel and Palestine, for example, is not going to be successful. Neither will there be peace at home or at work if we do not honor our promises. Our calling is to be consistently true to the promises of our covenants.

Have you experienced broken relationships because of the loss of trust?

---

24. Ibid., 7–8.

Day 327

Treat all persons with equal respect and concern as beloved children of God.[25]

I continue to be amazed and deeply troubled that, in this age of violence, human life often appears to have so little value. In a single act of terrorism, hundreds of innocent people are killed. In many cases, it does so little to advance some political cause or to be faithful to a distorted religious command; in fact, it completely alienates the rest of the world from the fanatical ideology. If there is a claim to being obedient within one's religion, it indirectly may cast aspersions on religion in general. Nearly all religions teach the value of not only human life, but all of life. There is a theme within the Abrahamic religions that humans are created in the image of God and have infinite value and worth. The command in these texts is clear: to "love our neighbor" and our neighbor in a global context is all of human life.

The ethical teaching in "Standards of Ethical Conduct" of the PCUSA is very clear as well, and has three essential components. The first is to show respect for all people, not just those in one community or nation, or in one culture or ethnicity, nor only with those who speak my language, dress like I do, and who have my religious and political convictions. We are to respect all persons. I have some discomfort, even in my faith community, when we appear to undervalue people whose religious and political beliefs are different from ours, especially if they say that God's love is not present for them. We sometimes forget our favorite Bible verse, "God so loved the world" (John 3:16). We are to show respect and, secondly, concern. Our mindful spirituality calls us to expand outward in compassion, care for the needs of marginalized people, find ways for all people to have their needs met, and live in a just society that seeks the common good. We get involved in the hard work of loving others just as we love ourselves. We do so, thirdly, because it is the will and way of God. We reach out because all people are the beloved children of God.

What makes loving those different from us so difficult?

---

25. Ibid., 8.

Day 328

Do not be conformed to this world, but be transformed by the renewing of your minds, so that you may discern what is the will of God—what is good and acceptable and perfect. (Rom 12:2)

Ethical standards are not reached in a vacuum, but grow out of a total way of life. The PCUSA, as they prepared the ethical guidelines, knew that following them depended upon the total health of the person and the context in which a person lives. They address this concern in the next ethical standard. It says to maintain a healthy balance among one's work and ministry responsibilities, commitment to the family, and care in other primary relationships. It stresses the need to give attention to spiritual, physical, emotional, and intellectual renewal.

These admonitions may seem obvious, and we may too easily take them for granted. The Apostle Paul, as he writes to the Romans, urged them to be concerned about renewal. The term "mind" in his letter speaks not just about our intellectual capacities, but about how we look at the world around us, make sense of it, and how we live in it. He knows that it is easy to accept the values of one's culture and to crave power, pleasure, prestige, and possessions. He calls this way of life being "conformed to the world." He tells them not to be taken in by these cravings, and to renew their mind and change their outlook. Then, he says, you will be able to discern the will of God, that he calls "good and acceptable and perfect." As our minds are renewed, we are then able to clarify our values and give attention to what is important. We will be able to do our work well, sustain a healthy family life, and spend time with friends that meet our social and emotional needs. All too often, one or more of these dimensions of our lives is neglected. The ethical guideline reminds us that we need renewal in all aspects of our lives; we need to maintain a healthy spiritual life, utilizing the practices of mindful spirituality; we need to keep ourselves physically healthy by eating well and staying fit; we need to enjoy the arts and have some fun to stay emotionally tuned; we need to stimulate the mind and keep our brains active. As we do, we are better able to know and do the will of God.

Do you consider yourself reasonably healthy? What do you want to improve?

Day 329

Refrain from abusive, addictive, or exploitive behavior and seek help to overcome such behavior if it occurs. Maintain an attitude of repentance and humility, responsive to God's reconciling will.[26]

I have chosen to combine two statements on the list of ethical standards prepared by the PCUSA, in that one logically follows from the other. The first one deals with negative behavior, and the second one has a partial remedy. Note that the three types of negative behavior are bunched together, in part because they can easily flow together in a person, although they could exist separately as well. My experience, especially in family life, is that people who have these negative traits are often people who are emotionally ill and have deep needs that have not been met. One may be abusive in order to gain power and control over another person. It is a way of putting them down and asserting one's own superiority. If one has addictive tendencies, it is likely a compensation for excessive depression and anxiety, a quest for a few hours of peace. If one is exploitive, it likely grows out of the need to gain possessions or pleasure at the expense of others. It is possible to become aware of these tendencies in one's life, although this self-awareness does not come easily. The more likely response, if challenged, will be defensiveness. Progress will only come in a setting where there is a desire to change and a setting where there is acceptance and able guidance.

The second statement points to such a setting, one where the norm is to acknowledge our failures and limitations, and then to seek forgiveness and transformation. The Christian community, as it lives up to its standard of being a beloved community, is an ideal setting for repentance, humility, and a desire to be responsive to God's reconciling love. But church communities are human communities, and at times there are settings in which we pretend always to be okay. The Catholic practice of confession does offer a healthy way to seek forgiveness and transformation. Perhaps other churches might find an equivalent practice.

What ways have you found to make changes in your behavior?

---

26. Ibid., 10–11.

Day 330

> *God is light and in him there is no darkness at all. If we say that we have fellowship with him while we are walking in darkness, we lie and do not do what is true; but if we walk in the light as he himself is in the light, we have fellowship with one another.* (1 John 1:5b–7a)

There is a shift in the second section of the Standards of Ethical Conduct from concerns about personal behavior to our responsibilities in social settings. The verse from 1 John above uses the metaphor of light and darkness. I have found the insight of this metaphor to be profound. It is often what we hide (walking in the darkness) that is dishonest, harmful, and damaging to our social lives and work settings. It is not that we need to say or reveal everything, but we must resist the tendency to be deceptive. So the guideline for those Presbyterians in professional ministry reads: "I will conduct my ministry so that nothing need be hidden from a governing body or colleagues in ministry."[27] There are then seventeen stated ways that we are to carry out our ministries "in the light." I'll just give a few examples, though the guidelines are written to guide ordained clergy; yet the principles, for the most part, apply to all who seek a more mindful spirituality. There is guidance (1) to speak the truth in love; (2) to honor the sacred trust of the covenant relationships; (3) to be judicious in the exercise of power; (4) to avoid conflicts of interest in decision making; (5) to refrain from exploitive behavior; and (6) to respect the privacy of individuals who share information about their personal lives.

Notice that each guideline has to do with truth and love, the two statements describing God mentioned in 1 John: God is light and love, with light a symbol for truth. So our behavior, as it is transformed in our relationship with the God of light and love, will begin to reflect these fundamental virtues. These virtues begin to be present in my life as I give attention to the practices of mindful spirituality, and as I am inspired in my reading and association with those who take seriously their spiritual journey. My participation in a beloved community helps to sustain me.

What helps you as you seek to become a more truthful and loving person?

---

27. Ibid., 12.

Day 331

For by grace given to me I to say to everyone among you not to think of yourself more highly than you ought to think but to think with sober judgment, each according to the measure of faith God has assigned. (Rom 12:3)

The next group of guidelines has to do with personal awareness and the management of one's financial affairs. Again, in that they are written specifically for officers in the church, I will reword them slightly so that their application is more universal. I will list them and then invite us to reflect upon their application to our lives as we seek to live in a responsible way: (7) recognize the limits of our own abilities and training, and be sure to refer persons and tasks to others as appropriate; (8) be honest as you speak about your qualifications and be sure to give credit when using the sources and insight of others; (9) manage your money wisely and refrain from incurring indebtedness that will have adverse affects; (10) be wise and a good steward of all funds and property for which you have responsibility; (11) be sure to accept only what is appropriate for honoraria, business endeavors, and gifts of loans from persons other than family.

There are two qualities that stand out in this listing of ethical standards: humility and wisdom. I remember in an earlier period in my life, and occasionally even in the present, how I often felt a need to let others know what I had done and achieved. This tendency grew from a relatively poor self-image as a child and young person. I thought I might be more respected and better liked if they knew all that I achieved. But gradually, as I began to understand and even like myself, it became easier to just be who I am in the present moment and not worry about impressing others. It has been liberating and increased my self-esteem and sense of integrity. It also helped me to be wiser about what is important, how to manage resources, and how to make decisions. I became better able to manage the affairs of my life and my professional responsibilities, in terms of what was best for all involved, not on the basis of how it might improve my situation. I am now better able to weigh and measure options, and to make better choices based on reality.

How would you describe your growth toward humility and wisdom?

Day 332

Give instruction to the wise, and they will become wiser still; teach the righteous and they will gain in learning. (Prov 9:9)

The next set of guidelines in the Standards of Ethical Conduct speaks about the issues of accountability and relationships with colleagues. Again, I'll list them in a general way that makes them applicable to most situations: (12) accept the accountability of that organization in which you work and the guidance of those to whom you are responsible; (13) participate in continuing education and seek the counsel of mentors and professional advisors; (14) honor the person who is your predecessor and speak and act in ways that support the work of the one who is your successor; (15) participate in that setting from which you have come only as invited and suggested by the new leadership; (16) offer services to those whom you previously served with the consent of and as directed by the new leadership; (17) honor the guidance and counsel of that the organization from which you have retired.[28]

I have not always been as sensitive in my accountability to others in my work as I should have been. There were times when I made mistakes of judgment and action, and I would now do things differently. I failed primarily because I was overly confident in my vision of what should be done, and went ahead without checking with the persons to whom I reported. I wanted to lead, but failed to lead with consent and consultation. Over time, I began to learn that I truly needed the guidance of others, and I became more open to learning from their wisdom and experience. These guidelines touched me in another way, as I began to assume more responsibility in the positions that I held and the Boards on which I served. With experience, I had more empathy for those with energy and enthusiasm, and was able to guide them in using it in wise and constructive ways. I learned how to give oversight, less by correcting and more by conversations based on trust and affirmation.

Are there some experiences in your past work that you would like to do over?

---

28. Ibid., 18–21.

Day 333

> *[The Lord] has told you, O mortal, what is good: and what does the Lord require of you but to do justice, and to love kindness, and to walk humbly with your God.* (Mic 6:8)

There is one final section in the Standards of Ethical Conduct, one that expresses the need to collaborate as a partner with the mission of the church universal. There is language that underscores the need to be a global partner. It recognizes that we are all inhabitants of the planet earth. If, in our practice of mindful spirituality, we seek to expand outward in responsible living, we must expand beyond our region, our state, and our country, and begin to think globally. There is little that we now do that doesn't have an impact on how others live in different parts of the world. There are four exhortations in this third section, ones that I will paraphrase to make them more applicable to settings apart from the church. They are: (1) participate in the mission of compassion and justice in ways that cooperate with those who engage in similar missions in our global context; (2) show respect and provide encouragement for these global partners; (3) recruit people to engage in missions of love and justice in ways that honor partnerships and refrain from exploiting persons in vulnerable situations; (4) work globally for justice, compassion, and peace with those from other faith traditions.

I want to underline several themes that are emphasized in these exhortations. The first is to recognize that we live in a global context, and that we are interconnected with all of the world's people and with all living creatures. We live as planetary pilgrims and partners, facing the overwhelming challenge of caring for our threatened earth. Global warming is a reality, the oceans are rising, the world's population is increasing, and there are deep divisions and devastating conflicts among the peoples of the world. There are parts of the world where famine is widespread, water is scarce, and disease is rampant.

A second theme is that we must work together if we are to make progress in solving these overwhelming global problems. They cannot be solved in isolation from others, hiding behind the narrow distortion of extreme nationalism.

What steps of cooperation and collaboration should we take as a nation?

Day 334

Three great questions present themselves to those who travel and live upon this planet: "Where did I come from?" "Where am I going?" and "Why am I here?" To seek our sacred answer to these questions is to be a planetary pilgrim.[29]

We are reflecting together about how we maintain our ethical standards in extending outward in fulfilling our global responsibilities. We have been learning from the document entitled "Standards of Ethical Conduct," published by the Presbyterian Church (USA). The final section of this document deals with ethical behavior in a global context. A third major theme in this section of the document is that we must maintain partnerships of integrity and trust and avoid the exploitation of the vulnerable. It is all too easy for powerful nations of the world to exploit weaker nations by disguising financial assistance to poor nations, using it as leverage, and then slipping back into colonial practices. Fairness and reciprocity are essential in the partnership between nations. But when there is a need for products by farming the land and for oil by a large powerful country, then there will be a conflict between the farmers and the oil developers. Often, the power is with oil development, and this may result in exploitation and oppression. The challenge is to find ways for all to benefit.[30]

The final ethical guideline from the Presbyterian document speaks about the need to reach across the boundaries of faith in the formation of partnerships based on justice, compassion, and peace. We add the need to reach across the boundaries of ethnicity, culture, and language as well. Currently, the United States, in its attempts to provide security, is threatening to prohibit immigration that appears to be based on religious affiliation. It is a risky move, in that we are a nation of immigrants. Our founding documents are based on the freedom of religion. In my judgment, we will achieve more security if we focus on careful vetting of those who come to the United States without reference to religious affiliation. We will achieve a more just and peaceful country and world if we avoid religious categories and focus on behavior.

How do we preserve our values in international partnerships?

---

29. Hays, *Prayers for a Planetary Pilgrim*, 15.
30. We will say more about this issue in the December readings.

Study Guide for the November Readings

Questions for Contemplation and Discussion:

1. Which of the most pressing and urgent world problems motivates you to help? Why and how?
2. Which of the most challenging problems we face as a nation is the most difficult to solve? What makes it so difficult to find solutions?
3. How should we prepare ourselves to get involved? What will make our intervention effective and valuable?
4. What are some guidelines we should follow in finding just solutions to the problems we face as a nation and in our global context?
5. What are the different forms of justice, and which of them motivates you to care and act?
6. What kind of government and what sort of government leaders do we need in order to maintain a just social order?
7. Which government structure (authoritarian, democratic, socialist, etc.) is best suited to protect human rights and honor the dignity of all people?
8. Have you ever experienced some form of prejudice? If so, what form did it take and how did you react?
9. What fundamental values guide you when you extend outward and attempt to do so in a responsible way?
10. What are the essential components of the ethical life? And how are they applied locally in your regional, national, and global relationships?

THEME FOR DECEMBER

EXPANDING OUTWARD FOR JUSTICE, RECONCILIATON, AND PEACE

Day 335

True peace is not the absence of tension, it is the presence of justice.

—Dr. Martin Luther King Jr.

We begin a new section of our daily readings today, entitled "Expanding Outward for Justice, Reconciliation, and Peace." As I have mentioned along the way, the discussions and writings about spirituality tend to focus more on the subjects of our first two sections: "Reaching Upward" and "Opening Inward." However, there are several thoughtful books and innumerable people that have integrated social ministries with the spiritual way.[1] There is a strong case to be made that those who are deeply grounded in a spiritual way have the sensitive conscience, the commitment, and the compassion to be effective in the pursuit of justice, reconciliation, and peace. It does require a profound grasp of the issues, the patience to stay with the slow pace of change, and the emotional maturity to deal with different forms of pressure and risk.

I think about several people who were models for me as I have endeavored to understand the connection between my spiritual center and practices with a life of service. One of these is Mother Teresa of Calcutta, who consistently spoke of her spiritual center as the reason for her life of dedicated service and sacrifice. She acknowledged that she had limitations, and even a lack of feeling God's presence in her work with the poorest of the poor. She wrote: "My poor ones in the world's slums are like the suffering Christ. In them God's Son lives and dies, and through them God shows me his true face. Prayer for me means becoming twenty-four hours a day at one with the will of Jesus to live for him, through him and with him. If we pray we will believe, if we believe, we will love, if we love, we will serve. Only then can we put our love for God into living action through service of Christ in the distressing disguise of the poor."[2]

How do you connect your spiritual center and the life of service? Or do you?

---

1. See for example, Merton, *Contemplation in a World of Action*, and the current Pope Francis, *The Name of God is Mercy*.
2. Mother Teresa, *Life in the Spirit*, 1.

Day 336

In an extinction event of our own making, what happens to us? One possibility—the possibility implied by the Hall of Biodiversity—is that we, too, will eventually be undone by our transformation of the ecological landscape.[3]

Our world faces a range of overwhelming problems, perhaps more serious than ever because we have not seen them before, nor do we have the global infrastructure with which to solve them. Elizabeth Kolbert, whom I quote above, makes the case that we have caused and allowed the earth environment to deteriorate so severely that the human race is facing extinction. The case she makes is not just a newspaper headline; it is a serious scholarly and scientific study. It traces the trends that have been set in place over the last few decades that point in the direction of "the sixth extinction," not unlike the extinction of the dinosaur age eons ago. Human beings are threatened, and if we continue in the same patterns that we have followed in recent past, we may not be able to inhabit the earth. It may become uninhabitable.

Global warming is one of those concerns in the category of overwhelming. There are other concerns as well. We continue trying to solve our conflicts with violence and warfare, and even use our creativity to design a theology of redemptive violence, an irony of the first order. There are the challenges of the rapidly expanding population, the inequity in the distribution of wealth, severe hunger in many parts of the world, huge populations without clean or running water, oppressive governments, continuing prejudice based on gender, race, and religion, and unmet educational and health needs. I am not suggesting that, as individuals, we can solve these extraordinary problems; rather, I am suggesting that we should be aware of them and find ways to do our part. Our mindful spirituality calls us to lend a hand as we have the education, the talents, the resources, and the time. We can find a way to help relieve suffering in our corner of the earth, and perhaps on a grander scale. There are ways to partner with God and join with others in creating a more just and humane world.

In what way can you make a contribution to solving the earth's problems?

---

3. Kolbert, *The Sixth Extinction*, 267.

Day 337

Now consider a thought experiment: Suppose that when we gather to choose the principles, we don't know where we will wind up in society. Imagine that we choose behind a "veil of ignorance" that temporarily prevents us from knowing anything about who in particular we are. . . . If no one knew any of these things, we would choose, in effect, from an original position of equality.[4]

In Michael Sandel's book on justice, he explores the question of the right thing to do in our society and world. His approach is to examine the theme of justice. In the case of the quote above, he studies the theory that equality is the heart of justice, a case made by an American philosopher named John Rawls. It provides a place to start, although we could have begun without "the veil of ignorance" and advocated from our vested interests and informed starting points. I might start with the golden rule or the Ten Commandments. However, he says that even these perspectives get loaded down with presuppositions. I want to explore the notion of equality that he suggests. As I do, I will be up front about my Christian frame of reference and say, "God wants us all to have an equal chance for the good life." Let's take a moment and remember what we have explored together about this position.

We have said that having a sensitive and informed spiritual center gives us motivation to care about others, and especially those who suffer. We have said that that the primary expression of a deep and enlightened spirituality is to demonstrate compassion for those who suffer and are marginalized. We need to find ways to relieve that suffering, motivated by *agape* love, which is without limits and unconditional in character. We have reflected together in our readings about how to act in love toward others, caring for them as individuals and finding ways to challenge, change, and improve the environments in which they live. We may devote ourselves to helping a single individual, and then we may want to get engaged in seeking a more just social order, one that is committed to the common good. We move toward enabling all people to have an equal opportunity for a good life.

What can I do to help give all people an equal chance in life? Be specific.

---

4. Sandel, *Justice*, 141.

Day 338

> *More recently, Yale ethicist Gene Outka argued that we should define Christian love as equal regard. Love means that we value all persons equally, regardless of their special traits, actions, merits, or what they can do for us. Of course, the appropriate way for me to express my love to various equally regarded people may differ.*[5]

Our concern in this month's reading is to understand how we can expand outward in seeking justice, reconciliation, and peace. We are beginning with the attempt to better understand justice. Let's return for a moment to what we have already said about justice. Our definition was that justice is the effort to ensure that all people receive their due, or as we say in the founding documents of the United States, the rights of life, liberty, and the pursuit of happiness. We have maintained that to deny people justice is to harm and hurt them, deny them respect, and fail to honor their dignity. We have maintained that a just society, at a minimum, leads to the common good and enables people to pursue the good life as far as possible, however they understand it, as long as it doesn't harm others. We noted three kinds of justice: (1) commutative justice, or trust and honesty in a transaction between two people or social entities; (2) social justice, or that which individuals and social institutions owe the society for the common good; and (3) distributive justice, or the fair allocation of goods and duties among its citizens. We went on to explore how these forms of justice take shape in laws and governments, public institutions, economic systems, and religious entities.

As we look at these different forms of justice and their expressions in our setting, our spirituality calls us to explore how we can ensure that those people near and dear to us have an equal opportunity for a good life based on justice. If love and compassion are what motivates us, we might ask ourselves how we relieve the suffering of our family, friends, and neighbors that is caused by injustice. What might we do to make sure these people have equal opportunity to enjoy and find meaning in life? What might we do, given our talents and interests? How might we volunteer to help those in need? How might we resist injustice wherever it is present?

What would you most like to do to help others improve their lives?

---

5. Gushee and Stassen, *Kingdom Ethics*, 112.

Day 339

> *For the past 200 years, Jews have been involved in virtually all organized attempts to improve human life. Sometimes* tikkun olam *takes a specifically Jewish form. . . . However, a commitment to* tikkun olam *also requires, almost by definition, attention to many issues that are not strictly limited to Jewish interest, among them, the environment and ecology, nuclear disarmament and international peace, and equal protection for all, regardless of race, sex, sexual orientation, or national origin.*[6]

I am quite drawn to the Jewish concept of *tikkun olam,* which can be defined as "taking responsibility for correcting damage done by people to each other and the planet. Hebrew for repairing the world."[7] There is an organization by that name that has the mission statement: "To Heal, Repair, and Transform the World." It has some similarity with our three words (justice, reconciliation, and peace), in that we seek to overcome the fear, mistrust, and anger between people by seeking justice. As we make progress and move toward justice, there is reconciliation with the diminishment of fear, the recovery of trust, and the emergence of peace. It is always a long process, and it is easy to slip back into conflict because people do not easily forget hurt and pain. In addition, the learned prejudice about the other is not easily removed from the consciousness of many people. It takes time to heal and repair. The transformation into a just and peaceful social order is often a slow and demanding process.

In the 1990s, I was involved into a program that had the goal of healing the hurt and mistrust that existed between Protestants and Catholics in Northern Ireland. It was a modest contribution to restoring trust and peace, and complemented a wide range of other initiatives. Yet it illustrates the movement from anger and mistrust to approximate justice, and to some reconciliation and peace. I worked for a mainline Protestant denomination in the United States, and was invited by a senior staff member of the economic development department of the government of Northern Ireland to consider developing a program that was later to be called "The Business Education Initiative." We were told by nearly everyone that it would never work.

Have you ever been told that what you want to do will never work?

---

6. Diamant and Cooper, *Living a Jewish Life,* 77.
7. Ibid., 322.

Day 340

Men and women are made in the image and likeness of God. So people may never be regarded as mere objects, nor may they be sacrificed for political, economic, or social gain. We must never allow them to be manipulated or enslaved by ideologies or technology. Their God-given dignity and worth as human beings forbid this.[8]

Yesterday, I was illustrating the flow of human affairs from fear and mistrust to justice, reconciliation, and peace. My colleague from the British government and I started by getting approval from the person to whom he reported, and by informing the church leadership of my denomination (Presbyterian Church USA). With these approvals, we jumped in, in part because we were both relatively bold, and in part because we had a deep commitment to a just peace in Northern Ireland (and maybe because we were sort of naïve). He arranged for some funds, and together we began calling colleges and universities. Our proposal was to bring students from Northern Ireland to study American business practices, with the goal that the students would return to help revitalize the struggling economy in Northern Ireland. A collateral concern was that the Catholic population was poor and had high unemployment, and the Protestant population had the power and wealth, and was mostly employed. We sold the program with the clear goal of improving the economy, although another clear goal was to improve Catholic and Protestant relations. We were bold enough to believe that we could engage Catholic and Protestant colleges and universities to participate, that the supporting churches could work together, and that the Catholic and Protestant students would put the prejudices of the previous generations aside. As we began the conversation, few thought that we could do it. The divisions were five hundred years old and deep, Catholic and Protestants leaders would be cautious around each other and barely polite, and the costs were too great! We gathered a group of them together for dinner in Belfast, told them about our plan, and asked for their support. Much to our surprise, the Catholic Bishop and the Protestant pastor said, "Let's do it!"

Is there another way of looking at a problem that you haven't thought of?

---

8. John Paul II, *In My Own Words*, 75.

Day 341

Mercy is divine and has to do with the judgment of sin. Compassion has a more human face. It means to suffer with, to suffer together, and to not remain indifferent to the pain and suffering of others.[9]

The first year we had seventeen Irish students in Presbyterian-related colleges and universities, the next year seventy-five Irish students in Presbyterian, Methodist, and Catholic institutions, and in the third year, one hundred and fifty students in the program, equally distributed. The colleges and universities waived tuition, and the British government paid for transportation, room and board, and basic expenses. Each student had a year of education in a fine American college or university, the limit permitted by Northern Ireland to avoid any brain drain. This project has continued for over twenty years. We have tracked what the students have done, their understanding of American business practices, and their feelings for others in the program, whether Catholic or Protestant. Currently, most are making a contribution to the economy in Northern Ireland and the Republic of Ireland. When we started, both Irish economies faced economic challenges, and now the economies are dramatically improved. Regarding their fellow students, the general spirit has been that, after the first week, they did not even notice whether their fellow students were Catholic or Protestant, because they had become a good and trusted friends. Did the program turn the economy around? Not by itself, but many young people started careers that advanced the economy. Did the program bring peace to Northern Ireland? Not by itself, but there is now a semblance of peace. Did it improve relations between Northern Ireland and the Republic of Ireland? It helped, as students from both locations initially participated in the program. Did it improve relations between the United States and the United Kingdom? The relations were already very good, and both Tony Blair and Bill Clinton spoke about the value of the program. Can a person or two make a phone call and arrange a lunch or dinner to talk about a program worth twenty thousand dollars times one hundred and fifty students, or three million dollars, and expect to make it happen? Yes, it happened.

Do you have an idea that might make a contribution to world peace?

---

9. Pope Francis, *The Name of God is Mercy*, 91.

Day 342

Before we can generate compassion and love, it is important to have a clear understanding of what we understand compassion to be. . . . in the Buddhist tradition, compassion and love are seen as two aspects of the same thing: compassion is the wish for another to be free from suffering; love is wanting them to have happiness.[10]

We are reflecting together about how we might expand outward to improve the lives of others. The Dalai Lama is quite clear about the goals of improving the lives of others: it is to show compassion by relieving the suffering of others, and to love in ways that make others happy. "Happy," in this case, may not be exactly the word we would use, although it is one with which we can easily identify, if we mean deeply contented and at peace. If you will forgive another personal illustration, let me say a word about how these goals have motivated me in the last few years.

When in retirement, having moved to a setting in the state of Washington, I asked myself the question about how I might engage in ministries that would relieve suffering and bring deep happiness to others. I was not altogether saintly, and had other plans as well. I wanted to hike in the glorious mountains of the Northwest, walk on its beaches, enjoy friends, be with my family, and have a comfortable home. I did think, as well, about how I might make a contribution to relieving suffering and increase the happiness of others. I thought the best way to do it was to use the skills I had developed over the years, the experience in the church and higher education, and knowledge that I had accumulated with extensive travel in other parts of the world. So I did get involved in education by teaching and consulting in educational institutions. I also engaged in a range of peace and justice initiatives in other parts of the world. I have enjoyed the opportunities to continue to learn and share some of what I have learned in my writing. These have been wonderful learning years, and I want to share one conviction that has grown out of this experience: if we are going to help suffering people, we not only need to help individuals, but also must engage in social change and move the social order toward justice and peace.

What goals motivate you in reference to helping others?

10. Dalai Lama, *The Compassionate Life*, 17.

Day 343

We live in an age of empathy. So announces a manifesto by the eminent primatologist Frans de Waal, one of a spate of books that have championed this human capability at the end of the first decade of the new millennium.[11]

We live in a very complex world filled with many trends and forces shaping our existence and way of life. It is difficult to lift up just a few of these trends and make them the definers of an age. What is encouraging, even with these extraordinary challenges we are facing, such as global warming, is that there has been a turn toward compassion and empathy. There are so many people who are suffering and will continue to suffer if we cannot find ways to solve our problems. Steven Pinker, the Johnstone Professor of Psychology at Harvard University, maintains that the human family has made a shift in its outlook, allowing "the better angels of our nature" to emerge. His marvelous book makes the case that there is now, percentage-wise, at least, less oppression and violence toward others than in previous eras. Jeremy Rifkin, in *The Empathic Civilization: The Race to Global Consciousness in a World in Crisis*, makes a similar point and urges that we find ways for this global consciousness to take form and action. Both authors make the obvious point that we have stressed, that our efforts must be more than helping individuals who suffer, but also changing the conditions of oppressive settings, societies, and world structures that both allow and even create suffering. I have been helped by the assessments of many authors, who have described the conditions causing suffering, and have suggested ways to change the planetary infrastructure to create a more just and peaceful world. One of those people, Jeremy Lent, in his book *The Patterning Instinct: A Cultural History of Humanity's Search for Meaning*, speaks about structural flaws in our outlook. I want to borrow a few points that he calls "structural flaws of the Western worldview."[12] He argues that part of the problem is our flawed thinking, which is not always conscious.

What presuppositions, often below the surface, guide us in our assessments?

---

11. Pinker, *The Better Angels of Our Nature*, 571.
12. In a paper published by Lent, "House on Shaky Ground."

Day 344

> *There has been a steady rise of interest in the import and impact of empathy on consciousness and social development over the past century. The interest that has mushroomed in the past decade as empathy has become a hot-button in professional fields ranging from medical care to human resources management.*[13]

My presuppositions are in line with those of both Steven Pinker and Jeremy Rifkin in that I believe that empathy, that capacity to understand and identify with those who are oppressed and suffer, is a critical starting point. I also assume that this empathy can lead to caring about justice. It will inspire us to see that injustice, when it is corrected can lead to reconciliation and a more peaceful world and less suffering. But my fear is that this formula may be flawed with hidden preconceptions, and Jeremy Lent's list of structural flaws may be a helpful correction, making the formula less of an empty platitude and more of a design for a better world. He lists eight structural flaws in what he calls "the Western worldview."[14]

The first of these is the assumption that humans are fundamentally selfish. Such a view can be traced back to an interpretation of the Bible and the notion of a cosmic fall. It is also related to economic and biological theories, and what these theories suggest is that self-interest and collective self-serving actions result in the best outcomes for society. We do not need to interfere, and should let the human survival instincts and the economic market have their way. There is, however, another way of reading human history, which is to maintain that cooperation and fair play are equally present in human experience. We need to shift to the model of justice (fair play), reconciliation (cooperation), and the resulting peace that serves the common good.

The second flaw in our thinking, according to Lent, is that we basically believe that genes are fundamentally selfish. Richard Dawkins, the British biologist, did make the case for this in his book titled *The Selfish Gene*.[15] But perhaps some self-interest is acceptable and not selfish. In fact, it may be integral to the developing view of evolution that is leading to collective health and well-being.

Are you basically despairing or basically hopeful about the human future?

---

13. Rifkin, *The Empathic Civilization*, 14.
14. Lent, "House on Shaky Ground." This source is referenced from Day 344 to 346.
15. Dawkins, *The Selfish Gene*, 4.

Day 345

> *The greatest obstacle to a more unified, just, and peaceful world is a religious belief that God and the world are in conflict and that doing good in earthly life will reap a reward in eternal life. Catholicity is stifled by the polar opposites of heaven and hell and many people live fearfully in between.*[16]

There is a great deal of Christian thought and some generic religious thought that understands nature as our challenge, and that it must be tamed. Further, our natural instincts must be controlled in order to live the virtuous life and receive an eternal reward. The truth in these preconceptions is that the virtuous life is a good life, but the rest, if not fundamentally challenged or at least restated, could lead us astray. Jeremy Lent argues that a third flaw in our thinking is that humans are separate from nature and need to subdue it and have control over it. Western history has been influenced by the belief that we have an eternal soul imprisoned in our bodies, and that we have reason that enables us to prevail over our natural state. In fact, we are part of nature, and share the world with other creatures and all that is alive. Our future is tied to the ways we live interdependently and in harmony with nature.

Still another flaw in our thinking and linked to the flawed notion that we are separate from nature is that nature is a machine. Lent maintains that it is not a machine, but a self-organized, self-regenerating living and global system of which we are an integral part. We may even be guests of nature, and need to be polite. The world is alive, and we need to do our part to ensure that it stays alive, acknowledge the interdependency built into the global system, and work in harmony with nature.

A fifth flaw in our thinking, according to Lent, has to do with money and the way we measure prosperity and value success. He says, "Structural Flaw #5: GDP is a good measure of prosperity."[17] In fact, the Gross Domestic Product only measures money, but does not accurately measure a country's genuine progress. It does not tell us how we are doing with global warming and the crime rate. It is only one factor, and many other factors need to be considered to measure the success of our country.

What do you think is the best way to measure the progress of a country?

---

16. Delio, *Making All Things New*, 92–93.
17. Lent, "House on Shaky Ground," para. 27.

Day 346

No one would deny that human consciousness has changed over history. When we look closer, however, we see that shifts in consciousness accompany shifts in the way human beings organize their relationships to the natural world and, in particular, the way people harness the energies of the planet.[18]

We are asking ourselves whether our way of viewing the world is a sound starting point from which to make judgments about the future. We are reviewing Jeremy Lent's reflections on structural flaws in the way that Western world understands reality. He suggests that we should guard against eight flaws in our assumptions. We now turn to number six: the earth can support limitless growth. He notes that our financial systems assume growth indefinitely, and that our natural resources are unlimited. It may have been felt by people a hundred years ago that these assumptions were accurate. However we now know that we are reaching the limits of our earth's capacities. The challenge is whether we can move toward growth in quality and away from unrestricted consumption. If we don't, then we increase human suffering and further deteriorate the environment.

The seventh structural flaw in our outlook is that "technology has the solution." Technology can certainly help, and it does provide immediate relief for some of our problems. But it doesn't solve the larger issues that crowd the earth's capacities. In fact, there are many unintended consequences of the high-tech strategy, such as the ubiquitous use of artificial fertilizer that has led to "dead zones" in the ocean. Fundamentally, the technology solution is a move away from our partnership with nature to the older idea of conquering nature. We need solutions that look at the big picture, and not immediate fixes that lead to unpredictable outcomes.

His last and eighth item on the list of structural flaws is that the universe has no meaning. The assumption is that human beings create meaning, both in particular areas, but also on a cosmic scale. Perhaps a better way of reading the universe is to discern that it has a web of meaning, one with which we need to live in harmony.

What is the purpose of the universe? Does it have a discernable meaning?

---

18. Rifkin, *The Empathic Civilization*, 181.

Day 347

Consciousness is simply what depth looks like from the inside, from within. So yes, depth is everywhere, consciousness is everywhere, Spirit is everywhere. As depth increases, consciousness increasingly awakens. Spirit increasingly unfolds. To say that evolution produces greater depth is simply to say that it unfolds greater consciousness.[19]

It was in the sixties that I was first introduced to the word "consciousness," and I remember being quite interested in the ways it was being used to describe how people from different times, cultures, and backgrounds looked at the world. I developed a great interest in this phenomenon, and exposed myself to the literature that was describing the changing consciousness of the sixties and the influence of a counter-culture and new-age thought. I began to explore the history of human thought, read about patterns of culture, the lonely crowd, and the organization man, pictures of past and current ways of understanding. I sensed that there was a change as we moved from the fifties to the sixties. I read with great interest the fine histories of the mind of the Middle Ages, the mind of East Asia, and the making of the modern mind. My library is still filled with dozens of these books, and also with the books that describe the shift to the postmodern outlook and the emergence of the counter culture. Increasingly, I was beginning to fully grasp our new way of looking at the world, making sense of it, and how to live in it. It was a description of our consciousness. I began to realize that our consciousness was our lens through which we see the world, and that this lens is shaded.

I did my doctoral dissertation on the theme of "Preunderstanding in Historical and Biblical Interpretation," and maintained that our knowledge (knowing the truth) was always shaped by our proverbial sunglasses. We participate in describing what is and in creating knowledge, an observation that Immanuel Kant made at an earlier point in history. I was in the stimulating mix of hermeneutics with regard to interpreting history, and also making sense of my time in history. Where all of this has led me is to be a bit cautious about absolutes, and more inclined to use words like "approximate."

How much are your views shaped by the times in which you live?

---

19. Wilber, *A Brief History of Everything*, 37.

Day 348

> *We live in an extraordinary time: all of the world's cultures, past and present, are to some degree available to us, either in historical records or as living entities. In the history of planet Earth, this has never happened before.*[20]

Ken Wilber, a thoughtful philosopher and scientist, has developed a persuasive description of the unfolding and development of human consciousness. Not everyone agrees with his nearly cosmic descriptions. Nor do I, yet I still find his work informative and suggestive. It has led me to a way of looking at ethics and values, and how they have an evolutionary development. More specifically, it has invited me to look at our current theme ("Expanding Outward for Justice, Reconciliation, and Peace") in a more evolutionary and developmental pattern. To say that one direction is better than another is a risk, because we do not have absolute knowledge, although it is a risk worth taking because we can now see better than we could at an earlier time.

We propose ethical guidelines about justice, reconciliation, and peace from a consciousness that we hope has been refined and matured. In order to better describe this pattern of development, I want to draw upon Ken Wilber and the authors of *Spiral Dynamics: Mastering Values, Leadership, and Change* (Don Edward Beck and Christopher C. Cowan), and see how they trace the development of consciousness. They use the term "meme" to describe the way we put information together, and how it forms into a collective consciousness and gives our minds the categories of understanding. It is how we see things. Beck and Cowan describe how these memes form, change, and develop. Over history, these memes have evolved, and have become the pattern of understanding for individuals, organizations, and societies. Beck and Cowan use colors to identify them. The first color is beige, and it describes primitive people who lived in caves or "the bush," and whose basic outlook and goal in life was to survive. Their genes drove them to seek food and procreate in order to replace themselves. The pattern of life was "just making it through the day and night."[21]

Are human beings evolving in a positive way, becoming better human beings?

---

20. Wilber, *A Theory of Everything*, 1.
21. Beck and Cowan, *Spiral Dynamics*, 197.

Day 349

Human nature alternates through spurts of growth and periods of consolidation. Each transition is a state of dynamic tension between a more complex MEME, which is brightening and the preceding one is fading to less influence.[22]

The second meme, labeled with the color purple, began to develop when those at the beige state became curious about all that was around them and how it was influencing and threatening them. Those at the beige level began to think about why survival (gathering food and perpetuating the race) was so difficult. Over time, they began to wonder if the world around them was alive and filled with spirits or demons. Life became sufficiently complex, so that survival demanded organizing the clan with elders and socializing customs. Certain events and places became sacred, and were set apart for rituals. They sought ways to live in harmony with nature, and began to honor ancestors, which they believed continued to influence the present. There was a movement from instincts and biology to a more conscious mind.[23]

People with the purple meme, or consciousness, essentially lived in a sacred community, led by elders and guided by shamans as they found their way in the world of nature. We might ask ourselves whether any parts of their way of life continue into the present, and whether some of their beliefs and practices might teach us. The answer is that there are traces of this way that continue in some tribal regions of the world. There is a great challenge for these people, as modernity presses in on them. Perhaps some positive features of this way of life can be preserved. For example, they did honor nature and, as far as possible, lived in harmony with nature. Their lives were less fragmented, and more coherent and centered. But other characteristics of this way of life were very difficult. For example, they were tribal and often xenophobic, living at risk as they competed with other tribes. They were subject to hunger, disease, and the changing climate of the seasons. It was not an easy life. I find myself reflecting, however, on its simplicity and closeness to nature.

What might we bring forward into our lives from the purple meme?

---

22. Ibid., 201.
23. Ibid., 203.

Day 350

> *In the classical tradition, being human means standing between nature and spirit, between finite limits and infinite possibilities. Our ability to be spirit—that is, to be more than our physical or biological nature—is exactly what is necessary for us to be historic. But it is also the case that we cannot be historic without our physical or biological nature. It is because nature anchors us so resolutely in the concrete that we are actors capable of forming a history.*[24]

As we move from a purple meme to a red meme, we are in the process of leaving the absolute control of nature and toward creating our own history. As I reflect on the characteristics of the red consciousness, I see much that continues with us as we evolve. The reality is that a certain part of the population moves to a more mature consciousness, while other people and clusters remain with a less mature consciousness, one that is not moving toward justice and the common good.

The red meme illustrates our point—that different segments of the human family remain less able to support the quest of a more just and peaceful world. Those with the red meme understand the world as a sort of jungle in which we must survive. In order to survive, we must seek and use power and wealth, even if we leave the "have nots" behind. It is a world that rewards those who seek power, wealth, privilege, prestige, and pleasure. There are winners and losers. To be a winner, one must be aggressive (a warrior) and even predatory, break constraints of customs and laws, and not worry about consequences (at least for others).

I have some fear that, occasionally, the political life of the United States, and even some of its leaders, continue to stagnate at the red level. The object is to win and advance one's own agenda, rather than to seek the common good, although the language used may be a disguise. Without in any way diminishing individual initiative, I hope that our government can find ways of wisely pursuing a just social order and the common good. For our part, the burden is to extend outward for justice, reconciliation, and peace, both in terms of domestic policy and international affairs. Our mindful spirituality prepares us and nudges us toward the welfare of all.

Are there ways for us to participate in politics and seek the common good?

---

24. Hauerwas, *The Peaceable Kingdom*, 35.

Day 351

> *We are facing a situation in economics today similar to that in astronomy when Copernicus arrived on the scene, a time when it was believed that the sun revolved around the earth. Just as Copernicus had to formulate a new astronomical worldview after several decades of celestial observations and mathematical calculations, we too must formulate a new economic worldview based on several decades of environmental observations and analyses.*[25]

We are using a developmental model called spiral dynamics, which traces the way human consciousness evolves and changes in response to new challenges and discoveries. This model gives a color to each level or phase of the pattern of change. We have looked briefly at the beige, the purple, and the red, and we now turn to the blue phase. As we do, we are asking ourselves how our changing consciousness might lead us to solutions for the overwhelming problems we currently face. Is it possible to have a consciousness that values justice, reconciliation, and peace? While our answer may not always be yes, it is nevertheless encouraging that we see evidence of a shift by many of our leaders who are seeking the common good and reversing the trend that could lead to an uninhabitable world with poisoned oceans, perpetual war, and economic collapse.

As we turn to the characteristics of the blue meme, of emerging consciousness, we see some signs of hope. This consciousness is characterized by understanding our life conditions, and it proposes a way forward. It is a consciousness that says life has meaning, and that we must discern it and sacrifice ourselves to it. This will bring order and stability. Often, this meme is filled with religious concepts, maintaining that God calls us to righteous living and assigns us to a certain role. The obvious risk in the blue meme is that there may be more than one proposed way to save the earth. For example, the well-known historian Samuel Huntington, in his book *The Clash of Civilizations: Remaking the World Order*, speaks about how the Western world may be in dramatic clash with Jihadist Islam, a clash of two civilizations. It is not an altogether hopeful book, and it invites reflection.

Does your consciousness have shades of blue in it? Are they helpful or risky?

---

25. Brown, *World on the Edge*, 9.

Day 352

Political leaders imbued with the hubris to think that they can fundamentally reshape the culture of their societies are destined to fail. While they may introduce elements of the Western culture, they are unable permanently to suppress or to eliminate the core elements of their indigenous culture.[26]

The next meme, labeled orange by Beck and Cowan, stays with the blue focus on analyzing basic life conditions on earth, but is less sure that that there is only one way to solve problems and create order. It is a movement away from central control, and toward finding a life with autonomy and independence.[27] The orange consciousness is more individualistic, and stresses that an individual can achieve the good life as one achieves material abundance. It affirms that, to achieve abundance, one must search for and find good solutions. Often these solutions are in the realm of science and technology. As one enters fully into the world of technology, and finds a means to solve problems and advance one's own aims, then the good life may be possible. But one must play to win, enjoy competition, and make a better iMac than the Hewlett-Packard PC. Beck and Cowan list five forces that have been at work since the industrial revolution, leading to this consciousness:

1. The market economy
2. The utilitarian political philosophy
3. The scientific method, rather than myths and superstitions
4. The rise of advanced machines to replace human labor
5. The rise of the individual, with guarantees of freedom, liberty, rights, and personal autonomy

It is to say to oneself that I can trust my own abilities, make a difference in the world, gather the information I need, set a strategic plan, and strive for excellence in all dimensions of my life. "Just do it," as Nike suggests. The risk, of course, is that a majority of the population who can't "just do it" get set aside.

Are there aspects of the orange meme in your outlook on life?

---

26. Huntington, *The Clash of Civilizations*, 154.
27. Beck and Cowan, *Spiral Dynamics*, 244.

Day 353

Interpersonal skills are often at a peak because constructive, warm interaction is so integral to self-satisfaction. Intuition and insight are valuable commodities here, so individuals strive to polish skills like empathetic listening. In organizations, moving through this range, human relations, sensitivity, and cultural awareness reading and training are often mandatory.[28]

As we move from the orange meme to the green meme, we shift the focus to more collaboration and cooperation, rather than individual initiative. It is the meme that stresses positive human bonding. This occurs when everyone is treated with respect and has equal importance in addressing the concerns of justice and social change. Those engaging in the mission of justice, reconciliation, and peace model the values inherent in a social order that seeks the common good. If there are those in positions of governmental power, for example, who display ambition to advance their own personal wealth and exploit those within the system, then there will be no trust and change will be resisted. Leadership must promote a sense of community and unity, endeavor to share society's resources, liberate humans from greed and dogma, and reach decisions through a careful process of consensus.[29]

There is often an attempt to create the feeling of psychological well-being and safety. Edgar Schein, in his book titled *Organizational Culture and Leadership*, lists eight components of this kind of transformation in organizations: (1) a compelling positive vision; (2) formal training in group skills; (3) involvement of the learners and participants; (4) arrangement of people in small groups and teams; (5) practice sessions with coaches and feedback; (6) positive role models from the leadership; (7) support groups for solving problems and airing frustrations; (8) structuring the systems in the organization in ways that the organization can engage in social change.[30] This green consciousness is undergirded with attractive ideals, but may not be able to manage conflict or opposition, or make hard decisions for change.

What elements of the green meme appeal to you? What are its limitations?

---

28. Ibid., 261.
29. Ibid., 260.
30. Ibid., 305–7.

Day 354

Injustice anywhere is a threat to justice everywhere.

—Martin Luther King Jr.

We are exploring the concept of consciousness, the way one perceives the world, makes sense of it, and functions in it. We are using the excellent tracing of the development of consciousness in human evolution, material developed by Don Beck and Christopher Cowan in their book *Spiral Dynamics*. They draw from a range of sources, and often reference the influence of Ken Wilber. Their use of colors to describe a particular consciousness gives us a way to speak about these different levels and patterns of human consciousness or memes. We last spoke about the green meme, that way of looking at and functioning in the world that stresses the respect for each person and the need to build consensus to move forward in creating a more just and peaceful world. At the next level of development, Beck and Cowan talk about moving on to a second tier. It is a move in human development from those outlooks (memes) that are part of our primal senses, survival, and subsistence, to those that have more freedom and can be chosen as a better way forward. Those with this level of consciousness must deal with the given and then make choices for the common good. It is possible to put Humpty Dumpty together and give him hope for a better life.[31] Humpty Dumpty's life is still precarious, but is now hopeful because he knows where he sits and can be wise and careful.

The yellow meme is more systemic, factoring in nature's ways and finding constructive patterns for the good life. It requires knowledge, competence, and flexibility. It allows for uncertainties, personal freedom, and alternative choices, as long as there is no harm to others. The yellow meme is integrative, collaborative, and maximizes open systems. Instead of closed systems that control, there is a shift to open systems that value change, transparency, diversity, questioning, discussing, reflecting, and direct communication. The leaders in these open systems have points of view, but are open to having their views changed and improved.

Have you been in organizations that have a yellow meme?

---

31. Beck and Cowan, *Spiral Dynamics*, 274–75.

Day 355

> *When we create competitive environments, organizations develop as contexts in which it is valued and rewarded to withhold information and mislead to gain status and authority. Collaborative practices cannot succeed in that environment. Instead, they demand that we act in an authentic manner. Being authentic means being straightforward, genuine, honest, and truthful about one's plans, opinions, and motivations.*[32]

In order to assist in the process of increasing justice, reconciliation, and peace, we maintain that where and how we start and proceed are of fundamental importance. It is essential that we be informed and committed to a just peace that leads to the common good. We must also cultivate the right spirit and attitude, or as we are saying, the right consciousness, or meme. Our thesis is that this consciousness is nurtured in the practices of mindful spirituality. We have reviewed the way authors Beck and Cowan outline the evolution of human consciousness and maintain that a new human consciousness is developing, giving human beings the freedom to chose their preferred future, one in which there can be a just peace and a commitment to the common good. We thought together about the yellow (or systemic) meme that is aware of nature's ways and human needs, and works with them in charting a course for the future. This meme is a clear statement about how we are now participants in evolution and thinking and planning with open and inclusive systems. A second step in this direction is an emerging new consciousness that is holistic and global in outlook. This turquoise meme has the following dimensions: Those who have this consciousness want to bring together many people from around the world, and address common problems such as global warming. They suggest integrated systems that bring all the factors shaping human life into consideration. They urge using the latest scientific and technological advances to aid in solving such difficult questions as climate change, world hunger, and the resort to violence. It is a clear statement that all of us (all living entities) are in this quest for a just and peaceful future.

Are you hopeful about the future of our world, or despairing?

---

32. Anderson, *Organization Development*, 42–43.

Day 356

When scanning previous world orders, periodically stop to clean your lenses. Slip on "their" colored glasses to see reality as "they" do. We only see what we can see, not all that is there; so no wonder we revise history every time a new "Meme" awakens and rewrite the books through our new-found filters.[33]

The last edition of *Spiral Dynamics* was published in 2006. So much has happened since then. New memes are taking shape, and our consciousness is changing even if at times we do not notice it. The turquoise meme asks the human family to review the deep and profound needs of planet earth and enter more directly into planetary management. We certainly need to fix and shape the communities and regions in which we live. We also need to grapple with problems of the world; we live in it! What color should our new meme be? Perhaps gold, and moving toward platinum? What sort of features will the new emerging consciousness have? The answer is somewhat elusive. Perhaps a few suggestions may be helpful as we search for our preferred future. One characteristic of any new meme will be to factor in the realities of nature and human behavior. We are profoundly challenged by our threatened earth and by the vast majority of the world's population still living with blue, red, and purple memes, ones pointing to individual futures, not our future. How do we make change within this reality? It will require a new level of leadership.

A second characteristic and need of the emerging new consciousness is to continue an aggressive educational initiative that will awaken the mind and heart of those who do not have a global and holistic outlook. We need to become a community of nations, not in competition for our own country. We must learn that we are in it together. A third quality of the new meme is to find ways to address our global problems in ways that are not overly dependent upon government initiative. Ask those with private wealth to help. This strategy can complement the work of governments. A fourth quality is to see in what ways the divine or transcendent presence may be understood as involved in our quest and guiding us.

What are items five through ten on this list?

---

33. Beck and Cowan, *Spiral Dynamics*, 297.

Day 357

> *Justice and compassion are sometimes regarded as antithetical or opposites. Justice may be seen as rigid, imposing certain standards or punishment without mercy or care for the well-being of those affected; and compassion can be seen as soft-hearted, if not soft-headed, sentimental, without regard for fairness or equity. In this book it is suggested that biblical concepts of justice and compassion may be seen as two sides of the same coin.*[34]

In this section of our readings we have been reflecting on how our mindful spirituality leads us to a life of service. We expand outward to work for justice, reconciliation, and peace. As we observe our world we are reminded that our work in this domain never ends. We have acknowledged that justice is a complex term and suggested that one way of viewing it is to give each person equal opportunity for a good life. We have noted that justice is not present everywhere and in fact its absence is very disturbing. There is a clear calling to *tikkun olam*, to repair the world. We noted that there is an increase of compassion and empathy in the emerging consciousness of many parts of the population, especially as the world's overwhelming problems are seen as a threat close to home. We then spent a few days thinking about how we should address our current situation, and explored some possible flaws in our thinking together. We then spoke about how our approach grows out of the way we look at the world and make sense of it, and how we live in it. We spoke about how our consciousness shapes our strategies and then reviewed the development of consciousness across human history and into our time. We used the term from *Spiral Dynamics*, "meme," and looked at the evolution of consciousness and how it impacts our ability to engage in repairing the world—how we expand outward for justice, reconciliation, and peace.

For the remainder of our readings through the year, we will continue this theme and reflect together on how we might pull all our themes into an integrated whole, bubbling up as a compassionate meme that leads us to care about creating a more just and humane world.

In what ways do I need to prepare myself so that I can lend a helping hand?

---

34. Hiers, *Justice and Compassion*, 4.

Day 358

So "being disciples" means at least two things. It means very simply going on asking ourselves whether what we do, how we think and speak and act, is open to Christ and Christ's Spirit . . . And it is also about how we as a Church go on being a learning community, how we grow in depth of relation with each other and God.[35]

As we move toward the completion of our readings for the year, I want to stress that we are called to a life of service, one that helps to heal, repair, and transform the world. We do not need to function at the level of being eligible for the Nobel Peace Prize. However we can do our part in our setting with our gifts, talents, and time. Once again, in that it is my pathway of mindful spirituality, I want to speak the language of the Christian faith, although much of what I want us to reflect upon can be translated across different worldviews.

In reflecting on how one becomes a mature and responsible Christian, the former Archbishop of Canterbury, Rowan Williams uses the language of discipleship to describe the way of Christian living. In his slender volume, from which our guiding thought for the day comes, he describes the pathway and the intended outcome of the life of discipleship. A disciple is one who learns from the Great Teacher, Jesus, and follows his teaching in a diligent way. Discipleship is more than just the act of believing; it is also how we live our lives; and it is a state of being. To be a disciple is to be a learner, continually reflecting on how one's life might follow the example of Jesus. We look for good ways to live, listen carefully for the voice of God, and respond to the situations in our pattern of life that need care, understanding, and compassion. If I were a disciple in another religious setting, the response to the call from the religion would be similar. Or if I were not religious, but more secular, in my outlook, I would nevertheless choose a life of responsible living, following the ethical norms I have chosen and living by these norms in a way that helps to build a just and peaceful world. One might say that Jesus cared about such a world and died trying to achieve it. We follow his example.

What are your deepest values, and how do they guide you?

---

35. Williams, *Being Disciples*, vii.

A CONCLUDING SUMMARY AND COURSE OF ACTION

Day 359

This reborn humanism will be the context in which religious studies will be carried out in the future. For the first time since its emergence in the historical process, Western culture has an opportunity to establish itself within a functional global complex of cultures in a spiritually cooperative attitude, rather than a spiritual antagonistic and competitive one.[1]

Thomas Berry argues persuasively that contemporary religious life must be fully engaged with current realities, and not just exhort disciples to look backward, wish for another time, and harshly judge the way we are managing the world. In its simplest form, what he is saying is that contemporary secular life in our new world needs religious depth, and that traditional religious thought must fully engage the outlook of the present world order. Fear, judgment, and contrasting the Right Way with the current wrong way has more often been the posture of the world's religions. I am persuaded that Thomas Berry is correct in his assessment. We must turn to a more mindful spirituality to add depth, meaning, and universal values to the secular world in which most of us live.

I have been interested in this topic for many years, and as I did my doctoral studies at the University of Edinburgh, I chose the area that was called divinity, a course of study that was not directly Christian theology or Biblical Studies, but the way that religion intersects with the world. The particular focus was in hermeneutics, which I understood as the way the literature and the thought of the past jumps forward in time and gives us guidance in the present. When I read the small volume by Rowan Williams, I was quite taken by his thoughtful hermeneutical method. I would like to borrow some from him and suggest how the ancient literature of the Bible and the first-century Palestinian Jew (Jesus) speaks to our present situation. The Christian faith has many values; we have mentioned several, such as justice and peace. I turn now to three of the cardinal virtues: faith, hope, and love (1 Cor 13:13).[2]

How would you like to add or subtract from the seven cardinal virtues?

---

1. Berry, *The Sacred Universe*, 24.
2. Note that the remaining four cardinal virtues are justice, prudence, temperance, and fortitude.

Day 360

We have got to grow into mature stillness, a poise and an openness to others and the world, so that it can also be a transformative mode of living in which the act of God can come through, so as to change ourselves, our immediate environment, our world.[3]

I want us to think and move today into the world in which we live, not the world that has passed, by doing some exploration of the word "faith." Faith has many of the qualities of consciousness; it is open, fully present, and a way of being and acting. I have often spoken of faith as having three components: knowledge/understanding, trust, and action. Frequently, when I speak with people about faith, only one of these components of faith is mentioned. For example a person will say what they believe but not move on to trust and action. Or they will point to their actions, not realizing that the foundation for their actions remains below the surface. On the first of these components, knowledge and understanding, I am persuaded that an essential part of sustaining the life of faith is making it credible, having a view of God that is not exclusively tied to an ancient worldview. I have been exploring ways of understanding God in reference to our evolutionary development, not over against it[4] and in reference to contemporary physics and cosmology. These explorations occasionally challenge my faith, although more often explain and deepen it. As my understanding increases, so too does my trust. Concepts such as God's will, guidance, and comfort take on new meaning. I trust in different ways than I did with my childhood faith. As my understanding and trust expand, so too does my desire to get on board and be God's partner in the continuing creation of the earth and the cosmos. My images and metaphors for God are less creations of a god in my own image and more journeys of understanding that invite me to a way of life and being. God is engaged in cosmic formation, that vast majority of the multiverse about which we know so little. I have faith in this God.

How has your understanding of God, or transcendence, changed?

---

3. Williams, *Being Disciples*, 17.

4. Of course, the works of Pierre Teilhard de Chardin have been helpful, and so have the works of Delio, such as *The Unbearable Wholeness of Being*.

Day 361

Hope, then, is not simply confidence in the future; it is confidence that past, present and future are held in one relationship so that the confusions about memory—Who were we? Who was I? Who am I, and who are we?—become bearable because of the witness in heaven, a witness who does not abandon.[5]

The cardinal virtues of faith, hope, and love are interrelated and part of a larger reality. They are part of the Christian worldview. To a large extent, my hope rests on my faith and becomes a positive experience because of love. As I mature in my understanding, my faith becomes more credible and foundational. From this platform I can more easily move to hope. If I am a hopeful person, then I can, by an act of the will, more easily lead a life of love. One missing corner of this triangle makes being a disciple very difficult.

We often think of hope as having to do with the future, and it certainly does. It also has a lot to do with the past. We hope that next year's vacation will be enjoyable because the one last year was such a positive experience. The great biblical characters, from Abraham to Moses and from Moses to Jesus, were people of hope. They were inclined to reference their hope (anticipating the future) because of their past. Abraham ventured out, going without knowing, and was hopeful because God had been faithful in the past. Moses went back to Egypt with hope and said "Let my people go!" because he had encountered God and his faith was secure. Jesus could say in the Garden of Gethsemane, "Not my will, but yours be done," because God had been trustworthy all of his life, especially in his public ministry. At the end of his life, he could say, "Into thy hands, I commit my spirit."

Hope, then, has this double connection, gaining reassurance from the past because of God's faithfulness, and being open to the future because God will continue to be faithful. I don't want to pretend that it is always easy; in fact, it is common for us to lose hope, but my understanding of God gives me hope. I am ready for what life might bring my way. I live in hope.

What are the inner dynamics of your hope, or lack of it?

---

5. Williams, *Being Disciples*, 30.

Day 362

All the most intractable problems in human relationships can be traced back to what I call the mood of unlove—a deep-seated suspicion most of us harbor within ourselves that we cannot be loved, or that we are not truly lovable, just for who we are.[6]

We are reflecting together about the foundation of mindful spirituality. We are drawing from the Christian frame of reference, not because there are not other secure foundations, but because it is the one with which I am most familiar.[7] I turn to the Apostle Paul's first letter to the Corinthian church for a succinct statement for Christians: "And now faith, hope, and love abide, these three; and the greatest of these is love" (1 Cor 13:13). The word that Paul chose as he wrote in Greek is *agape*, often defined as unlimited and unconditional love. We have used this concept of love frequently in our readings. I bring it up again as we close our readings, because it is the fundamental value in the Christian faith, and one that is foundational in many of the religions of the human family. It is also given a central place in some more secular worldviews. Like many fundamental human values, it is not always practiced, because it is difficult to love in an unlimited way. John Welwood, from whom we quoted above, explains that love is difficult because of us and them, which is to say that loving deeply and profoundly requires great maturity on our part, and the challenge that many people whom we encounter daily are not all that lovable.

My capacity to love, and especially to love those who are unlovable, is limited, but has increased over the years with experience, and by being intentional to cultivate a mindful spirituality. I still have miles to go before I sleep, but I am on my way. I still make mistakes, inadvertently hurt others, and remain unresponsive to situations needing love. I am growing as a disciple, as my faith deepens, as my hope feels secure, and I choose to love.

What are the factors in your life that empower you to be more loving?

---

6. Welwood, *Perfect Love*, 4.

7. Goldstein's book, *Mindfulness*, provides an excellent statement of the Buddhist foundations for a mindful life. Chopra, in his book *The Path to Love*, speaks of the centrality of love in Hindu thought.

Day 363

> *Islam states that God is Love, since this is one of His Divine Names, but it does not identify God solely with love, for He is also Knowledge and Light, Justice and Mercy, as well as Peace and Beauty, but He is never without love and His Love is essential to the creation of the universe and our relation with Him.*[8]

I quote the excellent Muslim scholar, Seyyed Hossein Nasr, because Islam is often identified in the Western world as a religion that tolerates violence. In fact, one can demonstrate that nearly all of the world's religions occasionally resorted to violence; it is a human trait. What I want to underline is that, deep at its heart, Islam is a religion of love. It values love in approximately the same way that Jews and Christians do; they all share the belief that ultimate reality is Love. In their spiritual practices, the followers of the Abrahamic religions cultivate their capacity to love by drawing close to God and being transformed by God into more loving people.

Do we fail in in our quest to be more loving? Yes, almost daily, and we are often reminded of our failures by those who see hypocrisy in our behavior. Our only answer is to say that we are sorry and will continue to try to find ways of being more loving. We are currently exploring one of those ways as part of our mindful spirituality, namely, to expand outward for justice, reconciliation, and peace. If we truly love others, we will seek to redress injustices and use all of the resources available to create a more just society and world. Even if we have limited resources, we can be engaged. Further, we must work to overcome mistrust and prejudice and invite people to be reconciled to each other. Often, it is injustice that separates us, and it is also our fear of the other. We too easily judge those who are different from us in custom and culture, stereotyping them, and playing out these prejudices in ways that divide us. As those who love, we seek to find ways of reconciling those who are divided by mistrust, prejudice, and injustice. We also need to be peacemakers as wisely and intentionally as we can. There are ways to resolve conflicts and divisions. We must utilize every means available to us.

What steps are you able to take toward justice, reconciliation, and peace?

---

8. Nasr, *The Heart of Islam*, 210–11.

Day 364

In everything do to others as you would have them do to you; for this is the law and the prophets. (Matt 7:12)

At this point in our readings, we are briefly reviewing where we have been and where we still need to go. I return to the golden rule taught by Jesus, one that Luke simplifies: "Do to others as you would have them do to you" (Luke 6:31). I have in front of me comparable statements from the teachings of Hinduism, Buddhism, Judaism, Islam, and Baha'i. I believe these statements capture the essence of what these religions teach us about how to live. We have maintained that this pattern of love and compassion is difficult, and often confusing and complex. But it can be cultivated by the practices in mindful spirituality. We have spoken about mindful spirituality by using three spatial metaphors:

- We reach upward to that which is beyond us, to God, or Transcendence, and give this linkage the highest priority. We relate to ultimate reality in love and with faith, cultivating a transforming union. We use all of the means available to us within our religious or philosophical understanding, such as prayer, meditation, ardency, intentionality, attentiveness, living in the present, and concentration.

- We open inward in this relationship with God or the ground of being, and seek healing, wholeness, and clarity about our values and the ethical norms that guide us. Gradually, we begin to find inner peace, serenity, and a purposeful direction for our lives.

- We then expand outward to express love and compassion. We do so within a community that supports and guides us. We move outward from our community to responsible living and join with others in the quest for justice at all levels. We work for reconciliation between those that live with fear and anger toward others. We seek to overcome violence and become peacemakers, committed to a more just and humane world. We ask,

What phases of mindful spirituality need the most attention in my life?

Day 365

You have heard that it was said, "You shall love your neighbor and hate your enemy." But I say to you, Love your enemies and pray for those who persecute you. (Matt 5:43–44)

I find myself often reflecting on how it is that I make choices and decisions about the direction of my life. I have read extensively about this complex pattern in our lives and have observed it in those who have taught me and guided me. Again, it is a book-length subject, but if I had to summarize it, I would use the following explanation:

I am exposed to a new way of understanding, and find patterns of cause and effect in the circumstances of my life and the world around me. I begin to think about what I have learned, and find that my mind provides me with categories and explanations that help me to understand, or least begin to understand. My mind gets around the swirl of information and puts it into some kind of order. As this pattern continues, I become educated. I get it, but it may not move me to action.

Gradually, as my understanding increases and I see signs of suffering, oppression, violence, and injustice, my emotions kick in. I begin to care about what is happening. I may have positive emotions if I learn that people are being helped, educated, fed, and healed. There are efforts to address global warming and offers to receive refugees. There is joy in learning that life is better for a particular group of people. Often, as I learn about a tragedy, violence, and injustice, I begin to care and wonder what I might do to help. The feelings of sadness and outrage emerge, and I want to do something to get involved and reduce human suffering.

The third level of this process inside of me points toward my will and the intention to get involved in some way. I know I can't do everything, but perhaps I can do something. I can write a check, volunteer, or join with a service agency that is addressing the concern. First my mind understands, then my heart is awakened, and I decide to act. This process is not always a neat and tidy linear pattern. Over time, it has become a way for me to intelligently care and wisely act. It is the way that my spiritual mindfulness develops: learn, care, act; head to heart to hand.

What sort of pattern unfolds in your life that causes you to tangibly care?

Day 366

Are all apostles? Are all prophets? Are all teachers? Do all work miracles? Do all speak in tongues? Do all interpret? But I strive for the greater gifts. And I will show you a more excellent way. (1 Cor 12:29–31)

The Apostle Paul founded a number of churches across the Roman Empire, one of which was in the Greek city of Corinth. It was a lively place, a typical seaport, with some wealth and a relatively well-educated population. The new church in Corinth was having some difficulty with their mindful spirituality; it was quite unmindful, and not very spiritual. They drank too much during the communion service, and liked to be in competition about who was the ideal leader and who had the best gifts to lead. Paul wisely reminds them that their respective gifts are for the common good, and that the real issue is following a more excellent way. He says in the next chapter of his letter that to have all the gifts in the world but be without love makes life empty and meaningless. Love is the more excellent way. It is not too hard to figure out; it is patient and kind, not boastful or rude, and it is glad when truth prevails. Because it is God-given, it never ends. All other gifts end, such as prophecy, the gift of tongues, and even knowledge, but not love. So, don't act like children. Be mature, and recognize the true expression of being spiritual. Faith is important, and to have hope brings joy and reassurance. These qualities along with love abide, but the greatest of these is love. To live with love as the center of life is the more excellent way.

As we close the year, it is a time for us to ponder about how the past year has gone and a time to reflect on the ways to do better in the coming year. The custom of making New Year's resolutions has some merit. We ask, "How might I do better in managing life and fulfilling my responsibilities?" I have lots of areas of my life that need attention. If I had to choose one, it would involve being more mindful about my spiritual life and finding ways to be more loving and compassionate, to care more deeply, and to be less preoccupied with my needs. I will try to stay focused on the present, reduce my stress and anxiety, and be ardent and attentive to the ways I stay in union with God and in love with all the people who surround me.

What might you do differently this coming year?

Study Guide for the December Readings

Questions for Contemplation and Discussion

1. What is the connection between inner spiritual vitality and a responsible life of service? How does one lead to the other?
2. Do you think that with all the problems we are facing, such as global warming, that there is the risk of human extinction? How should we respond to this threat?
3. How would you define justice? Are there different forms of justice? At what point do you feel the pinch of injustice, and how do you respond?
4. Do you believe that every person should have an equal opportunity for a good life, or does the opportunity for the good life have to be earned?
5. As you think about your life and abilities, what part might you play in following the Jewish belief that we have responsibility for healing and repairing the earth?
6. What do you think are the reasons why one culture will value human life and protect it, and why another culture will not give that much value to human life? What makes the difference?
7. Do you think that there is a gradual shift in human consciousness toward empathy and compassion?
8. In looking at American culture (and there are many sub-cultures), do you see some flaws in the assumptions that most of us make when assessing the quality of life and proposing solutions for improving the quality of our lives?
9. As you look around you and engage in some introspection, what color meme (consciousness) do those around you have, and that you share with them? Is your meme evolving?
10. What do you think are the best ways to make social change? Is our government system working so that changes can be made fairly and efficiently?

Study Guide

Section Three: Expanding Outward

Questions to Ponder and Discuss

1. What is your understanding of love? Are there many kinds of love? How do love and compassion differ? How can we increase our capacity to be more loving and compassionate? Is love an outgrowth of mindful spirituality?

2. How would you describe a healthy community, one in which you would like to be active? What are the characteristics of a healthy community? In what ways does the community in which you live contribute to your outlook and life?

3. The Christian faith, and nearly all of the religions of the human family, ask their adherents to live a responsible and ethical life. In what ways has your religion or more secular outlook influenced your behavior and led you to take more responsibility in your family and the region in which you live?

4. How do you understand the concept of justice? Does it mean that everyone should have an equal opportunity in life and be treated fairly? Where are the pockets of injustice in our region, country, and around the world?

5. In what ways do your mindful spirituality or your fundamental values lead you to work for justice, reconciliation, and peace?

Key Terms and Concepts

1. *Agape*: A Greek word for love that means unconditional acceptance and unlimited care and compassion.

2. Justice: A term meaning that every person should get their due (be treated fairly) and have an equal opportunity for a good life.

3. Consciousness: A word describing one's outlook on life, often used in reference to a particular group of people at a particular time and place in history

4. Meme: A term that is a description of the way one looks at the world, makes sense of it, and how one lives in it; it is similar to the words consciousness, outlook, and even worldview

5. *Tikkam*: A Hebrew word meaning to heal, repair, and transform the world

Study Resources:

1. Berry, Thomas. *The Great Work: Our Way into the Future.* New York: Three Rivers, 1999.
2. Dalai Lama. *How to Expand Love.* New York: Atria, 2005.
3. Ferguson, Duncan S. *Lovescapes: Mapping the Geography of Love.* Eugene, OR: Cascade, 2012.
4. Gushee, David P., and Glen H. Stassen. *Kingdom Ethics: Following Jesus in Contemporary Context.* Grand Rapids, MI: Eerdamans, 2016.
5. Thich Nhat Hanh. *Creating True Peace.* New York: Atria, 2003.
6. Post, Stephen G. *Unlimited Love: Altruism, Compassion, and Service.* Radnor, PA: Templeton Foundation, 2003.
7. Sandel, Michael J. *Justice: What's the Right Thing to Do?* New York: Farrar, Straus and Giroux, 2009.

Bibliography

Achtemeier, Paul, ed. *Harper's Bible Dictionary*. Revised edition. New York: HarperCollins, 1985.

à Kempis, Thomas. *The Imitation of Christ*. Translated by William Benham. Overland Park, KS: Digireads, 2016.

Albert, Ethel M., Theodore C. Denise, and Sheldon Peterfreund. *Great Traditions in Ethics*. 3rd ed. New York: Nostrand, 1975.

Allison, Dale C., Jr. *Night Comes: Death, Imagination, and the Last Things*. Grand Rapids: Eerdmans, 2016.

Amen, Daniel G. *Change Your Brain, Change Your Life*. New York: Three Rivers, 1998.

Anderson, Donald L. *Organizational Development: The Process of Leading Organizational Change*. Los Angeles: Sage, 2010.

Aristotle. *The Ethics of Aristotle*. Translated by J. A. K. Thomson. New York: Penguin, 1958.

Armstrong, Karen. *Buddha*. New York: Penguin, 2004.

Augustine. *The City of God*. Trans. by Marcus Dods. New York: Random House, 1950.

———. *The Confessions of St. Augustine*. Edited by E. B. Pusey. London: Dent & Sons, 1906.

Aurobindo, Sri. *The Aim of Life*. Auroville, IN: International Institute for Educational Research, 1986.

Barbour, Ian. *Religion and Science*. San Francisco: HarperOne, 1997.

Baer, Greg. *Real Love: The Truth about Finding Unconditional Love & Fulfilling Relationships*. New York: Gotham, 2003.

Barasch, Marc Ian. *The Compassionate Life: Walking the Path of Kindness*. San Francisco: Berrett-Koehler, 2009.

Barclay, William. *The Plain Man's Book of Prayers*. London: Fontana, 1959.

Bardacke, Nancy. *Mindful Birthing: Training the Mind, Body, and Heart for Childbirth and Beyond*. San Francisco: HarperOne, 2012.

Bartley, Trish. *Mindfulness: A Kindly Approach to Being with Cancer*. Malden, MA: Wiley & Sons: 2017.

Bass, Diana Butler. *Christianity after Religion*. San Francisco: HarperOne, 2013.

———. *Grounded: Finding God in the World, A Spiritual Revolution*. New York: HarperCollins, 2015.

Beck, Don Edward, and Christopher C. Cowan. *Spiral Dynamics: Mastering Values, Leadership, and Change*. Malden, MA: Blackwell, 2006.

Berry, Thomas. *The Great Work: Our Way into the Future*. New York: Three Rivers, 1999.

———. *The Sacred Universe: Earth, Spirituality, and Religion in the Twenty-First Century*. New York: Columbia University Press, 2009.

Blakney, Raymond B., trans. *Meister Eckhart*. New York: Harper & Row, 1941.

Blomfield, Vishvapani. *Gautama Buddha: The Life and Times of the Awakened One.* London: Quercus, 2011.

Bloom, Howard. *The God Problem: How a Godless Cosmos Creates.* Amherst, NY: Prometheus, 2012.

Bohler, Carolyn Jane. *God the What? What Our Metaphors for God Reveal about Our Beliefs in God.* Woodstock, VT: Skylight Paths, 2008.

Borg, Marcus. *Convictions: How I Learned What Matters Most.* New York: HarperOne, 2014.

———. *Jesus: Uncovering the Life, Teachings, and Relevance of a Religious Revolutionary.* San Francisco: Harper, 2006.

Brother Lawrence. *The Practice of the Presence of God: Being Conversations and Letters of Nicholas Herman of Lorraine.* Translated from French. Westwood, NJ: Revell, 1958.

Brown, Lester B. *World on Edge: How to Prevent Environmental and Economic Collapse.* New York: Norton, 2011.

Brueggemann, Walter. *Journey to the Common Good.* Louisville, KY: Knox, 2010.

———. *Theology of the Old Testament.* Minneapolis: Fortress, 1997.

Buber, Martin. *Moses.* Oxford: Oxford University Press, 1944.

Bultmann, Rudolf. *The Theology of the New Testament, Volume 1: The Ministry of Jesus in its Theological Significance.* Translated by Kendrick Grobel. London: SCM, 1952.

Bunyan, John. *The Pilgrim's Progress.* New York: Grosset & Dunlap, n.d.

Butcher, Carmen Acevedo, trans. *Cloud of Unknowing.* Boulder: Shambhala, 1991.

Cahalan, Kathleen A., and Douglas J. Schuurman. *Calling in Today's World: Voices from Eight Faith Perspectives.* Grand Rapids: Eerdmans, 2016.

Campbell, Joseph. *Oriental Mythology: The Masks of God.* New York: Penguin, 1962.

Chödrön, Pema. *Comfortable with Uncertainty.* Boston: Shambhala, 2003.

———. *No Time to Lose: A Timely Guide to the Way of the Bodhisattva.* Boston: Shambhala, 2005.

Chopra, Deepak. *The Future of God.* New York: Harmony, 2014.

———. *The Path to Love: Renewing the Power of Spirit in Your Life.* New York: Harmony, 1997.

Christopher, David. *The Holy Universe: A New Story of Creation for the Heart, Soul, and Spirit.* Santa Rosa, CA: New Story, 2014.

Coakley, Sarah. *God, Sexuality, and the Self.* Cambridge, UK: Cambridge University Press, 2013.

Cobb, John. *Jesus' Abba: The God Who Has Not Failed.* Minneapolis: Fortress, 2015.

Colledge, Edmund, and Bernard McGinn, trans. *Meister Eckhart: The Essential Sermons, Commentaries, Treatises and Defense.* Mahwah, NJ: Paulist, 1981.

Confucius. *The Wisdom of Confucius.* New York: Citadel, 1968.

Cox, Harvey. *The Future of Faith.* New York: HarperCollins, 2009.

Crossan, John Dominic. *The Historical Jesus: The Life of a Mediterranean Jewish Peasant.* New York: HarperCollins, 1991.

Dalai Lama. *The Compassionate Life.* Boston: Wisdom, 2003.

———. *Ethics for the New Millennium.* New York: Riverhead, 1999.

———. *The Four Noble Truths.* London: Thorsons, 1997.

———. *How to Expand Love.* New York: Atria, 2005.

Das, Surya. *Awakening the Buddha Within.* New York: Broadway, 1997.

Dawkins, Richard. *The God Delusion.* New York: Houghton Mifflin, 2006.

———. *The Selfish Gene.* Oxford: Oxford University Press, 1977.

Davids, T. W. Rhys. *Buddhism*. London: SPCK, 1903.

Delio, Ilia. *Making All Things New: Catholicity, Cosmology, Consciousness*. Maryknoll, NY: Orbis, 2015.

———. *The Unbearable Wholeness of Being: God, Evolution, and the Power of Love*. Maryknoll, NY: Orbis, 2013.

Diamant, Anita, and Howard Cooper. *Living a Jewish Life*. New York: HarperCollins, 1991.

Diamond, Jarod. *Guns, Germs, and Steel: The Fates of Human Societies*. New York: Norton, 1999.

Dickinson, Emily. *Modern American Poetry*. Edited by Louis Untermeyer. New York: Harcourt, 1936.

Dykstra, Craig. *Growing in the Life of Faith*. 2nd edition. Louisville: Westminster John Knox Press, 2005.

Echegaray, Hugo. *The Practice of Jesus*. Translated by Matthew J. O'Connell. Maryknoll, NY: Orbis, 1984.

Eckhart, Meister. *Meister Eckhart*. Translated Raymond B. Blakney. New York: Harper, 1941.

Eliade, Mircea. *The Quest: History and Meaning in Religion*. Chicago: The University of Chicago Press, 1969.

Ellwood, Walter, ed. *Dictionary of Evangelical Theology*. Ada, MI: Baker Academic, 2001.

Esposito, John L. *Islam: The Straight Path*. 3rd ed. New York: Oxford University Press, 2005.

Ferguson, Duncan. *Biblical Hermeneutics: An Introduction*. Atlanta: Knox, 1986.

———. *Exploring the Spirituality of the World Religions*. New York: Continuum, 2010.

———. *Lovescapes: Mapping the Geography of Love*. Eugene, OR: Cascade, 2012.

———. *The Radical Teaching of Jesus*. Eugene, OR: Wipf & Stock, 2016.

Finley, James. *Christian Meditation: Experiencing the Presence of God*. New York: HarperOne, 2005.

Foster, Richard J. *The Celebration of Discipline: The Path to Spiritual Growth*. San Francisco: Harper and Row. 1978.

Fowler, James W. *Stages of Faith: The Psychology of Human Development and the Quest for Meaning*. New York: Harper & Row, 1981.

Francis, Pope. *The Name of God is Mercy*. New York: RandomHouse, 2016.

Fromm, Eric. *The Art of Loving*. New York: Bantam, 1962.

Gabriel, Ralph Henry. *The Course of American Democratic Thought*. New York: Ronald, 1940.

Gadamer, Hans-Georg. *Truth and Method*. New York: Crossroads, 1975.

Gibran, Kahill. *The Prophet*. New York: Knopf, 2003.

Goldstein, Joseph. *Mindfulness: A Practical Guide to Awakening*. Boulder, CO: Sounds True, 2013.

Greeley, Andrew M., and Mary G. Durkin, eds. *The Book of Love*. New York: Forge, 2002.

Gushee, David P., and Glen H. Stassen. *Kingdom Ethics: Following Jesus in Contemporary Context*. 2nd ed. Grand Rapids: Eerdmans, 2016.

Haidt, Jonathan. *The Righteous Mind*. New York: Vintage, 2013.

Hanson, Rick. *Buddha's Brain: The Practical Neuroscience of Happiness, Love, & Wisdom*. Oakland, CA: New Harbinger, 2009.

Harris, Sam. *The End of Faith*. New York: Norton, 2004.

Hart, David Bently. *The Experience of God: Being Consciousness, Bliss*. New Haven, CT: Yale University Press, 2013.

Hauerwas, Stanley. *The Peaceable Kingdom*. South Bend, IN: University of Notre Dame Press, 1991.

BIBLIOGRAPHY

Hauerwas, Stanley, and John H. Westerhoff, eds. *Schooling Christians.* Grand Rapids: Eerdmans, 1992.

Hays, Edward. *Prayers of a Planetary Pilgrim.* Easton, KS: Forest of Peace, 1989.

Heschel, Abraham Joshua. *God in Search of Man.* New York: Farrar, 1976.

Hiers, Richard H. *Justice and Compassion in Biblical Law.* New York: Continuum, 2009.

Hitchens, Christopher. *God Is Not Great: How Religion Poisons Everything.* New York: Twelve, 2007.

Hjelm, Titus, ed. *Is God Back? Reconsidering the New Visibility of Religion.* London: Bloomsbury, 2015.

Huntington, Samuel P. *The Clash of Civilizations: Remaking the World Order.* New York: Touchstone, 1996.

Hutchison, John A. *Paths of Faith.* 3rd ed. New York: McGraw-Hill, 1981.

"Introduction to Hinduism." *Hinduism Today,* April/May/June, 2004.

John Paul II, Pope. *In My Own Words.* New York: Gramercy, 1998.

Kabat-Zinn, Jon. *Full Catastrophe Living.* Revised edition. New York: Bantam, 2013.

Kant, Immanuel. *Critique of Practical Reason.* Cambridge, UK: Cambridge University Press, 2015.

Keating, Thomas. "The Method of Centered Prayer." https://www.cpt.org/files/WS%20-%20 Centering%20Prayer.pdf.

Keepin, William. *Belonging to God: Spirituality, Science & a Universal Path of Divine Love.* Woodstock, VT: Skylight Paths, 2016.

Kelsey, Morton. *The Other Side of Silence.* Mahwah, NJ: Paulist, 1997.

Kierkegaard, Soren. *Works of Love.* Translated by Howard and Edna Hong. New York: Harper Perennial, 1962.

King, Martin Luther, Jr. *Where Do We Go From Here: Chaos or Community?* New York: Bantam, 1968.

Kirkpatrick, Thomas. *Communication in the Church.* Lanham, MD: Rowman & Littlefield, 2016.

Kittel, Gerhard, ed. *Theological Dictionary of the Bible, Vol. II.* Translated by Geoffrey Bromiley. Grand Rapids: Eerdmans, 1965.

Kohlberg, Lawrence. *The Philosophy of Moral Development.* New York: Harper & Row, 1981.

Kolbert, Elizabeth. *The Sixth Extinction: An Unnatural History.* New York: Henry Holt, 2014.

Kornfield, Jack. *A Path with Heart.* New York: Bantam, 1993.

———. *The Wise Heart.* New York: Bantam, 2008.

Lao Tzu. *Tao Te Ching.* New York: Barnes and Noble, 2005.

Lent, Jeremy. *The Patterning Instinct: A Cultural History of Humanity's Search for Meaning.* Amherst, NY: Prometheus, 2017.

———. "A House on Shaky Ground: Eight Structural Flaws of the Western Worldview." http://www.tikkun.org/nextgen/a-house-on-shaky-ground-eight-structural-flaws-of-the-western-worldview.

Lewis, C. S. *Mere Christianity.* New York: Macmillan, 1952.

Levison, John. *Filled with the Spirit.* Grand Rapids, MI: Eerdmans, 2009.

Lonergan, Bernard. *Method in Theology.* New York: Seabury, 1972.

Mafi, Maryam. *Rumi Day by Day.* Charlottesville, VA: Hampton Roads, 2014.

Maguire, Daniel C. *Christianity without God: Moving Beyond the Dogmas and Retrieving the Epic Moral Narrative.* New York: SUNY, 2014.

———. *Ethics: A Complete Guide for Moral Choice.* Minneapolis: Fortress, 2010.

Marion, Jim. *Putting on the Mind of Christ: The Inner Life of the Spirit.* Newburyport, MA: Hampton Roads, 2011.

McGinn, Bernard, ed. *The Essential Writings of Christian Mysticism.* New York: Modern Library, 2006.

McGrath, Alister. *The Big Questions: Why We Can't Stop Talking about Science Faith and God.* New York: St. Martin's, 2015.

McIntosh, Steve. *The Presence of the Infinite: The Spiritual Experience of Goodness, Truth, and Beauty.* Wheaton, IL: Quest, 2015.

McLaren, Brian D. *Naked Spirituality: A Life with God in 12 Simple Words.* New York: HarperOne, 2011.

———. *A New Kind of Christianity.* New York: HarperOne, 2010.

Medina, John. *Brain Rules: 12 Principles for Surviving and Thriving at Work, Home, and School.* Seattle: Pear, 2008.

Meier, John P. *Mentor, Message, and Miracles.* Vol. 2 of *The Marginal Jew: Rethinking the Historical Jesus.* New York: Doubleday, 1994.

Merrett, Carol Howard. *Healing Spiritual Wounds.* New York: HarperOne, 2017.

Merton, Thomas. *Contemplation in a World of Action.* Garden City, NY: Image, 1973.

———. *Contemplative Prayer.* Garden City, NY: Image, 1971.

———. *New Seeds of Contemplation.* New York: New Directions, 1961.

Michael, Chester P., and Marie C. Norrisey. *Prayer and Temperament.* Ballston Spa, NY: Open Door, 1991.

Migliore, Daniel L. *Faith Seeking Understanding: An Introduction to Christian Theology.* Grand Rapids: Eerdmans, 1991.

Mitchell, Stephen, trans. *Bhagavad Gita, A New Translation.* New York: Three Rivers, 2000.

Moltmann, Jürgen. *The Church in the Power of the Holy Spirit.* Translated by Margaret Kohl. New York: Harper & Row, 1977.

Moore, Thomas. *The Care of the Soul.* New York: HarperCollins, 1992.

Morris, Leon. *Testaments of Love: A Study of Love in the Bible.* Grand Rapids, MI: Eerdmans, 1981.

Mother Teresa. *Life in the Spirit: Reflections, Meditations, Prayers.* San Francisco: Harper & Row, 1983.

Mott, Stephen Charles. *Biblical Ethics and Social Change.* Oxford: Oxford University Press, 1982.

Murphy, Nancey, and George Ellis. *On the Moral Nature of the Universe.* Minneapolis: Fortress, 1996.

Murray, Gilbert. *Five Stages of Greek Religion.* Garden City, NY: Doubleday, 1955.

Nasr, Seyyed Hossein. *The Heart of Islam: Enduring Values for Humanity.* San Francisco: Harper, 2002.

Nerburn, Kent, ed. *The Wisdom of Native Americans.* New York: MJF, 1999.

Newell, John Philip. *The Rebirthing of God: Christianity's Struggle for New Beginnings.* Woodstock, VT: Skylight Paths, 2015.

Nygren, Anders. *Agape and Eros.* London: SPCK, 1953.

Oord, Thomas Jay. *Defining Love: A Philosophical, Scientific, and Theological Engagement.* Grand Rapids: Brazos, 2010.

The Order of Carmelites. "What is Lectio Divina?" http://ocarm.org/en/content/lectio/what-lectio-divina.

Osmer, Richard Robert. *A Teachable Spirit: Recovering the Teaching Office in the Church.* Louisville: Knox, 1990.

Ottati, Douglas. *Theology for Liberal Protestants: God the Creator.* Grand Rapids, MI: Eerdmans, 2013.

Pagels, Elaine. *Beyond Belief: The Secret Gospel of Thomas.* New York: Random House, 2005.

Palmer, Parker J. *The Courage to Teach.* San Francisco: Jossey-Bass, 1998.

———. *A Hidden Wholeness: The Journey Toward the Undivided Life.* San Francisco: Jossey-Bass, 2004.

———. *To Know as We are Known: A Spirituality of Education.* San Francisco: Harper & Row, 1983.

———. *Let Your Life Speak: Listening the Voice of Vocation.* San Francisco: Jossey-Bass, 2000.

Peacocke, Arthur. *Theology for a Scientific Age.* Minneapolis: Augsburg, 1993.

Peck, M. Scott. *The Road Less Traveled.* New York: Simon & Schuster, 1978.

Peters, Ted. *God: The World's Future.* Minneapolis: Fortress, 1992.

Pinker, Stephen. *The Better Angels of Our Nature: Why Violence Has Declined.* New York: Penguin, 2011.

Plato. *Great Dialogues of Plato.* Translated by W. H. D. Rouse. New York: Mentor, 1958.

———. *The Republic.* Translated by Francis MacDonald Cornford. London: Oxford University Press, 1977.

Polkinghorne, John. *Belief in God in an Age of Science.* New Haven, CT: Yale University Press, 2003.

Post, Stephen G. *Unlimited Love: Altrusim, Compassion, and Service.* Philadelphia: Templeton Foundation, 2003.

Rahman, Jamal. *The Spiritual Gems of Islam.* Nashville, TN: SkyLight Paths, 2013.

Reynolds, Stefan Gillow. *Living with the Mind of Christ: Mindfulness in Christian Spirituality.* London: Darton, Longman & Todd, 2016.

Rifkin, Jeremy. *The Empathic Civilization: The Race to Global Consciousness in a World in Crisis.* New York: Penguin, 2009.

Riley, Laurie. *Practical Compassion.* Self-published, 2008.

Russell, Letty M., ed. *The Liberating Word: A Guide to the Nonsexist Interpretation of the Bible.* Philadelphia: Westminster Seminary Press, 1976.

Sacks, Jonathan. *Not in God's Name: Confronting Religious Violence.* New York: Schocken, 2015.

Sandel, Michael J. *Justice: What's the Right Thing to Do?* New York: Farrar, Straus and Giroux, 2009.

Sanders, E. P. *The Historical Figure of Jesus.* New York & London: Penguin, 1993.

Schein, Edgar H. *Organizational Culture and Leadership.* 4th ed. San Francisco: Jossey-Bass, 2010.

Schleiermacher, Friedrich. *On Religion: Speeches to Cultured Despisers.* Cambridge, UK: Cambridge University Press, 1998.

Schonert-Reichl, Kimberly A., and Robert W. Roeser. *Handbook of Mindfulness in Education: Integrating Theory and Practice.* New York: Springer-Verlag, 2016.

Siegel, Daniel J. *The Developing Mind: How Relationships and the Brain Interact to Shape Who We Are.* New York, 1999.

———. *The Mindful Brain.* New York: Norton, 2007.

Sonderegger, Katherine. *Systematic Theology.* Vol 1. Minneapolis: Fortress, 2015.

Spohn, William C. *Go and Do Likewise: Jesus and Ethics.* New York: Continuum, 2000.

"Standards of Ethical Conduct, Approved by the 210th General Assembly (1998)." Louisville: General Assembly of the Presbyterian Church (USA), 1998.
Stella, Tom. *Finding God Beyond Religion*. Woodstock, VT: Skylight Paths, 2013.
Swineburne, Richard. *The Coherence of Theism*. Oxford, UK: Oxford University Press, 2016.
Teilhard de Chardin, Pierre. *The Phenomenon of Man*. London: Collins, 1959.
Thich Nhat Hanh. *The Heart of the Buddha's Teaching*. New York: Broadway, 1998.
———. *Creating True Peace: Ending Violence in Yourself, Your Family, Your Community, and the World*. New York: Atria, 2004.
———. *How to Love*. Berkeley: Parallax, 2015.
———. *Teachings on Love*. Berkeley: Parallax, 1998.
———. *True Love*. Boston: Shambhala, 2006.
Tolle, Eckhart. *The Power of Now*. Vancouver, BC: Namaste, 2004.
Tracy, David. *The Analogical Imagination*. New York: Crossroad, 1981.
———. *Plurality and Ambiguity: Hermeneutics, Religion, Hope*. San Francisco: Harper & Row, 1987.
Underhill, Evelyn. *Mysticism*. New York: New American Library, 1974.
Walsh, Roger. *Essential Spirituality: The 7 Central Practices to Awaken Heart and Mind*. New York: John Wiley & Sons, 1999.
Wassmer, Thomas S. *Christian Ethics for Today*. Milwaukee: Bruce, 1969.
Watson, Burton, trans. *Lotus Sutra*. New York: Columbia University Press, 1993.
Weatherhead, Lesley. *The Will of God*. Nashville: Abingdon, 1999.
Welwood, John. *Perfect Love, Imperfect Relationships: Healing the Wound of the Heart*. Boston: Trumpeter, 2006.
Westneat, Danny, and Karen Matthews. "Attack on Muslim Shakes London." *The Seattle Times*, June 23, 2017.
———. "Questions and Anger after Mother Killed by Police." *The Seattle Times*, June 20, 2017.
"What is Lectio Divina?" http://ocarm.org/en/content/lectio/what-lectio-divina.
Wilber, Ken. *A Brief History of Everything*. Boston: Shambhala, 2001.
———. *Integral Spirituality: A Startling New Role for Religion in the Modern and Postmodern World*. Boston: Integral, 2006.
———. *The Marriage of Sense and Soul: Integrating Science and Religion*. New York: Random House, 1998.
———. *A Theory of Everything*. Boston: Shambhala, 2001.
Williams, Daniel Day. *The Spirit and Forms of Love*. New York: University Press of America, 1981.
Williams, Rowan. *Being Disciples*. Grand Rapids: Eerdmans, 2016.
Wilson, Edward O. *The Meaning of Human Existence*. New York: Liveright, 2014.
Woolfolk, Anita. *Educational Psychology*. 11th ed. Columbus, OH: Merrill, 2010.
Wright, N. T. *The New Testament and the People of God*. Minneapolis: Fortress, 1992.

www.ingramcontent.com/pod-product-compliance
Lightning Source LLC
Chambersburg PA
CBHW060505300426
44112CB00017B/2551